The Practice of Criticism

SHELDON P. ZITNER
JAMES D. KISSANE
M. M. LIBERMAN
Grinnell College

SCOTT, FORESMAN AND COMPANY

Chicago   Atlanta   Dallas   Palo Alto   Fair Lawn, N.J.

Library of Congress Catalog Card No. 66-14835
Copyright © 1966 by Scott, Foresman and Company
Printed in the United States of America
All Rights Reserved

Foreword

The Practice of Criticism is designed as an introductory text in literary criticism for students and for general readers. By presenting criticism as a set of specific tasks, it permits an evaluation of "schools" of criticism and their procedures, and also of theories of criticism which attempt to relate those schools. The collection is also a *vade mecum* to major works in English and American literature. The rationale of the work may be found in the Introduction. It is enough to say here that the general plan of the work is inductive—that is, it raises questions of metacriticism last and relies on examples to define the tasks and categories of criticism. Finally, its goal is not only to present literary criticism but to stimulate critical writing by students.

For help in preparing the collection we are greatly indebted to our colleagues in the Department of English at Grinnell College, particularly to Curtis Bradford, and to the staff of the Grinnell College Library, especially Mr. Richard Ryan. Our students Ellen Crandall and Annette Gould have also given us invaluable aid. In the course of preparing the essays for the press, it has been necessary to correct some obvious misprints and, in one or two instances, emend errors with the permission of the author. In the case of earlier criticism, we have depended on authoritative early texts, emended in a few instances to reflect the author's intention as it is revealed in subsequent printings. Excerpting has been clearly indicated in all cases.

Contents

Introduction

The Plan and Aims of the Collection

We are frequently told, by way of criticism no doubt, that ours is an Age of Criticism. It is also an age of excerpts, digests, and anthologies. And, to complete this catalog of literary parasitism, it is also a time when one may have a modest career decrying all this endless making of books out of books about books. So whoever offers us another anthology of literary criticism must do so on the ground that the selections are the very best available or that their arrangement permits some illumination of criticism in general.

The selections which follow need no apology. Literary criticism in English is "God's plenty." Yet it would be presumptuous to believe that any collection can bring together only the paramount achievements. Moreover, such a collection, even if it could be made, would not be definitive. What T. S. Eliot stated about poetry—that one new master-work rearranges the relations among all the earlier ones—is true of literary criticism as well. Who will deny, for example, that Northrop Frye's discussion of myth in his *Anatomy of Criticism* (1957) forces us to see in a new light Maurice Morgann's eighteenth-century essay on the character of Falstaff? On more practical grounds, a collection of the best, the very, very best, might be a distortion of the nature of criticism. Some works, as Pope wrote, "may have more wit than does them good," blinding us by their brilliance to the considerable accomplishments effected by sound method and patient observation. So we have not hesitated to place side by side here the workmanlike and the magisterial. Our primary considerations were that the pieces chosen should illustrate how one might go about solving a particular problem in criticism, that they should deal with works which a great many readers are likely to know, and, above all, that they should be provocative, opening questions as well as answering them.

A few selections may seem unrepresentative of influential work on their respective topics. Interested students will, of course, want to compare Lee Lemon's novel approach to plot, for example, with the approach in such a classic study as R. S. Crane's essay on the plot of *Tom Jones* (reprinted in *Critics and Criticism,* 1952, 1957). And the implied definition and treatment of myth by Ian Watt may be usefully contrasted with the discussion in Frederick Gose's article on *Lord Jim.* Gose's approach to symbol and myth is closer to that of Maude Bodkin's influential *Archetypal Patterns in Poetry* (1934). In any case, the selections are designed to raise important questions concerning the topics rather than to present a survey of all their aspects.

It follows from this that we have aimed at making an anthology whose strength depends as much on its arrangement as on its selections. This aim grew out of our estimate of some of the limitations of the many excellent anthologies of criticism now available. These collections fall into several categories:

Masterworks of criticism arranged chronologically
Selections designed to illustrate the so-called "schools" of criticism
Selections centering around a single period, author, or topic
Selections arranged according to the categories suggested by a particular "school" of criticism or critical theory

All these schemes have strengths which are apparent enough that they need not be stated. It is their limitations that we were forced to contend with in the course of introducing fairly sophisticated students to the problems of understanding criticism and writing it themselves. There is some pedagogical value, therefore, in examining these limitations.

The chronological arrangement of masterpieces of criticism is more convenient than instructive, for the topics which the great works treat, though they may be perennial, appear in such a variety of contexts that the student comes away more often with a bewildering impression of flux than with a clear sense of what is changing. The sequential examination of critical documents falls in the category of what the philosopher C. S. Peirce calls "secondness." One ought, logically, to talk about the history of criticism only after one has some schematic sense of the problems to which critics may address themselves. These problems emerge in the history of criticism, but the scheme itself is obscured by the necessity of coping with the relation of one document to another.

The anthology organized around the "schools" or "theories" of criticism similarly obscures the problems all criticism faces. It forces a concentration on the differing assumptions underlying the way particular critics go about solving particular problems. Despite their usefulness for some purposes, such anthologies lead the student to concentrate on abstract and often remote metaphysical questions (alternative extraliterary value systems, for example), and they suggest by their organization a position of relativism in which all critical "schools" represented are on a par. One may conclude that a relativist position is correct, but the position is unearned if it results merely from the format in which criticism is presented.

The other types of collection are more obviously limited as introductions to literary criticism. They are useful but partial views—of greater use in the study of a particular period or author than in the general study of critical practice.

Such impressions of the limitations of current anthologies have led us to the plan of this collection. We asked ourselves—with as much freedom from predisposition as we could—what are the tasks and problems that critics actually deal with? What, in short, is the behavior of criticism? We then organized our answers into the categories of this collection. The critic, we said, treats genres and styles, traditions and eras, authors and techniques, whole works and their parts, ideas and evaluations; and, finally, as is appropriate to an activity so self-conscious as criticism, he speculates on criticism itself. For each of what we conceived to be the major tasks of criticism, we have chosen an essay dealing with major literary works[1] that is provocative and that implies the relatedness of the various critical tasks. If there is one underlying theoretical assumption of this collection it is Coleridge's: that literature provides us with 'the manyness in the one, the oneness in the many' and hence that a critical essay should appropriately suggest the connections of its major topic to other problems in the work it treats. Therefore we have avoided, for example, the sort of essay on imagery, popular a decade or two ago, that treats the images of a lyric as though these had an organization and meaning apart from the rest of the poem. But we have avoided such essays at what may seem to be the peril of ill-defined categories.

Our categories—genre, style, theme, diction, and so on—are not rigidly conceived, and the essays which represent them may seem to spill over into other categories. An essay on diction may show how language is affected by meter and symbol; how a style, a genre, an era, or an author "demands" diction or meter of a specific sort. But we do not regret our avoidance of a "hardening of the categories." Such rigidity would be inconsistent with the search for a whole significance in works and with the nature of the literary work itself which, when excellent, appears seamless. Our apology for the possible incompleteness of categories is even more perfunctory. This is a book to be carried, not wheeled about; it is a *vade mecum* to masterworks of literature in English.

The relevance of the organization of this collection to the study of criticism should be apparent. Criticism is, finally, the sum of what critics do. Understanding the major tasks of criticism and understanding them one at a time, the student is prepared to understand the history of criticism, the particular characteristics of eras and authors, and, perhaps most important, the achievements and limitations of "schools" and "theories" of criticism. The history of criticism is characterized by a shifting concentration on some tasks to the exclusion of others. Thus the dominant criticism of the thirties concentrated on the problems of theme, audience, author, and age, and the topics excluded from its discussions clearly marked the character and limitations of the criticism of that period. Thus the school of so-called "myth-criticism" may also be judged in terms of its apparent powerlessness to deal adequately with the relation between author and work or to suggest ways of evaluating the achievement of individual works. Put most simply, the pedagogical principle of the collection is this: sensing what can and ought to be done, the student is in a position to judge what has been done.

Finally, we offer this collection as a group of specimen essays which the student may emulate in his own writing about literature. Experience has led us to conclude that literary criticism is best taught as an activity related to, not remote from, the student's effort to write about the works

---

1. The only exception is T. S. Eliot's "Tradition and the Individual Talent." Our reasons for including this essay will be obvious to those who know it. Our reasons for excluding others dealing with questions of tradition concern the degree of scholarly expertise needed to understand the best of such essays.

he reads. The plan of this collection, we believe, has the virtue of presenting the range of criticism in a series of steps that make the tasks
of criticism comprehensible and in a series of essays that invite response
and emulation.

Approaching the Selections: Primarily for the Student

Even if one accepts the view of impressionist criticism that at bottom
"a good critic is one who narrates the adventures of his mind among
masterpieces" (the formulation is Anatole France's), one must agree
that the critic is obliged to give us more than a bare statement of his
preferences. He is expected to define, illustrate, and explain them. And
the definition and explanation are necessarily more important than the
statement. Criticism, in short, is a variety of inquiry. Therefore we may
judge it on its clarity, organization, and logic.

The obvious point has been obscured by the manner of some recent
criticism. As John Crowe Ransom remarks:

> There is a criticism which is literary in the double sense; the
> literary quality attaches to the object of criticism, of course, but
> it attaches to the work of criticism too. The indubitable art work
> invites a low-grade and lesser art work to celebrate as well as
> judge it. The critic never ceases to be impressed with his fine
> object. He starts with a spontaneous surge of piety, and is in-
> ducted by the contagion of art into a composition of his own,
> which sustains the warmth unashamed, and probably manages
> a rounded literary effect, having a beginning, a middle, and an
> end.[2]

Although Mr. Ransom remarks that such pseudo-art "is likely to seem
unprofessional to the academic critic," he seems at first to give it a
better welcome than it may deserve. There has been much confusion
wrought by whimsical or anecdotal organization, quasi-poetic ambiguity
of statement, private allusion, or straining after stylistic "beauties."
Some current critical writing is rendered useless by the intruding tone
and method of the artist *manqué*. If one wants poetry, one reads Keats,
not his critics. It is to the credit of such poets as T. S. Eliot and W. H.
Auden that when they write criticism they write as critics. That is,
they state a thesis, make the necessary distinctions and definitions,
and then proceed to demonstrate their point by the analysis of specific
works.

If a mistakenly "poetic" tone in criticism is one undesirable extreme,
there is another extreme equally bad. Some critical writing defeats its
aim by a style so wooden and a procedure so mechanical as to call the
author's taste into question. It is to the credit of academic critics like
C. S. Lewis and Douglas Bush that their writing is often charming and
witty and manages to respect and even celebrate the literary possibilities

2. "The Literary Criticism of Aristotle," *Lectures in Criticism,* ed. Elliott Coleman (New
York: Pantheon Books, 1949), p. 17.

of language while remaining within the bounds of clear, logical statement. In evaluating the pieces that follow, one ought to ask how successfully the critic has avoided these two perils of critical writing: pointless effusion and pedantic dullness. The very best criticism provides us with both the soundness of knowledge and the grace of a minor art.

More apparent as a standard for judging criticism is the degree to which it actually illuminates the work under discussion and persuades us to experience it again or for the first time. Here the reader must ask himself (to use R. P. Blackmur's telling phrase) whether the critic has "done his homework." Has he, for example, worked with the most authoritative text of his author, or has he been misled by bad editions, by misconstructions of the text based on ignorance of the state of the language or the conventions of a given period, or by mere typographical errors? Is he aware of his assumptions and their limitations, or does he force the work he treats into a set of rigid categories he is unaware of? The sham battle of several decades ago between traditional scholars and New Critics has finally faded. It was, in any case, fought by irregulars, for most scholars knew that their labors were designed to enable readers to appreciate literature, and most esthetic critics knew that appreciation was impossible without knowledge and understanding. The student of criticism, then, is concerned with its accuracy in statement and citation and with the bearing of what the critic leaves untreated on the validity of what he actually gives us.

Equally important in good criticism are clear statements of aims, consistent argument, and adequate demonstration. Unfortunately, the language of literary criticism is complicated and uncodified. To trace the meaning and use of such a term as *allegory* is to discover that its boundaries are sometimes unclear (how does it precisely and always differ from symbol, myth, and metaphor?), its application and value different from one critic to another. Yet one ought not be overly dismayed by this. In large measure criticism is an enterprise in definition. And in examining literature, whose elements partake of one another, an iron terminology might well obscure or prohibit certain kinds of insights. In any case, innovations in critical thought often begin with an overthrow of the terminology which an older criticism uses as a shield. What one requires of the terminology of a given critical piece is that it be clear and self-consistent and that, if it is eccentric, the eccentricity be deliberate and useful rather than merely whimsical or uninformed. Finally, the need for what we have called an "iron terminology" is less arguable in literary criticism, which deals with works whose value lies, after all, in their uniqueness, than in the physical sciences, which deal with things or events whose common attributes provide their interest. However, students may wish to use handbooks of literary terms, of which there are many, or dip into some of the extended discussions of these terms, which are appearing with increasing frequency.

So far we have avoided suggesting that a hallmark of good literary criticism is the presence or implication of a fully worked-out philosophic position on the nature of knowledge and the question of value. For one thing, the gap between philosophy (even its esthetic branch) and criticism is greater than some would like to believe. It is only the mildest cynicism to say that we ought not expect more of an esthetic theory than that it will lead us to neglect as few masterpieces as possible. It was probably Oliver Edwards, Dr. Johnson's Pembroke College friend, who (according to Boswell) said:

> I have tried too in my time to be a philosopher; but I don't know how, cheerfulness was always breaking in.

The critic, too, may begin resolutely with grand generalizations, a definition of beauty, and a certainty about the limitations of this genre or that. But as he reads, he is brought up with a start by a phrase, a turn of plot, a revelation of character, and, despite his resolutions and certainties, the cheerfulness of recognizing a masterpiece breaks in. One would rather have a critic with few principles, or confused abstractions, or none, than a critic who fitted a text into a preconception. For essentially the critic attempts something parallel to the work of the writer, treating his object with sensitive openness and tact until it discloses itself.

Yet ultimately, sometimes even immediately, what the critic writes has implications for matters other than literature. To recognize what is effete or meretricious in literary expression, one must have some sense of what these qualities are in life. At their best, critics such as Samuel Johnson, Matthew Arnold, and Northrop Frye—to name only a few—allow us to conclude that their principles and values, consistent or not, are generous and humane. But these qualities lie more often in a sensitivity to "minute particulars" of existence than in an allegiance to high-minded abstractions.

A Final Word

If an anthology is, literally, a "gathering of flowers," this is a gathering of flowers dissected. "We murder to dissect," wrote Wordsworth. But a recent critic compared his art to those magician's acts in which a woman is sawed in half. After the show she walks offstage whole. Keats was not, to deny Byron's phrase, "killed off by one critique," nor was his poetry. Nor is the greatness of Shakespeare or Milton a conspiracy of critics. It is not works which are the final objects of literary criticism but the minds of readers.

What the critic does is to urge on us the logic and importance of seeing a work from this vantage and then that, like a good guide in Rome. His aim is to propose hypotheses and perceptions that will make a work more accessible to appreciation or, if it is a bad work, less. In short, the aim of the critic is to prompt and perfect the response of the reader. As I. A. Richards remarked, it is probably less important that we like good literature and dislike bad than that we employ both to organize our minds. Possibly this process of self-clarification is the ultimate reason for criticism. Viewed in this light, criticism becomes more than a parasitic activity; it becomes, like literature itself, a contribution to the scope and excellence of the mind.

Joseph Addison

PARADISE LOST *AS AN EPIC*

No. 267. SATURDAY, JANUARY 5.

CEDITE ROMANI SCRIPTORES, CEDITE GRAII
Propertius

There is nothing in nature more irksome than general discourses, especially when they turn chiefly upon words. For this reason I shall waive
the discussion of that point which was started some years since, Whether
Milton's *Paradise Lost* may be called an heroic poem? Those who will not
give it that title, may call it (if they please) a divine poem. It will be sufficient to its perfection, if it has in it all the beauties of the highest kind of
poetry; and as for those who allege it is not an heroic poem, they advance
no more to the diminution of it, than if they should say Adam is not Aeneas,
nor Eve, Helen.

I shall therefore examine it by the rules of epic poetry, and see whether
it falls short of the *Iliad* or *Aeneid*, in the beauties which are essential to
that kind of writing. The first thing to be considered in an epic poem is
the fable, which is perfect or imperfect, according as the action which it
relates is more or less so. This action should have three qualifications in
it. First, it should be but one action. Secondly, it should be an entire action. And thirdly, it should be a great action. To consider the action of
the *Iliad, Aeneid,* and *Paradise Lost,* in these three several lights. Homer,
to preserve the unity of his action, hastens into the midst of things, as
Horace has observed: had he gone up to Leda's egg, or begun much later,
even at the rape of Helen, or the investing of Troy, it is manifest that the
story of the poem would have been a series of several actions. He therefore opens his poem with the discord of his princes, and artfully inter-
weaves, in the several succeeding parts of it, an account of everything
material which relates to them, and had passed before this fatal dissen-
sion. After the same manner Aeneas makes his first appearance in the
Tyrrhene seas, and within sight of Italy, because the action proposed to

From *The Spectator* (1712). Title supplied by the editors.

be celebrated was that of his settling himself in Latium. But because it was necessary for the reader to know what had happened to him in the taking of Troy, and in the preceding parts of his voyage, Virgil makes his hero relate it by way of episode in the second and third books of the *Aeneid*. The contents of both which books come before those of the first book in the thread of the story, though, for preserving of this unity of action, they follow it in the disposition of the poem. Milton, in imitation of these two great poets, opens his *Paradise Lost* with an infernal council plotting the fall of man, which is the action he proposed to celebrate; and as for those great actions, the battle of the angels, and the creation of the world, (which preceded in point of time, and which, in my opinion, would have entirely destroyed the unity of his principal action, had he related them in the same order that they happened,) he cast them into the fifth, sixth, and seventh books, by way of episode to this noble poem.

Aristotle himself allows, that Homer has nothing to boast of as to the unity of his fable, though at the same time, that great critic and philosopher endeavours to palliate this imperfection in the Greek poet, by imputing it in some measure to the very nature of an epic poem. Some have been of opinion, that the *Aeneid* also labours in this particular, and has episodes which may be looked upon as excrescences rather than as parts of the action. On the contrary, the poem which we have now under our consideration, hath no other episodes than such as naturally arise from the subject, and yet is filled with such a multitude of astonishing incidents, that it gives us at the same time a pleasure of the greatest variety, and of the greatest simplicity; uniform in its nature, though diversified in the execution.

I must observe, also, that as Virgil, in the poem which was designed to celebrate the original of the Roman empire, has described the birth of its great rival, the Carthaginian commonwealth; Milton, with the like art, in his poem on the Fall of Man, has related the fall of those angels who are his professed enemies. Beside the many other beauties in such an episode, its running parallel with the great action of the poem hinders it from breaking the unity so much as another episode would have done, that had not so great an affinity with the principal subject. In short, this is the same kind of beauty which the critics admire in the *Spanish Friar, or the Double Discovery,* where the two different plots look like counterparts and copies of one another.

The second qualification required in the action of an epic poem is, that it should be an entire action: an action is entire when it is complete in all its parts; or, as Aristotle describes it, when it consists of a beginning, a middle, and an end. Nothing should go before it, be intermixed with it, or follow after it, that is not related to it; as, on the contrary, no single step should be omitted in that just and regular process which it must be supposed to take from its original to its consummation. Thus we see the anger of Achilles in its birth, its continuance, and effects; and Aeneas's settlement in Italy, carried on through all the oppositions in his way to it both by sea and land. The action in Milton excels (I think) both the former in this particular; we see it contrived in hell, executed upon earth, and punished by heaven. The parts of it are told in the most distinct manner, and grow out of one another in the most natural order.

The third qualification of an epic poem is its greatness. The anger of Achilles was of such consequence, that it embroiled the kings of Greece, destroyed the heroes of Asia, and engaged all the gods in factions. The settlement of Aeneas in Italy produced the Caesars, and gave birth to the Roman empire. Milton's subject was still greater than either of the former; it does not determine the fate of single persons or nations, but of a whole species. The united powers of hell are joined together for the destruction of mankind, which they effected in part, and would have completed, had not Omnipotence itself interposed. The principal actors are, man in his greatest perfection, and woman in her highest beauty. Their enemies are the fallen angels: the Messiah their friend, and the Almighty their protector. In short, everything that is great in the whole circle of being, whether within the verge of nature or out of it, has a proper part assigned it in this admirable poem.

In poetry, as in architecture, not only the whole, but the principal members, and every part of them, should be great. I will not presume to say, that the book of Games in the *Aeneid,* or that in the *Iliad,* are not of this nature; nor to reprehend Virgil's simile of a top and many other of the same kind in the *Iliad,* as liable to any censure in this particular; but I think we may say, without derogating from those wonderful performances, that there is an indisputable and unquestioned magnificence in every part of *Paradise Lost,* and, indeed, a much greater than could have been formed upon any Pagan system.

But Aristotle, by the greatness of the action, does not only mean that it should be great in its nature, but also in its duration; or, in other words, that it should have a due length in it, as well as what we properly call greatness. The just measure of this kind of magnitude, he explains by the following similitude. An animal, no bigger than a mite, cannot appear perfect to the eye, because the sight takes it in at once, and has only a confused idea of the whole, and not a distinct idea of all its parts; if, on the contrary, you should suppose an animal of ten thousand furlongs in length, the eye would be so filled with a single part of it, that it could not give the mind an idea of the whole. What these animals are to the eye, a very short or a very long action would be to the memory. The first would be, as it were, lost and swallowed up by it, and the other difficult to be contained in it. Homer and Virgil have shown their principal art in this particular; the action of the *Iliad,* and that of the *Aeneid,* were in themselves exceeding short; but are so beautifully extended and diversified by the invention of episodes, and the machinery of gods, with the like poetical ornaments, that they make up an agreeable story sufficient to employ the memory without overcharging it. Milton's action is enriched with such variety of circumstances, that I have taken as much pleasure in reading the contents of his books, as in the best invented story I ever met with. It is possible, that the traditions on which the *Iliad* and *Aeneid* were built, had more circumstances in them than the history of the Fall of Man, as it is related in Scripture. Besides, it was easier for Homer and Virgil to dash the truth with fiction, as they were in no danger of offending the religion of their country by it. But as for Milton, he had only a very few circumstances upon which to raise his poem, but was also obliged to proceed with the greatest caution in everything that he added out of his own invention. And, indeed, notwithstanding all the restraints he was under, he has filled his story with so many surprising incidents, which bear so close an analogy with what is delivered in holy writ, that it is capable of pleasing the most delicate reader, without giving offence to the most scrupulous.

The modern critics have collected, from several hints in the *Iliad* and *Aeneid,* the space of time which is taken up by the action of each of those poems; but as a great part of Milton's story was transacted in regions that lie out of the reach of the sun and the sphere of day, it is impossible to gratify the reader with such a calculation, which, indeed, would be more curious than instructive; none of the critics, either ancient or modern, having laid down rules to circumscribe the action of an epic poem with any determined number of years, days, or hours.

But of this more particularly hereafter.

No. 273. Saturday, January 12.

—NOTANDI SUNT TIBI MORES
Horace

Having examined the action of *Paradise Lost,* let us in the next place consider the actors. This is Aristotle's method of considering, first the fable, and secondly the manners; or, as we generally call them in English, the fable and the characters.

Homer has excelled all the heroic poets that ever wrote, in the multitude and variety of his characters. Every god that is admitted into his poem, acts a part which would have been suitable to no other deity. His princes are as much distinguished by their manners as by their dominions; and even those among them, whose characters seem wholly made up of courage, differ from one another as to the particular kinds of courage in which they excel. In short, there is scarce a speech or action in the *Iliad,* which the reader may not ascribe to the person that speaks or acts, without seeing his name at the head of it.

Homer does not only outshine all other poets in the variety, but also in the novelty of his characters. He hath introduced among his Grecian princes a person who had lived thrice the age of man, and conversed with Theseus, Hercules, Polyphemus, and the first race of heroes. His principal actor is the son of a goddess, not to mention the offspring of other deities, who have likewise a place in his poem, and the venerable Trojan prince, who was the father of so many kings and heroes. There is in these several characters of Homer, a certain dignity as well as novelty, which adapts them in a more peculiar manner to the nature of an heroic poem. Though at the same time, to give them the greater variety, he has described a Vulcan, that is, a buffoon among his gods, and a Thersites among his mortals.

Virgil falls infinitely short of Homer in the characters of his poem, both as to their variety and novelty. Aeneas is, indeed, a perfect character; but as for Achates, though he is styled the hero's friend, he does nothing in the whole poem which may deserve that title. Gyas, Mnestheus, Sergestus, and Cloanthus, are all of them men of the same stamp and character.

—FORTEMQUE GYAN, FORTEMQUE CLOANTHUM
Virgil

There are, indeed, several natural incidents in the part of Ascanius: as that of Dido cannot be sufficiently admired. I do not see anything new or particular in Turnus. Pallas and Evander are remote copies of Hector and Priam, as Lausus and Mezentius are almost parallels to Pallas and Evander. The characters of Nisus and Euryalus are beautiful, but common. We must not forget the parts of Sinon, Camilla, and some few others, which are fine improvements on the Greek poet. In short, there is neither that variety nor novelty in the persons of the *Aeneid,* which we meet with in those of the *Iliad.*

If we look into the characters of Milton, we shall find that he has introduced all the variety his fable was capable of receiving. The whole species of mankind was in two persons at the time to which the subject of his poem is confined. We have, however, four distinct characters in these two persons. We see man and woman in the highest innocence and perfection, and in the most abject state of guilt and infirmity. The two last characters are, indeed, very common and obvious; but the two first are not only more magnificent, but more new, than any characters either in Virgil or Homer, or indeed in the whole circle of nature.

Milton was so sensible of this defect in the subject of his poem, and of the few characters it would afford him, that he has brought into it two actors of a shadowy fictitious nature, in the persons of Sin and Death, by which means he has wrought into the body of his fable a very beautiful and well-invented allegory. But, notwithstanding the fineness of this allegory may atone for it in some measure, I cannot think that persons of such a chimerical existence are proper actors in an epic poem; because there is not that measure of probability annexed to them, which is requisite in writings of this kind, as I shall show more at large hereafter.

Virgil has, indeed, admitted Fame as an actress in the *Aeneid,* but the part she acts is very short, and none of the most admired circumstances in that divine work. We find in mock-heroic poems, particularly in the *Dispensary* and the *Lutrin,* several allegorical persons of this nature, which are very beautiful in those compositions, and may, perhaps, be used as an argument, that the authors of them were of opinion, such characters might have a place in an epic work. For my own part, I should be glad the reader would think so, for the sake of the poem I am now examining; and must further add, that if such empty, unsubstantial beings may be ever made use of on this occasion, never were any more nicely imagined, and employed in more proper actions, than those of which I am now speaking.

Another principal actor in this poem is the great enemy of mankind. The part of Ulysses in Homer's *Odyssey* is very much admired by Aristotle, as perplexing that fable with very agreeable plots and intricacies, not only by the many adventures in his voyage, and the subtilty of his behaviour, but by the various concealments and discoveries of his person in several parts of that poem. But the crafty being I have now mentioned makes a much longer voyage than Ulysses, puts in practice many more wiles and stratagems, and hides himself under a greater variety of shapes and appearances, all of which are severally detected, to the great delight and surprise of the reader.

We may likewise observe with how much art the poet has varied several characters of the persons that speak in his infernal assembly. On the contrary, how has he represented the whole Godhead exerting itself towards man in its full benevolence, under the three-fold distinction of a Creator, a Redeemer, and a Comforter!

Nor must we omit the person of Raphael, who, amidst his tenderness and friendship for man, shows such a dignity and condescension in all his speech and behaviour, as are suitable to a superior nature. The angels are, indeed, as much diversified in Milton, and distinguished by their proper parts, as the gods are in Homer or Virgil. The reader will find nothing ascribed to Uriel, Gabriel, Michael, or Raphael, which is not in a particular manner suitable to their respective characters.

There is another circumstance in the principal actors of the *Iliad* and *Aeneid*, which gives a peculiar beauty to those two poems, and was therefore contrived with very great judgment. I mean the authors having chosen for their heroes, persons who were so nearly related to the people for whom they wrote. Achilles was a Greek, and Aeneas the remote founder of Rome. By this means their countrymen (whom they principally proposed to themselves for their readers) were particularly attentive to all parts of their story, and sympathized with their heroes in all their adventures. A Roman could not but rejoice in the escapes, successes, and victories of Aeneas, and be grieved at any defeats, misfortunes, or disappointments that befell him; as a Greek must have had the same regard for Achilles. And it is plain, that each of those poems have lost this great advantage, among those readers to whom their heroes are as strangers, or indifferent persons.

Milton's poem is admirable in this respect, since it is impossible for any of its readers, whatever nation, country, or people he may belong to, not to be related to the persons who are the principal actors in it; but what is still infinitely more to its advantage, the principal actors in this poem are not only our progenitors, but our representatives. We have an actual interest in everything they do, and no less than our utmost happiness is concerned and lies at stake in their behaviour.

I shall subjoin, as a corollary to the foregoing remark, an admirable observation out of Aristotle, which hath been very much misrepresented in the quotations of some modern critics. "If a man of perfect and consummate virtue falls into a misfortune, it raises our pity, but not our terror, because we do not fear that it may be our own case, who do not resemble the suffering person. But (as that great philosopher adds) if we see a man of virtue, mixt with infirmities, fall into any misfortune, it does not only raise our pity, but our terror; because we are afraid that the like misfortune may happen to ourselves, who resemble the character of the suffering person."

I shall only remark in this place, that the foregoing observation of Aristotle, though it may be true in other occasions, does not hold in this; because in the present case, though the persons who fall into misfortune are of the most perfect and consummate virtue, it is not to be considered as what may possibly be, but what actually is our own case; since we are embarked with them on the same bottom, and must be partakers of their happiness or misery.

In this, and some other very few instances, Aristotle's rules for epic poetry (which he had drawn from his reflections upon Homer) cannot be supposed to square exactly with the heroic poems which have been made since his time; since it is evident to every impartial judge, his rules would still have been more perfect, could he have perused the *Aeneid,* which was made some hundred years after his death.

In my next I shall go through other parts of Milton's poem; and hope that what I shall there advance, as well as what I have already written, will not only serve as a comment upon Milton, but upon Aristotle.

No. 279. Saturday, January 19.

REDDERE PERSONAE SCIT CONVENIENTIA CUIQUE
Horace

We have already taken a general survey of the fable and characters in Milton's *Paradise Lost:* the parts which remain to be considered, according to Aristotle's method, are the sentiments and the language. Before I enter upon the first of these, I must advertise my reader, that it is my design, as soon as I have finished my general reflections on these four several heads, to give particular instances out of the poem now before us, of beauties and imperfections which may be observed under each of them, as also of such other particulars as may not properly fall under any of them. This I thought fit to premise, that the reader may not judge too hastily of this piece of criticism, or look upon it as imperfect, before he has seen the whole extent of it.

The sentiments in an epic poem are the thoughts and behaviour which the author ascribes to the persons whom he introduces, and are just when they are conformable to the characters of the several persons. The sentiments have likewise a relation to things as well as persons, and are then perfect when they are such as are adapted to the subject. If in either of these cases the poet endeavours to argue or explain, magnify or diminish, to raise love or hatred, pity or terror, or any other passion, we ought to consider whether the sentiments he makes use of are proper for those ends. Homer is censured by the critics for his defect as to this particular in several parts of the *Iliad* and *Odyssey;* though at the same time, those who have treated this great poet with candour, have attributed this defect to the times in which he lived. It was the fault of the age, and not of Homer, if there wants that delicacy in some of his sentiments, which now appears in the works of men of a much inferior genius. Besides, if there are blemishes in any particular thoughts, there is an infinite beauty in the greatest part of them. In short, if there are many poets who would not have fallen into the meanness of some of his sentiments, there are none who could have risen up to the greatness of others. Virgil has excelled all others in the propriety of his sentiments. Milton shines likewise very much in this particular: nor must we omit one consideration which adds to his honour and reputation. Homer and Virgil introduced persons whose characters are commonly known among men, and such as are to be met with either in history, or in ordinary conversation. Milton's characters, most of them, lie out of nature, and were to be formed purely by his own invention. It shows a greater genius in Shakspeare to have drawn his Caliban, than his Hotspur or Julius Caesar: the one was to be supplied out of his own imagination, whereas the other might have been formed upon tradition, history, and observation. It was much easier, therefore, for Homer to find proper sentiments for an assembly of Grecian generals, than for Milton to diversify his infernal council with proper characters, and inspire them with a variety of sentiments. The loves of Dido and Aeneas are only copies of what has passed between other persons. Adam and Eve, before the fall, are a different species from that of mankind who are descended from them; and none but a poet of the most unbounded invention, and the most exquisite judgment, could have filled their conversation and behaviour with so many circumstances during their state of innocence.

Nor is it sufficient for an epic poem to be filled with such thoughts as are natural, unless it abound also with such as are sublime. Virgil in this particular falls short of Homer. He has not, indeed, so many thoughts that are low and vulgar; but at the same time has not so many thoughts that are sublime and noble. The truth of it is, Virgil seldom rises into very astonishing sentiments, where he is not fired by the *Iliad*. He everywhere charms and pleases us by the force of his own genius; but seldom elevates and transports us where he does not fetch his hints from Homer.

Milton's chief talent, and, indeed, his distinguishing excellence, lies in the sublimity of his thoughts. There are others of the moderns who rival him in every other part of poetry; but in the greatness of his sentiments he triumphs over all the poets both modern and ancient, Homer only excepted. It is impossible for the imagination of man to distend itself with greater ideas, than those which he has laid together in his first, second, and sixth books. The seventh, which describes the creation of the world, is likewise wonderfully sublime, though not so apt to stir up emotion in the mind of the reader, nor consequently so perfect in the epic way of writing, because it is filled with less action. Let the judicious reader compare what Longinus has observed on several passages in Homer, and he will find parallels for most of them in the *Paradise Lost*.

From what has been said we may infer, that as there are two kinds of sentiments, the natural and the sublime, which are always to be pursued in an heroic poem, there are also two kinds of thoughts which are carefully to be avoided. The first are such as are affected and unnatural; the second, such as are mean and vulgar. As for the first kind of thoughts, we meet with little or nothing that is like them in Virgil; he has none of those trifling points and puerilities that are so often to be met with in Ovid, none of the epigrammatic turns of Lucan, none of those swelling sentiments which are so frequently in Statius and Claudian, none of those mixed embellishments of Tasso. Everything is just and natural. His sentiments show that he had a perfect insight into human nature, and that he knew everything which was the most proper to affect it.

Mr. Dryden has in some places, which I may hereafter take notice of, misrepresented Virgil's way of thinking as to this particular, in the translation he has given us of the *Aeneid*. I do not remember that Homer anywhere falls into the faults above-mentioned, which were, indeed, the false refinements of later ages. Milton, it must be confest, has sometimes erred in this respect, as I shall show more at large in another paper; though, considering all the poets of the age in which he writ were infected with this wrong way of thinking, he is rather to be admired that he did not give more into it, than that he did sometimes comply with the vicious taste which still prevails so much among modern writers.

But since several thoughts may be natural which are low and grovelling, an epic poet should not only avoid such sentiments as are unnatural or affected, but also such as are mean and vulgar. Homer has opened a great field of raillery to men of more delicacy than greatness of genius, by the homeliness of some of his sentiments. But, as I have before said, these are rather to be imputed to the simplicity of the age in which he lived, to which I may also add, of that which he described, than to any imperfection in that divine poet. Zöilus among the ancients, and Monsieur Perrault among the moderns, pushed their ridicule very far upon him, on account of some such sentiments. There is no blemish to be observed in Virgil under this head, and but a very few in Milton.

I shall give but one instance of this impropriety of thought in Homer, and at the same time compare it with an instance of the same nature, both in Virgil and Milton. Sentiments which raise laughter can very seldom be admitted with any decency into an heroic poem, whose business is to excite passions of a much nobler nature. Homer, however, in his characters of Vulcan and Thersites, in his story of Mars and Venus, in his behaviour of Irus, and in other passages, has been observed to have lapsed into the burlesque character, and to have departed from that serious air which seems essential to the magnificence of an epic poem. I remember but one laugh in the whole *Aeneid,* which rises in the fifth book, upon Monoetes, where he is represented as thrown overboard, and drying himself upon a rock. But this piece of mirth is so well timed, that the severest critic can have nothing to say against it, for it is in the book of games and diversions, where the reader's mind may be supposed to be sufficiently relaxed for such an entertainment. The only piece of pleasantry in *Paradise Lost,* is where the evil spirits are described as rallying the angels upon the success of their newly invented artillery. This passage I look upon to be the most exceptionable in the whole poem, as being nothing else but a string of puns, and those too very indifferent.

> —Satan beheld their plight,
> And to his mates thus in derision called.
> O friends, why come not on these victors proud!
> Ere while they fierce were coming, and when we,
> To entertain them fair with open front
> And breast, (what could we more?) propounded terms
> Of composition, straight they changed their minds,
> Flew off, and into strange vagaries fell,
> As they would dance; yet for a dance they seemed
> Somewhat extravagant and wild, perhaps
> For joy of offered peace; but I suppose
> If our proposals once again were heard,
> We should compel them to a quick result.
> To whom thus Belial, in like gamesome mood.
> Leader, the terms we sent were terms of weight,
> Of hard contents, and full of force urged home,
> Such as we might perceive amused them all,
> And stumbled many; who receives them right
> Had need, from head to foot, well understand;
> Not understood, this gift they have besides,
> They show us when our foes walk not upright.
> Thus they among themselves in pleasant vein
> Stood scoffing—

No. 285. Saturday, January 26.

NE QUICUNQUE DEUS, QUICUNQUE ADHIBEBITUR HEROS,
REGALI CONSPECTUS IN AURO NUPER ET OSTRO,
MIGRET IN OBSCURAS HUMILI SERMONE TABERNAS:
AUT DUM VITAT HUMUM, NUBES ET INANIA CAPTET
Horace

Having already treated of the fable, the characters, and sentiments in the *Paradise Lost*, we are in the last place to consider the language; and as the learned world is very much divided upon Milton as to this point, I hope they will excuse me if I appear particular in any of my opinions, and incline to those who judge the most advantageously of the author.

It is requisite that the language of an heroic poem should be both perspicuous and sublime. In proportion as either of these two qualities are wanting, the language is imperfect. Perspicuity is the first and most necessary qualification; insomuch, that a good-natured reader sometimes overlooks a little slip even in the grammar or syntax, where it is impossible for him to mistake the poet's sense. Of this kind is that passage in Milton, wherein he speaks of Satan:

—God and his Son except,
Created thing nought valued he nor shunn'd.

And that in which he describes Adam and Eve:

Adam the goodliest man of men since born
His sons, the fairest of her daughters Eve.

It is plain, that in the former of these passages, according to the natural syntax, the divine persons mentioned in the first line are represented as created beings; and that in the other, Adam and Eve are confounded with their sons and daughters. Such little blemishes as these, when the thought is great and natural, we should, with Horace, impute to a pardonable inadvertency, or to the weakness of human nature, which cannot attend to each minute particular, and give the last finishing to every circumstance in so long a work. The ancient critics, therefore, who were acted by a spirit of candour, rather than that of cavilling, invented certain figures of speech, on purpose to palliate little errors of this nature in the writings of those authors who had so many greater beauties to atone for them.

If clearness and perspicuity were only to be consulted, the poet would have nothing else to do but to clothe his thoughts in the most plain and natural expressions. But since it often happens, that the most obvious phrases, and those which are used in ordinary conversation, become too familiar to the ear, and contract a kind of meanness by passing through the mouths of the vulgar, a poet should take particular care to guard himself against idiomatic ways of speaking. Ovid and Lucan have many poornesses of expression upon this account, as taking up with the first phrases that offered, without putting themselves to the trouble of looking after such as would not only be natural, but also elevated and sublime. Milton has but a few failings in this kind, of which, however, you may meet with some instances, as in the following passages.

Embryos and Idiots, Eremites and Friars,
White, black, and grey, with all their trumpery,
Here pilgrims roam—

—Awhile discourse they hold,
No fear lest dinner cool; when thus began
Our author—

Who of all ages to succeed, but feeling
The evil on him brought by me, will curse
My head, ill fare our ancestor impure,
For this we may thank Adam—

The great masters in composition know very well that many an elegant phrase becomes improper for a poet or an orator, when it has been debased by common use. For this reason the works of ancient authors, which are written in dead languages, have a great advantage over those which are written in languages that are now spoken. Were there any mean phrases or idioms in Virgil and Homer, they would not shock the ear of the most delicate modern reader so much as they would have done that of an old Greek or Roman, because we never hear them pronounced in our streets, or in ordinary conversation.

It is not, therefore, sufficient, that the language of an epic poem be perspicuous, unless it be also sublime. To this end it ought to deviate from the common forms and ordinary phrases of speech. The judgment of a poet very much discovers itself in shunning the common roads of expression, without falling into such ways of speech as may seem stiff and unnatural; he must not swell into a false sublime, by endeavoring to avoid the other extreme. Among the Greeks, Aeschylus, and sometimes Sophocles, were guilty of this fault; among the Latins, Claudian and Statius; and among our own countrymen, Shakspeare and Lee. In these authors the affectation of greatness often hurts the perspicuity of the style, as in many others the endeavour after perspicuity prejudices its greatness.

Aristotle has observed, that the idiomatic style may be avoided, and the sublime formed, by the following methods. First, by the use of metaphors: such are those in Milton.

Imparadised in one another's arms.

—And in his hand a reed
Stood waving, tipt with fire.—

The grassy clods now calved.—

Spangled with eyes—

In these, and innumerable other instances, the metaphors are very bold, but just; I must, however, observe, that the metaphors are not thick-sown in Milton, which always savours too much of wit; that they never clash with one another, which, as Aristotle observes, turns a sentence into a kind of an enigma or riddle; and that he seldom has recourse to them where the proper and natural words will do as well.

Another way of raising the language, and giving it a poetical turn, is to make use of the idioms of other tongues. Virgil is full of the Greek forms of speech, which the critics call Hellenisms, as Horace in his Odes abounds with them, much more than Virgil. I need not mention the several dialects which Homer has made use of for this end. Milton, in conformity with the practice of the ancient poets, and with Aristotle's rule, has infused a great many Latinisms, as well as Graecisms, and sometimes Hebraisms, into the language of his poem; as towards the beginning of it,

Nor did they not perceive the evil plight
In which they were, or the fierce pains not feel,
Yet to their general's voice they soon obeyed.

—Who shall tempt with wandering feet
The dark, unbottomed, infinite abyss,
And through the palpable obscure find out
His uncouth way, or spread his airy flight,
Upborne with indefatigable wings
Over the vast abrupt!

—So both ascend
In the visions of God—
          B. ii.

Under this head may be reckoned the placing the adjective after the substantive, the transposition of words, the turning the adjective into a substantive, with several other foreign modes of speech, which this poet has naturalized to give his verse the greater sound, and throw it out of prose.

The third method mentioned by Aristotle, is what agrees with the genius of the Greek language more than with that of any other tongue, and is therefore more used by Homer than by any other poet. I mean the lengthening of a phrase by the addition of words, which may either be inserted or omitted, as also by the extending or contracting of particular words by the insertion or omission of certain syllables. Milton has put in practice this method of raising his language, as far as the nature of our tongue will permit, as in the passage above-mentioned, eremite for what is hermite in common discourse. If you observe the measure of his verse, he has with great judgment suppressed a syllable in several words, and shortened those of two syllables into one, by which method, besides the above-mentioned advantage, he has given a greater variety to his numbers. But this practice is more particularly remarkable in the names of persons and of countries, Beëlzebub, Hessebon, and in many other particulars, wherein he has either changed the name, or made use of that which is not the most commonly known, that he might the better depart from the language of the vulgar.

The same reason recommended to him several old words, which also makes his poem appear the more venerable, and gives it a greater air of antiquity.

I must likewise take notice, that there are in Milton several words of his own coining, as *Cerberean, miscreated, hell-doom'd, embryon* atoms, and many others. If the reader is offended at this liberty in our English poet, I would recommend him to a discourse in Plutarch, which shows us how frequently Homer has made use of the same liberty.

Milton, by the above-mentioned helps, and by the choice of the noblest words and phrases which our tongue would afford him, has carried our language to a greater height than any of the English poets have ever done before or after him, and made the sublimity of his style equal to that of his sentiments.

I have been the more particular in these observations on Milton's style, because it is that part of him in which he appears the most singular. The remarks I have here made upon the practice of other poets, with my observations out of Aristotle, will perhaps alleviate the prejudice which some have taken to his poem upon this account; though, after all, I must confess, that I think his style, though admirable in general, is in some places too much stiffened and obscured by the frequent use of those methods, which Aristotle has prescribed for the raising of it.

This redundancy of those several ways of speech which Aristotle calls foreign language, and with which Milton has so very much enriched, and in some places darkened, the language of his poem, was the more proper for his use, because his poem is written in blank verse. Rhyme, without any other assistance, throws the language off from prose, and very often makes an indifferent phrase pass unregarded; but where the verse is not built upon rhymes, there pomp of sound, and energy of expression, are indispensably necessary to support the style, and keep it from falling into the flatness of prose.

Those who have not a taste for this elevation of style, and are apt to ridicule a poet when he goes out of the common forms of expression, would do well to see how Aristotle has treated an ancient author, called Euclid, for his insipid mirth upon this occasion. Mr. Dryden used to call this sort of men his prose-critics.

I should, under this head of the language, consider Milton's numbers, in which he has made use of several elisions, that are not customary among other English poets, as may be particularly observed in his cutting off the letter Y, when it precedes a vowel. This, and some other innovations in the measure of his verse, has varied his numbers, in such a manner, as makes them incapable of satiating the ear and cloying the reader, which the same uniform measure would certainly have done, and which the perpetual returns of rhyme never fail to do in long narrative poems. I shall close these reflections upon the language of *Paradise Lost,* with observing that Milton has copied after Homer, rather than Virgil, in the length of his periods, the copiousness of his phrases, and the running of his verses into one another.

Maynard Mack

THE MUSE OF SATIRE

It grows plainer every year that literary study in our part of the twenti-eth century has been very considerably stimulated by one important event. This event is the gradual reëmergence of rhetoric—by which I mean the reëmergence of a number of interpretive skills and assumptions about literature that under the name of rhetoric once formed part of the medieval trivium and together with grammar made up a study somewhat resembling what we now call literary explication. As we begin the second half of the century, the signs of this rhetorical quickening seem to me to be multiplying very fast.

To begin with a whimsical example, I notice that my reprint of Puttenham's "Arte of English Poesie" (1589), frequently on loan to students, is well thumbed chiefly at the twelve chapters where the rhetorical figures are named and illustrated. Forty-five years ago, when Gregory Smith reprinted Puttenham in his collection of "Elizabethan Critical Essays," these were precisely the chapters, and the only chapters, he chose to leave out. This is a straw in the wind from readers.

There is ampler evidence from writers. One might cite, at the level of research, the speedy proliferation of studies dealing with aspects of rhetorical history: investigations like J. W. H. Atkins' of classical, medieval, and Renaissance criticism, or T. W. Baldwin's of Shakespeare's grammar school training, or Miss Tuve's of sixteenth-century rhetorical manuals. At the level of practical criticism, one could point to the reappearance of rhetorical concepts in literary discourse. One hears the word *decorum* used nowadays without a sneer; one comes across mentions, though as yet no illuminating discussions, of the "three styles" —high, middle, and low; one even hears the admission that there may be something in genre: "Paradise Lost," Mr. C. S. Lewis has been trying to persuade us, is what it is at least as much because it is a *heroic* poem as because it was written by John Milton.

But doubtless the climactic evidence at the critical level is the so-called—the so ineptly called—"new" criticism. The enormous influence of this body of writing can only be properly understood, I think, if we

From *The Yale Review*, XLI (1951), 80–92. Copyright 1951 by Yale University Press.

realize that it has been the pioneering phase—that is to say, the most applied and "practical" phase—in a general revival of rhetorical interests and disciplines. Evoked by the absence of a continuing tradition of rhetorical analysis (for the classical tradition was unfortunately discredited by the time the new critics began to write), this criticism has been an effort, often fumbling, often brilliant, to recapture some of the older exegetical skills, or at any rate to formulate their equivalents, for modern use.

Now rhetoric being a body of learning that insists on the recognition of artifice, one of the effects of its renascence is bound to be the reinvigoration of our sense of distinctions between art and life. If we compare ourselves with the nineteenth century in this respect, we realize that we no longer write, or care to read, books like Mrs. Cowden Clarke's on "The Girlhood of Shakespeare's Heroines" (1850–2); nor do we care to inquire, even with so great a critic as A. C. Bradley, where Hamlet was when his father was being murdered, or with Ellen Terry, how the Boy in Henry V learned French: "Did he learn to speak the lingo from Prince Hal, or from Falstaff in London, or did he pick it up during his few weeks in France with the army?" We realize, too, that unlike the nineteenth century we can no longer speak of Shakespeare's "Dark Period" or his "Joyous Comedies," except by enclosing the words in quotation marks. We acknowledge, to be sure, that a playwright and his plays are involved with each other in important ways, but we are much too conscious of artifice to be willing to risk a direct reading from comedy or tragedy to the author's states of mind.

In our dealings with the drama, in fact, most of us are now willing to add to the study of how a work grows or what it does the study of what it is. Inquiries into biographical and historical origins, or into effects on audiences and readers, can and should be supplemented, we are beginning to insist, by a third kind of inquiry treating the work with some strictness as a rhetorical construction: as a "thing made," which, though it reaches backward to an author and forward to an audience, has its artistic identity in between—in the realm of artifice and artifact. With respect to drama, there has lately been building a valuable even if by no means uniformly sound criticism of this kind. But outside the drama, and a few other areas recently invaded, we cannot point to very much. On the subject of poetry in general, Mr. Ricardo Quintana has complained, most of our commentary still "turns out to be either description of our impressions" (i.e., effects), "or reconstruction—largely imaginary—of a precise moment in the poet's emotional history with which we have chosen to equate the poem" (i.e., origins).

One need not share Mr. Quintana's doubt as to the effectiveness of other approaches to feel that in the case of satire, at any rate, what is desperately needed today is inquiry that deals neither with origins nor effects, but with artifice. Criticism of satiric literature has barely begun to budge from the position of Macaulay, Elwin, Leslie Stephen—all of whom seem, at one time or another, to have regarded it as a kind of dark night of the soul (dank with poisonous dews) across which squibs of envy, malice, hate, and spite luridly explode. Here is a sample from 1880, referring to Pope's "Sporus": "that infusion of personal venom"; "the poet is writing under some bitter mortification"; he is "trying with concentrated malice to sting his adversary"; he is "a tortured victim screaming out the shrillest taunts at his tormentor" (Sir Leslie Stephen). Here is a sample from 1925, referring to Pope's epistles and satires in general: at the time of their creation, "they resembled nothing so much as spoonsful of boiling oil, ladled out by a fiendish monkey at an upstairs window upon such of the passers-by whom the wretch had a grudge against" (Lytton Strachey). And here is a sample from 1941, referring to the "Dunciad"—if anything the tone is shriller: "impossible to admire it without an unenviable pleasure in sheer spite"; "the tone of furious indiscriminate hatred"; "the half-crazed misanthropy of the whole poem"; "a general indictment of the human race"; "this universal shriek of loathing and despair" (Gilbert Highet).

In this essay, I should like to ventilate this fetid atmosphere a little by opening a window on one or two rhetorical observations. These observations will be commonplaces, but the record suggests that they can bear repetition. My illustrations will be drawn from Pope, especially from his formal satires, such as the "Epistle to Dr. Arbuthnot"; and my thesis will be that even in these apparently very personal poems, we overlook what is most essential if we overlook the distinction between the historical Alexander Pope and the dramatic Alexander Pope who speaks them.

It is to underscore this distinction that I have ventured in my title to name the Muse. For the Muse ought always to be our reminder that it is not the author as man who casts these shadows on our printed page, but the author as poet: an instrument possessed by and possessing—Plato would have said a god, we must at any rate say an art. And, moreover, the Muse ought to remind us that in any given instance the shadow may not delineate even the whole poet, but perhaps only that angle of his sensibility which best refracts the light from epic, elegy, pastoral, lyric, satire. The fact is not without significance, it seems to me, that though Pope, following the great victories of naturalism in the seventeenth century, had to make do with a minimum of mythology and myth, he never discarded the Muse, either the conception or the term. She appears with remarkable regularity even in his satires, and there, for my present purposes, I am choosing to regard her as a not entirely playful symbol of the impersonality of the satiric genre—of its rhetorical and dramatic character.

Rhetorically considered, satire belongs to the category of *laus et vituperatio*, praise and blame. It aims, like all poetry, in Sidney's phrase, through the "fayning notable images of vertues [and] vices," to achieve "that delightful teaching which must be the right describing note to know a Poet by." And it has, of course, its own distinctive means to this. Prominent among them to a casual eye is the *exemplum* in the form of portrait, like Dryden's Zimri, or Pope's Atticus; and the middle style, which stresses conversational speech (more than passion or grandiloquence) along with aphoristic phrasings, witty turns, and ironical indirections. Less prominent but more important than either of these is the satiric fiction into which such materials must be built.

All good satire, I believe it is fair to say, exhibits an appreciable degree of fictionality. Where the fiction inheres in familiar elements like plot, as in "Absalom and Achitophel" or "The Rape of the Lock" or "The Dunciad" or "The Beggar's Opera," its presence is, of course, unmistakable; and it is unmistakable, too, in such satires as Swift's "Argument against Abolishing Christianity" or his "Modest Proposal," where the relation of the speaker to the author is extremely oblique, not to say antithetical. But when the relation is only slightly oblique, as in Pope's formal satires, the fictionality takes subtler forms and resides in places where, under the influence of romantic theories of poetry as the spontaneous overflow of powerful emotions, we have become unaccustomed to attend to it. (How far unaccustomed is seen if we reflect that the extraordinary views of Gulliver in Houyhnhnmland have been repeatedly cited as identical with Swift's. And this despite the fact that the incidents of the book show the author to be studiedly undercutting his hero-gull and to be using the metaphor of the rational *animal*, the Houyhnhnm, to make it plain that pure rationality is neither available nor appropriate to the human species—just as in the "Essay on Man" Pope's fully rational angels show "a Newton as we show an Ape.")

One aspect of the fictionality in Pope's case resides in the general plan of the formal satiric poem. This, as Miss Randolph has observed in the work of Horace, Persius, and Juvenal, contains always two layers. There is a thesis layer attacking vice and folly, elaborated with every kind of rhetorical device, and, much briefer, an antithesis layer illustrating or implying a philosophy of rational control, usually embodied in some more or less ideal norm like the Stoic *vir bonus,* the good plain man. The contours of formal verse satire, in other words, are not established entirely or even principally by a poet's rancorous sensibility; they are part of a fiction.

We encounter a further aspect of this fiction when we pause to consider that the bipartite structure just mentioned apparently exists to reflect a more general fictive situation. This situation is the warfare of good and evil—differentiated in satire from the forms it might take in, say, lyric, by being viewed from the angle of social solidarity rather than private introspection; and from the forms it might take in, say, tragedy, by being carried on in a context that asserts the primacy of moral decision, as tragedy asserts the primacy of moral understanding.

Tragedy and satire, I suspect, are two ends of a literary spectrum. Tragedy tends to exhibit the inadequacy of norms, to dissolve systematized values, to precipitate a meaning containing— but not necessarily contained by—recognizable ethical codes. Satire, on the contrary, asserts the validity and necessity of norms, systematic values, and meanings that *are* contained by recognizable codes. Where tragedy fortifies the sense of irrationality and complexity in experience because it presents us a world in which man is more victim than agent, in which our commodities prove to be our defects (and vice versa), and in which blindness and madness are likely to be symbols of insight, satire tends to fortify our feeling that life makes more immediate moral sense. In the world it offers us, madness and blindness are usually the emblems of vice and folly, evil and good are clearly distinguishable, criminals and fools are invariably responsible (therefore censurable), and standards of judgment are indubitable. All this, too, results from a slant of the glass, a fictional perspective on the real world—which, as we know, does not wholly correspond either with the tragic outlook or the satiric one.

Finally, we must note, among these general and pervasive aspects of fictionality in satire, the *ethos* of the satirist. Classical rhetoric, it is well to recall, divides the persuasive elements in any communication from one man to another into three sorts: the force of the arguments employed, the appeal to the interest and emotions of the hearer, and the weight of authority that comes from the hearer's estimate of the speaker's character, his *ethos*. For the satirist especially, the establishment of an authoritative *ethos* is imperative. If he is to be effective in "that delightful teaching," he must be accepted by his audience as a fundamentally virtuous and tolerant man, who challenges the doings of other men not whenever he happens to feel vindictive, but whenever they deserve it. On this account, the satirist's *apologia* for his satire is one of the stock subjects of both the classical writers and Pope: the audience must be assured that its censor is a man of good will, who has been, as it were, *forced* into action. *Difficile est saturam non scribere:* "It is difficult *not* to write satire."

Moreover, the satirist's *ethos* is the *rhetorical* occasion (even though vanity may be among the *motives)* of his frequent citations of himself. As a candid fellow, for instance, and no pretender to be holier than thou:

> I love to pour out all myself, as plain
> As downright Shippen, or as old Montaigne. . . .
> In me what Spots, (for Spots I have) appear,
> Will prove at least the Medium must be clear.

A man, too, of simple tastes, persistent loyalties:

> Content with little, I can piddle here
> On Broccoli and mutton, round the Year;
> But ancient friends, (tho' poor, or out of play)
> That touch my Bell, I cannot turn away.

A man whose character was formed in the good old-fashioned way by home instruction and edifying books:

> Bred up at home, full early I begun
> To read in Greek, the Wrath of Peleus' Son.
> Besides, My Father taught me from a Lad,
> The better Art, to know the good from bad.

Consequently, a man who honors the natural pieties:

> Me, let the tender Office long engage
> To rock the Cradle of reposing Age:

who is sensible of life's true ends:

> Farewell then Verse, and Love, and ev'ry Toy,
> The rhymes and rattles of the Man or Boy,
> What right, what true, what fit, we justly call,
> Let this be all my Care—for this is All:

and who is valued by distinguished friends. If the friends happen to be out of power, or drawn in part from a vanished Golden Age, so much the better for *ethos:* our satirist is guaranteed to be no time-server.

> But does the Court a worthy Man remove?
> That instant, I declare, he has my love.
> I shun his Zenith, court his mild Decline;
> Thus Sommers once, and Halifax were mine.
> Oft in the clear, still Mirrour of Retreat
> I study'd Shrewsbury, the wise and great. . . .
> How pleasing Atterbury's softer hour!
> How shin'd the Soul, unconquer'd in the Tow'r!
> How can I Pult'ney, Chesterfield forget
> While Roman Spirit charms, and Attic Wit? . . .
> Names which I long have lov'd, nor lov'd in vain,
> Rank'd with their Friends, not number'd with their Train.

By passages of this kind in Pope's satires, the rhetorically innocent are habitually distressed. They remark with surprise that Pope insists on portraying himself in these poems as "lofty, good-humored, calm, disinterested." Or they grow indignant that an epistle like "Arbuthnot" reveals "not what Pope really was, but what he wished others to think him." They fail to notice that he speaks this way only in a certain kind of poem, and so enlarge irrelevantly—though to be sure with biographical truth enough—upon the subject of his vanity. Meantime, on a rhetorical view, the real point remains, which is simply that in passages of this sort, as also in his notes to the "Dunciad," and probably, to some extent, in the publication of his letters (both these enterprises, significantly, accompanied his turning satirist), Pope felt the necessity of supporting the *ethos* a satirical poet must have.

Obviously, the two agents to be considered in the fictive situation are the person speaking and the person addressed. We may, however, dismiss the second, for though he is often a true *adversarius*—a friend calculated like Job's friends to be egregiously mistaken in his views and values—no one, I think, has ever seriously misinterpreted a satire because he failed to see that the *adversarius* was a fiction. It is with the satiric speaker that the difficulty has come. We may call this speaker Pope, if we wish, but only if we remember that he always reveals himself as a character in a drama, not as a man confiding in us. The distinction is apparent if we think of Wordsworth's use of the word *young* in a famous passage from "The Prelude" about the early days of the French Revolution: "Bliss was it in that dawn to be alive, And to be young was very heaven"— and then compare it with Pope's remark to the friend with whom he professes to be conversing in the first dialogue of the "Epilogue to the Satires": "Dear Sir, forgive the Prejudice of Youth." Wordsworth's *young* is determined by something outside the poem, something true (in the years to which the poet refers) of himself in real life. But in real life, when Pope wrote his dialogue, he was already fifty; his *youth* is true only of the satiric speaker of the poem, who is an assumed identity, a *persona*.

This *persona* or speaker has almost always in Pope's formal satires three distinguishable voices. One is the voice of the man I have partly described in connection with *ethos:* the man of plain living, high thinking, lasting friendships; who hates lies, slanders, lampoons; who laughs at flatteries of himself; who is "soft by Nature, more a Dupe than Wit"; who loves of all things best "the Language of the Heart"; and who views his own poetry with amused affection qualified with Virgilian tenderness for the tears of things in general:

> Years foll'wing Years, steal something ev'ry day,
> At last they steal us from ourselves away;
> In one our Frolicks, one Amusements end,
> In one a Mistress drops, in one a Friend:
> This subtle Thief of Life, this paltry Time,
> What will it leave me, if it snatch my Rhime?

Then, secondly, there is the voice of the *naïf,* the *ingénu,* the simple heart: "the Prejudice of Youth." The owner of this voice is usually the vehicle of ironies about matters he professes not to understand, and is amazed by his own involvement in the literary arts. "I lisp'd in Numbers, for the Numbers came"—says this voice, speaking of one of the most carefully meditated poetries in literature. Or else: "Why did I write? What sin to me unknown Dipt me in Ink . . . ?" To the owner of this voice, his proficiency in satire is particularly puzzling. Should it be explained as the by-product of insomnia?

> I nod in Company, I wake at Night,
> Fools rush into my Head, and so I write;

a scheme of personal defense like jiujitsu?

> Satire's my weapon . . .
> Its proper pow'r to hurt each Creature feels,
> Bulls aim their Horns, and Asses lift their Heels;

or is it a species of harmless madness, a kind of psychosomatic twitch that nothing short of death will stop?

> Whether the darken'd Room to Muse invite,
> Or whiten'd Wall provoke the Skew'r to write,
> In Durance, Exile, Bedlam, or the Mint,
> Like Lee and Budgell, I will Rhyme and Print.

Pope's third voice is that of the public defender. If the first voice gives us the satirist as *vir bonus,* the plain good private citizen, and the second, the satirist as *ingénu,* this one brings us the satirist as hero. A peculiar tightening in the verse takes place whenever this *persona* begins to speak, whether he speaks of the mysterious purposes of

> The God of Nature, who, within us still,
> Inclines our Action, not constrains our Will;

or of the time when

> Inexorable Death shall level all,
> And Trees, and Stones, and Farms, and Farmer fall;

or of his own calling:

> Yes, I am proud; I must be proud to see
> Men not afraid of God, afraid of me.

The satirist as *vir bonus* was content to laugh at flatteries, but the satirist as hero feels differently:

> Fr. This filthy Simile, this beastly Line,
> Quite turns my Stomach—P. So does Flatt'ry mine;
> And all your Courtly Civet Cats can vent,
> Perfume to you, to me is Excrement.

Similarly, the satirist as *ingénu* chose to find the motives of satire in a nervous reflex; the satirist as hero has other views:

> O sacred Weapon! left for Truth's defence,
> Sole dread of Folly, Vice, and Insolence!
> To all but Heav'n-directed hands deny'd,
> The Muse may give thee, but the Gods must guide.

   Without pretending that these are the only voices Pope uses, or that they are always perfectly distinguishable, we may observe that the total dramatic development of any one of his formal satires is to a large extent determined by the way they succeed one another, modulate and qualify one another, and occasionally fuse with one another. In a poem like Pope's imitation of the first satire of Horace's second book, the structure is in a very real sense no more than a function of the modulations in tone that it takes to get from the opening verses, where the *naïf* shows up with his little slingshot and his five smooth pebbles from the brook:

> Tim'rous by Nature, of the Rich in awe,
> I come to Council learned in the Law;

through the point, about a hundred lines later, at which we realize that this fellow has somehow got Goliath's head in his hand (and also, the hero's accents in his voice):

> Hear this, and tremble! you, who 'scape the Laws.
> Yes, while I live, no rich or noble knave
> Shall walk the World, in credit, to his grave;

then back down past a window opening on the unimpeachable integrity of the *vir bonus,* instanced in his ties with men whom it is no longer fashionable to know: "Chiefs, out of War, and Statesmen, out of Place"; and so, finally, to a reassumption of the voice of the *ingénu,* surprised and pained that he should be thought to have any but the noblest aims. "Libels and Satires!" he exclaims, on learning the category into which his poems are thrust—"lawless things indeed!"

> But grave Epistles, bringing Vice to light,
> Such as a King might read, a Bishop write,
> Such as Sir Robert would approve——?

Indeed? says the friend; well to be sure, *that's* different: "You may then proceed."

Though the construction in Pope's satires is by no means always so schematic as in this example, it seems almost invariably to invoke the three voices of the *naïf,* the *vir bonus,* and the hero. And their presence need not perhaps surprise us, if we pause to consider that they sum up, between them, most of what is essential in the satirist's position. As *naïf,* the satirist educates us. He makes us see the ulcer where we were accustomed to see the rouge. He is the child in the fairy story forever crying, "But mamma, the king *is* naked." As *vir bonus,* on the other hand, he wins our confidence in his personal moral insight. He shows us that he is stable, independent, urbane, wise—a man who knows there is a time to laugh, a time to weep: "Who would not weep, if Atticus were he?" And finally, as hero, he opens to us a world where the discernment of evil is always accompanied, as it is not always in the real world, by the courage to strike at it. He invites us, in an excellent phrase of Mr. Bredvold's, to join "the invisible church of good men" everywhere, "few though they may be—for whom things matter." And he never lets us forget that we *are* at war; there *is* an enemy.

We should never have made, I think, so many mistakes about a portrait like "Sporus" if we had grasped the fact that it is primarily a portrait of the enemy (one of the finest Pope ever drew), evoked in a particular context at a particular point. We know, of course, that the lines were based on Pope's contemporary, Lord Hervey, whom he passionately disliked; and therefore we may justly infer that personal animus entered powerfully into their motivation.

But to read with this animus as our center of interest is to overlook the fact that, though the lines may be historically about Hervey, they are rhetorically about the enemy. It is to fail to see that they sum up in an *exemplum* (of which the implications become very pointed in the references to Satan) the fundamental attributes of the invader in every garden: his specious attractiveness—as a butterfly, a painted child, a dimpling stream; his nastiness—as a bug, a creature generated in dirt, a thing that stinks and stings, a toad spitting froth and venom; his essential impotence—as a mumbling spaniel, a shallow stream, a puppet, a hermaphrodite; and yet his perpetual menace as the tempter, powerless himself but always lurking "at the ear of Eve," as Pope puts it, to usurp the powers of good and pervert them. Because the lines associate Sporus with Evil in this larger sense, his portrait can be the ladder by which Pope mounts, in the evolution of the epistle as a whole, from the studiedly personal impatience of the pestered private citizen in the opening lines: " 'Shut, shut the door, good John!' fatigu'd I said," to the impersonal trumpet tones of the public defender on the walls of *Civitas Dei*—"Welcome for thee, fair Virtue, all the past." Without Sporus prostrate on the field behind him, the satiric speaker could never have supported this heroic tone. Something pretty close to the intensity exhibited by this portrait was called for, at just this point, not by the poet's actual feelings about a contemporary, but by the drama of feelings that has been building inside the poem—the fictive war—"the strong Antipathy of Good to Bad," here projected in its climactic symbol.

Northrop Frye

TOWARDS DEFINING AN AGE OF SENSIBILITY

The period of English literature which covers roughly the second half of the eighteenth century is one which has always suffered from not having a clear historical or functional label applied to it. I call it here the age of sensibility, which is not intended to be anything but a label. This period has the 'Augustan' age on one side of it and the 'Romantic' movement on the other, and it is usually approached transitionally, as a period of reaction against Pope and anticipation of Wordsworth. The chaos that results from treating this period, or any other, in terms of reaction has been well described by Professor Crane in a recent article in the Toronto Quarterly.[1] What we do is to set up, as the logical expression of Augustanism, some impossibly pedantic view of following rules and repressing feelings, which nobody could ever have held, and then treat any symptom of freedom or emotion as a departure from this. Our students are thus graduated with a vague notion that the age of sensibility was the time when poetry moved from a reptilian Classicism, all cold and dry reason, to a mammalian Romanticism, all warm and wet feeling.

As for the term 'pre-romantic,' that, as a term for the age itself, has the peculiar demerit of committing us to anachronism before we start, and imposing a false teleology on everything we study. Not only did the 'pre-romantics' not know that the Romantic movement was going to succeed them, but there has probably never been a case on record of a poet's having regarded a later poet's work as the fulfilment of his own. However, I do not care about terminology, only about appreciation for an extraordinarily interesting period of English literature, and the first stage in renewing that appreciation seems to me the gaining of a clear sense of what it is in itself.

Some languages use verb-tenses to express, not time, but the difference between completed and continuous action. And in the history of litera-

From *Journal of English Literary History* (June 1956), 144–152. Reprinted by permission of The Johns Hopkins Press.

1. R. S. Crane, 'On Writing the History of English Criticism, 1650–1800,' *University of Toronto Quarterly,* July 1953, pp. 376–91.

ture we become aware, not only of periods, but of a recurrent opposition of two views of literature. These two views are the Aristotelian and the Longinian, the aesthetic and the psychological, the view of literature as product and the view of literature as process. In our day we have acquired a good deal of respect for literature as process, notably in prose fiction. The stream of consciousness gets careful treatment in our criticism, and when we compare Arnold Bennett and Virginia Woolf on the subject of Mrs. Brown we generally take the side of Virginia Woolf. So it seems that our age ought to feel a close kinship with the prose fiction of the age of sensibility, when the sense of literature as process was brought to a peculiarly exquisite perfection by Sterne, and in lesser degree by Richardson and Boswell.

All the great story-tellers, including the Augustan ones, have a strong sense of literature as a finished product. The suspense is thrown forward until it reaches the end, and is based on our confidence that the author knows what is coming next. A story-teller does not break his illusion by talking to the reader as Fielding does, because we know from the start that we are listening to Fielding telling a story—that is, Johnson's arguments about illusion in drama apply equally well to prose fiction of Fielding's kind. But when we turn to *Tristram Shandy* we not only read the book but watch the author at work writing it: at any moment the house of Walter Shandy may vanish and be replaced by the author's study. This does break the illusion, or would if there were any illusion to break, but here we are not being led into a story, but into the process of writing a story: we wonder, not what is coming next, but what the author will think of next.

Sterne is, of course, an unusually pure example of a process-writer, but even in Richardson we find many of the same characteristics. Johnson's well-known remark that if you read Richardson for the story you would hang yourself indicates that Richardson is not interested in a plot with a quick-march rhythm. Richardson does not throw the suspense forward, but keeps the emotion at a continuous present. Readers of *Pamela* have become so fascinated by watching the sheets of Pamela's manuscript spawning and secreting all over her master's house, even into the recesses of her clothes, as she fends off assault with one hand and writes about it with the other, that they sometimes overlook the reason for an apparently clumsy device. The reason is, of course, to give the impression of literature as process, as created on the spot out of the events it describes. And in the very beginning of *Boswell in London* we can see the boy of twenty-one already practising the art of writing as a continuous process from experience. When he writes of his adventure with Louisa he may be writing several days after the event, but he does not use his later knowledge.

In poetry the sense of literature as a finished product normally expresses itself in some kind of regularly recurring metre, the general pattern of which is established as soon as possible. In listening to Pope's couplets we have a sense of continually fulfilled expectation which is the opposite of obviousness: a sense that eighteenth-century music also often gives us. Such a technique demands a clear statement of what sound-patterns we may expect. We hear at once the full ring of the rhyming couplet, and all other sound-patterns are kept to a minimum. In such a line as:

And strains from hard-bound brains eight lines a year,

the extra assonance is a deliberate discord, expressing the difficulties of constipated genius. Similarly with the alliteration in:

Great Cibber's brazen, brainless brothers stand,

and the fact that these are deliberate discords used for parody indicates that they are normally not present. Johnson's disapproval of such devices in serious contexts is written all over the *Lives of the Poets*.

When we turn from Pope to the age of sensibility, we get something of the same kind of shock that we get when we turn from Tennyson or Matthew Arnold to Hopkins. Our ears are assaulted by unpredictable assonances, alliterations, inter-rhymings and echolalia:

Mie love ys dedde,
Gon to hys death-bedde . . .

With brede ethereal wove,
O'erhang his wavy bed . . .

The couthy cracks begin whan supper's o'er,
The cheering bicker gars them glibly gash.

But a pebble of the brook
  Warbled out these metres meet . . .

In many of the best-known poems of the period, in Smart's *Song to David,* in Chatterton's elegies, in Burns's songs and Blake's lyrics, even in some of the Wesley hymns, we find a delight in refrain for refrain's sake. Sometimes, naturally, we can see the appropriate literary influences helping to shape the form, such as the incremental repetition of the ballad, or Old Norse alliteration in *The Fatal Sisters.* And whatever may be thought of the poetic value of the Ossianic poems, most estimates of that value parrot Wordsworth, and Wordsworth's criticisms of Ossian's imagery are quite beside the point. The vague generalized imagery of Ossian, like the mysterious resonant names and the fixed epithets, are part of a deliberate and well unified scheme. *Fingal* and *Temora* are long poems for the same reason that *Clarissa* is a long novel: not because there is a complicated story to be told, as in *Tom Jones* or an epic of Southey, but because the emotion is being maintained at a continuous present by various devices of repetition.

The reason for these intensified sound-patterns, is, once again, an interest in the poetic process as distinct from the product. In the composing of poetry, where rhyme is as important as reason, there is a primary stage in which words are linked by sound rather than sense. From the point of view of sense this stage is merely free or uncontrolled association, and in the way it operates it is very like the dream. Again like the dream, it has to meet a censor-principle, and shape itself into intelligible patterns. Where the emphasis is on the communicated product, the qualities of consciousness take the lead: a regular metre, clarity of syntax, epigram and wit, repetition of sense in antithesis and balance rather than of sound. Swift speaks with admiration of Pope's ability to get more 'sense' into one couplet than he can into six: concentration of sense for him is clearly a major criterion of poetry. Where the emphasis is on the original process, the qualities of subconscious association take the lead, and the poetry becomes hypnotically repetitive, oracular, incantatory, dreamlike and in the original sense of the word charming. The response to it includes a subconscious factor, the surrendering to a spell. In Ossian, who carries this tendency further than anyone else, the aim is not concentration of sense but diffusion of sense, hence Johnson's remark that anybody could write like Ossian if he would abandon his mind to it. Literature as product may take a lyrical form, as it does in the sublime ode about which Professor Maclean has written so well, but it is also the conception of literature that makes the longer continuous poem possible. Literature as process, being based on an irregular and unpredictable coincidence of sound-patterns, tends to seek the brief or even the fragmentary utterance, in other words to centre itself on the lyric, which accounts for the feeling of a sudden emergence of a lyrical impulse in the age of sensibility.

The 'pre-romantic' approach to this period sees it as developing a conception of the creative imagination, which became the basis of Romanticism. This is true, but the Romantics tended to see the poem as the *product* of the creative imagination, thus reverting in at least one respect to the Augustan attitude. For the Augustan, art is posterior to nature because nature is the art of God; for the Romantic, art is prior to nature because God is an artist; one deals in physical and the other in biological analogies, as Professor Abrams' *Mirror and the Lamp* has shown. But for the Romantic poet the poem is still an artefact: in Coleridge's terms, a secondary or productive imagination has been imposed on a primary imaginative process. So, different as it is from Augustan poetry, Romantic poetry is like it in being a conservative rhetoric, and in being founded on relatively regular metrical schemes. Poe's rejection of the continuous poem does not express anything very central in Romanticism itself, as nearly every major Romantic poet composed poems of considerable, sometimes immense, length. Poe's theory is closer to the practice of the age of sensibility before him and the *symbolistes* after him.

In the age of sensibility most of the long poems, of course, simply carry on with standard continuous metres, or exploit the greater degree of intensified recurrent sound afforded by stanzaic forms, notably the Spenserian. But sometimes the peculiar problems of making associative poetry continuous were faced in a more experimental way, experiments largely ignored by the Romantics. Oracular poetry in a long form often tends to become a series of utterances, irregular in rhythm but strongly marked off one from the other. We notice in Whitman, for instance, that the end of every line has a strong pause—for when the rhythm is variable there is no point in a run-on line. Sometimes this oracular rhythm takes on at least a typographical resemblance to prose, as it does in Rimbaud's *Saison en Enfer,* or, more frequently, to a discontinuous blend of prose and verse in which the sentence, the paragraph and the line are much the same unit. The chief literary influence for this rhythm has always been the translated Bible, which took on a new impetus in the age of sensibility; and if we study carefully the rhythm of Ossian, of Smart's *Jubilate Agno* and of the Blake Prophecies, we can see three very different but equally logical developments of this semi-Biblical rhythm.

Where there is a strong sense of literature as aesthetic product, there is also a sense of its detachment from the spectator. Aristotle's theory of catharsis describes how this works for tragedy: pity and fear are detached from the beholder by being directed towards objects. Where there is a sense of literature as process, pity and fear become states of mind without objects, moods which are common to the work of art and the reader, and which bind them together psychologically instead of separating them aesthetically.

Fear without an object, as a condition of mind prior to being afraid of anything, is called *Angst* or anxiety, a somewhat narrow term for what may be almost anything between pleasure and pain. In the general area of pleasure comes the eighteenth-century conception of the sublime, where qualities of austerity, gloom, grandeur, melancholy or even menace are a source of romantic or penseroso feelings. The appeal of Ossian to his time on this basis needs no comment. From here we move through the graveyard poets, the Gothic-horror novelists and the writers of tragic ballads to such *fleurs du mal* as Cowper's *Castaway* and Blake's Golden Chapel poem in the Rossetti MS.

Pity without an object has never to my knowledge been given a name, but expresses itself as an imaginative animism, or treating everything in nature as though it had human feelings or qualities. At one end of its range is the apocalyptic exultation of all nature bursting into human life that we have in Smart's *Song to David* and the ninth Night of *The Four Zoas.* Next comes an imaginative sympathy with the kind of folklore that peoples the countryside with elemental spirits, such as we have in Collins, Fergusson, Burns and the Wartons. Next we have the curiously intense awareness of the animal world which (except for some poems of D. H. Lawrence) is unrivalled in this period, and is expressed in some of its best realized writing: in Burns's *To a Mouse,* in Cowper's exquisite snail poem, in Smart's superb lines on his cat Geoffrey, in the famous starling and ass episodes in Sterne, in the opening of Blake's *Auguries of Innocence.* Finally comes the sense of sympathy with man himself, the sense that no one can afford to be indifferent to the fate of anyone else, which underlies the protests against slavery and misery in Cowper, in Crabbe and in Blake's *Songs of Experience.*

This concentration on the primitive process of writing is projected in two directions, into nature and into history. The appropriate natural setting for much of the poetry of sensibility is nature at one of the two poles of process, creation and decay. The poet is attracted by the ruinous and the mephitic, or by the primeval and 'unspoiled'—a picturesque subtly but perceptibly different from the Romantic picturesque. The projection into history assumes that the psychological progress of the poet from lyrical through epic to dramatic presentations, discussed by Stephen at the end of Joyce's *Portrait*, must be the historical progress of literature as well. Even as late as the preface to Victor Hugo's *Cromwell* this assumption persists. The Ossian and Rowley poems are not simple hoaxes: they are pseudepigrapha, like the Book of Enoch, and like it they take what is psychologically primitive, the oracular process of composition, and project it as something historically primitive.

The poetry of process is oracular, and the medium of the oracle is often in an ecstatic or trance-like state: autonomous voices seem to speak through him, and as he is concerned to utter rather than to address, he is turned away from his listener, so to speak, in a state of rapt self-communion. The free association of words, in which sound is prior to sense, is often a literary way of representing insanity. In Rimbaud's terrifyingly accurate phrase, poetry of the associative or oracular type requires a 'dérèglement de tous les sens.' Hence the qualities that make a man an oracular poet are often the qualities that work against, and sometimes destroy, his social personality. Far more than the time of Rimbaud and Verlaine is this period of literature a period of the *poète maudit*. The list of poets over whom the shadows of mental breakdown fell is far too long to be coincidence. The much publicized death of Chatterton is certainly one of the personal tragedies of the age, but an easier one to take than the kind of agony which is expressed with an almost definitive poignancy by Smart in *Jubilate Agno:*

> For in my nature I quested for beauty, but God, God, hath sent me to sea for pearls.

It is characteristic of the age of sensibility that this personal or biographical aspect of it should be so closely connected with its central technical feature. The basis of poetic language is the metaphor, and the metaphor, in its radical form, is a statement of identity: 'this is that.' In all our ordinary experience the metaphor is non-literal: nobody but a savage or a lunatic can take metaphor literally. For Classical or Augustan critics the metaphor is a condensed simile: its real or common-sense basis is likeness, not identity, and when it obliterates the sense of likeness it becomes barbaric. In Johnson's strictures on the music and water metaphor of Gray's *Bard* we can see what intellectual abysses, for him, would open up if metaphors ever passed beyond the stage of resemblance. For the Romantic critic, the identification in the metaphor is ideal: two images are identified within the mind of the creating poet.

But where metaphor is conceived as part of an oracular and half-ecstatic process, there is a direct identification in which the poet himself is involved. To use another phrase of Rimbaud's, the poet feels not 'je pense,' but 'on me pense.' In the age of sensibility some of the identifications involving the poet seem manic, like Blake's with Druidic bards or Smart's with Hebrew prophets, or depressive, like Cowper's with a scapegoat figure, a stricken deer or castaway, or merely bizarre, like Macpherson's with Ossian or Chatterton's with Rowley. But it is in this psychological self-identification that the central 'primitive' quality of this age really emerges. In Collins's *Ode on the Poetical Character*, in Smart's *Jubilate Agno*, and in Blake's *Four Zoas*, it attains its greatest intensity and completeness.

In these three poems, especially the last two, God, the poet's soul and nature are brought into a white-hot fusion of identity, an imaginative fiery furnace in which the reader may, if he chooses, make a fourth. All three poems are of the greatest complexity, yet the emotion on which they are founded is of a simplicity and directness that English literature has rarely attained again. With the 1800 edition of *Lyrical Ballads*, secondary imagination and recollection in tranquillity took over English poetry and dominated it until the end of the nineteenth century. The primitivism of Blake and Smart revived in France with Rimbaud and Gérard de Nerval, but even this development had become conservative by the time its influence reached England, and only in a few poems of Dylan Thomas, and those perhaps not his best, does the older tradition revive. But contemporary poetry is still deeply concerned with the problems and techniques of the age of sensibility, and while the latter's resemblance to our time is not a merit in it, it is a logical enough reason for re-examining it with fresh eyes.

Walter Jackson Bate

KEATS'S STYLE:
EVOLUTION TOWARD QUALITIES OF PERMANENT VALUE

With the decline of neoclassicism, poetry was faced with some relatively new problems and a new uneasiness about its value and function. The problems and the uneasiness have persisted; and the principal ways of meeting them have not changed radically from those the greater romantics adopted. Whether we like our legacy or not, the present literary generation is very much the heir of the romantics.

On the other hand, of course, much of the poetry as well as critical effort of the last forty years has been written in a spirit of conscious protest against the idiom of romantic poetry. Some of the rather confused distinctions which this militant protest created at its start seem now to have become domesticated into academic orthodoxy, and we have begun to take them for granted, as we do most domestic phenomena, without any very searching revision of our first impressions. We especially follow the confusion of poetic form with mere idiom, and feel that we are describing or analyzing poetry according to the first when we are really thinking only of the latter. We hold academic symposia now on differences in the 'metaphysical,' 'Augustan,' 'romantic,' and 'modern modes'; and the word 'mode,' because it is open and fluid, gives us the feeling that we are being comprehensive. But it usually turns out to be restricted to special problems of metaphor, syntax, and phrasing. Like good Alexandrian rhetoricians, we have begun to play close to the ground.

No brief discussion of the style of a romantic poet can hope to improve on the situation. There are, after all, genuine differences between the idiom of the romantics and the poetry of the last forty years; and some of them are quite fundamental. But any discussion that could make place for these acknowledged differences, and then subsume them within larger considerations would involve a more pluralistic, leisurely, less compartmentalized procedure that would permit us to review the total achievement of a poet. This is particularly the case with Keats. He has

"Keats's Style: Evolution Toward Qualities of Permanent Value" by Walter Jackson Bate, from *The Major English Romantic Poets: A Symposium in Reappraisal* edited by Clarence D. Thorpe, Carlos Baker and Bennett Weaver. Copyright © 1957 by Southern Illinois University Press. Reprinted by permission of Southern Illinois University Press.

worn very well. He has continued to stir the imagination of poets and critics for a century and a half. On the other hand, the idiom of much of his earlier poetry is hardly at the present time a model or even much of an encouragement. Indeed, to a good many younger readers, some of it is not even very congenial. Of course the language of his greatest poetry has always held a magnetic attraction; for there we reach, if only for a brief while, a high plateau where in mastery of phrase he has few equals in English poetry, and only one obvious superior. A very important part of the more general significance of Keats is the fact that he was able to reach that level. But this, by itself, is not enough to explain the large, at times almost personal, relevance that we feel. He is a part of our literary conscience. Leaving aside the poignant appeal (and with it the sense of difference) of his own peculiar circumstances— the fact that he started with so little, the manner in which he strug- gled his way into poetry, his early death, and the like—we sense that this gifted young poet was working his way through problems that any honest poet of the last century and a half has faced.

Nothing less than a fairly capacious and imaginative consideration of his achievement, then, could get very far in capturing, or even begin- ning to suggest, the relevance of Keats's art to poetry since his death, and especially during the last generation. Still, the assigned purpose of this essay is to concentrate briefly on the stylistic character of Keats's poetry. Hard put to compartmentalize in this way, I should be forced to resort to the term 'honesty.' Certainly this is what now appeals to us most when we think of Keats as a whole, especially in the context of the letters. And we feel this impression confirmed in his stylistic development. Considering his short life, there is no parallel to the diver- sity of styles with which he experimented. Yet it was never experimenta- tion for its own sake. The experimentation moves constantly toward great honesty—greater openness to concrete life and the claims of expe- rience, toward greater fullness and richness of expression, and at the same time a growing strength of control and sensitivity to the formal claims of poetic art.

II

The early verse of Keats, down through the writing of *Isabella* (early in 1818), shows little selectivity of subject in either its themes or its imagery when it is measured by a really high standard. The impulse towards self-absorption in the object is associated with having the 'soul,' as he said, 'lost in pleasant smotherings.' It finds its outlet, that is, in a luxurious abandonment to the conventionally 'poetic' objects and images that intrigued a youthful romantic poet, and that Keats found ready at hand in the verse of his mentor, Leigh Hunt, and in the poets Hunt held up as a model. This sort of poetry, as it is developed by Hunt and the youthful Keats, and as it is continued throughout the poorer verse of the nineteenth century, is essentially a reaction, of course, against neo-classic conventions: an attempt to substitute for the stock themes and stock diction of the preceding century a conception of 'poetic' material even more confined, a diction equally liable to stereo- type, and a versification—as Keats later learned—of equal monotony.

We need not retrace in any detail the characteristics of Keats's early diction and imagery: his use of *y*-ending adjectives ('sphery,' 'lawny,' 'bloomy,' 'surgy,' and the like); the unfortunate predilection for adverbs made from participles ('lingeringly,' 'dyingly,' 'cooingly'), and for abstract nouns that have little intellectual content ('languishment,' 'designments,' 'soft ravishment'); the use of such conventional props in his imagery as 'Pink robes, and wavy hair,' the 'silvery tears of April,' and monotonously recurring nymphs with 'downward' glances, the habitual appearance of objects with 'pillowy' softness, and the frequently embarrassing attempts to introduce action ('madly I kiss/The wooing arms') into this smothering world of rose-leaves, doves, 'almond vales,' and 'blooming plums/Ready to melt between an infant's gums.'

These characteristics and their sources have been frequently discussed, are familiar to every student of English poetry, and have little interest to present-day readers except as a steppingstone in Keats's chronological development. And they are accompanied not only by a lack of structural control but by a deliberately cultivated slackness of manner—except in his early sonnets, written in the Petrarchan form and employing diverse and not too effective structural peculiarities drawn from Hunt, occasionally Wordsworth, and the Miltonic imitators of the late eighteenth century. One is almost tempted to conclude that if Pope, in his versification, went in one direction and employed a device to secure economy and tightness, then Hunt—and the youthful Keats—not only discarded it but, in some instances, deliberately adopted an opposite device. Examples of this would take us into the by-roads of prosody—particularly caesural-placing, where Keats followed Hunt very closely. It is perhaps enough to note how forcibly Keats, even more than Hunt, broke the couplet. In fact, when a pause is needed at the end of a line, he frequently put it at the end of the *first* line of the couplet, and then tried to run on the second line, without break, into the next couplet:

> Full of sweet dreams, and health, and quiet breathing./
> Therefore, on every morrow, are we wreathing
> A flowery band to bind us to the earth,/
> Spite of despondence, of the inhuman dearth
> Of noble natures, of the gloomy days,/
> Of all the unhealthy and o'er-darken'd ways
> Made for our searching: yes, in spite of all,/
> Some shape of beauty moves away the pall
> From our dark spirits. Such the sun, the moon,/
> Trees old, and young, sprouting a shady boon
> For simple sheep . . . .

Endymion, 1, 4–15

The style of *Isabella,* written a few months after Keats became twenty-three, shows an embarrassed and confused attempt by Keats to rid himself of the influences of Hunt and of the 'sickening stuff' he later associated with Hunt's taste. 'I shall have,' he wrote, 'the Reputation of

Hunt's elevé. His corrections and amputations will by the knowing ones be traced.' He had grown 'tired' of the 'slipshod' *Endymion;* his opinion of it was 'very low,' and he wanted to 'forget' it. Abandoning the loose, run-on couplet he had taken over from Hunt, Keats selected the tight ottava rima stanza (perhaps better fitted for satire, because of the snap of its concluding couplet); and though the story has limited possibilities, to say the least, and though there is still (as he himself was to say) a mawkish sentimentality of phrase and image, the versification shows an energetic struggle to impose a disciplined control.

III

It is during the year or more following the writing of *Isabella* that the maturer style of Keats developed so rapidly. Among the primary characteristics of this style is a suggestive power of image capable of securing from the reader an unusually intense emotional and imaginative identification. This quality has become widely recognized in recent years, particularly since the implications of Keats's own conception of the poet's character, and of his puzzling term, 'Negative Capability,' have been discussed. We need not here make distinctions between the romantic theory of sympathetic identification, in which the poet takes on, through participation, the qualities and character of his object, and the more recent theory of *Einfühlung* (or empathy), with its suggestion that many of these qualities are merely the subjective creation of the poet or observer, and are bestowed upon the object rather than descried in it. The poetry of Keats contains abundant examples that might be used to substantiate either, or both at once, as a guiding characteristic of his verse.

Certainly, in the verse written before *Hyperion,* a subjective element —more empathic than sympathetic—often characterizes this imaginative identification ('sweet peas, on *tiptoe* for a flight,' the foam crawling along the back of the wave with a 'wayward indolence'). But a more sympathetic in-feeling is equally apparent (minnows 'staying their wavy bodies 'gainst the stream,' lions with 'nervy tails,' or the organic in-feeling in 'Ere a lean bat could plump its wintry skin'). The verse from *Hyperion* through the great odes is replete with such imagery, ranging from 'The hare *limp'd trembling* through the frozen grass' to the agonies of the huge figures in *Hyperion:* 'horrors, portion'd to a giant nerve,/Oft made Hyperion ache'; or

> *through all his bulk* an agony
> *Crept* gradual, from the feet unto the crown,
> Like a lithe serpent *vast and muscular,*
> Making *slow way*, with head and neck *convuls'd*
> *From over strainèd might* . . .
> (1, 259–63)

Such lines remind us of the passages in both Shakespeare and Milton that evoked so strong a sympathetic participation in Keats—as, for example, when he wrote in the margin beside *Paradise Lost,* IX, 179 ff., where Satan enters the serpent without arousing him from sleep:

Satan having entered the Serpent, and inform'd his brutal sense—might seem sufficient—but Milton goes on *'but his sleep disturbed not.'* Whose spirit does not ache at the smothering and confinement . . . the *'waiting close?'* Whose head is not dizzy at the possible speculations of Satan in the serpent prison? No passage of poetry ever can give a greater pain of suffocation.

Or again there is his enthusiastic mention, in one of his letters (November 22, 1817), of Shakespeare's image of the sensitive retreat of a snail:

> As the snail, whose tender horns being hit,
> Shrinks back into his shelly cave with pain.

And we may recall Charles Cowden Clarke's story of Keats's reaction, while reading the *Faerie Queene* as a boy, to the phrase, 'sea-shouldering whales': as if raising himself against the pressure of the waves, 'he hoisted himself up, and looked burly and dominant. . . .'

This kinaesthetic gift of image, if one wishes to call it that, this organically felt participation, is further revealed in Keats's ability to bring into focus several diverse sense-impressions of an object, and—in transmuting them into a single image or series of images—present a more valid, rounded, and fully realized apperception. This unifying interplay of sense-impressions should not be confused with synaesthesia. Keats's imagery, to be sure, is perhaps as richly packed with examples of suggestive synaesthesia as any that can be found (*'fragrant* and enwreathèd light,' 'pale and silver silence,' 'scarlet pain,' 'the *touch* of *scent'*), and Keats's use of it had more effect on the synaesthetic imagery of later English poetry than any other one model. But the really distinctive quality in Keats—and a quality his Victorian imitators rarely attained—is less the *substitution* than it is the *substantiation* of one sense by another in order to give, as it were, additional dimension and depth, as in 'the *moist scent* of flowers,' 'embalmèd darkness,' or in making incense tangibly 'soft' and visible:

> I cannot see what flowers are at my feet,
> Nor what *soft* incense *hangs* upon the boughs.

A further example is Keats's predilection for tactile qualities: his craving for touch ('Touch,' he wrote, 'has a memory'), and for a firm grasp of the concrete as it exists in space. Thus images directly or indirectly connected with the sense of taste are sustained and deepened, in their vitality, through associations with tactile and muscular response: the 'purple-stainèd mouth,' the nightingale singing of summer 'in *full-throated* ease,' or the closing stanza of the *Ode on Melancholy,* with its

> *aching* Pleasure nigh,
> Turning to poison while the *bee-mouth sips* . . .
> Though seen of none save him whose *strenuous tongue*
> Can *burst* Joy's *grape against his palate* fine . . . .

This tactile strength gives a three-dimensional grasp to Keats's images. Perhaps the most notable instance is the famous 'wealth of *glob̀ed* peonies,' in the same ode: here the hand is virtually enclosing the peony, further assuring itself of the three-dimensional roundness.

There is, in short, a *centering* in Keats's imagery of the various qualities of an object into a single apperception; and as a result the object emerges as a totality with its several aspects resolved into a unified whole rather than delineated or suggested separately. The use of strong tactile associations that give a firmer hold, a more definitely felt outline, is one means by which this centering of impressions, into an amalgamated whole, is secured and anchored. His general amassing and condensing of sense-impressions is another. And the result is an imagery that is less 'synaesthetic,' in the ordinary sense, than it is a gifted illustration of what Hazlitt meant by 'gusto'—that is, a state in which the imagination, through sympathetic excitement, draws out and expresses the total character of its object. In this intense identification, the impressions made on one sense 'excite by affinity those of another'; the object is grasped as a vital whole. And accompanying this sympathetic gusto, with its resolving of diverse impressions into a unified and immediate experience, is a discerning ability to sense organic motion, with a vivid fellow-feeling, and as an unfolding and continuing process. One is reminded of Severn's account:

> 'a wave . . . billowing through a tree,' as he described the uplifting surge of air among swaying masses of chestnuts or oak foliage, or when, afar off, he heard the wind coming across woodlands. 'The tide! the tide!' he would cry delightedly, and spring on to some stile, or upon the bough of a wayside tree, and watch the passage of the wind upon the meadow grasses or young corn, not stirring till the flow of air was all around him, while an expression of rapture made his eyes gleam and his face glow.

IV

It is especially through a rapidly developed mastery of idiom and versification that Keats acquired the control of impact and the formal sense of structure that restrains the concrete richness of his mature verse and thus contributes to its massive and interwoven firmness. It is here that the powerful influence of Milton—against which he was later to react in some ways—had so salutary an effect, lifting him far beyond the weak and fitful devices with which he had tried to tighten his versification in *Isabella*. The first *Hyperion*, begun a few months after *Isabella*, immediately reveals that no apprentice, at once so gifted and eager, ever sat at the feet of Milton; certainly none ever learned from Milton more quickly and with greater ultimate profit. To be sure, much that he took over consists merely of the obvious mannerisms that all Miltonic imitators have used. One example is the frequent use of the adjective in place of the adverb ('Shook *horrid* with such aspen malady,' 'Crept *gradual*, from the foot unto the crown'). And there are the 'Miltonic inversions' with which Keats later thought *Hyperion* was disfigured: the epithet after the noun ('omens drear,' 'palace bright,' 'metal sick'), and the verb before the subject ('Pale wox I,' 'There saw she direst strife'). But other devices less mannered and more generally helpful were adopted. Among them should be noted the Milton ellipsis ('still snuff'd the incense, teeming up/From man to the sun's God; yet unsecure'); a condensed asyndeton ('some also shouted; Some wept, some wail'd, all bow'd with reverence'); and a use of repetition more effective than the crude repetition that Keats had taken over from Fairfax in his attempt to tighten *Isabella*. In versification, Keats closely followed Milton, and acquired metrical qualities that were to remain as a strengthening support in his verse. Chief among these are an increased slowing and weighting of the line with spondees, and also the use of the majestic sixth-syllable caesura, which Keats alone among Milton's imitators seems to have had the ear to catch. A growing sense of stanzaic structure is apparent in the *Eve of St. Agnes*, which, in contrast to other eighteenth- and nineteenth-century poems in the Spenserian stanza, often preserves the quatrain division that Spenser himself used in the stanza (*abab bcbc c*). In his sonnets, Keats now abandoned the Petrarchan form, which had been the dominant sonnet form since Milton; and he went back instead to the Shakespearian rhyme scheme, consisting of three heroic, or elegiac, quatrains and a couplet. But the sonnet was now only an incidental and casual form for Keats. If his poetic temper was still mainly lyrical, it was becoming too richly weighted to be couched in the brief space of the sonnet. In fact, he not only wished for a more lengthy form, which would permit a more leisurely development, but he desired a different rhyme pattern. In the first eight lines of the Petrarchan form, the three couplets (*a bb aa bb a*), he felt, had a 'pouncing' quality, the second line of each couplet leaping out, as it were, to match the first. In the Shakespearian form, on the other hand, the three alternate-rhyming quatrains (the heroic, and in the eighteenth century the traditional 'elegiac' quatrain) often had an 'elegiac' languor as well; and the concluding couplet, with which even Shakespeare had difficulty, 'has seldom a pleasing effect' (May 3, 1819). Keats wanted, therefore, 'a better sonnet stanza than we have,' and wrote an experimental sonnet, 'If by dull rhymes,' the theme of which is

> Let us find out, if we must be constrained,
> Sandals more interwoven and complete
> To fit the naked foot of Poesy.

After experimenting in the *Ode to Psyche*, he finally developed a ten-line stanza (in the later ode, *To Autumn,* eleven lines). This stanza is essentially constructed from the *disjecta membra* of both sonnet forms, and was possibly influenced also by some of the ten-line ode-stanzas common in the eighteenth century. Avoiding the 'pouncing rhymes' of the Petrarchan octave, the continual alternate rhyming of the Shakespearian form, and its concluding couplet, this new ode-stanza—though there are variations—consists basically of one alternate-rhyming quatrain (*abab*) from the three that make up the Shakespearean sonnet, with the addition of something like the ordinary sestet (*cde cde*) of the Petrarchan form. And here, in these closely knit and restraining stanzas, Keats certainly achieved a lyrical form 'more interwoven and complete.'

In the odes, moreover, may be seen a masterful use of the assonance and vowel-interplay, first employed in *Hyperion* and continued throughout the *Eve of St. Agnes* and many of the sonnets, with an intricacy hardly equalled in the history of English verse. Keats informed his friend, Benjamin Bailey, that he had a 'principle of melody in verse,' upon which he had his own motives, particularly in the management of open and close vowels:

> Keats's theory was that the vowels should be . . . interchanged like differing notes in music, to prevent monotony. . . . I well remember his telling me that, had he studied music, he had some notions of the combinations of sounds, by which he thought he could have done something as original as his poetry.

And when Keats turned to the writing of *Hyperion,* in the autumn of 1818, he began to make use of an elaborate patterning both of open and close vowels and also of assonance. This use of assonance and vowel-arrangement is extraordinarily complex at times, and cannot be described in any detail in this essay. A few examples of assonance patterning, however, may be cited:

And still she slept an azure-lidded sleep.

Nor let the beetle, nor the death-moth be.

Or, to take a somewhat more complicated example:

And bid old Saturn take his throne again.

Patterns of vowel repetition occur, in an even more complex manner, throughout series of more than one line, and easily substantiate Saintsbury's assertion that the deliberate and frequent use of assonance in English poetry starts with Keats.

V

With the great odes, we are probably at the apex of Keats's poetic art. A discussion of the relevance of Keats's stylistic craftsmanship to the present day could quite justifiably turn into simply an explication of one or two of these odes. But the procedure taken here, rightly or wrongly, has been to stress the rather rapid experimentation with styles, the interests that led to it, and some of the more general aspects of Keats's development in this series of experiments. Hence, there would be place for only the briefest explication; and considering the care with which the odes have been examined, especially in the last twenty years, a short impressionistic explication would be presumptuous. Nor could we get very far in discussing the form of these odes even in general terms unless we spent time in reminding ourselves of the underpart of the iceberg—of what was going on in the mind of Keats throughout the year before the great odes and especially the last two or three months of it.

But we can certainly note in these odes—especially the *Ode on a Grecian Urn* and the *Ode to a Nightingale*—what I can only call a successful intrusion of the dramatic. In each we are dealing with a miniature drama. In each the poet seeks at the start—in the *Ode to a Nightingale* shortly after the start—to identify himself with an object that can lift himself beyond a world of flux. In each there is a gradual disengagement, an inability to follow completely the implications of sympathetic absorption, and a return back (implicit in the *Grecian Urn,* more obvious in the *Nightingale*) to the world of process and the claims of the human heart. So, a century later with Yeats, there may be the paeans to Byzantium; but the drama lies in the return back—the descent down the ladder, as in 'The Circus Animals' Desertion'—to the human condition, and the assertive, unstilled desires of the dying animal, from which 'all ladders start.' The structure of the odes cannot be considered apart from this drama. Nor can the massive richness and the courageous openness to the full concrete expression, be considered apart from the drama, especially at a time like the present when fear of the welter, the quick unpredictable decay or change of concrete life has so intimidated the imagination of writers. There is courage here, in this welcome of concrete amplitude by Keats; and the courage is not apart from the poetic art.

The poems of the summer and early autumn of 1819 add important nuances to the situation. The questioning, before the odes, of the value and function of poetry in such a world as we find ourselves becomes more articulate in the letters. Energetic changes in style and form follow. *Lamia* drops, for the time being, many of the stylistic qualities of Keats from *Hyperion* through the odes. We have now a fairly open allegory, in some ways impetuously ironic and mocking in tone, which had, he hoped, a new energy that would 'take hold of people in some way—give them either pleasant or unpleasant sensations.' As if in a deliberate attempt to put things at arm's length, he surprisingly reverts to the crisp heroic couplet (the 'rocking-horse' meter he had once shied away from) of Dryden and Pope, though with a vivid color all of his own. The couplet is not so closed as in Dryden or Pope; but there are many closer similarities of a minor prosodic nature. Whatever else may be said of *Lamia,* it treats the effect of a Circian enchantment upon the impressionable mind of a young man (Lycius) who is open to the appeal of a magic world, and who is unable to withstand reality when it is pointed out to him. This general theme is closely related to the style which Keats, within two months, has suddenly evolved in contrast to the odes.

But at the same time he has begun to disengage himself from this new style, and to turn to still another, though the fragmentary form of the *Fall of Hyperion*—the revised *Hyperion*—hardly shows it to advantage. For, leaving aside all the psychological difficulties of this impetuous period, he was dealing with a discarded fragment. Little can be said about the style of this recast and warmed-up fragment except about meter and idiom. Stripped of its original allegory, the poem indicts the 'dreamer' who makes poetry a means of escape from the concrete world. Keats strips the poem, too, of many of its Miltonic mannerisms. In the place of the grandeur of the first *Hyperion,* we have now a more mellow blank verse, Virgilian and half-pastoral in tone:

> Still was more plenty than the fabled horn
> Thrice emptied could pour forth, at banqueting
> For Proserpine return'd to her own fields,
> Where the white heifers low.
>   I, 35–38

> When in mid-May the sickening East Wind
> Shifts sudden to the South, the small warm rain
> Melts out the frozen incense from all flowers.
>   I, 97–99

Despite the uncertainty of the poem as a whole, there is a relaxed, even confident, quietness in the opening hundred lines or so of this revision. This opening can be said to suggest a style unlike anything else in the nineteenth century: a style towards which Keats might well have moved—or through which he would have passed to something else—had he continued to write for a few more years. Meanwhile, Keats's last great poem—the ode *To Autumn*—is, of course, a return to the full and dense richness that characterized the great odes of the preceding May, but a richness now harmonized and lifted to a serenity quite unequalled elsewhere in romantic poetry.

VI

The range and variety of Keats's style are perhaps greater than can be found in other nineteenth-century English poets. This is a large tribute; the brevity of Keats's career makes it larger. This variety partly explains Keats's continued appeal despite changes of taste during the past century. Victorian poets, for example, could find in Keats a veritable treasure house of the qualities they valued. Even when the romantic emphasis on 'suggestiveness' in poetry—on qualities in poetry that will stimulate the imagination into a creative activity of its own—developed into a cult of subjective revery, with the poem serving merely as a backdrop to one's own personal mood, Keats, particularly in the early verse, could furnish the Victorians with as striking a precedent or model as Shelley. More specialized developments in Victorian poetry could find in him an even better stimulus than Wordsworth, Coleridge, Byron, or Shelley. Among two such developments one may mention a tendency— as in Tennyson, or in a different and cruder way, Swinburne—to sacrifice metaphor and concentrated imagery almost completely in order to exploit the musical qualities of verse; and Keats, as was said earlier— though without sacrificing metaphor and image—offers as dexterous and skillful a use of sound, especially in assonance, as can be found in English verse since the beginning of the romantic era. Similarly, the pre-Raphaelites, with their interest in single pictures, and in their effort to string a poem about a set of hangings or tapestries, usually to the neglect of any organic development of the poem as a whole, could find in Keats better examples to imitate than in any other romantic. Because Keats's images often attain remarkable clarity, as well as the condensation and the suggestive magic that the pre-Raphaelites liked, his poetry, more than that of the other romantics, remained popular with the Imagists when they revolted against pre-Raphaelite vagueness.

In the shift in stylistic taste, of which the revival of metaphysical poetry was a symptom, Keats was left relatively unscathed during the general barrage directed at nineteenth-century poetry. One explanation is the tensely braced and formal tightness of his mature verse, particularly the odes, which is hard to match in other verse of the century. Another is a growing experimental use of disparates and of sketched, suggestive metaphor in his phrasing: 'branchèd thoughts, new grown'; lightning viewed as 'crooked strings of fire' that 'singe away the swollen clouds'; or the now famous cancelled stanza of the *Ode on Melancholy:*

> Though you should build a bark of dead men's bones,
> And rear a phantom gibbet for a mast,
> Stitch creeds together for a sail, with groans
> To fill it out, blood stainèd and aghast;
> *Although your rudder be a dragon's tail*
> *Long sever'd, yet still hard with agony* . . . .

This active associative suggestion through compressed metaphor, when joined with an emphatic in-feeling that is comparatively weaker in metaphysical poetry, provides us with an idiom that at its best approximates that of Shakespeare. The combination, at least, is rare since Shakespeare.

The point is the variety, and a variety that consists not only in a successive series of styles but also in the diverse appeal of formal and stylistic qualities that are coalesced in the greatest poetry of Keats. It has stood him very well throughout some rather serious changes in stylistic taste during the past century, and throughout the growing, self-conscious fastidiousness that Johnson describes as 'elegance refined into impatience.' It is possible that what we think of as current tastes in poetry may continue for another generation, further refined. In this case the best of Keats will retain its relevance. But it may be that we are about to undergo another shift, a shift into a new romanticism, more sophisticated, of course, and more formally conscious than the old, but, I can only hope, with equal courage and openness to amplitude of emotion and experience. Indeed it may be a natural human craving for courage and openness, sharpened by long claustrophobia, that will have prodded us into such a shift and sustained it.

Should this be so, it would be difficult to imagine any poet since the mid-seventeenth century who could mean more. The help, the encouragement—the desire of which leads us constantly to reshuffle and re-evaluate our predecessors, when we are not doing so simply as an academic exercise—will not, of course, come from using even the greatest verse of Keats as a model. He that imitates the *Iliad*, said Edward Young, is not imitating Homer. The relevance is in what we catch from the example.

Samuel Johnson

PREFACE *TO THE 1765 EDITION OF SHAKESPEARE'S WORKS*

That praises are without reason lavished on the dead, and that the honors due only to excellence are paid to antiquity, is a complaint likely to be always continued by those who, being able to add nothing to truth, hope for eminence from the heresies of paradox; or those who, being forced by disappointment upon consolatory expedients, are willing to hope from posterity what the present age refuses and flatter themselves that the regard which is yet denied by envy will be at last bestowed by time.

Antiquity, like every other quality that attracts the notice of mankind, has undoubtedly votaries that reverence it, not from reason, but from prejudice. Some seem to admire indiscriminately whatever has been long preserved, without considering that time has sometimes cooperated with chance; all perhaps are more willing to honor past than present excellence; and the mind contemplates genius through the shades of age, as the eye surveys the sun through artificial opacity. The great contention of criticism is to find the faults of the moderns and the beauties of the ancients. While an author is yet living, we estimate his powers by his worst performance; and when he is dead, we rate them by his best.

To works, however, of which the excellence is not absolute and definite, but gradual and comparative; to works not raised upon principles demonstrative and scientific, but appealing wholly to observation and experience, no other test can be applied than length of duration and continuance of esteem. What mankind have long possessed they have often examined and compared; and if they persist to value the possession, it is because frequent comparisons have confirmed opinion in its favor. As among the works of nature no man can properly call a river deep or a mountain high, without the knowledge of many mountains and many rivers; so, in the productions of genius, nothing can be styled excellent till it has been compared with other works of the same kind. Demonstration immediately displays its power and has nothing to hope or fear from the flux of years; but works tentative and experimental must be estimated by their proportion to the general and collective ability of man, as it is discovered in a long succession of endeavors.

Excerpt from the *Preface* to the 1765 edition of Shakespeare's work, Samuel Johnson.

Of the first building that was raised, it might be with certainty determined that it was round or square, but whether it was spacious or lofty must have been referred to time. The Pythagorean scale of numbers was at once discovered to be perfect; but the poems of Homer we yet know not to transcend the common limits of human intelligence but by remarking that nation after nation, and century after century, has been able to do little more than transpose his incidents, new-name his characters, and paraphrase his sentiments.

The reverence due to writings that have long subsisted arises, therefore, not from any credulous confidence in the superior wisdom of past ages or gloomy persuasion of the degeneracy of mankind, but is the consequence of acknowledged and indubitable positions, that what has been longest known has been most considered, and what is most considered is best understood.

The poet of whose works I have undertaken the revision may now begin to assume the dignity of an ancient and claim the privilege of established fame and prescriptive veneration. He has long outlived his century, the term commonly fixed as the test of literary merit. Whatever advantages he might once derive from personal allusions, local customs, or temporary opinions have for many years been lost; and every topic of merriment or motive of sorrow which the modes of artificial life afforded him now only obscure the scenes which they once illuminated. The effects of favor and competition are at an end; the tradition of his friendships and his enmities have perished; his works support no opinion with arguments nor supply any faction with invectives; they can neither indulge vanity nor gratify malignity; but are read without any other reason than the desire of pleasure and are therefore praised only as pleasure is obtained; yet, thus unassisted by interest or passion, they have passed through variations of taste and changes of manners, and, as they devolved from one generation to another, have received new honors at every transmission.

But because human judgment, though it be gradually gaining upon certainty, never becomes infallible; and approbation, though long continued, may yet be only the approbation of prejudice or fashion; it is proper to inquire by what peculiarities of excellence Shakespeare has gained and kept the favor of his countrymen.

Nothing can please many, and please long, but just representations of general nature. Particular manners can be known to few, and therefore few only can judge how nearly they are copied. The irregular combinations of fanciful invention may delight awhile by that novelty of which the common satiety of life sends us all in quest; but the pleasures of sudden wonder are soon exhausted, and the mind can only repose on the stability of truth.

Shakespeare is, above all writers, at least above all modern writers, the poet of nature, the poet that holds up to his readers a faithful mirror of manners and of life. His characters are not modified by the customs of particular places, unpracticed by the rest of the world; by the peculiarities of studies or professions which can operate but upon small numbers; or by the accidents of transient fashions or temporary opinions: they are the genuine progeny of common humanity, such as the world will always supply, and observation will always find. His persons act and speak by the influence of those general passions and principles by which all minds are agitated and the whole system of life is continued in motion. In the writings of other poets a character is too often an individual; in those of Shakespeare it is commonly a species.

It is from this wide extension of design that so much instruction is derived. It is this which fills the plays of Shakespeare with practical axioms and domestic wisdom. It was said of Euripides that every verse was a precept; and it may be said of Shakespeare that from his works may be collected a system of civil and economical prudence. Yet his real power is not shown in the splendor of particular passages, but by the progress of his fable and the tenor of his dialogue; and he that tries to recommend him by select quotations will succeed like the pedant in Hierocles, who, when he offered his house to sale, carried a brick in his pocket as a specimen.

It will not easily be imagined how much Shakespeare excels in accommodating his sentiments to real life but by comparing him with other authors. It was observed of the ancient schools of declamation that the more diligently they were frequented, the more was the student disqualified for the world, because he found nothing there which he should ever meet in any other place. The same remark may be applied to every stage but that of Shakespeare. The theater, when it is under any other direction, is peopled by such characters as were never seen, conversing in a language which was never heard, upon topics which will never arise in the commerce of mankind. But the dialogue of this author is often so evidently determined by the incident which produces it, and is pursued with so much ease and simplicity, that it seems scarcely to claim the merit of fiction, but to have been gleaned by diligent selection out of common conversation and common occurrences.

Upon every other stage the universal agent is love, by whose power all good and evil is distributed and every action quickened or retarded. To bring a lover, a lady, and a rival into the fable; to entangle them in contradictory obligations, perplex them with oppositions of interest, and harass them with violence of desires inconsistent with each other; to make them meet in rapture and part in agony, to fill their mouths with hyperbolical joy and outrageous sorrow, to distress them as nothing human ever was distressed, to deliver them as nothing human ever was delivered, is the business of a modern dramatist. For this, probability is violated, life is misrepresented, and language is depraved. But love is only one of many passions; and as it has no great influence upon the sum of life, it has little operation in the dramas of a poet who caught his ideas from the living world and exhibited only what he saw before him. He knew that any other passion, as it was regular or exorbitant, was a cause of happiness or calamity.

Characters thus ample and general were not easily discriminated and preserved, yet perhaps no poet ever kept his personages more distinct from each other. I will not say with Pope that every speech may be assigned to the proper speaker, because many speeches there are which have nothing characteristical; but, perhaps, though some may be equally adapted to every person, it will be difficult to find any that can be properly transferred from the present possessor to another claimant. The choice is right, when there is reason for choice.

Other dramatists can only gain attention by hyperbolical or aggravated characters, by fabulous and unexampled excellence or depravity, as the writers of barbarous romances invigorated the reader by a giant and a dwarf; and he that should form his expectations of human affairs from the play, or from the tale, would be equally deceived. Shakespeare has no heroes; his scenes are occupied only by men, who act and speak as the reader thinks that he should himself have spoken or acted on the same occasion. Even where the agency is supernatural, the dialogue is level with life. Other writers disguise the most natural passions and most frequent incidents; so that he who contemplates them in the book will not know them in the world. Shakespeare approximates the remote and familiarizes the wonderful; the event which he represents will not happen, but, if it were possible, its effects would probably be such as he has assigned; and it may be said that he has not only shown human nature as it acts in real exigencies, but as it would be found in trials to which it cannot be exposed.

This, therefore, is the praise of Shakespeare, that his drama is the mirror of life; that he who has mazed his imagination in following the phantoms which other writers raise up before him, may here be cured of his delirious ecstasies by reading human sentiments in human language, by scenes from which a hermit may estimate the transactions of the world and a confessor predict the progress of the passions.

His adherence to general nature has exposed him to the censure of critics who form their judgments upon narrower principles. Dennis and Rymer think his Romans not sufficiently Roman; and Voltaire censures his kings as not completely royal. Dennis is offended that Menenius, a senator of Rome, should play the buffoon; and Voltaire perhaps thinks decency violated when the Danish usurper is represented as a drunkard. But Shakespeare always makes nature predominate over accident; and, if he preserves the essential character, is not very careful of distinctions superinduced and adventitious. His story requires Romans or kings, but he thinks only on men. He knew that Rome, like every other city, had men of all dispositions; and wanting a buffoon, he went into the senate house for that which the senate house would certainly have afforded him. He was inclined to show an usurper and a murderer not only odious, but despicable; he therefore added drunkenness to his other qualities, knowing that kings love wine like other men, and that wine exerts its natural power upon kings. These are the petty cavils of petty minds; a poet overlooks the casual distinction of country and condition, as a painter, satisfied with the figure, neglects the drapery.

The censure which he has incurred by mixing comic and tragic scenes, as it extends to all his works, deserves more consideration. Let the fact be first stated and then examined.

Shakespeare's plays are not in the rigorous and critical sense either tragedies or comedies, but compositions of a distinct kind; exhibiting the real state of sublunary nature, which partakes of good and evil, joy and sorrow, mingled with endless variety of proportion and innumerable modes of combination; and expressing the course of the world, in which the loss of one is the gain of another; in which, at the same time, the reveller is hasting to his wine, and the mourner burying his friend; in which the malignity of one is sometimes defeated by the frolic of another; and many mischiefs and many benefits are done and hindered without design.

Out of this chaos of mingled purposes and casualties the ancient poets, according to the laws which custom had prescribed, selected some the crimes of men, and some their absurdities; some the momentous vicissitudes of life, and some the lighter occurrences; some the terrors of distress, and some the gaieties of prosperity. Thus rose the two modes of imitation, known by the names of *tragedy* and *comedy*, compositions intended to promote different ends by contrary means, and considered as so little allied that I do not recollect among the Greeks or Romans a single writer who attempted both.

Shakespeare has united the powers of exciting laughter and sorrow not only in one mind but in one composition. Almost all his plays are divided between serious and ludicrous characters, and, in the successive evolutions of the design, sometimes produce seriousness and sorrow, and sometimes levity and laughter.

That this is a practice contrary to the rules of criticism will be readily allowed; but there is always an appeal open from criticism to nature. The end of writing is to instruct; the end of poetry is to instruct by pleasing. That the mingled drama may convey all the instruction of tragedy or comedy cannot be denied, because it includes both in its alternations of exhibition and approaches nearer than either to the appearance of life, by showing how great machinations and slender designs may promote or obviate one another, and the high and the low co-operate in the general system by unavoidable concatenation.

It is objected that by this change of scenes the passions are interrupted in their progression, and that the principal event, being not advanced by a due gradation of preparatory incidents, wants at last the power to move, which constitutes the perfection of dramatic poetry. This reasoning is so specious that it is received as true even by those who in daily experience feel it to be false. The interchanges of mingled scenes seldom fail to produce the intended vicissitudes of passion. Fiction cannot move so much but that the attention may be easily transferred; and though it must be allowed that pleasing melancholy be sometimes interrupted by unwelcome levity, yet let it be considered likewise that melancholy is often not pleasing, and that the disturbance of one man may be the relief of another; that different auditors have different habitudes; and that, upon the whole, all pleasure consists in variety.

The players, who in their edition divided our author's works into comedies, histories, and tragedies, seem not to have distinguished the three kinds by any very exact or definite ideas.

An action which ended happily to the principal person, however serious or distressful through its intermediate incidents, in their opinion constituted a comedy. This idea of a comedy continued long amongst us; and plays were written which, by changing the catastrophe, were tragedies today and comedies tomorrow.

Tragedy was not in those times a poem of more general dignity or elevation than comedy; it required only a calamitous conclusion, with which the common criticism of the age was satisfied, whatever lighter pleasure it afforded in its progress.

History was a series of actions, with no other than chronological succession, independent of each other, and without any tendency to introduce or regulate the conclusion. It is not always very nicely distinguished from tragedy. There is not much nearer approach to unity of action in the tragedy of *Antony and Cleopatra* than in the history of *Richard the Second*. But a history might be continued through many plays; as it had no plan, it had no limits.

Through all these denominations of the drama, Shakespeare's mode of composition is the same: an interchange of seriousness and merriment, by which the mind is softened at one time and exhilarated at another. But whatever be his purpose, whether to gladden or depress, or to conduct the story, without vehemence or emotion, through tracts of easy and familiar dialogue, he never fails to attain his purpose; as he commands us, we laugh or mourn, or sit silent with quiet expectation, in tranquility without indifference.

When Shakespeare's plan is understood, most of the criticisms of Rymer and Voltaire vanish away. The play of *Hamlet* is opened, without impropriety, by two sentinels; Iago bellows at Brabantio's window without injury to the scheme of the play, though in terms which a modern audience would not easily endure; the character of Polonius is seasonable and useful; and the gravediggers themselves may be heard with applause.

Shakespeare engaged in dramatic poetry with the world open before him; the rules of the ancients were yet known to few; the public judgment was unformed; he had no example of such fame as might force him upon imitation, nor critics of such authority as might restrain his extravagance; he therefore indulged his natural disposition; and his disposition, as Rymer has remarked, led him to comedy. In tragedy he often writes, with great appearance of toil and study, what is written at last with little felicity; but, in his comic scenes, he seems to produce, without labor, what no labor can improve. In tragedy he is always struggling after some occasion to be comic; but in comedy he seems to repose, or to luxuriate, as in a mode of thinking congenial to his nature. In his tragic scenes there is always something wanting, but his comedy often surpasses expectation or desire. His comedy pleases by the thoughts and the language, and his tragedy for the greater part by incident and action. His tragedy seems to be skill, his comedy to be instinct.

The force of his comic scenes has suffered little diminution, from the changes made by a century and a half, in manners or in words. As his personages act upon principles arising from genuine passion, very little modified by particular forms, their pleasures and vexations are communicable to all times and to all places; they are natural, and therefore durable. The adventitious peculiarities of personal habits are only superficial dyes, bright and pleasing for a little while, yet soon fading to a dim tinct, without any remains of former lustre; but the discriminations of true passion are the colors of nature; they pervade the whole mass and can only perish with the body that exhibits them. The accidental compositions of heterogeneous modes are dissolved by the chance which combined them; but the uniform simplicity of primitive qualities neither admits increase nor suffers decay. The sand heaped by one flood is scattered by another, but the rock always continues in its place. The stream of time, which is continually washing the dissoluble fabrics of other poets, passes without injury by the adamant of Shakespeare.

If there be, what I believe is, in every nation a style which never becomes obsolete, a certain mode of phraseology so consonant and congenial to the analogy and principles of its respective language as to remain settled and unaltered; this style is probably to be sought in the common intercourse of life, among those who speak only to be understood, without ambition of elegance. The polite are always catching modish innovations, and the learned depart from established forms of speech in hope of finding or making better; those who wish for distinction forsake the vulgar, when the vulgar is right; but there is a conversation above grossness and below refinement, where propriety resides, and where this poet seems to have gathered his comic dialogue. He is therefore more agreeable to the ears of the present age than any other author equally remote and among his other excellencies deserves to be studied as one of the original masters of our language.

These observations are to be considered not as unexceptionably constant, but as containing general and predominant truth. Shakespeare's familiar dialogue is affirmed to be smooth and clear, yet not wholly without ruggedness or difficulty; as a country may be eminently fruitful, though it has spots unfit for cultivation; his characters are praised as natural, though their sentiments are sometimes forced and their actions improbable; as the earth upon the whole is spherical, though its surface is varied with protuberances and cavities.

Shakespeare with his excellencies has likewise faults, and faults sufficient to obscure and overwhelm any other merit. I shall show them in the proportion in which they appear to me, without envious malignity or superstitious veneration. No question can be more innocently discussed than a dead poet's pretensions to renown; and little regard is due to that bigotry which sets candor higher than truth.

His first defect is that to which may be imputed most of the evil in books or in men. He sacrifices virtue to convenience and is so much more careful to please than to instruct that he seems to write without any moral purpose. From his writings indeed a system of social duty may be selected, for he that thinks reasonably must think morally; but his precepts and axioms drop casually from him; he makes no just distribution of good or evil, nor is always careful to show in the virtuous a disapprobation of the wicked; he carries his persons indifferently through right and wrong and at the close dismisses them without further care and leaves their examples to operate by chance. This fault the barbarity of his age cannot extenuate; for it is always a writer's duty to make the world better, and justice is a virtue independent on time or place.

The plots are often so loosely formed that a very slight consideration may improve them, and so carelessly pursued that he seems not always fully to comprehend his own design. He omits opportunities of instructing or delighting which the train of his story seems to force upon him, and apparently rejects those exhibitions which would be more affecting, for the sake of those which are more easy.

It may be observed that in many of his plays the latter part is evidently neglected. When he found himself near the end of his work, and in view of his reward, he shortened the labor to snatch the profit. He therefore remits his efforts where he should most vigorously exert them, and his catastrophe is improbably produced or imperfectly represented.

He had no regard to distinction of time or place, but gives to one age or nation, without scruple, the customs, institutions, and opinions of another, at the expense not only of likelihood but of possibility. These faults Pope has endeavored, with more zeal than judgment, to tranfer to his imagined interpolators. We need not wonder to find Hector quoting Aristotle, when we see the loves of Theseus and Hippolyta combined with the Gothic mythology of fairies. Shakespeare, indeed, was not the only violator of chronology, for in the same age Sidney, who wanted not the advantages of learning, has, in his *Arcadia,* confounded the pastoral with the feudal times, the days of innocence, quiet, and security, with those of turbulence, violence and adventure.

In his comic scenes he is seldom very successful when he engages his characters in reciprocations of smartness and contests of sarcasm; their jests are commonly gross, and their pleasantry licentious; neither his gentlemen nor his ladies have much delicacy nor are sufficiently distinguished from his clowns by any appearance of refined manners. Whether he represented the real conversation of his time is not easy to determine. The reign of Elizabeth is commonly supposed to have been a time of stateliness, formality, and reserve; yet perhaps the relaxations of that severity were not very elegant. There must, however, have been always some modes of gaiety preferable to others, and a writer ought to choose the best.

In tragedy his performance seems constantly to be worse as his labor is more. The effusions of passion which exigence forces out are for the most part striking and energetic; but whenever he solicits his invention, or strains his faculties, the offspring of his throes is tumor, meanness, tediousness, and obscurity.

In narration he affects a disproportionate pomp of diction and a wearisome train of circumlocution and tells the incident imperfectly in many words which might have been more plainly delivered in few. Narration in dramatic poetry is naturally tedious, as it is unanimated and inactive and obstructs the progress of the action; it should therefore always be rapid and enlivened by frequent interruption. Shakespeare found it an incumbrance and, instead of lightening it by brevity, endeavored to recommend it by dignity and splendor.

His declamations or set speeches are commonly cold and weak, for his power was the power of nature; when he endeavored, like other tragic writers, to catch opportunities of amplification, and, instead of inquiring what the occasion demanded, to show how much his stores of knowledge could supply, he seldom escapes without the pity or resentment of his reader.

It is incident to him to be now and then entangled with an unwieldy sentiment, which he cannot well express and will not reject; he struggles with it awhile, and, if it continues stubborn, comprises it in words such as occur and leaves it to be disentangled and evolved by those who have more leisure to bestow upon it.

Not that always where the language is intricate the thought is subtle, or the image always great where the line is bulky; the equality of words to things is very often neglected, and trivial sentiments and vulgar ideas disappoint the attention to which they are recommended by sonorous epithets and swelling figures.

But the admirers of this great poet have most reason to complain when he approaches nearest to his highest excellence and seems fully resolved to sink them in dejection and mollify them with tender emotions by the fall of greatness, the danger of innocence, or the crosses of love. What he does best, he soon ceases to do. He is not long soft and pathetic without some idle conceit or contemptible equivocation. He no sooner begins to move than he counteracts himself; and terror and pity, as they are rising in the mind, are checked and blasted by sudden frigidity.

A quibble is to Shakespeare what luminous vapors are to the traveler; he follows it at all adventures; it is sure to lead him out of his way and sure to engulf him in the mire. It has some malignant power over his mind, and its fascinations are irresistible. Whatever be the dignity or profundity of his disquisition, whether he be enlarging knowledge or exalting affection, whether he be amusing attention with incidents or enchaining it in suspense, let but a quibble spring up before him, and he leaves his work unfinished. A quibble is the golden apple for which he will always turn aside from his career or stoop from his elevation. A quibble, poor and barren as it is, gave him such delight that he was content to purchase it by the sacrifice of reason, propriety, and truth. A quibble was to him the fatal Cleopatra for which he lost the world and was content to lose it.

It will be thought strange that in enumerating the defects of this writer I have not yet mentioned his neglect of the unities, his violation of those laws which have been instituted and established by the joint authority of poets and critics.

For his other deviations from the art of writing, I resign him to critical justice, without making any other demand in his favor than that which must be indulged to all human excellence: that his virtues be rated with his failings. But from the censure which this irregularity may bring upon him, I shall, with due reverence to that learning which I must oppose, adventure to try how I can defend him.

His histories, being neither tragedies nor comedies, are not subject to any of their laws; nothing more is necessary to all the praise which they expect than that the changes of action be so prepared as to be understood, that the incidents be various and affecting, and the characters consistent, natural, and distinct. No other unity is intended, and therefore none is to be sought.

In his other works he has well enough preserved the unity of action. He has not, indeed, an intrigue regularly perplexed and regularly unraveled; he does not endeavor to hide his design only to discover it, for this is seldom the order of real events, and Shakespeare is the poet of nature; but his plan has commonly, what Aristotle requires, a beginning, a middle, and an end; one event is concatenated with another, and the conclusion follows by easy consequence. There are perhaps some incidents that might be spared, as in other poets there is much talk that only fills up time upon the stage; but the general system makes gradual advances and the end of the play is the end of expectation.

To the unities of time and place he has shown no regard; and perhaps a nearer view of the principles on which they stand will diminish their value and withdraw from them the veneration which, from the time of Corneille, they have very generally received, by discovering that they have given more trouble to the poet than pleasure to the auditor.

The necessity of observing the unities of time and place arises from the supposed necessity of making the drama credible. The critics hold it impossible that an action of months or years can be possibly believed to pass in three hours; or that the spectator can suppose himself to sit in the theater while ambassadors go and return between distant kings, while armies are levied and towns besieged, while an exile wanders and returns, or till he whom they saw courting his mistress shall lament the untimely fall of his son. The mind revolts from evident falsehood, and fiction loses its force when it departs from the resemblance of reality.

From the narrow limitation of time necessarily arises the contraction of place. The spectator, who knows that he saw the first act at Alexandria, cannot suppose that he sees the next at Rome, at a distance to which not the dragons of Medea could, in so short a time, have transported him; he knows with certainty that he has not changed his place; and he knows that place cannot change itself; that what was a house cannot become a plain; that what was Thebes can never be Persepolis.

Such is the triumphant language with which a critic exults over the misery of an irregular poet, and exults commonly without resistance or reply. It is time, therefore, to tell him by the authority of Shakespeare, that he assumes as an unquestionable principle, a position which, while his breath is forming it into words, his understanding pronounces to be false. It is false, that any representation is mistaken for reality; that any dramatic fable in its materiality was ever credible, or, for a single moment, was ever credited.

The objection arising from the impossibility of passing the first hour at Alexandria and the next at Rome, supposes that when the play opens the spectator really imagines himself at Alexandria and believes that his walk to the theater has been a voyage to Egypt, and that he lives in the days of Antony and Cleopatra. Surely he that imagines this may imagine more. He that can take the stage at one time for the palace of the Ptolemies may take it in half an hour for the promontory of Actium. Delusion, if delusion be admitted, has no certain limitation; if the spectator can be once persuaded that his old acquaintance are Alexander and Caesar, that a room illuminated with candles is the plain of Pharsalia or the bank of Granicus, he is in a state of elevation above the reach of reason or of truth, and from the heights of empyrean poetry may despise the circumscriptions of terrestrial nature. There is no reason why a mind thus wandering in ecstasy should count the clock, or why an hour should not be a century in that calenture of the brains that can make the stage a field.

The truth is that the spectators are always in their senses and know, from the first act to the last that the stage is only a stage, and that the players are only players. They come to hear a certain number of lines recited with just gesture and elegant modulation. The lines relate to some action, and an action must be in some place; but the different actions that complete a story may be in places very remote from each other; and where is the absurdity of allowing that space to represent first Athens and then Sicily which was always known to be neither Sicily nor Athens, but a modern theater.

By supposition, as place is introduced, time may be extended; the time required by the fable elapses for the most part between the acts; for, of so much of the action as is represented, the real and poetical duration is the same. If in the first act preparations for war against Mithridates are represented to be made in Rome, the event of the war may, without absurdity, be represented in the catastrophe as happening in Pontus; we know that there is neither war nor preparation for war; we know that we are neither in Rome nor Pontus; that neither Mithridates nor Lucullus are before us. The drama exhibits successive imitations of successive actions; and why may not the second imitation represent an action that happened years after the first, if it be so connected with it that nothing but time can be supposed to intervene? Time is, of all modes of existence, most obsequious to the imagination; a lapse of years is as easily conceived as a passage of hours. In contemplation we easily contract the time of real actions and therefore willingly permit it to be contracted when we only see their imitation.

It will be asked how the drama moves if it is not credited. It is credited with all the credit due to a drama. It is credited, whenever it moves, as a just picture of a real original; as representing to the auditor what he would himself feel if he were to do or suffer what is there feigned to be suffered or to be done. The reflection that strikes the heart is not that the evils before us are real evils, but that they are evils to which we ourselves may be exposed. If there be any fallacy, it is not that we fancy the players, but that we fancy ourselves unhappy for a moment; but we rather lament the possibility than suppose the presence of misery, as a mother weeps over her babe when she remembers that death may take it from her. The delight of tragedy proceeds from our consciousness of fiction; if we thought murders and treasons real, they would please no more.

Imitations produce pain or pleasure, not because they are mistaken for realities, but because they bring realities to mind. When the imagination is recreated by a painted landscape, the trees are not supposed capable to give us shade, or the fountains coolness; but we consider how we should be pleased with such fountains playing beside us and such woods waving over us. We are agitated in reading the history of _Henry the Fifth_, yet no man takes his book for the field of Agincourt. A dramatic exhibition is a book recited with concomitants that increase or diminish its effect. Familiar comedy is often more powerful in the theater than on the page; imperial tragedy is always less. The humor of Petruchio may be heightened by grimace; but what voice or what gesture can hope to add dignity or force to the soliloquy of Cato?

A play read affects the mind like a play acted. It is therefore evident that the action is not supposed to be real; and it follows that between the acts a longer or shorter time may be allowed to pass, and that no more account of space or duration is to be taken by the auditor of a drama than by the reader of a narrative, before whom may pass in an hour the life of a hero or the revolutions of an empire.

Whether Shakespeare knew the unities and rejected them by design, or deviated from them by happy ignorance, it is, I think, impossible to decide and useless to inquire. We may reasonably suppose that, when he rose to notice, he did not want the counsels and admonitions of scholars and critics, and that he at last deliberately persisted in a practice, which he might have begun by chance. As nothing is essential to the fable but unity of action, and as the unities of time and place arise evidently from false assumptions, and, by circumscribing the extent of the drama, lessen its variety, I cannot think it much to be lamented that they were not known by him, or not observed; nor, if such another poet could arise, should I very vehemently reproach him that his first act passed at Venice and his next in Cyprus. Such violations of rules merely positive become the comprehensive genius of Shakespeare, and such censures are suitable to the minute and slender criticism of Voltaire:

> Non usque adeo permiscuit imis
> Longus summa dies, ut non, si voce Metelli
> Serventur leges, malint a Caesare tolli.

Yet when I speak thus slightly of dramatic rules, I cannot but recollect how much wit and learning may be produced against me; before such authorities I am afraid to stand, not that I think the present question one of those that are to be decided by mere authority, but because it is to be suspected that these precepts have not been so easily received but for better reasons than I have yet been able to find. The result of my inquiries, in which it would be ludicrous to boast of impartiality, is that the unities of time and place are not essential to a just drama; that, though they may sometimes conduce to pleasure, they are always to be sacrificed to the nobler beauties of variety and instruction; and that a play written with nice observation of critical rules is to be contemplated as an elaborate curiosity, as the product of superfluous and ostentatious art, by which is shown, rather what is possible, than what is necessary.

He that, without diminution of any other excellence, shall preserve all the unities unbroken deserves the like applause with the architect who shall display all the orders of architecture in a citadel without any deduction from its strength; but the principal beauty of a citadel is to exclude the enemy, and the greatest graces of a play are to copy nature and instruct life.

Perhaps what I have here not dogmatically but deliberatively written may recall the principles of the drama to a new examination. I am almost frighted at my own temerity and, when I estimate the fame and the strength of those that maintain the contrary opinion, am ready to sink down in reverential silence; as Aeneas withdrew from the defense of Troy when he saw Neptune shaking the wall and Juno heading the besiegers.

Those whom my arguments cannot persuade to give their approbation to the judgment of Shakespeare will easily, if they consider the condition of his life, make some allowance for his ignorance.

Every man's performances, to be rightly estimated, must be compared with the state of the age in which he lived and with his own particular opportunities; and though to a reader a book be not worse or better for the circumstances of the author, yet as there is always a silent reference of human works to human abilities, and as the inquiry how far man may extend his designs, or how high he may rate his native force, is of far greater dignity than in what rank we shall place any particular performance, curiosity is always busy to discover the instruments as well as to survey the workmanship, to know how much is to be ascribed to original powers and how much to casual and adventitious help. The palaces of Peru or Mexico were certainly mean and incommodious habitations if compared to the houses of European monarchs; yet who could forbear to view them with astonishment who remembered that they were built without the use of iron?

The work

G. Robert Stange

EXPECTATIONS WELL LOST:
DICKENS' FABLE FOR HIS TIME

Great Expectations is a peculiarly satisfying and impressive novel. It is un-usual to find in Dickens' work so rigorous a control of detail, so simple and organic a pattern. In this very late novel the usual features of his art—proliferating sub-plots, legions of minor grotesques—are almost entirely absent. The simplicity is that of an art form that belongs to an ancient type and concentrates on permanently significant issues. *Great Expectations* is conceived as a moral fable; it is the story of a young man's development from the moment of his first self-awareness, to that of his mature acceptance of the human condition.

So natural a theme imposes an elemental form on the novel: the over-all pattern is defined by the process of growth, and Dickens employs many of the motifs of folklore. The story of Pip falls into three phases which clearly display a dialectic progression. We see the boy first in his natural condition in the country, responding and acting instinctively and therefore virtuously. The second stage of his career involves a nega-tion of child-like simplicity; Pip acquires his "expectations," renounces his origins, and moves to the city. He rises in society, but since he acts through calculation rather than through instinctive charity, his moral values deteriorate as his social graces improve. This middle phase of his career culminates in a sudden fall, the beginning of a redemptive suffering which is dramatically concluded by an attack of brain fever leading to a long coma. It is not too fanciful to regard this illness as a symbolic death; Pip rises from it regenerate and percipient. In the final stage of growth he returns to his birthplace, abandons his false expectations, accepts the limitations of his condition, and achieves a partial synthesis of the virtue of his innocent youth and the melancholy insight of his later experience.

Variants of such a narrative are found in the myths of many heroes. In Dickens' novel the legend has the advantage of providing an action which appeals to the great primary human affections and serves as unifying center for the richly conceived minor themes and images which form the body of the novel. It is a signal virtue of this simple structure that it saves *Great Expectations* from some of the startling weaknesses of such excellent

From *College English*, XVI (1954), 9-17. Reprinted with the permission of the National Council of Teachers of English and G. Robert Stange.

but inconsistently developed novels as *Martin Chuzzlewit* or *Our Mutual Friend*.

The particular fable that Dickens elaborates is as interesting for its historical as for its timeless aspects. In its particulars the story of Pip is the classic legend of the nineteenth century: *Great Expectations* belongs to that class of education or development-novels which describe the young man of talents who progresses from the country to the city, ascends in the social hierarchy, and moves from innocence to experience. Stendhal in *Le Rouge et le Noir*, Balzac in *Le Père Goriot* and *Les Illusions perdues*, use the plot as a means of dissecting the post-Napoleonic world and exposing its moral poverty. This novelistic form reflects the lives of the successful children of the century, and usually expresses the mixed attitudes of its artists. Dickens, Stendhal, Balzac communicate their horror of a materialist society, but they are not without admiration for the possibilities of the new social mobility; *la carrière ouverte aux talents* had a personal meaning for all three of these energetic men.

Pip, then, must be considered in the highly competitive company of Julien Sorel, Rubempré, and Eugène de Rastignac. Dickens' tale of lost illusions, however, is very different from the French novelists'; *Great Expectations* is not more profound than other development-novels, but it is more mysterious. The recurrent themes of the genre are all there: city is posed against country, experience against innocence; there is a search for the true father; there is the exposure to crime and the acceptance of guilt and expiation. What Dickens' novel lacks is the clarity and, one is tempted to say, the essential tolerance of the French. He could not command either the saving ironic vision of Stendhal or the disenchanted practicality and secure Catholicism of Balzac. For Dickens, always the Victorian protestant, the issues of a young man's rise or fall are conceived as a drama of the individual conscience; enlightenment (partial at best) is to be found only in the agony of personal guilt.

With these considerations and possible comparisons in mind I should like to comment on some of the conspicuous features of *Great Expectations*. The novel is interesting for many reasons: it demonstrates the subtlety of Dickens' art; it displays a consistent control of narrative, imagery, and theme which gives meaning to the stark outline of the fable, and symbolic weight to every character and detail. It proves Dickens' ability (which has frequently been denied) to combine his genius for comedy with his fictional presentation of some of the most serious and permanently interesting of human concerns.

The principal themes are announced and the mood of the whole novel established in the opening pages of *Great Expectations*. The first scene with the boy Pip in the graveyard is one of the best of the superbly energetic beginnings found in almost all Dickens' mature novels. In less than a page we are given a character, his background, and his setting; within a few paragraphs more we are immersed in a decisive action. Young Pip is first seen against the background of his parents' gravestones—monuments which communicate to him no clear knowledge either of his parentage or of his position in the world. He is an orphan who must search for a father and define his own condition. The moment

of this opening scene, we learn, is that at which the hero has first realized his individuality and gained his "first most vivid and broad impression of the identity of things." This information given the reader,
the violent meeting between Pip and the escaped convict abruptly takes
place.

The impression of the identity of things that Pip is supposed to have
received is highly equivocal. The convict rises up like a ghost from
among the graves, seizes the boy suddenly, threatens to kill him, holds
him upside down through most of their conversation, and ends by forc-
ing the boy to steal food for him. The children of Dickens' novels always
receive rather strange impressions of things, but Pip's epiphany is the
oddest of all, and in some ways the most ingenious. This encounter in
the graveyard is the germinal scene of the novel. While he is held by
the convict, Pip sees his world upside down; in the course of Dickens'
fable the reader is invited to try the same view. This particular change
of viewpoint is an ancient device of irony, but an excellent one: Dickens'
satire asks us to try reversing the accepted senses of innocence and guilt,
success and failure, to think of the world's goods as the world's evils.

A number of ironic reversals and ambiguous situations develop out
of the first scene. The convict, Magwitch, is permanently grateful to
Pip for having brought him food and a file with which to take off his
leg-iron. Years later he expresses his gratitude by assuming in secrecy
an economic parenthood; with the money he has made in Australia he
will, unbeknownst to Pip, make "his boy" a gentleman. But the money
the convict furnishes him makes Pip not a true gentleman, but a cad.
He lives as a *flâneur* in London, and when he later discovers the disrepu-
table source of his income is snobbishly horrified.

Pip's career is a parable which illustrates several religious paradoxes:
he can gain only by losing all he has; only by being defiled can he be
cleansed. Magwitch returns to claim his gentleman, and finally the convict's devotion and suffering arouse Pip's charity; by the time Magwitch has been captured and is dying Pip has accepted him and come
to love him as a true father. The relationship is the most important
one in the novel: in sympathizing with Magwitch Pip assumes the
criminal's guilt; in suffering with and finally loving the despised and
rejected man he finds his own real self.

Magwitch did not have to learn to love Pip. He was naturally devoted
to "the small bundle of shivers," the outcast boy who brought him the
stolen food and the file in the misty graveyard. There is a natural
bond, Dickens suggests, between the child and the criminal; they are
alike in their helplessness; both are repressed and tortured by established society, and both rebel against its incomprehensible authority.
In the first scene Magwitch forces Pip to commit his first "criminal"
act, to steal the file and food from his sister's house. Though this theft
produces agonies of guilt in Pip, we are led to see it not as a sin but
as an instinctive act of mercy. Magwitch, much later, tells Pip: "I first
become aware of myself, down in Essex, a thieving turnips for my living." Dickens would have us, in some obscure way, conceive the illicit
act as the means of self-realization.

In the opening section of the novel the view moves back and forth between the escaped criminal on the marshes and the harsh life in the house of Pip's sister, Mrs. Joe Gargery. The "criminality" of Pip and the convict is contrasted with the socially approved cruelty and injustice of Mrs. Joe and her respectable friends. The elders who come to the Christmas feast at the Gargerys' are pleased to describe Pip as a criminal: the young are, according to Mr. Hubble, "naterally vicious." During this most bleak of Christmas dinners the child is treated not only as outlaw, but as animal. In Mrs. Joe's first speech Pip is called a "young monkey"; then, as the spirits of the revellers rise, more and more comparisons are made between boys and animals. Uncle Pumblechook, devouring his pork, toys with the notion of Pip's having been born a "Squeaker":

> "If you had been born such, would you have been here now? Not you. . . ."
> "Unless in that form," said Mr. Wopsle, nodding towards the dish.
> "But I don't mean in that form, sir," returned Mr. Pumblechook, who had an objection to being interrupted; "I mean, enjoying himself with his elders and betters, and improving himself with their conversation, and rolling in the lap of luxury. Would he have been doing that? No, he wouldn't. And what would have been your destination?" turning on me again. "You would have been disposed of for so many shillings according to the market price of the article, and Dunstable the butcher would have come up to you as you lay in your straw, and he would have whipped you under his left arm, and with his right he would have tucked up his frock to get a penknife from out of his waistcoat-pocket, and he would have shed your blood and had your life. No bringing up by hand then. Not a bit of it!"

This identification of animal and human is continually repeated in the opening chapters of the novel, and we catch its resonance throughout the book. When the two convicts—Pip's "friend" and the other fugitive, Magwitch's ancient enemy—are captured, we experience the horror of official justice, which treats the prisoners as if they were less than human: "No one seemed surprised to see him, or interested in seeing him, or glad to see him, or sorry to see him, or spoke a word, except that somebody in the boat growled as if to dogs, 'Give way, you!'" And the prison ship, lying beyond the mud of the shore, looked to Pip "like a wicked Noah's ark."

The theme of this first section of the novel—which concludes with the capture of Magwitch and his return to the prison ship—might be called "the several meanings of humanity." Only the three characters who are in some way social outcasts—Pip, Magwitch, and Joe Gargery the child-like blacksmith—act in charity and respect the humanity of others. To Magwitch Pip is distinctly not an animal, and not capable of adult wickedness: "You'd be but a fierce young hound indeed, if at your time of life you could help to hunt a wretched warmint." And when, after he is taken, the convict shields Pip by confessing to have stolen the Gargerys' pork pie, Joe's absolution affirms the dignity of man:

> "God knows you're welcome to it—so far as it was ever mine," returned Joe, with a saving remembrance of Mrs. Joe. "We don't know what you have done, but we wouldn't have you starved to death for it, poor miserable fellow-creatur.—Would us, Pip?"

The next section of the narrative is less tightly conceived than the introductory action. Time is handled loosely; Pip goes to school, and becomes acquainted with Miss Havisham of Satis House and the beautiful Estella. The section concludes when Pip has reached early manhood, been told of his expectations, and has prepared to leave for London. These episodes develop, with variations, the theme of childhood betrayed. Pip himself renounces his childhood by coming to accept the false social values of middle-class society. His perverse development is expressed by persistent images of the opposition between the human and the non-human, the living and the dead.

On his way to visit Miss Havisham for the first time, Pip spends the night with Mr. Pumblechook, the corn-chandler, in his lodgings behind his shop. The contrast between the aridity of this old hypocrite's spirit and the viability of his wares is a type of the conflict between natural growth and social form. Pip looks at all the shopkeeper's little drawers filled with bulbs and seed packets and wonders "whether the flower-seeds and bulbs ever wanted of a fine day to break out of those jails and bloom." The imagery of life repressed is developed further in the descriptions of Miss Havisham and Satis House. The first detail Pip notices is the abandoned brewery where the once active ferment has ceased; no germ of life is to be found in Satis House or in its occupants:

> . . . there were no pigeons in the dove-cot, no horses in the stable, no pigs in the sty, no malt in the storehouse, no smells of grains and beer in the copper or the vat. All the uses and scents of the brewery might have evaporated with its last reek of smoke. In a by-yard, there was a wilderness of empty casks. . . .

On top of these casks Estella dances with solitary concentration, and behind her, in a dark corner of the building, Pip fancies that he sees a figure hanging by the neck from a wooden beam, "a figure all in yellow white, with but one shoe to the feet; and it hung so, that I could see that the faded trimmings of the dress were like earthy paper, and that the face was Miss Havisham's."

Miss Havisham *is* death. From his visits to Satis House Pip acquires his false admiration for the genteel; he falls in love with Estella and fails to see that she is the cold instrument of Miss Havisham's revenge on human passion and on life itself. When Pip learns he may expect a large inheritance from an unknown source he immediately assumes (incorrectly) that Miss Havisham is his benefactor; she does not undeceive him. Money, which is also death, is appropriately connected with the old lady rotting away in her darkened room.

Conflicting values in Pip's life are also expressed by the opposed imagery of stars and fire. Estella is by name a star, and throughout the novel stars are conceived as pitiless: "And then I looked at the stars, and considered how awful it would be for a man to turn his face up to them as he froze to death, and see no help or pity in all the glittering multitude." Estella and her light are described as coming down the dark passage of Satis House "like a star," and when she has become a woman she is constantly surrounded by the bright glitter of jewelry.

Joe Gargery, on the other hand, is associated with the warm fire of the hearth or forge. It was his habit to sit and rake the fire between the lower bars of the kitchen grate, and his workday was spent at the forge. The extent to which Dickens intended the contrast between the warm and the cold lights—the vitality of Joe and the frigid glitter of Estella—is indicated in a passage that describes the beginnings of Pip's disillusionment with his expectations:

> When I woke up in the night . . . I used to think, with a weariness on my spirits, that I should have been happier and better if I had never seen Miss Havisham's face, and had risen to manhood content to be partners with Joe in the honest old forge. Many a time of an evening, when I sat alone looking at the fire, I thought, after all, there was no fire like the forge fire and the kitchen fire at home.
>
> Yet Estella was so inseparable from all my restlessness and disquiet of mind, that I really fell into confusion as to the limits of my own part in its production.

At the end of the novel Pip finds the true light on the homely hearth, and in a last twist of the father-son theme, Joe emerges as a true parent —the only kind of parent that Dickens could ever fully approve, one that remains a child. The moral of this return to Joe sharply contradicts the accepted picture of Dickens as a radical critic of society: Joe is a humble countryman who is content with the place in the social order he has been appointed to fulfill. He fills it "well and with respect"; Pip learns that he can do no better than to emulate him.

The second stage of Pip's three-phased story is set in London, and the moral issues of the fiction are modulated accordingly. Instead of the opposition between custom and the instinctive life, the novelist treats the conflict between man and his social institutions. The topics and themes are specific, and the satire, some of it wonderfully deft, is more social than moral. Not all Dickens' social message is presented by means that seem adequate. By satirizing Pip and his leisure class friends (The Finches of the Grove, they call themselves) the novelist would have us realize that idle young men will come to a bad end. Dickens is here expressing the Victorian Doctrine of Work—a pervasive notion that both inspired and reassured his industrious contemporaries.

The difficulty for the modern reader, who is unmoved by the objects of Victorian piety, is that the doctrine appears to be the result, not of moral insight, but of didactic intent; it is presented as statement, rather than as experience or dramatized perception, and consequently it never modifies the course of fictional action or the formation of character.

The distinction is crucial: it is between the Dickens who *sees* and the Dickens who *professes;* often between the good and the bad sides of his art.

The novelist is on surer ground when he comes to define the nature of wealth in a mercantile society. Instead of moralistic condemnation we have a technique that resembles parable. Pip eventually learns that his ornamental life is supported, not by Miss Havisham, but by the labor and suffering of the convict Magwitch:

> "I swore arterwards, sure as ever I spec'lated and got rich, you should get rich. I lived rough, that you should live smooth; I worked hard that you should be above work. What odds, dear boy? Do I tell it fur you to feel a obligation? Not a bit. I tell it, fur you to know as that there dung-hill dog wot you kep life in, got his head so high that he could make a gentleman—and, Pip, you're him!"

The convict would not only make a gentleman but own him. The blood horses of the colonists might fling up the dust over him as he was walking, but, "I says to myself, 'If I ain't a gentleman, nor yet ain't got no learning, I'm the owner of such. All on you owns stock and land; which on you owns a brought-up London gentleman?'"

In this action Dickens has subtly led us to speculate on the connections between a gentleman and his money, on the dark origins of even the most respectable fortunes. We find Magwitch guilty of trying to own another human being, but we ask whether his actions are any more sinful than those of the wealthy *bourgeois*. There is a deeper moral in the fact that Magwitch's fortune at first destroyed the natural gentleman in Pip, but that after it was lost (it had to be forfeited to the state when Magwitch was finally captured) the "dung-hill dog" did actually make Pip a gentleman by evoking his finer feelings. This ironic distinction between "gentility" and what the father of English poetry meant by "gentilesse" is traditional in our literature and our mythology. In *Great Expectations* it arises out of the action and language of the fiction; consequently it moves and persuades us as literal statement never can.

The middle sections of the novel are dominated by the solid yet mysterious figure of Mr. Jaggers, Pip's legal guardian. Though Jaggers is not one of Dickens' greatest characters he is heavy with implication; he is so much at the center of this fable that we are challenged to interpret him—only to find that his meaning is ambiguous. On his first appearance Jaggers strikes a characteristic note of sinister authority:

> He was a burly man of an exceedingly dark complexion, with an exceedingly large head and a correspondingly large hand. He took my chin in his large hand and turned up my face to have a look at me by the light of the candle. . . . His eyes were set very deep in his head, and were disagreeably sharp and suspicious. . . .
>
> "How do *you* come here?"
>
> "Miss Havisham sent for me, sir," I explained.
>
> "Well! Behave yourself. I have a pretty large experience of

boys, and you're a bad set of fellows. Now mind!" said he, biting the side of his great forefinger, as he frowned at me, "you behave yourself."

Pip wonders at first if Jaggers is a doctor. It is soon explained that he is a lawyer—what we now ambiguously call a *criminal* lawyer—but he is like a physician who treats moral malignancy, with the doctor's necessary detachment from individual suffering. Jaggers is interested not in the social operations of the law, but in the varieties of criminality. He exudes an antiseptic smell of soap and is described as washing his clients off as if he were a surgeon or a dentist.

Pip finds that Jaggers has "an air of authority not to be disputed . . . with a manner expressive of knowing something secret about every one of us that would effectually do for each individual if he chose to disclose it." When Pip and his friends go to dinner at Jaggers' house Pip observes that he "wrenched the weakest parts of our dispositions out of us." After the party his guardian tells Pip that he particularly liked the sullen young man they called Spider: "'Keep as clear of him as you can. But I like the fellow, Pip; he is one of the true sort. Why if I was a fortune-teller. . . . But I am not a fortune-teller,' he said. . . . 'You know what I am, don't you?'" This question is repeated when Pip is being shown through Newgate Prison by Jaggers' assistant, Wemmick. The turnkey says of Pip: "Why then . . . he knows what Mr. Jaggers is."

But neither Pip nor the reader ever fully knows what Mr. Jaggers is. We learn, along with Pip, that Jaggers has manipulated the events which have shaped the lives of most of the characters in the novel; he has, in the case of Estella and her mother, dispensed a merciful but entirely personal justice; he is the only character who knows the web of secret relationships that are finally revealed to Pip. He dominates by the strength of his knowledge the world of guilt and sin—called Little Britain—of which his office is the center. He has, in brief, the powers that an artist exerts over the creatures of his fictional world, and that a god exerts over his creation.

As surrogate of the artist, Jaggers displays qualities of mind—complete impassibility, all-seeing unfeelingness—which are the opposite of Dickens', but of a sort that Dickens may at times have desired. Jaggers can be considered a fantasy figure created by a novelist who is forced by his intense sensibility to relive the sufferings of his fellow men and who feels their agonies too deeply.

In both the poetry and fiction of the nineteenth century there are examples of a persistent desire of the artist *not to care*. The mood, which is perhaps an inevitable concomitant of Romanticism, is expressed in Balzac's ambivalence toward his great character Vautrin. As arch-criminal and Rousseauistic man, Vautrin represents all the attitudes that Balzac the churchman and monarchist ostensibly rejects, yet is presented as a kind of artist-hero, above the law, who sees through the social system with an almost noble cynicism.

Related attitudes are expressed in the theories of art developed by such different writers as Flaubert and Yeats. While—perhaps because

—Flaubert himself suffered from hyperaesthesia, he conceived the ideal novelist as coldly detached, performing his examination with the deft impassivity of the surgeon. Yeats, the "last Romantic," found the construction of a mask or anti-self necessary to poetic creation, and insisted that the anti-self be cold and hard—all that he as poet and feeling man was not.

Dickens' evocation of this complex of attitudes is less political than Balzac's, less philosophical than Flaubert's or Yeats'. Jaggers has a complete understanding of human evil but, unlike the living artist, can wash his hands of it. He is above ordinary institutions; like a god he dispenses justice, and like a god displays infinite mercy through unrelenting severity:

> "Mind you, Mr. Pip," said Wemmick, gravely in my ear, as he took my arm to be more confidential; "I don't know that Mr. Jaggers does a better thing than the way in which he keeps himself so high. He's always so high. His constant height is of a piece with his immense abilities. That Colonel durst no more take leave of *him*, than that turnkey durst ask him his intentions respecting a case. Then between his height and them, he slips in his subordinate—don't you see?—and so he has 'em soul and body."

Pip merely wishes that he had "some other guardian of minor abilities."

The final moral vision of *Great Expectations* has to do with the nature of sin and guilt. After visiting Newgate, Pip, still complacent and self-deceived, thinks how strange it was that he should be encompassed by the taint of prison and crime. He tries to beat the prison dust off his feet and to exhale its air from his lungs; he is going to meet Estella, who must not be contaminated by the smell of crime. Later it is revealed that Estella, the pure, is the bastard child of Magwitch and a murderess. Newgate is figuratively described as a greenhouse, and the prisoners as plants carefully tended by Wemmick, assistant to Mr. Jaggers. These disturbing metaphors suggest that criminality is the condition of life. Dickens would distinguish between the native, inherent sinfulness from which men can be redeemed, and that evil which destroys life: the sin of the hypocrite or oppressor, the smothering wickedness of corrupt institutions. The last stage of Pip's progression is reached when he learns to love the criminal and to accept his own implication in the common guilt.

Though Dickens' interpretation is theologically heterodox, he deals conventionally with the ancient question of free will and predestination. In one dramatic paragraph Pip's "fall" is compared with the descent of the rock slab on the sleeping victim in the Arabian Nights tale: Slowly, slowly, "all the work, near and afar, that tended to the end, had been accomplished; and in an instant the blow was struck, and the roof of my stronghold dropped upon me." Pip's fall was the result of a chain of predetermined events but he was, nevertheless, responsible for his own actions; toward the end of the novel Miss Havisham gravely informs him: "You have made your own snares. I never made them."

The patterns of culpability in *Great Expectations* are so intricate that the whole world of the novel is eventually caught in a single web of awful responsibility. The leg-iron, for example, which the convict removed with the file Pip stole for him is found by Orlick and used as a weapon to brain Mrs. Joe. By this fearsome chain of circumstance Pip shares the guilt for his sister's death.

Profound and suggestive as is Dickens' treatment of guilt and expiation in this novel, to trace its remoter implications is to find something excessive and idiosyncratic. A few years after he wrote *Great Expectations* Dickens remarked to a friend that he felt always as if he were wanted by the police—"irretrievably tainted." Compared to most of the writers of his time the Dickens of the later novels seems to be obsessed with guilt. The way in which his development-novel differs from those of his French compeers emphasizes an important quality of Dickens' art. The young heroes of *Le Rouge et le Noir* and *Le Père Goriot* proceed from innocence, through suffering to learning. They are surrounded by evil, and they can be destroyed by it. But Stendhal, writing in a rationalist tradition, and Balzac displaying the worldliness that only a Catholic novelist can command, seem astonishingly cool, even callous, beside Dickens. *Great Expectations* is outside either Cartesian or Catholic rationalism; profound as only an elementally simple book can be, it finds its analogues not in the novels of Dickens' English or French contemporaries, but in the writings of that other irretrievably tainted artist, Fyodor Dostoevski.

The work and the author

John Wain

BYRON: THE SEARCH FOR IDENTITY

Slowly, the literary biographies of the English nineteenth century are being steamrollered by those of the American twentieth. Dowden's two bulky volumes on Shelley were nudged aside, some years ago, by Newman Ivy White's even bulkier two; and now it is the turn of Tom Moore's three volumes on Byron to be replaced by Professor Marchand's.[1] Actually, the surprising thing is how much still remains of the obsolete ones: White discovered and/or incorporated much detail that had come to light since Dowden wrote, and yet it remains true that there is no important facet of Shelley's character that can't be found in Dowden, if you read him carefully enough. It is the same with Moore; his biography was a scissors-and-paste job (its full title is *Letters and Journals of Lord Byron, with Notices of his Life*), and there is hardly any individual flavor, hardly any unifying presence of the biographer himself, in its pages. But for the person who simply wants "a good read," without caring too much whether the information he is getting is the last word in completeness, Moore is likely to survive.

The question for a reviewer, however, is nothing so cosy. What (he must ask) does the Marchand biography add to our understanding of Byron's character? The answer is plain: not a great deal. Its usefulness is that it marshals everything into one book (albeit a tripartite and ruinously expensive book) and so makes for convenience. Anyone who has attentively read the huge compilation of eye-witness accounts of Byron, edited by Mr. E. J. Lovell, Jr., under the title *His Very Self and Voice*, and followed that up with his letters, and followed those in turn with his poems (which, we might remind ourselves, constitute the reason why we are interested in him at all)—such a reader, if he exists, could safely assume that he understands Byron, or has the means of understanding him, as well as Professor Marchand does. The one really big fact which, if I am not mistaken, sees the light for the first time in Professor Marchand's book comes near the beginning of the first volume,

From *Essays on Literature and Ideas* by John Wain (London and Toronto: Macmillan & Co., Ltd., 1963). Reprinted by permission of St. Martin's Press, Inc., and Macmillan & Co. Ltd.

1. *Byron* by Leslie A. Marchand.

and concerns Mary Gray. This Scots lass, a pious Calvinist, had charge of Byron in early boyhood, succeeding her equally pious sister Agnes, and the niche into which the pair of them have always been fitted is "early Bible training." They it was who instilled that knowledge of the Old Testament which came out in *Hebrew Melodies,* and also inoculated him with what the *Encyclopaedia Britannica* pithily calls "too much Calvinism for faith or unfaith in Christianity." We can now add one more fact about Mary Gray: namely, that (to use the words of a memorandum written by Byron's friend Hobhouse) she "used to come to bed to him and play tricks with his person." Byron was nine years old at this time, and Hobhouse did not hesitate to trace a direct link between this nursely *divertissement* and the poet's own statement, "My passions were developed very early—so early, that few would believe me, if I were to state the period, and the facts which accompanied it." We may go further and trace two more links: one to Byron's lifelong distaste for the Pharisaisms of churchgoing people, the other to his repulsive treatment of women—repulsive not merely because of his promiscuity, but because of the give-and-take-away pattern his feelings seem to have most easily fallen into. Byron would display himself before a woman until he provoked her to make the first move; then, when it was all over, he would pass harsh judgment on her for having thrown herself at him.

But there, I think, the influence of Mary Gray ends, or becomes inextricably blended with more general influences. The real root of Byron's impossible treatment of women was his failure to establish his own true identity. The friendships Byron seems to have kept longest were male ones of the hearty, pistol-shooting, all-boys-together type, in which he could wear an easily assumed mask which did not drop off every time his inner feelings underwent a change. In the more seismographic and intimate relationships offered by women—and, for that matter, by the various youths with whom he had homosexual entanglements—this was impossible to sustain.

I want now to suggest—and I know there is nothing very original about the suggestion—that it was not possible for Byron to have a fully successful relationship with his poetic imagination, either, and for the same reasons.

Byron was a poet who worked through, by means of, self-consciousness. That is to say, he projected an image of himself and then let the image do the writing. Composition, to him, was a dramatic performance: the poet, having called an audience together, walked on to the stage and delivered an oration. The subject matter of this oration scarcely mattered. Its real purpose, from first to last, was to present the character of the poet.

Naturally this character was to some extent a false one. It was assumed, edited, deliberately posed. What man could ever present his real personality, with all its doubts, its inward hesitations, ambiguities, and contradictions, in such a way as to make *dramatic* sense of it? In Byron's time, and for half a century before, a number of authors made it their life's work to present the inner working of their minds with complete frankness. The most celebrated of these attempts was Rousseau's; it is a brave effort, and yet the figure held up for our inspection in the *Con-*

fessions doesn't give much impression of spontaneity. It seems in many ways as posed, as consciously staged, as the Byron-figure. Stendhal likened Byron to Rousseau: to that acute and disenchanted man, neither seemed very genuine. Boswell came nearer to complete self-revelation, especially in the records he had no intention of publishing. For my money, the best of these attempts to lift the lid off a man's mind is Wordsworth's: the quickest way to make oneself realize the true greatness of *The Prelude* is to approach it after a diet of these lesser predecessors.

To return to Byron: he had no idea of attempting this kind of self-dissection. He put as much energy into covering up those sides of his character that wouldn't fit into the pattern, as he did into revealing the ones that would. Fundamentally, Byron lacked the confidence to disclose, even to himself, the basic mechanisms of his mind. He was mystified by life, and more than a trifle repelled by it: and, like many neurotics, he had no means of facing it except by fitting himself out with a character that was partly assumed. Partly, but not wholly, since no one can maintain, for more than a few minutes at a time, a character which bears no relation at all to his real one. The two characters Byron assumed during his brief life were both built up from recognizably genuine elements within his character, but they were both simplifications. They existed by virtue of suppression, rather than fabrication.

And this, of course, was the rock on which he split as a poet. He created, in turn, two over-simplified characters to write his poetry for him. He could not write it himself because he did not, in the deeper sense, have a self. His attitudinizing was a short cut to arriving at a sense of his own tangible existence. As long as he had a mold into which his emotional lava could pour, he could escape the torturing contradictions that beset him, and he seems to have discovered this very early. Professor Marchand's pages provide abundant illustration. A notable one (which, incidentally, is taken from Moore) concerns a party at which the school-boy Byron lapsed into bashfulness in the presence of some vivacious girls.

"The first time I was introduced to him," Elizabeth Pigot recalled, "was at a party at his mother's, when he was so shy that she was forced to send for him three times before she could persuade him to come into the drawing-room, to play with the young people at a round game. He was then a fat, bashful boy, with his hair combed straight over his forehead, and extremely like a miniature picture that his mother had painted by M. de Chambruland. The next morning Mrs. Byron brought him to call at our house, when he still continued shy and formal in his manner. The conversation turned upon Cheltenham where we had been staying . . . and I mentioned that I had seen the character of Gabriel Lackbrain very well performed. His mother getting up to go, he accompanied her, making a formal bow, and I, in allusion to the play, said 'Goodby, Gaby.' His countenance lighted up, his handsome mouth displayed a broad grin, all his shyness vanished, never to return, and, upon his mother's saying, 'Come, Byron, are you ready?'—no, she might go by herself, he would stay and talk a little longer."

In other words, she had provided him with a role into which, however fleetingly, he could throw himself. Obviously he would not wish to be cast as "Gaby" for long—but it was enough to get started.

Most people are agreed that Byron failed to become the great poet that he potentially was: I do not see how else we can account for this failure than by relating it to the deeper and more intimate failure to discover his own true identity. It takes courage, after all, to abandon one's neatly carved *persona* and surrender to the contradictory richness of life itself. A little too much defensiveness in one's make-up, and it is impossible. We all know the kind of author who adopts a set of outward characteristics that make it easy to assimilate him to the characters he imagines; everything he writes has the effect of strengthening this central *persona,* until the books themselves become mere adjuncts to a personal legend. And what happens? His work becomes more and more rigidly patterned, more and more dry and predictable. The imaginative life simply cannot be contained in this way.

Not that Byron fell a victim to this kind of desiccation and repetitiveness. He was too vital, too impetuously inventive, for that to be much of a danger. In any case, he died so young that the onrush of new material kept his pen busy and produced an impression of inexhaustible fertility. This impression, I believe, was illusory. Another ten years and Byron would have been forced to come to terms with this central imaginative and emotional hiatus. The result, I imagine—though of course one is frankly guessing here—would have been a crisis which would either have silenced him altogether or set him up as a new, and very much greater, poet.

As it is, we are left with an *œuvre* which breaks into two halves. The conventional division, which seems perfectly adequate, is that the "romantic" Byron holds the stage until 1816, in which year the accumulated scandals of the poet's private life drove him from England, never to return; then, after a few months in which his romantic poetry sings its swan-song, the "satiric" Byron takes over. This classification will serve well enough, provided we notice two things. First, that the two Byrons are not different characters, but different arrangements of the same character. Insistence on the division can only encourage the pointless diversion of finding veins of satire in the romantic poems, veins of romance in the satiric. *Hours of Idleness,* the first published volume, shows clearly enough that the young Byron was fully capable of developing in either direction; there is one poem, *To a Lady Who Presented to the Author a Lock of Hair,* which Professor Marchand singles out as "amazingly" like the later satiric work, but I don't see what is amazing about it. This leads us to the second noteworthy point: that Byron, in choosing to adopt first one vein and then the other, allowed circumstances to lead him: his choice was not made from literary motives, but simply imposed by the events of his life and the pressures of his *milieu.* When he made his first appearance, it was in the entirely conventional romantic guise of the day. Except for his greater energy, there is nothing in his earlier work that cannot be paralleled in Scott, Moore, or James Beatty—except, indeed, for the handful of couplet satires which he wrote to an Augustan formula.

It was the same story with the switch to the satiric *persona.* The romantic mask had to be put aside, and Byron acted as soon as he perceived this. He did not lead; he followed. It became impossible for him to embody, in his own person, the "Byronic hero" (Mark I), because that hero was a figure of mystery—wronged, perhaps, by the world, and with a nameless sin or two stacked away in the cupboard, but mainly an unknown quantity. And when the extraordinary deluge of moral righteousness suddenly swamped Byron, the mystery was swept away. (I know, of course, that technically speaking there is still a mystery—that it is still possible to argue over whether Byron's wife left him because he was committing incest with Augusta Leigh, as Harriet Beecher Stowe claimed in 1869, or because he was compelling her to "enact the Ganymede," as Professor Wilson Knight insists. But this kind of concrete puzzle is not at all the kind of "mystery" demanded by the Byronic hero.) Once the earlier pose had become impossible, there was nothing for it but to accept the later one. Overnight, Byron became irreverent, caustic, savagely fleering, the well-appointed unmasker of hypocrisy, the anti-cant man.

Before going on to discuss the merits of the poetry written by either of these two fantasy-figures, there are one or two considerations that must detain us a little longer. The first is an obvious one: how very Scotch all this is! Every Scot—and this is a fact that can be checked by ordinary day-to-day observation—has the gift of projecting a *persona* which simplifies his real character and allows it to make a more dramatic impact. Whether or not it is true that every Irishman is a stage Irishman, every Scotsman is certainly a stage Scotsman. If we look back over the half-century before Byron was born, there can be no doubt as to who is the best poet there; it is Burns; and Burns has a gift of self-dramatization as strongly marked as Byron's. The typical poem by Burns is a speech in character, and the character is always an important part of the poetry. When he writes a tender love poem, or an earthy piece of shrewd humorous comment on life, the character he is using is one of the conventional projections of himself. When he writes a satire such as "Holy Willie's Prayer," the mouthpiece-figure is presented in vividly economical fashion. (How the nineteenth century English could ever have admired Browning's "dramatic" pieces so much, when "Holy Willie's Prayer" was available for comparison, must remain enigmatic.) Burns also had the trick of writing in compartments; almost as strongly as Byron, he split his poetry down the middle, with satiric and sophisticated pieces on one side, "spontaneous" lyrics on the other. He even pinpointed this by issuing two volumes in successive years, the Kilmarnock edition of 1786 and the Edinburgh edition of 1787, in which the weighting is radically different.

The example of Burns, then, should make Byron's life and work seem less difficult to comprehend; particularly as they both asserted, with a sincerity there is no reason to doubt, that poetry was to them a direct and uncomplicated reaction to life. The poet finds himself in a situation, the situation throws up an emotion, and the emotion throws up a poem. Everyone knows Burns's statement, in the autobiographical letter to Dr. Moore, of how he first discovered within himself the impulse to song. "Thus with me began love and poetry." Byron might have used the same words. So, it is true, might any adolescent versifier; but these two excellent poets never broke away from the pattern, and never felt the need to break away.

A poetry directly geared to the events of one's life, and expressed through *personae* which are themselves simplifications of one's own character; that is the formula. If Byron had to adopt more challenging attitudes than those of Burns, and discard the first more dramatically in favor of the second, that in turn is due to his more complicated position. The one was a crofter's son who became an exciseman; the other, the child of a shabby-genteel mother and a raffish father, nurtured in an Edinburgh side street and suddenly flung into the life of an English *milord*.

The "romantic" Byron and the "satiric," then, seem to me too nearly the same poet to make it worth distinguishing between them. They both have the same gifts—energy, sweep, pace, scope. And in each case the deficiencies are related to this central timidity.

Let us take a quotation which shows Byron at his best—and there is no need to be afraid of using a hackneyed one. The "Dying Gladiator" set piece, from *Childe Harold*, is probably the one passage which has been oftenest quoted.

> I see before me the Gladiator lie;
> He leans upon his hand—his manly brow
> Consents to death, but conquers agony,
> And his droop'd head sinks gradually low—
> And through his side the last drops, ebbing slow
> From the red gash, fall heavy, one by one,
> Like the first of a thunder-shower: and now
> The arena swims around him—he is gone.
> Ere ceased the inhuman shout which hail'd the wretch who won.
>
> He heard it, but he heeded not—his eyes
> Were with his heart, and that was far away:
> He reck'd not of the life he lost nor prize,
> But where his rude hut by the Danube lay.
> *There* were his young barbarians all at play,
> *There* was their Dacian mother—he, their sire,
> Butcher'd to make a Roman holiday—
> All this rush'd with his blood—Shall he expire
> And unavenged?—Arise! ye Goths, and glut your ire!

A quotation of only two stanzas is, strictly speaking, too short to do justice to a long narrative poem; still, given that we are reasonably familiar with the whole, we can make some use even of these few lines. We can find, even here, the chief characteristics of Byron's poetry. Probably the first thing that meets the eye is the energy with which he sets about a conventional subject. Walking pensively among the ruins of Rome (the very phrase, *The Ruins of Rome,* is the title of a popular eighteenth century romantic poem), the poet thinks of the tumultuous scenes once witnessed by the now silent and deserted arena. A dying gladiator!—what could be more conventional? And yet, after all, gladiators *did* fight and die there, and it is reasonable that somebody should write poetry about the fact. If Byron had not existed, there would be a huge gap right down the middle of English romanticism. So we have the gladiator dying; and what does he think about? *His wife and children.* Yes, Byron actually dares one of the enormous platitudes that no modern writer would touch with a barge pole.

The people watching the gladiatorial contest are "inhuman," and this is linked with a certain tit-for-tat moralizing, never far away in Byron (his "shocking" side, as no one has ever failed to note, is merely the obverse of this). It is all very fine for the inhuman spectators to shout with glee, but we know something that they don't: Rome is going to fall, and what is more it is these same Goths who will push it over, *so there*. This mechanical (and not very accurate) moral-drawing from history is an eighteenth century taste, and the other major poets of Byron's day have hardly a trace of it. Here as elsewhere, he is less up-to-date than they are.

The conventionality, the energy, the conviction, the willingness to play on easily aroused responses in his audience—all these are obvious marks of Byron's poetry. His technical characteristics, too, are easy to recognize. The verse is impetuous but lumpy. For all its energy and rapidity, it moves in a stumbling way. Byron makes no attempt to capture those long wave-like rhythms which best justify the use of the Spenserian stanza; instead, he provides excellent single lines—strong, pithy, and quotable to an extent hardly to be matched except in Dryden—and links them with more or less inert passages. Rhymes are a bit of a nuisance, too: "He reck'd not of the life he lost nor prize," is very poor, but it has to stay because "prize" must go at the end of a line; something must rhyme with "eyes" in the magnificent opening lines of the stanza.

Similarly,

> *There* was their Dacian mother—he, their sire,
> Butcher'd to make a Roman holiday,

is a very typical piece of Byron; the introductory line, which exists for the sake of the one it leads to, is clumsy and stilted; Byron has to italicize *There* in the hope of getting the reader to stress it enough to set it apart from the two-fold repetition of "their" immediately afterwards. "Dacian" is a pure fill-in; having said that the man's hut was by the Danube, there is no need to go on and particularize—neither do we really need to be told that the gladiator was the "sire" of his children. All the line is doing is to carry us over ten syllables so that we can be there in time to receive the big punch from the second line—which, as usual with Byron, is one that no reader, having once met it, ever forgets.

Again, in the first of these two stanzas, there are numb and mechanical passages; the comparison between the last drops of blood from the gladiator's mortal wound with the first drops of a thundershower is not particularly illuminating; but the fact is that, having given us a line as magnificent as

> Consents to death, but conquers agony,

Byron can fill the rest of the stanza with anything he chooses—we're with him, whatever he does.

In fact that line, when one comes to think about it, is one of the very few lines of English verse that one cannot imagine any critic, of any period, failing to rate high. Sidney would have liked it; so would Dryden, so would Johnson; so, one presumes, would Mr. Eliot, despite his somewhat harsh verdict that Byron is at his best when being sardonic, bantering, not "poetic." This line is "poetic"; we can say of it that it unmistakably represents the poetic use of language, and what is more it is entirely non-ironic; but it is poetic in the manner of the unselfconscious Dryden, rather than the superpoetical nineteenth century.

If we turn to Byron's later satiric work, much the same qualities will be apparent; there is no need to go over the ground twice. Obviously, it was opportune for him to adopt the stance of a searingly honest man, impatient with cant from whatever source it came. For one thing, it fitted the facts. After fondling Byron for a season or two, "England" (i.e. London society) had cast him out with exaggerated protestations of horror; and in this, there were undeniable elements of cant. London in 1816 was not renowned for its strict morality; the Victorian age had not yet set in. Professor Marchand has made it plain that Byron was a shade paranoiac about the extent of his persecution: it was not so universal or so virulent as he thought; still, he *did* think so, and that is the important fact. He was in a mood to hate hypocrisy because he had been hurt, and the people who had hurt him had acted hypocritically.

Secondly, the Europe to which he turned his face was the Europe of the Congress of Vienna. The spectacle that met his eyes was one of pompous coalitions and committees sitting with the idea of restoring the pre-Napoleonic *status quo*. As Elizabeth Barrett Browning put it,

And kings crept out again to feel the sun.

Internationally, it was a time of windy protestations, of crocodile tears, of all the detestable humbug of professional politicians. For the six years that remained of his life, Byron stalked through this landscape, pushing over the lath-and-plaster buildings, withering the paper foliage, puncturing the gasbags, in the biggest one-man debunking spree the world has ever seen. Sober historians have gone on record as saying that Byron, single-handed, had a demonstrable influence in neutralizing the effect of the Congress of Vienna. He was certainly—to take one example—the imaginative inspiration of the Russian "Decembrist" rising, in 1825, the first revolt against the Tsars; one of its leaders, the poet Ryleyev, went to the scaffold with a volume of Byron's poems in his hand.

We need not doubt the sincerity of all this. To assume such a *persona* was within Byron's power, and he made full use of the opportunity. Like many people of his demonstrative type, he was more at ease before a large audience than a small one. He could act a part in public, but individuals often dried him up. In the same way, he was more generous and considerate to underdogs—children, servants, anyone who was not in a position to challenge him in any way—than to social and intellectual equals. One recalls that letter of Claire Clairmont's, written in 1818, in which she contrasted his gentle bearing towards dependants with his cold and suspicious reception of people "on a par" with him.

The psychology of the thing is quite plain. Byron found it easier to identify emotionally with the underdog because, deep down, he had cast himself in the same rôle. A childhood spent in genteel poverty, suddenly cut across by the entirely unexpected reversion of the title, had left him with a basic uncertainty as to which world he really belonged in. The scandal and ostracism of 1816 resolved that doubt. There had always been a tinsel artificiality about the welcome he had received from the *beau monde*, and now they had revealed themselves in their true colors. The very haste with which he concluded this, and took himself off, is symptomatic of a kind of relief at having his dilemma settled for him. Henceforth, his most consistent public face was that of the champion of the oppressed, the stripper away of the pretences with which greed and tyranny cover themselves. Already, in 1812, he had delivered his great speech in the House of Lords, resisting the bill which would make machine-wrecking a capital offence; already he had written his fiercely compassionate "Song for the Luddites." But after the *débâcle* of 1816, his tone became less exalted, more cynical and vitriolic. He developed a vein of satire which, while it derives directly from the great couplet satirists of the Augustan age, is a mirror image rather than a straight copy. Where their assumption is the classical one—"I, the satirist, am a better man than you"—his is "You, the righteous one, are no better than I am." The Augustan satirist knocks his opponent down from above; Byron lies in the mud, like a crocodile, and pulls his victim down from below. All his most direct statements, after 1816, are made in terms of irony, even burlesque. Thus, in 1820, after he had become finally identified with the cause of European liberty, he summed up his attitude in the idiom of the music hall.

> When a man has no freedom to fight at home,
> Let him combat for that of his neighbours.
> Let him think of the glories of Greece and of Rome,
> And get knocked on the head for his labours.

Once again, in this phase of his creative life, Byron's technical expedients were of the simplest. The Italian burlesque epic attracted him, as also did that previous attempt to reproduce its tone in English, that of J. H. Frere in his two poems, *Whistlecraft* and *Monks and Giants*.[2] His power of rapid assimilation was always remarkable; within a few months he had mastered the *genre*, and the new tone was fully developed.

> "England! with all thy faults I love thee still,"
>   I said at Calais, and have not forgot it;
> I like to speak and lucubrate my fill;
>   I like the government (but that is not it);
> I like the freedom of the press and quill;
>   I like the Habeas Corpus (when we've got it);
> I like a parliamentary debate,
> Particularly when 'tis not too late.
>
> I like the taxes, when they're not too many;
>   I like a seacoal fire, when not too dear;

2. In strict fact, the first attempt to acclimatize the Italian burlesque epic in English was in a poem Byron had not read, William Tennant's *Anster Fair* (1812).

I like a beef-steak, too, as well as any;
    Have no objection to a pot of beer;
I like the weather, when it is not rainy,
    That is, I like two months of every year.
And so God save the Regent, Church, and King!
Which means that I like all and every thing.

Our standing army, and disbanded seamen,
    Poor's rate, Reform, my own, the nation's debt,
Our little riots just to show we are free men,
    Our trifling bankruptcies in the Gazette,
Our cloudy climate, and our chilly women,
    All these I can forgive, and those forget,
And greatly venerate our recent glories,
And wish they were not owing to the Tories.

That is from *Beppo*. It is worth quoting a fragment to show how completely Byron was at ease with the new manner before he began the composition of *Don Juan*.

Of *Don Juan* itself there is no need to say much. With its quick changes of scene, proliferation of incident, frequent ribaldry, patches of picturesque description and continuous festal *panache*, it must be one of the very few long narrative poems that can still attract readers in an age like ours, when the long narrative poem is the deadest of all forms. It is more to our present purpose to note the profound moral seriousness which looks out now and then, especially in the descriptions of war, which Byron was inclined to regard as a murderous confidence trick played on the common man by his rulers.

There the still varying pangs, which multiply
    Until their very number makes men hard
By the infinities of agony,
    Which meet the gaze, whate'er it may regard—
The groan, the roll in dust, the all-white eye
    Turn'd back within its socket—these reward
Your rank and file by thousands, while the rest
May win perhaps a riband at the breast!

Yet I love glory:—glory's a great thing—
    Think what it is to be in your old age
Maintain'd at the expense of your good king:
    A moderate pension shakes full many a sage.
And heroes are but made for bards to sing,
    Which is still better; thus in verse to wage
Your wars eternally, besides enjoying
Half-pay for life, make mankind worth destroying.

His address to the Duke of Wellington has a deadliness which suggests that Byron had, at last, found something other than himself to be serious about:

You are "the best of cut-throats":—do not start;
 The phrase is Shakespeare's, and not misapplied:—
War's a brain-spattering, windpipe-slitting art,
 Unless her cause by right be sanctified.
If you have acted *once* a generous part,
 The world, not the world's masters, will decide,
And I shall be delighted to learn who,
Save you and yours, have gain'd by Waterloo?

I am no flatterer—you've supp'd full of flattery:
 They say you like it too—'tis no great wonder.
He whose whole life has been assault and battery,
 At last may get a little tired of thunder;
And swallowing eulogy much more than satire, he
 May like being praised for every lucky blunder,
Call'd "Saviour of the Nations"—not yet saved,
And "Europe's Liberator"—still enslaved.

I've done. Now go and dine from off the plate
 Presented by the Prince of the Brazils.
And send the sentinel before your gate
 A slice or two from your luxurious meals:
He fought, but has not fed so well of late.
 Some hunger, too, they say the people feels:—
There is no doubt that you deserve your ration,
But pray give back a little to the nation.

And so this second *persona* satisfied him for a time, releasing a vein of satire and fantasy which he had still not exhausted when he died. What he would have done when driven, finally, to relate the two, no one can know.

Byron's early death thus interrupts a story which was just approaching its denouement. Reading the lives of other romantic poets who died young, from Keats to Hart Crane, one is conscious chiefly of the pathos of that premature silence: with Byron, I, at any rate, feel a sense of annoyance, of baffled disappointment, when I get to that final scene—Missolonghi, the fever-ridden swamp, the deathbed surrounded by scared and weeping servants, the thunderstorm which burst in the moment that life departed. I feel cheated. I want to know what Byron would have *done* —as a man, and with that quick spontaneity of his, as a poet immediately afterwards—when time finally drove him into a corner and brought him face to face with the riddle of his own character. He would have done something, we know that; he was a man of action, and self-knowledge is the most decisive form of action; once Byron realized that, he would have made some decisive move. But what move, not even Professor Marchand can tell us.

Byron is very much of his time, in fact it is difficult to imagine him living in any other. He sums up so perfectly the crossroads at which European and English culture then stood. He seems fully typical in his unwillingness to go down either of the two available roads to the complete neglect of the other. If he has the color, sweep, and *brio* of romanticism, he also has the ironical appraising eye of the Augustan, together with the Augustan gift of writing a line whose content is "obvious" and which nevertheless strikes one with utterly disarming freshness ("Consents to death, but conquers agony"). One is tempted to say that he was ideally fortunate to live when he did.

I believe, however, that this would be a mistake. Every considerable artist (leaving aside the very greatest, who give the unmistakable impression of having the energy to triumph over any circumstances), strikes one as fortunate in this way. Dryden, for example, seems to us just as fortunate to have lived at the moment when classicism was closing in, as Byron does to have lived at the moment when it was opening out. He has an Elizabethan richness and fullness which we feel would have been dried out of him if he had lived fifty years later. In fact, of course, it is merely that Dryden was a good enough poet to pick up the materials nearest to hand and use them with such assurance that his work seems to have been created by its idiom, and to have cost its author nothing. Whereas, in fact, it was the work which created the idiom, and the cost to the author was no less than a lifetime's devotion.

In the same way, Byron, whose working life overlaps with those of Peacock and Jane Austen as well as Shelley, Keats, and Wordsworth, gives the impression of having been placed by chance in the very position where his full range of gifts could be employed. But one does not, in such a case, speak of chance. One speaks only, and with such perceptiveness as one can muster, of the gifts.

The work and the reader

Kenneth Burke

PSYCHOLOGY AND FORM

It is not until the fourth scene of the first act that Hamlet confronts the ghost of his father. As soon as the situation has been made clear, the audience has been, consciously or unconsciously, waiting for this ghost to appear, while in the fourth scene this moment has been definitely promised. For earlier in the play Hamlet had arranged to come to the platform at night with Horatio to meet the ghost, and it is now night, he is with Horatio and Marcellus, and they are standing on the platform. Hamlet asks Horatio the hour.

> Hor.   I think it lacks twelve.
> Mar.   No, it is struck.
> Hor.   Indeed? I heard it not: then it draws near the season
>   Wherein the spirit held his wont to walk.

Promptly hereafter there is a sound off-stage. "A flourish of tumpets, and ordnance shot off within." Hamlet's friends have established the hour as twelve. It is time for the ghost. Sounds off-stage, and of course it is not the ghost. It is, rather, the sound of the king's carousal, for the king "keeps wassail." A tricky, and useful, detail. We have been waiting for a ghost, and get, startlingly, a blare of trumpets. And, once the trumpets are silent, we feel how desolate are these three men waiting for a ghost, on a bare "platform," feel it by this sudden juxtaposition of an imagined scene of lights and merriment. But the trumpets announcing a carousal have suggested a subject of conversation. In the darkness Hamlet discusses the excessive drinking of his countrymen. He points out that it tends to harm their reputation abroad, since, he argues, this one showy vice makes their virtues "in the general censure take corruption." And for this reason, although he himself is a native of this place, he does not approve of the custom. Indeed, there in the gloom he is talking very intelligently on these matters, and Horatio answers, "Look, my Lord, it comes." All this time we had been waiting for a ghost, and it comes at the one moment which was not pointing towards it. This ghost, so assiduously prepared for, is yet a surprise. And now that the ghost

Originally published in *Counter-Statement;* Harcourt, Brace and World, Inc., New York, 1931. Second Edition, Revised: Hermes Publications, Los Altos, California, 1953.

has come, we are waiting for something further. Program: a speech from Hamlet. Hamlet must confront the ghost. Here again Shakespeare can feed well upon the use of contrast for his effects. Hamlet has just been talking in a sober, rather argumentative manner—but now the flood-gates are unloosed:

> Angels and ministers of grace defend us!
> Be thou a spirit of health or goblin damn'd,
> Bring with thee airs from heaven or blasts from hell . . .

and the transition from the matter-of-fact to the grandiose, the full-throated and full-voweled, is a second burst of trumpets, perhaps even more effective than the first, since it is the rich fulfilment of a promise. Yet this satisfaction in turn becomes an allurement, an itch for further developments. At first desiring solely to see Hamlet confront the ghost we now want Hamlet to learn from the ghost the details of the murder—which are, however, with shrewdness and husbandry, reserved for "Scene V.— Another Part of the Platform."

I have gone into this scene at some length, since it illustrates so perfectly the relationship between psychology and form, and so aptly indicates how the one is to be defined in terms of the other. That is, the psychology here is not the psychology of the *hero*, but the psychology of the *audience*. And by that distinction, form would be the psychology of the audience. Or, seen from another angle, form is the creation of an appetite in the mind of the auditor, and the adequate satisfying of that appetite. This satisfaction—so complicated is the human mechanism—at times involves a temporary set of frustrations, but in the end these frustrations prove to be simply a more involved kind of satisfaction, and furthermore serve to make the satisfaction of fulfilment more intense. If, in a work of art, the poet says something, let us say, about a meeting, writes in such a way that we desire to observe that meeting, and then, if he places that meeting before us—that is form. While obviously, that is also the psychology of the audience, since it involves desires and their appeasements.

The seeming breach between form and subject-matter, between technique and psychology, which has taken place in the last century is the result, it seems to me, of scientific criteria being unconsciously introduced into matters of purely aesthetic judgment. The flourishing of science has been so vigorous that we have not yet had time to make a spiritual readjustment adequate to the changes in our resources of material and knowledge. There are disorders of the social system which are caused solely by our undigested wealth (the basic disorder being, perhaps, the phenomenon of overproduction: to remedy this, instead of having all workers employed on half time, we have half working full time and the other half idle, so that whereas overproduction could be the greatest reward of applied science, it has been, up to now, the most menacing condition our modern civilization has had to face). It would be absurd to suppose that such social disorders would not be paralleled by disorders of culture and taste, especially since science is so pronouncedly a spiritual factor. So that we are, owing to the sudden wealth science has thrown upon us, all *nouveaux-riches* in matters of culture, and most poignantly in that field where lack of native firmness is most readily exposed, in matters of aesthetic judgment.

One of the most striking derangements of taste which science has temporarily thrown upon us involves the understanding of psychology in art. Psychology has become a body of information (which is precisely what psychology in science should be, or must be). And similarly, in art, we tend to look for psychology as the purveying of information. Thus, a contemporary writer has objected to Joyce's *Ulysses* on the ground that there are more psychoanalytic data available in Freud. (How much more drastically he might, by the same system, have destroyed Homer's *Odyssey!*) To his objection it was answered that one might, similarly, denounce Cézanne's trees in favor of state forestry bulletins. Yet are not Cézanne's landscapes themselves tainted with the psychology of information? Has he not, by perception, *pointed out* how one object lies against another, *indicated* what takes place between two colors (which is the psychology of science, and is less successful in the medium of art than in that of science, since in art such processes are at best implicit, whereas in science they are so readily made explicit)? Is Cézanne not, to that extent, a state forestry bulletin, except that he tells what goes on in the eye instead of on the tree? And do not the true values of his work lie elsewhere—and precisely in what I distinguish as the psychology of form?

Thus, the great influx of information has led the artist also to lay his emphasis on the giving of information—with the result that art tends more and more to substitute the psychology of the hero (the subject) for the psychology of the audience. Under such an attitude, when form is preserved it is preserved as an annex, a luxury, or, as some feel, a downright affectation. It remains, though sluggish, like the human appendix, for occasional demands are still made upon it; but its true vigor is gone, since it is no longer organically required. Proposition: The hypertrophy of the psychology of information is accompanied by the corresponding atrophy of the psychology of form.

In information, the matter is intrinsically interesting. And by intrinsically interesting I do not necessarily mean intrinsically valuable, as witness the intrinsic interest of backyard gossip or the most casual newspaper items. In art, at least the art of the great ages (Æschylus, Shakespeare, Racine) the matter is interesting by means of an extrinsic use, a function. Consider, for instance, the speech of Mark Antony, the "Brutus is an honourable man." Imagine in the same place a very competently developed thesis on human conduct, with statistics, intelligence tests, definitions; imagine it as the finest thing of the sort ever written, and as really being at the roots of an understanding of Brutus. Obviously, the play would simply stop until Antony had finished. For in the case of Antony's speech, the value lies in the fact that his words are shaping the future of the audience's desires, not the desires of the Roman populace, but the desires of the pit. This is the psychology of form as distinguished from the psychology of information.

The distinction is, of course, absolutely true only in its non-existent extremes. Hamlet's advice to the players, for instance, has little of the quality which distinguishes Antony's speech. It is, rather, intrinsically interesting, although one could very easily prove how the play would benefit by some such delay at this point, and that anything which made delay possible without violating the consistency of the subject would have, in this, its formal justification. It would, furthermore, be absurd to rule intrinsic interest out of literature. I wish simply to have it restored to its properly minor position, seen as merely one out of many possible elements of style. Goethe's prose, often poorly imagined, or neutral, in its line-for-line texture, especially in the treatment of romantic episode—perhaps he felt that the romantic episode in itself was enough?—is strengthened into a style possessing affirmative virtues by his rich use of aphorism. But this is, after all, but one of many possible facets of appeal. In some places, notably in *Wilhelm Meister's Lehrjahre* when Wilhelm's friends disclose the documents they have been collecting about his life unbeknown to him, the aphorisms are almost rousing in their efficacy, since they involve the story. But as a rule the appeal of aphorism is intrinsic: that is, it satisfies without being functionally related to the context.[1] . . . Also, to return to the matter of Hamlet, it must be observed that the style in this passage is no mere "information-giving" style; in its alacrity, its development, it really makes this one fragment into a kind of miniature plot.

One reason why music can stand repetition so much more sturdily than correspondingly good prose is that music, of all the arts, is by its nature least suited to the psychology of information, and has remained closer to the psychology of form. Here form cannot atrophy. Every dissonant chord cries for its solution, and whether the musician resolves or refuses to resolve this dissonance into the chord which the body cries for, he is dealing in human appetites. Correspondingly good prose, however, more prone to the temptations of pure information, cannot so much bear repetition since the æsthetic value of information is lost once that information is imparted. If one returns to such a work again it is purely because, in the chaos of modern life, he has been able to forget it. With a desire, on the other hand, its recovery is as agreeable as its discovery. One can memorize the dialogue between Hamlet and Guildenstern, where Hamlet gives Guildenstern the pipe to play on. For, once the speech is known, its repetition adds a new element to compensate for the loss of novelty. We cannot take a recurrent pleasure in the new (in formation) but we can in the natural (in form). Already, at the moment when Hamlet is holding out the pipe to Guildenstern and asking him to play upon it, we "gloat over" Hamlet's triumphal descent upon Guildenstern, when, after Guildenstern has, under increasing embarrassment, protested three times that he cannot play the instrument, Hamlet launches the retort for which all this was preparation:

"Why, look you now, how unworthy a thing you make of me. You would play upon me, you would seem to know my stops; you would pluck out the heart of my mystery; you would sound me from my lowest note to the top of my compass; and there is much music, excellent

1. Similarly, the epigram of Racine is "pure art," because it usually serves to formulate or clarify some situation within the play itself. In Goethe the epigram is most often of independent validity, as in *Die Wahlverwandtschaften*, where the ideas of Ottilie's diary are obviously carried over bodily from the author's notebook. In Shakespeare we have the union of extrinsic and intrinsic epigram, the epigram growing out of its context and yet valuable independent of its context.

voice, in this little organ, yet cannot you make it speak. 'Sblood, do you think I am easier to be played on than a pipe? Call me what instrument you will, though you can fret me, you cannot play upon me."[2]

In the opening lines we hear the promise of the close, and thus feel the emotional curve even more keenly than at first reading. Whereas in most modern art this element is underemphasized. It gives us the gossip of a plot, a plot which too often has for its value the mere fact that we do not know its outcome.[3]

Music, then, fitted less than any other art for imparting information, deals minutely in frustrations and fulfilments of desire,[4] and for that reason more often gives us those curves of emotion which, because they are natural, can bear repetition without loss. It is for this reason that music, like folk tales, is most capable of lulling us to sleep. A lullaby is a melody which comes quickly to rest, where the obstacles are easily overcome—and this is precisely the parallel to those waking dreams of struggle and conquest which (especially during childhood) we permit ourselves when falling asleep or when trying to induce sleep. Folk tales are just such waking dreams. Thus it is right that art should be called a "waking dream." The only difficulty with this definition (indicated by Charles Baudouin in his *Psychoanalysis and Æsthetics,* a very valuable study of Verhaeren) is that today we understand it to mean art as a waking dream for the artist. Modern criticism, and psychoanalysis in particular, is too prone to define the essence of art in terms of the artist's weaknesses. It is, rather, the audience which dreams, while the artist oversees the conditions which determine this dream. He is the manipulator of blood, brains, heart, and bowels which, while we sleep, dictate the mould of our desires. This is, of course, the real meaning of artistic felicity—an exaltation at the correctness of the procedure, so that we enjoy the steady march of doom in a Racinian tragedy with exactly the same equipment as that which produces our delight with Benedick's "Peace! I'll stop your mouth. *(Kisses her)"* which terminates the imbroglio of *Much Ado About Nothing.*

The methods of maintaining interest which are most natural to the psychology of information (as it is applied to works of pure art) are surprise and suspense. The method most natural to the psychology of form is eloquence. For this reason the great ages of Æschylus, Shakespeare, and Racine, dealing as they did with material which was more or less a matter of common knowledge so that the broad outlines of the plot were known in advance (while it is the broad outlines which are

2. One might indicate still further appropriateness here. As Hamlet finishes his speech, Polonius enters, and Hamlet turns to him, "God bless you, sir!" Thus the plot is continued (for Polonius is always the promise of action) and a full stop is avoided: the embarrassment laid upon Rosencranz and Guildenstern is not laid upon the audience.

3. Yet modern music has gone far in the attempt to renounce this aspect of itself. Its dissonances become static, demanding no particular resolution. And whereas an unfinished modulation by a classic musician occasions positive dissatisfaction, the refusal to resolve a dissonance in modern music does not dissatisfy us, but irritates or stimulates. Thus, "energy" takes the place of style.

4. Suspense is the least complex kind of anticipation, as surprise is the least complex kind of fulfilment.

usually exploited to secure surprise and suspense) developed formal excellence, or eloquence, as the basis of appeal in their work.

Not that there is any difference in kind between the classic method and the method of the cheapest contemporary melodrama. The drama, more than any other form, must never lose sight of its audience: here the failure to satisfy the proper requirements is most disastrous. And since certain contemporary work is successful, it follows that rudimentary laws of composition are being complied with. The distinction is one of intensity rather than of kind. The contemporary audience hears the lines of a play or novel with the same equipment as it brings to reading the lines of its daily paper. It is content to have facts placed before it in some more or less adequate sequence. Eloquence is the minimizing of this interest in fact, *per se,* so that the "more or less adequate sequence" of their presentation must be relied on to a much greater extent. Thus, those elements of surprise and suspense are subtilized, carried down into the writing of a line or a sentence, until in all its smallest details the work bristles with disclosures, contrasts, restatements with a difference, ellipses, images, aphorism, volume, sound-values, in short all that complex wealth of minutiæ which in their line-for-line aspect we call style and in their broader outlines we call form.

As a striking instance of a modern play with potentialities in which the intensity of eloquence is missing, I might cite a recent success, Capek's *R.U.R.* Here, in a melodrama which was often astonishing in the rightness of its technical procedure, when the author was finished he had written nothing but the scenario for a play by Shakespeare. It was a play in which the author produced time and again the opportunity, the demand, for eloquence, only to move on. (At other times, the most successful moments, he utilized the modern discovery of silence, with moments wherein words could not possibly serve but to detract from the effect: this we might call the "flowering" of information.) The Adam and Eve scene of the last act, a "commission" which the Shakespeare of the comedies would have loved to fill, was in the verbal barrenness of Capek's play something shameless to the point of blushing. The Robot, turned human, prompted by the dawn of love to see his first sunrise, or hear the first bird-call, and forced merely to say "Oh, see the sunrise," or "Hear the pretty birds"—here one could do nothing but wring his hands at the absence of that æsthetic mould which produced the overslung "speeches" of Romeo and Juliet.

Suspense is the concern over the possible outcome of some specific detail of plot rather than for general qualities. Thus, "Will A marry B or C?" is suspense. In *Macbeth,* the turn from the murder scene to the porter scene is a much less literal channel of development. Here the presence of one quality calls forth the demand for another, rather than one tangible incident of plot awaking an interest in some other possible tangible incident of plot. To illustrate more fully, if an author managed over a certain number of his pages to produce a feeling of sultriness or oppression, in the reader, this would unconsciously awaken in the reader the desire for a cold, fresh northwind—and thus some aspect of a northwind would be effective if called forth by some aspect of stuffiness. A good example of this is to be found in a contemporary poem, T. S. Eliot's *The Waste Land,* where the vulgar, oppressively trivial conversation in the public house calls forth in the poet a memory of a line from Shakespeare. These slobs in a public house, after a desolately low-visioned conversation, are now forced by closing time to leave the saloon. They say good-night. And suddenly the poet, feeling his release, drops into another good-night, a good-night with *désinvolture,* a good-night out of what was, within the conditions of the poem at least, a graceful and irrecoverable past.

> "Well that Sunday Albert was home, they had a hot gammon,
> And they asked me in to dinner, to get the beauty of it hot"—
> [at this point the bartender interrupts: it is closing time]
> "Goonight Bill. Goonight Lou. Goonight May. Goonight. Ta ta.
> Goonight. Goonight.
> Good-night, ladies, good-night, sweet ladies, good-night, good-night."

There is much more to be said on these lines, which I have shortened somewhat in quotation to make my issue clearer. But I simply wish to point out here that this transition is a bold juxtaposition of one quality created by another, an association in ideas which, if not logical, is nevertheless emotionally natural. In the case of *Macbeth,* similarly, it would be absurd to say that the audience, after the murder scene, wants a porter scene. But the audience does want the quality which this porter particularizes. The dramatist might, conceivably, have introduced some entirely different character or event in this place, provided only that the event produced the same quality of relationship and contrast (grotesque seriousness followed by grotesque buffoonery). . . . One of the most beautiful and satisfactory "forms" of this sort is to be found in Baudelaire's *Femmes Damnées,* where the poet, after describing the business of a Lesbian seduction, turns to the full oratory of his apostrophe:

> *"Descendez, descendez, lamentables victimes,*
> *Descendez le chemin de l'enfer éternel . . ."*

while the stylistic efficacy of this transition contains a richness which transcends all moral (or unmoral) sophistication: the efficacy of appropriateness, of exactly the natural curve in treatment. Here is morality even for the godless, since it is a morality of art, being justified, if for no other reason, by its paralleling of that staleness, that disquieting loss of purpose, which must have followed the procedure of the two characters, the *femmes damnées* themselves, a remorse which, perhaps only physical in its origin, nevertheless becomes psychic.[5]

But to return, we have made three terms synonymous: form, psychology, and eloquence. And eloquence thereby becomes the essence of art, while pity, tragedy, sweetness, humor, in short all the emotions which

---

5. As another aspect of the same subject, I could cite many examples from the fairy tale. Consider, for instance, when the hero is to spend the night in a bewitched castle. Obviously, as darkness descends, weird adventures must befall him. His bed rides him through the castle; two halves of a man challenge him to a game of nine-pins played with thigh bones and skulls. Or entirely different incidents may serve instead of these. The quality comes first, the particularization follows.

we experience in life proper, as non-artists, are simply the material on which eloquence may feed. The arousing of pity, for instance, is not the central purpose of art, although it may be an adjunct of artistic effectiveness. One can feel pity much more keenly at the sight of some actual misfortune—and it would be a great mistake to see art merely as a weak representation of some actual experience.[6] That artists today are content to write under such an æsthetic accounts in part for the inferior position which art holds in the community. Art, at least in the great periods when it has flowered, was the conversion, or transcendence, of emotion into eloquence, and was thus a factor added to life. I am reminded of St. Augustine's caricature of the theatre: that whereas we do not dare to wish people unhappy, we do want to feel sorry for them, and therefore turn to plays so that we can feel sorry although no real misery is involved. One might apply the parallel interpretation to the modern delight in happy endings, and say that we turn to art to indulge our humanitarianism in a well-wishing which we do not permit ourselves towards our actual neighbors. Surely the catharsis of art is more complicated than this, and more reputable.

Eloquence itself, as I hope to have established in the instance from *Hamlet* which I have analyzed, is no mere plaster added to a framework of more stable qualities. Eloquence is simply the end of art, and is thus its essence. Even the poorest art is eloquent, but in a poor way, with less intensity, until this aspect is obscured by others fattening upon its leanness. Eloquence is not showiness; it is, rather, the result of that desire in the artist to make a work perfect by adapting it in every minute detail to the racial appetites.

The distinction between the psychology of information and the psychology of form involves a definition of æsthetic truth. It is here precisely, to combat the deflection which the strength of science has caused to our tastes, that we must examine the essential breach between scientific and artistic truth. Truth in art is not the discovery of facts, not an addition to human knowledge in the scientific sense of the word.[7] It

6. Could not the Greek public's resistance to Euripides be accounted for in the fact that he, of the three great writers of Greek tragedy, betrayed his art, was guilty of æsthetic impiety, in that he paid more attention to the arousing of emotion *per se* than to the sublimation of emotion into eloquence?

7. One of the most striking examples of the encroachment of scientific truth into art is the doctrine of "truth by distortion," whereby one aspect of an object is suppressed the better to emphasize some other aspect; this is, obviously, an attempt to *indicate* by art some fact of knowledge, to make some implicit aspect of an object as explicit as one can by means of the comparatively dumb method of art (dumb, that is, as compared to the perfect ease with which science can indicate its discoveries). Yet science has already made discoveries in the realm of this "factual truth," this "truth by distortion" which must put to shame any artist who relies on such matter for his effects. Consider, for instance, the motion picture of a man vaulting. By photographing this process very rapidly, and running the reel very slowly, one has upon the screen the most striking set of factual truths to aid in our understanding of an athlete vaulting. Here, at our leisure, we can observe the contortions of four legs, a head and a butt. This squirming thing we saw upon the screen showed up an infinity of factual truths anent the balances of an athlete vaulting. We can, from this, observe the marvelous system of balancing which the body provides for itself in the adjustments of movement. Yet, so far as the æsthetic truth is concerned, this on the screen was not an athlete, but a squirming thing, a horror, displaying every fact of vaulting except the exhilaration of the act itself.

is, rather, the exercise of human propriety, the formulation of symbols which rigidify our sense of poise and rhythm. Artistic truth is the externalization of taste.[8] I sometimes wonder, for instance, whether the "artificial" speech of John Lyly might perhaps be "truer" than the revelations of Dostoevsky. Certainly at its best, in its feeling for a statement which returns upon itself, which attempts the systole to a diastole, it *could* be much truer than Dostoevsky.[9] And if it is not, it fails not through a mistake of Lyly's æsthetic, but because Lyly was a man poor in character, whereas Dostoevsky was rich and complex. When Swift, making the women of Brobdingnag enormous, deduces from this discrepancy between their size and Gulliver's that Gulliver could sit astride their nipples, he has written something which is æsthetically true, which is, if I may be pardoned, profoundly "proper," as correct in its Euclidean deduction as any corollary in geometry. Given the companions of Ulysses in the cave of Polyphemus, it is true that they would escape clinging to the bellies of the herd let out to pasture. St. Ambrose, detailing the habits of God's creatures, and drawing from them moral maxims for the good of mankind, St. Ambrose in his limping natural history rich in scientific inaccuracies that are at the very heart of emotional rightness, St. Ambrose writes "Of night-birds, especially of the nightingale which hatches her eggs by song; of the owl, the bat, and the cock at cock-crow; in what wise these may apply to the guidance of our habits," and in the sheer rightness of that program there is the truth of art.

In introducing this talk of night-birds, after many pages devoted to other of God's creatures, he says,

"What now! While we have been talking, you will notice how the birds of night have already started fluttering about you, and, in this same fact of warning us to leave off with our discussion, suggest thereby a further topic"—and this seems to me to contain the best wisdom of which the human frame is capable, an address, a discourse, which can make our material life seem blatant almost to the point of despair. And when the cock crows, and the thief abandons his traps, and the sun lights up, and we are in every way called back to God by the well-meaning admonition of this bird, here the very blindnesses of religion become the deepest truths of art.

8. The procedure of science involves the elimination of taste, employing as a substitute the corrective norm of the pragmatic test, the empirical experiment, which is entirely intellectual. Those who oppose the "intellectualism" of critics like Matthew Arnold are involved in an hilarious blunder, for Arnold's entire approach to the appreciation of art is through delicacies of taste intensified to the extent almost of squeamishness.

9. As for instance, the "conceit" of Endymion's awakening, when he forgets his own name, yet recalls that of his beloved.

The work and its age: I

Charles Lamb

ON THE ARTIFICIAL COMEDY OF THE LAST CENTURY

The artificial Comedy, or Comedy of manners, is quite extinct on our stage. Congreve and Farquhar show their heads once in seven years only, to be exploded and put down instantly. The times cannot bear them. Is it for a few wild speeches, an occasional license of dialogue? I think not altogether. The business of their dramatic characters will not stand the moral test. We screw every thing up to that. Idle gallantry in a fiction, a dream, the passing pageant of an evening, startles us in the same way as the alarming indications of profligacy in a son or ward in real life should startle a parent or guardian. We have no such middle emotions as dramatic interests left. We see a stage libertine playing his loose pranks of two hours' duration, and of no after consequence, with the severe eyes which inspect real vices with their bearings upon two worlds. We are spectators to a plot or intrigue (not reducible in life to the point of strict morality) and take it all for truth. We substitute a real for a dramatic person, and judge him accordingly. We try him in our courts, from which there is no appeal to the *dramatis personæ*, his peers. We have been spoiled with—not sentimental comedy—but a tyrant far more pernicious to our pleasures which has succeeded to it, the exclusive and all devouring drama of common life; where the moral point is every thing; where, instead of the fictitious half-believed person-ages of the stage (the phantoms of old comedy) we recognise ourselves, our brothers, aunts, kinsfolk, allies, patrons, enemies,—the same as in life,—with an interest in what is going on so hearty and substantial, that we cannot afford our moral judgment, in its deepest and most vital results, to compromise or slumber for a moment. What is *there* transacting, by no modification is made to affect us in any other man-ner than the same events or characters would do in our relationships of life. We carry our fire-side concerns to the theatre with us. We do not go thither, like our ancestors, to escape from the pressure of reality, so much as to confirm our experience of it; to make assurance double, and take a bond of fate. We must live our toilsome lives twice over, as it was the mournful privilege of Ulysses to descend twice to the

Excerpt from "On the Artificial Comedy of the Last Century," Charles Lamb.

shades. All that neutral ground of character, which stood between vice and virtue; or which in fact was indifferent to neither, where neither properly was called in question; that happy breathing-place from the burthen of a perpetual moral questioning—the sanctuary and quiet Alsatia of hunted casuistry—is broken up and disfranchised, as injurious to the interests of society. The privileges of the place are taken away by law. We dare not dally with images, or names, of wrong. We bark like foolish dogs at shadows. We dread infection from the scenic representation of disorder; and fear a painted pustule. In our anxiety that our morality should not take cold, we wrap it up in a great blanket surtout of precaution against the breeze and sunshine.

I confess for myself that (with no great delinquencies to answer for) I am glad for a season to take an airing beyond the diocese of the strict conscience,—not to live always in the precincts of the law-courts,—but now and then, for a dream-while or so, to imagine a world with no meddling restrictions—to get into recesses, whither the hunter cannot follow me—

> ——————Secret shades
> Of woody Ida's inmost grove,
> While yet there was no fear of Jove—

I come back to my cage and my restraint the fresher and more healthy for it. I wear my shackles more contentedly for having respired the breath of an imaginary freedom. I do not know how it is with others, but I feel the better always for the perusal of one of Congreve's—nay, why should I not add even of Wycherley's—comedies. I am the gayer at least for it; and I could never connect those sports of a witty fancy in any shape with any result to be drawn from them to imitation in real life. They are a world of themselves almost as much as fairy-land. Take one of their characters, male or female (with few exceptions they are alike), and place it in a modern play, and my virtuous indignation shall rise against the profligate wretch as warmly as the Catos of the pit could desire; because in a modern play I am to judge of the right and the wrong. The standard of *police* is the measure of *political justice*. The atmosphere will blight it, it cannot live here. It has got into a moral world, where it has no business, from which it must needs fall headlong; as dizzy, and incapable of making a stand, as a Swedenborgian bad spirit that has wandered unawares into the sphere of one of his Good Men, or Angels. But in its own world do we feel the creature is so very bad?—The Fainalls and the Mirabels, the Dorimants and the Lady Touchwoods, in their own sphere, do not offend my moral sense; in fact they do not appeal to it at all. They seem engaged in their proper element. They break through no laws, or conscientious restraints. They know of none. They have got out of Christendom into the land—what shall I call it?—of cuckoldry—the Utopia of gallantry, where pleasure is duty, and the manners perfect freedom. It is altogether a speculative scene of things, which has no reference whatever to the world that is. No good person can be justly offended as a spectator, because no good person suffers on the stage. Judged morally, every character in these plays—the few exceptions only are *mistakes*—is alike essentially vain and worthless. The great art of Congreve is especially shown in this, that he has entirely excluded from his scenes,—some little generosities in the part of Angelica perhaps excepted,—not only any thing like a faultless character, but any pretensions to goodness or good feelings whatsoever. Whether he did this designedly, or instinctively, the effect is as happy, as the design (if design) was bold. I used to wonder at the strange power which his Way of the World in particular possesses of interesting you all along in the pursuits of characters, for whom you absolutely care nothing—for you neither hate nor love his personages—and I think it is owing to this very indifference for any, that you endure the whole. He has spread a privation of moral light, I will call it, rather than by the ugly name of palpable darkness, over his creations, and his shadows flit before you without distinction or preference. Had he introduced a good character, a single gush of moral feeling, a revulsion of the judgment to actual life and actual duties, the impertinent Goshen would have only lighted to the discovery of deformities, which now are none, because we think them none.

Translated into real life, the characters of his, and his friend Wycherley's dramas, are profligates and strumpets,—the business of their brief existence, the undivided pursuit of lawless gallantry. No other spring of action, or possible motive of conduct, is recognized; principles which, universally acted upon, must reduce this frame of things to a chaos. But we do them wrong in so translating them. No such effects are produced in *their* world. When we are among them, we are amongst a chaotic people. We are not to judge them by our usages. No reverend institutions are insulted by their proceedings,—for they have none among them. No peace of families is violated,—for no family ties exist among them. No purity of the marriage bed is stained,—for none is supposed to have a being. No deep affections are disquieted,—no holy wedlock bands are snapped asunder,—for affection's depth and wedded faith are not of the growth of that soil. There is neither right nor wrong,—gratitude or its opposite,—claim or duty,—paternity or sonship. Of what consequence is it to virtue, or how is she at all concerned about it, whether Sir Simon, or Dapperwit, steal away Miss Martha; or who is the father of Lord Froth's, or Sir Paul Pliant's children.

The whole is a passing pageant, where we should sit as unconcerned at the issues, for life or death, as at a battle of the frogs and mice. But, like Don Quixote, we take part against the puppets, and quite as impertinently. We dare not contemplate an Atlantis, a scheme, out of which our coxcombical moral sense is for a little transitory ease excluded. We have not the courage to imagine a state of things for which there is neither reward nor punishment. We cling to the painful necessities of shame and blame. We would indict our very dreams.

The work and its age: II

T. B. Macaulay

THE DRAMATIC WORKS OF
WYCHERLEY, CONGREVE, VANBRUGH AND FARQUHAR

The whole liberal education of our countrymen is conducted on the principle, that no book which is valuable, either by reason of the excellence of its style, or by reason of the light which it throws on the history, polity, and manners of nations, should be withheld from the student on account of its impurity. The *Athenian Comedies,* in which there are scarcely a hundred lines together without some passage of which Rochester would have been ashamed, have been reprinted at the Pitt Press, and the Clarendon Press, under the direction of Syndics, and delegates appointed by the Universities, and have been illustrated with notes by reverend, very reverend, and right reverend commentators. Every year the most distinguished young men in the kingdom are examined by bishops and professors of divinity in such works as the *Lysistrata* of Aristophanes and the *Sixth Satire* of Juvenal. There is certainly something a little ludicrous in the idea of a conclave of venerable fathers of the Church praising and rewarding a lad on account of his intimate acquaintance with writings compared with which the loosest tale in Prior is modest. But, for our own part, we have no doubt that the greatest societies which direct the education of the English gentry have herein judged wisely. It is unquestionable that an extensive acquaintance with ancient literature enlarges and enriches the mind. It is unquestionable that a man whose mind has been thus enlarged and enriched is likely to be far more useful to the State and to the Church than one who is unskilled or little skilled, in classical learning. On the other hand, we find it difficult to believe that, in a world so full of temptation as this, any gentleman whose life would have been virtuous if he had not read Aristophanes and Juvenal will be made vicious by reading them. A man who, exposed to all the influences of such a state of society as that in which we live, is yet afraid of exposing himself to the influences of a few Greek or Latin verses, acts, we think, much like the felon who begged the sheriffs to let him have an umbrella held over his head from the door of Newgate to the gallows, because it was a drizzling morning, and he was apt to take cold.

Excerpts from "The Dramatic Works of Wycherley, Congreve, Vanbrugh and Farquhar," *Edinburgh Review,* LXII (1841).

The virtue which the world wants is a healthful virtue, not a valetudinarian virtue, a virtue which can expose itself to the risks inseparable from all spirited exertion, not a virtue which keeps out of the common air for fear of infection, and eschews the common food as too stimulating. It would be indeed absurd to attempt to keep men from acquiring those qualifications which fit them to play their part in life with honour to themselves and advantage to their country, for the sake of preserving a delicacy which cannot be preserved, a delicacy which a walk from Westminster to the Temple is sufficient to destroy.

But we should be justly chargeable with gross inconsistency if, while we defend the policy which invites the youth of our country to study such writers as Theocritus and Catullus, we were to set up a cry against a new edition of the *Country Wife* or the *Way of the World*. The immoral English writers of the seventeenth century are indeed much less excusable than those of Greece and Rome. But the worst English writings of the seventeenth century are decent, compared with much that has been bequeathed to us by Greece and Rome. Plato, we have little doubt, was a much better man than Sir George Etherege. But Plato has written things at which Sir George Etherege would have shuddered. Buckhurst and Sedley, even in those wild orgies at the Cock in Bow Street for which they were pelted by the rabble and fined by the Court of King's Bench, would never have dared to hold such discourse as passed between Socrates and Phædrus on that fine summer day under the plane-tree, while the fountain warbled at their feet, and the cicadas chirped overhead. If it be, as we think it is, desirable that an English gentleman should be well informed touching the government and the manners of little commonwealths which both in place and time are far removed from us, whose independence has been more than two thousand years extinguished, whose language has not been spoken for ages, and whose ancient magnificence is attested only by a few broken columns and friezes, much more must it be desirable that he should be intimately acquainted with the history of the public mind of his own country, and with the causes, the nature, and the extent of those revolutions of opinion and feeling which, during the last two centuries, have alternately raised and depressed the standard of our national morality. And knowledge of this sort is to be very sparingly gleaned from Parliamentary debates, from State papers, and from the works of grave historians. It must either not be acquired at all, or it must be acquired by the perusal of the light literature which has at various periods been fashionable. We are therefore by no means disposed to condemn this publication, though we certainly cannot recommend the handsome volume before us as an appropriate Christmas present for young ladies.

We have said that we think the present publication perfectly justifiable. But we can by no means agree with Mr. Leigh Hunt, who seems to hold that there is little or no ground for the charge of immorality so often brought against the literature of the Restoration. We do not blame him for not bringing to the judgment-seat the merciless rigour of Lord Angelo; but we really think that such flagitious and impudent offenders as those who are now at the bar deserved at least the gentle rebuke of Escalus. Mr. Leigh Hunt treats the whole matter a little too much in the easy style of Lucio; and perhaps his exceeding lenity disposes us to be somewhat too severe.

And yet it is not easy to be too severe. For in truth this part of our literature is a disgrace to our language and our national character. It is clever, indeed, and very entertaining; but it is, in the most emphatic sense of the words, "earthly, sensual, devilish." Its indecency, though perpetually such as is condemned not less by the rules of good taste than by those of morality, is not, in our opinion, so disgraceful a fault as its singularly inhuman spirit. We have here Belial, not as when he inspired Ovid and Ariosto, "graceful and humane," but with the iron eye and cruel sneer of Mephistopheles. We find ourselves in a world, in which the ladies are like very profligate, impudent and unfeeling men, and in which the men are too bad for any place but Pandæmonium or Norfolk Island. We are surrounded by foreheads of bronze, hearts like the nether millstone, and tongues set on fire of hell.

Dryden defended or excused his own offences and those of his contemporaries by pleading the example of the earlier English dramatists; and Mr. Leigh Hunt seems to think there is force in the plea. We altogether differ from this opinion. The crime charged is not mere coarseness of expression. The terms which are delicate in one age become gross in the next. The diction of the English version of the Pentateuch is sometimes such as Addison would not have ventured to imitate; and Addison, the standard of moral purity in his own age, used many phrases which are now proscribed. Whether a thing shall be designated by a plain noun-substantive or by a circumlocution is mere matter of fashion. Morality is not at all interested in the question. But morality is deeply interested in this, that what is immoral shall not be presented to the imagination of the young and susceptible in constant connection with what is attractive. For every person who has observed the operation of the law of association in his own mind and in the minds of others knows that whatever is constantly presented to the imagination in connection with what is attractive will itself become attractive. There is undoubtedly a great deal of indelicate writing in Fletcher and Massinger, and more than might be wished even in Ben Jonson and Shakspeare, who are comparatively pure. But it is impossible to trace in their plays any systematic attempt to associate vice with those things which men value most and desire most, and virtue with every thing ridiculous and degrading. And such a systematic attempt we find in the whole dramatic literature of the generation which followed the return of Charles the Second. We will take, as an instance of what we mean, a single subject of the highest importance to the happiness of mankind, conjugal fidelity. We can at present hardly call to mind a single English play, written before the civil war, in which the character of a seducer of married women is represented in a favourable light. We remember many plays in which such persons are baffled, exposed, covered with derision, and insulted by triumphant husbands. Such is the fate of Falstaff, with all his wit and knowledge of the world. Such is the fate of Brisac in Fletcher's *Elder Brother,* and of Ricardo and Ubaldo in Massinger's *Picture.* Sometimes, as in the *Fatal Dowry* and *Love's Cruelty,* the outraged honour of families is repaired by a bloody revenge. If now and then the lover is represented as an accomplished man, and the husband as a person of weak or odious character, this only makes the triumph of female virtue the more signal, as in Johnson's Celia and Mrs. Fitzdottrel, and in Fletcher's Maria. In general we will venture to say that the dramatists of the age of Elizabeth and James the First either treat the breach of the marriage-vow as a serious crime, or, if they treat it as matter for laughter, turn the laugh against the gallant.

On the contrary, during the forty years which followed the Restoration, the whole body of the dramatists invariably represent adultery, we do not say as a peccadillo, we do not say as an error which the violence of passion may excuse, but as the calling of a fine gentleman, as a grace without which his character would be imperfect. It is as essential to his breeding and to his place in society that he should make love to the wives of his neighbours as that he should know French, or that he should have a sword at his side. In all this there is no passion, and scarcely anything that can be called preference. The hero intrigues just as he wears a wig; because, if he did not, he would be a queer fellow, a city prig, perhaps a Puritan. All the agreeable qualities are always given to the gallant. All the contempt and aversion are the portion of the unfortunate husband. Take Dryden for example; and compare Woodall with Brainsick, or Lorenzo with Gomez. Take Wycherley; and compare Horner with Pinchwife. Take Vanbrugh; and compare Constant with Sir John Brute. Take Farquhar; and compare Archer with Squire Sullen. Take Congreve; and compare Bellmour with Fondlewife, Careless with Sir Paul Plyant, or Scandal with Foresight. In all these cases, and in many more which might be named, the dramatist evidently does his best to make the person who commits the injury graceful, sensible, and spirited, and the person who suffers it a fool, or a tyrant, or both.

Mr. Charles Lamb, indeed, attempted to set up a defence for this way of writing. The dramatists of the latter part of the seventeenth century are not, according to him, to be tried by the standard of morality which exists, and ought to exist, in real life. Their world is a conventional world. Their heroes and heroines belong, not to England, not to Christendom, but to an Utopia of gallantry, to a Fairyland, where the Bible and Burn's Justice are unknown, where a prank which on this earth would be rewarded with the pillory is merely matter for a peal of elvish laughter. A real Horner, a real Careless, would, it is admitted, be exceedingly bad men. But to predicate morality or immorality of the Horner of Wycherley and the Careless of Congreve is as absurd as it would be to arraign a sleeper for his dreams. "They belong to the regions of pure comedy, where no cold moral reigns. When we are among them we are among a chaotic people. We are not to judge them by our usages. No reverend institutions are insulted by their proceedings, for they have none among them. No peace of families is violated, for no family ties exist among them. There is neither right nor wrong, gratitude or its opposite, claim or duty, paternity or sonship."

This is, we believe, a fair summary of Mr. Lamb's doctrine. We are sure that we do not wish to represent him unfairly. For we admire his genius; we love the kind nature which appears in all his writings; and we cherish his memory as much as if we had known him personally. But we must plainly say that his argument, though ingenious, is altogether sophistical.

Of course we perfectly understand that it is possible for a writer to create a conventional world in which things forbidden by the Decalogue and the Statute Book shall be lawful, and yet that the exhibition may be harmless, or even edifying. For example, we suppose that the most austere critics would not accuse Fénelon of impiety and immorality on account of his *Telemachus* and his *Dialogues of the Dead*. In *Telemachus* and the *Dialogues of the Dead* we have a false religion, and consequently a morality which is in some points incorrect. We have a right and a wrong differing from the right and the wrong of real life. It is represented as the first duty of men to pay honour to Jove and Minerva. Philocles, who employs his leisure in making graven images of these deities, is extolled for his piety in a way which contrasts singularly with the expressions of Isaiah on the same subject. The dead are judged by Minos, and rewarded with lasting happiness for actions which Fénelon would have been the first to pronounce splendid sins. The same may be said of Mr. Southey's Mahommedan and Hindoo heroes and heroines. In *Thalaba*, to speak in derogation of the Arabian impostor is blasphemy: to drink wine is a crime: to perform ablutions and to pay honour to the holy cities are works of merit. In the *Curse of Kehama*, Kailyal is commended for her devotion to the statue of Mariataly, the goddess of the poor. But certainly no person will accuse Mr. Southey of having promoted or intended to promote either Islamism or Brahminism.

It is easy to see why the conventional worlds of Fénelon and Mr. Southey are unobjectionable. In the first place, they are utterly unlike the real world in which we live. The state of society, the laws even of the physical world, are so different from those with which we are familiar, that we cannot be shocked at finding the morality also very different. But in truth the morality of these conventional worlds differs from the morality of the real world only in points where there is no danger that the real world will ever go wrong. The generosity and docility of Telemachus, the fortitude, the modesty, the filial tenderness of Kailyal, are virtues of all ages and nations. And there was very little danger that the Dauphin would worship Minerva, or that an English damsel would dance, with a bucket on her head, before the statue of Mariataly.

The case is widely different with what Mr. Charles Lamb calls the conventional world of Wycherley and Congreve. Here the garb, the manners, the topics of conversation are those of the real town and of the passing day. The hero is in all superficial accomplishments exactly the fine gentleman whom every youth in the pit would gladly resemble. The heroine is the fine lady whom every youth in the pit would gladly marry. The scene is laid in some place which is as well known to the audience as their own houses, in St. James's Park, or Hyde Park, or Westminster Hall. The lawyer bustles about with his bag, between the Common Pleas and the Exchequer. The Peer calls for his carriage to go to the House of Lords on a private bill. A hundred little touches are employed to make the fictitious world appear like the actual world. And the immorality is of a sort which never can be out of date, and which all the force of religion, law, and public opinion united can but imperfectly restrain.

In the name of art, as well as in the name of virtue, we protest against the principle that the world of pure comedy is one into which no moral enters. If comedy be an imitation, under whatever conventions, of real life, how is it possible that it can have no reference to the great rule which directs life, and to feelings which are called forth by every incident of life? If what Mr. Charles Lamb says were correct, the inference would be that these dramatists did not in the least understand the very first principles of their craft. Pure landscape-painting into which no light or shade enters, pure portrait-painting into which no expression enters, are phrases less at variance with sound criticism than pure comedy into which no moral enters.

But it is not the fact that the world of these dramatists is a world into which no moral enters. Morality constantly enters into that world, a sound morality, and an unsound morality; the sound morality to be insulted, derided, associated with everything mean and hateful; the unsound morality to be set off to every advantage, and inculcated by all methods, direct and indirect. It is not the fact that none of the inhabitants of this conventional world feel reverence for sacred institutions and family ties. Fondlewife, Pinchwife, every person in short of narrow understanding and disgusting manners, expresses that reverence strongly. The heroes and heroines, too, have a moral code of their own, an exceedingly bad one, but not, as Mr. Charles Lamb seems to think, a code existing only in the imagination of dramatists. It is, on the contrary, a code actually received and obeyed by great numbers of people. We need not go to Utopia or Fairyland to find them. They are near at hand. Every night some of them cheat at the hells in the Quadrant, and others pace the Piazza in Covent Garden. Without flying to Nephelococcygia or to the Court of Queen Mab, we can meet with sharpers, bullies, hard-hearted impudent debauchees, and women worthy of such paramours. The morality of the *Country Wife* and the *Old Bachelor* is the morality, not, as Mr. Charles Lamb maintains, of an unreal world, but of a world which is a great deal too real. It is the morality, not of a chaotic people, but of low town-rakes, and of those ladies whom the newspapers call "dashing Cyprians." And the question is simply this, whether a man of genius who constantly and systematically endeavours to make this sort of character attractive, by uniting it with beauty, grace, dignity, spirit, a high social position, popularity, literature, wit, taste, knowledge of the world, brilliant success in every undertaking, does or does not make an ill use of his powers. We own that we are unable to understand how this question can be answered in any way but one.

It must, indeed, be acknowledged, in justice to the writers of whom we have spoken thus severely, that they were to a great extent the creatures of their age. And if it be asked why that age encouraged immorality which no other age would have tolerated, we have no hesitation in answering that this great depravation of the national taste was the effect of the prevalence of Puritanism under the Commonwealth.

To punish public outrages on morals and religion is unquestionably within the competence of rulers. But when a government, not content with requiring decency, requires sanctity, it oversteps the bounds which mark its proper functions. And it may be laid down as a universal rule that a government which attempts more than it ought will perform less. A lawgiver who, in order to protect distressed borrowers, limits the rate of interest, either makes it impossible for the objects of his care to borrow at all, or places them at the mercy of the worst class of usurers. A lawgiver who, from tenderness for labouring men, fixes the hours of their work and the amount of their wages, is certain to make them far more wretched than he found them. And so a government which, not content with repressing scandalous excesses, demands from its subjects fervent and austere piety, will soon discover that, while attempting to render an impossible service to the cause of virtue, it has in truth only promoted vice.

For what are the means by which a government can effect its ends? Two only, reward and punishment; powerful means, indeed, for influencing the exterior act, but altogether impotent for the purpose of touching the heart. A public functionary who is told that he will be promoted if he is a devout Catholic, and turned out of his place if he is not, will probably go to mass every morning, exclude meat from his table on Fridays, shrive himself regularly, and perhaps let his superiors know that he wears a hair shirt next his skin. Under a Puritan government, a person who is apprised that piety is essential to thriving in the world will be strict in the observance of the Sunday, or, as he will call it, Sabbath, and will avoid a theatre as if it were plague-stricken. Such a show of religion as this the hope of gain and the fear of loss will produce, at a week's notice, in any abundance which a government may require. But under this show, sensuality, ambition, avarice, and hatred retain unimpaired power, and the seeming convert has only added to the vices of a man of the world all the still darker vices which are engendered by the constant practice of dissimulation. The truth cannot be long concealed. The public discovers that the grave persons who are proposed to it as patterns are more utterly destitute of moral principle and of moral sensibility than avowed libertines. It sees that these Pharisees are farther removed from real goodness than publicans and harlots. And, as usual, it rushes to the extreme opposite to that which it quits. It considers a high religious profession as a sure mark of meanness and depravity. On the very first day on which the restraint of fear is taken away, and on which men can venture to say what they think, a frightful peal of blasphemy and ribaldry proclaims that the short-sighted policy which aimed at making a nation of saints has made a nation of scoffers.

It was thus in France about the beginning of the eighteenth century. Lewis the Fourteenth in his old age became religious: he determined that his subjects should be religious too: he shrugged his shoulders and knitted his brows if he observed at his levee or near his dinner-table any gentleman who neglected the duties enjoined by the Church, and rewarded piety with blue ribands, invitations to Marli, governments, pensions, and regiments. Forthwith Versailles became, in everything but dress, a convent. The pulpits and confessionals were surrounded by swords and embroidery. The Marshals of France were much in prayer; and there was hardly one among the Dukes and Peers who did not carry good little books in his pocket, fast during Lent, and communicate at Easter. Madame de Maintenon, who had a great share in the blessed work, boasted that devotion had become quite the fashion. A fashion indeed it was; and like a fashion it passed away. No sooner had the old king been carried to St. Denis than the whole Court unmasked. Every man hastened to indemnify himself by the excess of licentiousness and impudence, for years of mortification. The same persons who, a few months before, with meek voices and demure looks, had consulted divines about the state of their souls, now surrounded the midnight table where, amidst the bounding of champagne corks, a drunken prince, enthroned between Dubois and Madame de Parabère, hiccoughed out atheistical arguments and obscene jests. The early part of the reign of Lewis the Fourteenth had been a time of licence; but the most dissolute men of that generation would have blushed at the orgies of the Regency.

It was the same with our fathers in the time of the Great Civil War. We are by no means unmindful of the great debt which mankind owes to the Puritans of that time, the deliverers of England, the founders of the American Commonwealths. But in the day of their power, those men committed one great fault, which left deep and lasting traces in the national character and manners. They mistook the end and overrated the force of government. They determined, not merely to protect religion and public morals from insult, an object for which the civil sword, in discreet hands, may be beneficially employed, but to make the people committed to their rule truly devout. Yet, if they had only reflected on events which they had themselves witnessed and in which they had themselves borne a great part, they would have seen what was likely to be the result of their enterprise. They had lived under a government which, during a long course of years, did all that could be done, by lavish bounty and by rigorous punishment, to enforce conformity to the doctrine and discipline of the Church of England. No person suspected of hostility to that Church had the smallest chance of obtaining favour at the Court of Charles. Avowed dissent was punished by imprisonment, by ignominious exposure, by cruel mutilations, and by ruinous fines. And the event had been that the Church had fallen, and had, in its fall, dragged down with it a monarchy which had stood six hundred years. The Puritan might have learned, if from nothing else, yet from his own recent victory, that governments which attempt things beyond their reach are likely not merely to fail, but to produce an effect directly the opposite of that which they contemplate as desirable.

All this was overlooked. The saints were to inherit the earth. The theatres were closed. The fine arts were placed under absurd restraints. Vices which had never before been even misdemeanours were made capital felonies. It was solemnly resolved by Parliament "that no person shall be employed but such as the House shall be satisfied of his real godliness." The pious assembly had a Bible lying on the table for reference. If they had consulted it they might have learned that the wheat and the tares grow together inseparably, and must either be spared together or rooted up together. To know whether a man was really godly was impossible. But it was easy to know whether he had a plain dress, lank hair, no starch in his linen, no gay furniture in his house; whether he talked through his nose, and showed the whites of his eyes; whether he named his children Assurance, Tribulation, Mahershalal-hash-baz; whether he avoided Spring Garden when in town, and abstained from hunting and hawking when in the country; whether he expounded hard scriptures to his troop of dragoons, and talked in a committee of ways and means about seeking the Lord. These were tests which could easily be applied. The misfortune was that they were tests which proved nothing. Such as they were, they were employed by the dominant party. And the consequence was that a crowd of impostors, in every walk of life, began to mimic and to caricature what were then regarded as the outward signs of sanctity. The nation was not duped. The restraints of that gloomy time were such as would have been impatiently borne, if imposed by men who were universally believed to be saints. Those restraints became altogether insupportable when they were known to be kept up for the profit of hypocrites. It is quite certain that, even if the royal family had never returned, even if Richard Cromwell or Henry Cromwell had been at the head of the administration, there would have been a great relaxation of manners. Before the Restoration many signs indicated that a period of licence was at hand. The Restoration crushed for a time the Puritan party, and placed supreme power in the hands of a libertine. The political counter-revolution assisted the moral counter-revolution, and was in turn assisted by it. A period of wild and desperate dissoluteness followed. Even in remote manor-houses and hamlets the change was in some degree felt; but in London the outbreak of debauchery was appalling; and in London the places most deeply infected were the Palace, the quarters inhabited by the aristocracy, and the Inns of Court. It was on the support of these parts of the town that the playhouses depended. The character of the drama became conformed to the character of its patrons. The comic poet was the mouthpiece of the most deeply corrupted part of a corrupted society. And in the plays before us we find, distilled and condensed, the essential spirit of the fashionable world during the anti-Puritan reaction.

The Puritan had affected formality; the comic poet laughed at decorum. The Puritan had frowned at innocent diversions; the comic poet took under his patronage the most flagitious excesses. The Puritan had canted; the comic poet blasphemed. The Puritan had made an affair of gallantry felony without benefit of clergy; the comic poet represented it as an honourable distinction. The Puritan spoke with disdain of the low standard of popular morality; his life was regulated by a far more rigid code; his virtue was sustained by motives unknown to men of the world. Unhappily it had been amply proved in many cases, and might well be suspected in many more, that these high pretensions were unfounded. Accordingly, the fashionable circles, and the comic poets who were the spokesmen of those circles, took up the notion that all professions of piety and integrity were to be construed by the rule of contrary; that it might well be doubted whether there was such a thing as virtue in the world; but that, at all events, a person who affected to be better than his neighbours was sure to be a knave.

In the old drama there had been much that was reprehensible. But whoever compares even the least decorous plays of Fletcher with those contained in the volume before us will see how much the profligacy which follows a period of overstrained austerity goes beyond the profligacy which precedes such a period. The nation resembled the demoniac in the New Testament. The Puritans boasted that the unclean spirit was cast out. The house was empty, swept, and garnished; and for a time the expelled tenant wandered through dry places seeking rest and finding none. But the force of the exorcism was spent. The fiend returned to his abode; and returned not alone. He took to him seven other spirits more wicked than himself. They entered in, and dwelt together; and the second possession was worse than the first.

The work and tradition

T. S. Eliot

TRADITION AND THE INDIVIDUAL TALENT

In English writing we seldom speak of tradition, though we occasionally apply its name in deploring its absence. We cannot refer to "the tradition" or to "a tradition"; at most, we employ the adjective in saying that the poetry of So-and-so is "traditional" or even "too traditional." Seldom, perhaps, does the word appear except in a phrase of censure. If otherwise, it is vaguely approbative, with the implication, as to the work approved, of some pleasing archaeological reconstruction. You can hardly make the word agreeable to English ears without this comfortable reference to the reassuring science of archaeology.

Certainly the word is not likely to appear in our appreciations of living or dead writers. Every nation, every race, has not only its own creative, but its own critical turn of mind; and is even more oblivious of the shortcomings and limitations of its critical habits than of those of its creative genius. We know, or think we know, from the enormous mass of critical writing that has appeared in the French language the critical method or habit of the French; we only conclude (we are such unconscious people) that the French are "more critical" than we, and sometimes even plume ourselves a little with the fact, as if the French were the less spontaneous. Perhaps they are; but we might remind ourselves that criticism is as inevitable as breathing, and that we should be none the worse for articulating what passes in our minds when we read a book and feel an emotion about it, for criticizing our own minds in their work of criticism. One of the facts that might come to light in this process is our tendency to insist, when we praise a poet, upon those aspects of his work in which he least resembles any one else. In these aspects or parts of his work we pretend to find what is individual, what is the peculiar essence of the man. We dwell with satisfaction upon the poet's difference from his predecessors, especially his immediate predecessors; we endeavour to find something that can be isolated in order to be enjoyed. Whereas if we approach a poet without this prejudice we shall often find that not only the best, but the most individual parts of his work may be those in which the dead poets, his ancestors, assert their immortality most vigorously. And I do not mean the impressionable period of adolescence, but the period of full maturity.

Yet if the only form of tradition, of handing down, consisted in following the ways of the immediate generation before us in a blind or timid adherence to its successes, "tradition" should positively be discouraged. We have seen many such simple currents soon lost in the sand; and novelty is better than repetition. Tradition is a matter of much wider significance. It cannot be inherited, and if you want it you must obtain it by great labour. It involves, in the first place, the historical sense, which we may call nearly indispensable to any one who would continue to be a poet beyond his twenty-fifth year; and the historical sense involves a perception, not only of the pastness of the past, but of its presence; the historical sense compels a man to write not merely with his own generation in his bones, but with a feeling that the whole of the literature of Europe from Homer and within it the whole of the literature of his own country has a simultaneous existence and composes a simultaneous order. This historical sense, which is a sense of the timeless as well as of the temporal and of the timeless and of the temporal together, is what makes a writer traditional. And it is at the same time what makes a writer most acutely conscious of his place in time, of his own contemporaneity.

No poet, no artist of any art, has his complete meaning alone. His significance, his appreciation is the appreciation of his relation to the dead poets and artists. You cannot value him alone; you must set him, for contrast and comparison, among the dead. I mean this as a principle of aesthetic, not merely historical, criticism. The necessity that he shall conform, that he shall cohere, is not onesided; what happens when a new work of art is created is something that happens simultaneously to all the works of art which preceded it. The existing monuments form an ideal order among themselves, which is modified by the introduction of the new (the really new) work of art among them. The existing order is complete before the new work arrives; for order to persist after the supervention of novelty, the *whole* existing order must be, if ever so slightly, altered; and so the relations, proportions, values of each work of art toward the whole are readjusted; and this is conformity between the old and the new. Whoever has approved this idea of order, of the form of European, of English literature will not find it preposterous that the past should be altered by the present as much as the present is directed by the past. And the poet who is aware of this will be aware of great difficulties and responsibilities.

In a peculiar sense he will be aware also that he must inevitably be judged by the standards of the past. I say judged, not amputated, by them; not judged to be as good as, or worse or better than, the dead; and certainly not judged by the canons of dead critics. It is a judgment, a comparison, in which two things are measured by each other. To conform merely would be for the new work not really to conform at all; it would not be new, and would therefore not be a work of art. And we do not quite say that the new is more valuable because it fits in; but its fitting in is a test of its value—a test, it is true, which can only be slowly and cautiously applied, for we are none of us infallible judges of conformity. We say: it appears to conform, and is perhaps individual, or it appears individual, and may conform; but we are hardly likely to find that it is one and not the other.

To proceed to a more intelligible exposition of the relation of the poet to the past: he can neither take the past as a lump, an indiscriminate bolus, nor can he form himself wholly on one or two private admirations, nor can he form himself wholly upon one preferred period. The first course is inadmissible, the second is an important experience of youth, and the third is a pleasant and highly desirable supplement. The poet must be very conscious of the main current, which does not at all flow invariably through the most distinguished reputations. He must be quite aware of the obvious fact that art never improves, but that the material of art is never quite the same. He must be aware that the mind of Europe—the mind of his own country—a mind which he learns in time to be much more important than his own private mind—is a mind which changes, and that this change is a development which abandons nothing *en route,* which does not superannuate either Shakespeare, or Homer, or the rock drawing of the Magdalenian draughtsmen. That this development, refinement perhaps, complication certainly, is not from the point of view of the artist, any improvement. Perhaps not even an improvement from the point of view of the psychologist or not to the extent which we imagine; perhaps only in the end based upon a complication in economics and machinery. But the difference between the present and the past is that the conscious present is an awareness of the past in a way and to an extent which the past's awareness of itself cannot show.

Some one said: "The dead writers are remote from us because we *know* so much more than they did." Precisely, and they are that which we know.

I am alive to a usual objection to what is clearly part of my programme for the *métier* of poetry. The objection is that the doctrine requires a ridiculous amount of erudition (pedantry), a claim which can be rejected by appeal to the lives of poets in any pantheon. It will even be affirmed that much learning deadens or perverts poetic sensibility. While, however, we persist in believing that a poet ought to know as much as will not encroach upon his necessary receptivity and necessary laziness, it is not desirable to confine knowledge to whatever can be put into a useful shape for examinations, drawing-rooms, or the still more pretentious modes of publicity. Some can absorb knowledge, the more tardy must sweat for it. Shakespeare acquired more essential history from Plutarch than most men could from the whole British Museum. What is to be insisted upon is that the poet must develop or procure the consciousness of the past and that he should·continue to develop this consciousness throughout his career.

What happens is a continual surrender of himself as he is at the moment to something which is more valuable. The progress of an artist is a continual self-sacrifice, a continual extinction of personality.

There remains to define this process of depersonalization and its relation to the sense of tradition. It is in this depersonalization that art may be said to approach the condition of science. I, therefore, invite you to consider, as a suggestive analogy, the action which takes place when a bit of finely filiated platinum is introduced into a chamber containing oxygen and sulphur dioxide.

II

Honest criticism and sensitive appreciation are directed not upon the poet but upon the poetry. If we attend to the confused cries of the newspaper critics and the *susurrus* of popular repetition that follows, we shall hear the names of poets in great numbers; if we seek not Bluebook knowledge but the enjoyment of poetry, and ask for a poem, we shall seldom find it. I have tried to point out the importance of the relation of the poem to other poems by other authors, and suggested the conception of poetry as a living whole of all the poetry that has ever been written. The other aspect of this Impersonal theory of poetry is the relation of the poem to its author. And I hinted, by an analogy, that the mind of the mature poet differs from that of the immature one not precisely in any valuation of "personality," not being necessarily more interesting, or having "more to say," but rather by being a more finely perfected medium in which special, or very varied, feelings are at liberty to enter into new combinations.

The analogy was that of the catalyst. When the two gases previously mentioned are mixed in the presence of a filament of platinum, they form sulphurous acid. This combination takes place only if the platinum is present; nevertheless the newly formed acid contains no trace of platinum, and the platinum itself is apparently unaffected; has remained inert, neutral, and unchanged. The mind of the poet is the shred of platinum. It may partly or exclusively operate upon the experience of the man himself; but, the more perfect the artist, the more completely separate in him will be the man who suffers and the mind which creates; the more perfectly will the mind digest and transmute the passions which are its material.

The experience, you will notice, the elements which enter the presence of the transforming catalyst, are of two kinds: emotions and feelings. The effect of a work of art upon the person who enjoys it is an experience different in kind from any experience not of art. It may be formed out of one emotion, or may be a combination of several; and various feelings, inhering for the writer in particular words or phrases or images, may be added to compose the final result. Or great poetry may be made without the direct use of any emotion whatever: composed out of feelings solely. Canto XV of the *Inferno* (Brunetto Latini) is a working up of the emotion evident in the situation; but the effect, though single as that of any work of art, is obtained by considerable complexity of detail. The last quatrain gives an image, a feeling attaching to an image, which "came," which did not develop simply out of what precedes, but which was probably in suspension in the poet's mind until the proper combination arrived for it to add itself to. The poet's mind is in fact a receptacle for seizing and storing up numberless feelings, phrases, images, which remain there until all the particles which can unite to form a new compound are present together.

If you compare several representative passages of the greatest poetry you see how great is the variety of types of combination, and also how completely any semi-ethical criterion of "sublimity" misses the mark. For it is not the "greatness," the intensity, of the emotions, the components, but the intensity of the artistic process, the pressure, so to speak, under which the fusion takes place, that counts. The episode of Paolo and Francesca employs a definite emotion, but the intensity of the poetry is something quite different from whatever intensity in the supposed experience it may give the impression of. It is no more intense, furthermore, than Canto XXVI, the voyage of Ulysses, which has not the direct dependence upon an emotion. Great variety is possible in the process of transmutation of emotion: the murder of Agamemnon, or the agony of Othello, gives an artistic effect apparently closer to a possible original than the scenes from Dante. In the *Agamemnon*, the artistic emotion approximates to the emotion of an actual spectator; in *Othello* to the emotion of the protagonist himself. But the difference between art and the event is always absolute; the combination which is the murder of Agamemnon is probably as complex as that which is the voyage of Ulysses. In either case there has been a fusion of elements. The ode of Keats contains a number of feelings which have nothing particular to do with the nightingale, but which the nightingale, partly, perhaps, because of its attractive name, and partly because of its reputation, served to bring together.

The point of view which I am struggling to attack is perhaps related to the metaphysical theory of the substantial unity of the soul: for my meaning is, that the poet has, not a "personality" to express, but a particular medium, which is only a medium and not a personality, in which impressions and experiences combine in peculiar and unexpected ways. Impressions and experiences which are important for the man may take no place in the poetry, and those which become important in the poetry may play quite a negligible part in the man, the personality.

I will quote a passage which is unfamiliar enough to be regarded with fresh attention in the light—or darkness—of these observations:

> And now methinks I could e'en chide myself
> For doating on her beauty, though her death
> Shall be revenged after no common action.
> Does the silkworm expend her yellow labours
> For thee? For thee does she undo herself?
> Are lordships sold to maintain ladyships
> For the poor benefit of a bewildering minute?
> Why does yon fellow falsify highways,
> And put his life between the judge's lips,
> To refine such a thing—keeps horse and men
> To beat their valours for her? . . .

In this passage (as is evident if it is taken in its context) there is a combination of positive and negative emotions: an intensely strong attraction toward beauty and an equally intense fascination by the ugliness which is contrasted with it and which destroys it. This balance of contrasted emotion is in the dramatic situation to which the speech is pertinent, but that situation alone is inadequate to it. This is, so to speak, the structural emotion, provided by the drama. But the whole effect, the dominant tone, is due to the fact that a number of floating feelings, having an affinity to this emotion by no means superficially evident, have combined with it to give us a new art emotion.

It is not in his personal emotions, the emotions provoked by particular events in his life, that the poet is in any way remarkable or interesting. His particular emotions may be simple, or crude, or flat. The emotion in his poetry will be a very complex thing, but not with the complexity of the emotions of people who have very complex or unusual emotions in life. One error, in fact, of eccentricity in poetry is to seek for new human emotions to express; and in this search for novelty in the wrong place it discovers the perverse. The business of the poet is not to find new emotions, but to use the ordinary ones and, in working them up into poetry, to express feelings which are not in actual emotions at all. And emotions which he has never experienced will serve his turn as well as those familiar to him. Consequently, we must believe that "emotion recollected in tranquillity" is an inexact formula. For it is neither emotion, nor recollection, nor, without distortion of meaning, tranquillity. It is a concentration, and a new thing resulting from the concentration, of a very great number of experiences which to the practical and active person would not seem to be experiences at all; it is a concentration which does not happen consciously or of deliberation. These experiences are not "recollected," and they finally unite in an atmosphere which is "tranquil" only in that it is a passive attending upon the event. Of course this is not quite the whole story. There is a great deal, in the writing of poetry, which must be conscious and deliberate. In fact, the bad poet is usually unconscious where he ought to be conscious, and conscious where he ought to be unconscious. Both errors tend to make him "personal." Poetry is not a turning loose of emotion, but an escape from emotion; it is not the expression of personality, but an escape from personality. But, of course, only those who have personality and emotions know what it means to want to escape from these things.

III

ὁ δὲ νοῦς ἴσως θειότερόν τι καὶ ἀπαθές ἐστιν.

This essay proposes to halt at the frontier of metaphysics or mysticism, and confine itself to such practical conclusions as can be applied by the responsible person interested in poetry. To divert interest from the poet to the poetry is a laudable aim: for it would conduce to a juster estimation of actual poetry, good and bad. There are many people who appreciate the expression of sincere emotion in verse, and there is a smaller number of people who can appreciate technical excellence. But very few know when there is an expression of *significant* emotion, emotion which has its life in the poem and not in the history of the poet. The emotion of art is impersonal. And the poet cannot reach this impersonality without surrendering himself wholly to the work to be done. And he is not likely to know what is to be done unless he lives in what is not merely the present, but the present moment of the past, unless he is conscious, not of what is dead, but of what is already living.

The work as myth

Ian Watt

ROBINSOE CRUSOE *AS MYTH*

We do not usually think of *Robinson Crusoe* as a novel. Defoe's first full-length work of fiction seems to fall more naturally into place with *Faust, Don Juan* and *Don Quixote,* the great myths of our civilization. What these myths are about it is fairly easy to say. Their basic plots, their enduring images, all exhibit a single-minded pursuit by the protagonist of one of the characteristic aspirations of Western man. Each of their heroes embodies an *arete* and a *hubris,* an exceptional prowess and a vitiating excess, in spheres of action that are peculiarly important in our culture. Don Quixote, the impetuous generosity and the limiting blindness of chivalric idealism; Don Juan, pursuing and at the same time tormented by the idea of boundless experience of women; Faustus, the great knower, his curiosity always unsatisfied, and therefore damned.

Crusoe does not at first seem a likely companion for these other culture-heroes. They lose the world for an idea; he for gain. Their aspirations are conscious, and defiant, so that when retribution comes it is half expected and already understood; whereas Robinson Crusoe disclaims either heroism or pride; he stolidly insists that he is no more than he seems, that you would do it too in the circumstances.

Yet of his apotheosis there can be no doubt. By the end of the nineteenth century, there had appeared at least 700 editions, translations and imitations, not to mention a popular eighteenth-century pantomime, and an opera by Offenbach.[1] There are other more picturesque examples of his fame. In 1848, an enterprising French industrialist started a restaurant up a tree, a particularly fine chestnut in a wood near Paris: he called it 'Robinson,' and now restaurateurs vie for the title in a village of that name.[2] In France, again, 'un robinson' has become a popular term for a large umbrella.

Nor, as Virginia Woolf has pointed out,[3] is he usually thought of as

From *Essays in Criticism* (April 1951), 95-119.

1. For a survey of the work done on this subject, with very full references, see Philip Babcock Gove, *The Imaginary Voyage in Prose Fiction...* (New York, 1941). The study of *Robinsonaden* is particularly connected with the name of Hermann Ullrich, author of *Robinson und Robinsonaden* (Weimar, 1898), and *Defoes Robinson Crusoe, Geschichte eines Weltbuches* (Leipzig, 1924). H. C. Hutchins has studied the early editions of *Robinson Crusoe* in his *Robinson Crusoe and Its Printing* (New York, 1925), and William-Edward Mann is responsible for a useful study of *Robinson Crusoë en France* (Paris, 1916).

a hero of fiction. Instead, partly because of Defoe's verisimilitude and partly for deeper reasons, his author's name has been forgotten, while he himself has acquired a kind of semi-historical status, like the traditional heroes of myth. When his story appeared it is reported to have been 'universally received and credited as a genuine history';[4] and we today can surely apply to it Malinowski's description of primitive myths: 'It is not of the nature of fiction, such as we read today in a novel, but it is a living reality, believed to have once happened in primeval times, and continuing ever since to influence the world and human destinies.'[5]

Almost universally known, almost universally thought of as at least half real, he cannot be refused the status of myth. But the myth of what?

It is at first difficult to answer, especially if we take into account the later portions of the Crusoe trilogy. For Defoe at once cashed in on the success of the *Strange and Surprising Adventures of Robinson Crusoe* with two other books, the *Farther Adventures* and the *Serious Reflections*. They complicate the answer because, though the character is the same, he is no longer on the island. But, perhaps, there is no need to consider them in detail. Myth always tends in transmission to be whittled down to a single, significant situation. Hardly anyone knows the later books of the trilogy; the stark facts of the hero's island existence occupy almost all our attention, and the rest is largely forgotten, or plays a very secondary role. Even the other portions of the first volume of the trilogy, comprising the early adventures and the eventual return to civilization, though better known, are hardly part of the myth, which retains only the island episode. But even if we ask what is the essential social meaning of that one episode, that solitude, many answers suggest themselves.

Defoe himself gives two main explanations for Crusoe's solitude. At times Crusoe feels he is being punished for irreligion;[6] at others for his filial disobedience in leaving home—in the *Farther Adventures* he even accuses himself of having 'killed his father.'[7] But Crusoe as a man isolated from God, or as a modern Oedipus, is not our subject here. For the myth as it has taken shape in our minds is surely not primarily about religious or psychological alienation, nor even about solitude as such. Crusoe lives in the imagination mainly as a triumph of human achievement and enterprise, and as a favourite example of the elementary processes of political economy. So, in our attempt to understand the causes for Crusoe's apotheosis, we will look first at the relationship of his story to some of the enduring traits of our social and economic history.

It is easy to see that *Robinson Crusoe* is related to three essential themes of modern civilization—which we can briefly designate as 'Back to Nature,' 'The Dignity of Labour' and 'Economic Man.' Robinson Crusoe seems to have become a kind of culture-hero representing all three of

2. René Pottier, *Histoire d'un Village* (Paris, 1941), pp. 171-4.

3. Defoe, *The Common Reader,* First Series (London, 1925).

4. Cit. Max Günther, *Entstehungsgeschichte von Defoes Robinson Crusoe* (Griefswald, 1909), p. 29.

5. *Myth in Primitive Psychology* (London, 1926), pp. 18-9.

6. *The Life and Strange Surprising Adventures of Robinson Crusoe,* ed. George A. Aitken (London, 1902), pp. 41-3, 95-100 and *passim.*

7. *The Farther Adventures of Robinson Crusoe,* ed. G. A. Aitken (London, 1902), pp. 149-50. Also, *Life,* p. 216.

these related but not wholly congruent ideas. It is true that if we examine what Defoe actually wrote, and may be thought to have intended, it appears that *Robinson Crusoe* hardly supports some of the symbolic uses to which the pressure of the needs of our society has made it serve. But this, of course, is in keeping with the status of *Robinson Crusoe* as a myth, for we learn as much from the varied shapes that a myth takes in men's minds, as from the form in which it first arose. It is not an author, but a society, that metamorphoses a story into a myth, by retaining only what its unconscious needs dictate, and forgetting everything else.

The term 'Back to Nature' covers the many and varied forms of primitivism, of revulsion from the contemporary complexities of civilization into a simpler and more 'natural' order. The movement necessarily features two forms of regress: technological and topographical; a simpler economic structure and its associated rural setting. Both are involved in *Robinson Crusoe*, and it is interesting to see that Rousseau, the great prophet of both these trends, was the first to see in it something which far transcended the status of a mere adventure story. The book played an important role in his imaginative experience, and he frequently referred to it. The most famous reference occurs in *Émile*.[8] There, after announcing that in principle 'he hates books' and that he is determined to correct the predominantly bookish tendency of traditional methods of education, Rousseau solemnly proclaims an exception. One book exists which teaches all that books can teach. It is 'the first that my Émile will read; it will for a long time be the whole contents of his library; and it will always hold an honoured place there . . . What then is this marvellous book? Is it Aristotle? Is it Pliny? Is it Buffon? No, it is *Robinson Crusoe.*'

The hero, alone on his island, deprived of all assistance from his fellows, and nevertheless able to look after himself, is obviously a figure that will enthral readers of all ages. The book's consequent entertainment value renders palatable its moral and philosophical merits which are Rousseau's main concern. We cannot here give a full account of them, but two are particularly relevant. One is based on the descriptions of Crusoe's labours: they will fire Émile's imagination with the practical, natural, and manual education to which he is destined. Bacon, Comenius and Locke had urged this change of emphasis, but Rousseau takes it very much further; Defoe's story, a box of tools, and the philosopher of Geneva, these will suffice Émile: anything more would be superfluous, nay vicious.

But the pattern which Émile must imitate is not only that of the simple life of toil. Crusoe also stands for another of Rousseau's favourite ideas—radical individualism. To attain this way of life, Rousseau believes that 'the surest way to raise oneself above prejudices and to order one's judgment on the real relationship between things, is to put oneself in the place of an isolated man, and to judge of everything as that man would judge of them, according to their actual usefulness.'[9] Hence,

8. *Émile, ou De L'Éducation*, ed. F. and P. Richard (Paris, 1939), pp. 210-4.
9. Ibid., p. 211.

again, the pre-eminent utility of *Robinson Crusoe* as a basic text: for the hero's life is its demonstration.

The book as Defoe wrote it (strictly speaking, the *Life and Strange Surprising Adventures* as Saint Hyacinthe and Van Effen transposed it into the more formal French literary tradition)[10] is not perfect. So Rousseau proposes a version freed of all 'fatras';[11] one which was in fact that of the myth. The story was to begin with the shipwreck and to end with the rescue: Émile's book would be less instructive if it ended in the way it actually does—with a return to civilization.

Defoe, of course, would have been surprised at this canonization of his story. His surprise would have been increased by Rousseau's other references where Crusoe becomes a sort of John the Baptist, who in his solitude made straight the ways of the final incarnation of the extravagancies of romantic individualism. For Crusoe is after all a 'solitaire malgré lui,' as Paul Nourrison points out in his *Jean-Jacques Rousseau et Robinson Crusoë*.[12] He is an involuntary and unappreciative prisoner of the beauties of nature. Rousseau was a botanist but Crusoe is a seed merchant: and the moral of his activities is quite different from that which Rousseau extracts. Indeed, if we, perhaps unwisely, attempt to draw any general conclusions from Crusoe's life on the island, it must surely be that out of humanity's repertoire of conceivable designs for living, rational economic behaviour alone is entitled to ontological status. Crusoe 'returns to nature' only according to Defoe's characteristic definition of that accommodating word: in his newspaper the *Review*, Defoe had written that 'Nothing follows the course of Nature more than Trade. There Causes and Consequences follow as directly as day and night.'[13] So in the island the nature of the universe is most importantly manifested in the rationality of the processes of economic life. There are the 'real relationships between things' which Crusoe discovers, relationships whose value and interest come from the way they help man to secure the maximum utility from his environment.

Defoe's 'nature' appeals not for adoration but for exploitation: the island solitude is an exceptional occasion not for undisturbed self-communion, but for strenuous efforts at self-help. Inspired with this belief, Crusoe observes nature, not with the eyes of a pantheist primitive, but with the calculating gaze of colonial capitalism; wherever he looks he sees acres that cry out for improvement, and as he settles down to the task he glows, not with noble savagery, but purposive possession.

The interest of Rousseau and Defoe in a 'state of nature' has only one motive in common: it and it alone will allow them to realize without interference their own thwarted vocations. The island offers exemplary opportunities for total *laisser-faire:* or perhaps we should say, for 'Laisse-

10. See Gove, *The Imaginary Voyage,* p. 36; Mann, *Robinson Crusoe en France,* pp. 51-5 and 102; W. J. B. Pienaar, *English Influences in Dutch Literature and Justus Van Effen as Intermediary* (Cambridge, 1929), pp. 248-9.

11. *Émile,* p. 211.

12. Paris, 1931, p. 30. This hostile and somewhat exaggerated polemic discusses Rousseau's other references to *Robinson Crusoe*.

13. *Review,* II, 26; cit., Walter Wilson, *Memoirs of the Life and Times of Daniel Defoe* (London, 1830), II, 319.

moi faire'—to put the doctrine in psychological terms, terms which help to explain its appeal to Rousseau.

But the vocations are different, and indeed contradictory. The primitive setting of the island which is Rousseau's goal is only a starting point for Crusoe. He finds himself on a desert island, but he has no intention of letting it remain as such. Rousseau wanted to flee the complication and corruptions of the town, to take refuge in a solitary pastoral retreat: Defoe's solution of the dilemma is much more deeply representative of our culture. If the pace gets too fast at home—go overseas. Not to pastoral retreats but to colonies. There the imagination is fired by a splendid prospect which shows the true and necessary conclusion of the ancient conflict between urban and rural ways of life. That conflict can only be resolved in one way—by the urbanization of the countryside. The new culture-hero's task is done only when he has taken possession of his colony and stocked it with an adequate labour force; presumably Rousseau did not read *The Farther Adventures of Robinson Crusoe* where his favourite hero rejoices that 'never was there such a little city in a wood.'[14] But this is the ultimate message of Defoe's story. The most desolate island cannot retain its natural order; wherever the white man brings his rational technology there can only be man-made order, and the jungle itself must succumb to the irresistible teleology of capitalism.

That is the direction which Defoe gives his story. It is fundamentally anti-primitivist. If many readers have interpreted it as a 'back to nature' story, they have done so to satisfy their own needs, and contrary to Defoe's general development of his theme. The implications of *Robinson Crusoe* are equally equivocal as regards the 'Dignity of Labour': but the immediate justification for seeing in it a panegyric of work is a good deal stronger.

Rousseau saw Defoe's story as an object lesson in the educational virtues of manual labour; and Crusoe does indeed draw the correct moral from this activity:

> By stating and squaring everything by reason, and by making the most rational judgment of things, every man may be in time master of every mechanic art. I had never handled a tool in my life, and yet in time, by labour, application and contrivance, I found at last that I wanted nothing but I could have made it, especially if I had had tools.[15]

The pleasures of this discovery to Crusoe and his readers are largely the result of the Division of Labour. The term is Adam Smith's, but he was to a large extent anticipated by Defoe's contemporary, Bernard Mandeville.[16] The process to which the term refers, and which, of course, began very early in human history, was at that time as far

14. p. 118.
15. *Life,* p. 74.
16. *The Fable of the Bees,* ed. F. B. Kaye (Oxford, 1924), I, cxxxiv-cxxxv, II, 142n.

advanced in England as anywhere. This advanced development of the division of labour is an important condition of the creation and immediate success of *Robinson Crusoe*, just as the later accelerated development of the process is a condition of the subsequent triumph of the myth. For the main processes by which man secures food, clothing, and shelter are only likely to become interesting when they have become alien to his common, everyday experience. To enjoy the description of the elementary productive processes reveals a sophisticated taste. Obviously, primitive peoples can never forget for a day what Crusoe announces with the tones of one making a discovery: 'It might be truly said that now I began to work for my bread. 'Tis a little wonderful, and what I believe few people have thought much upon, viz., the strange multitude of little things necessary in the providing, producing, curing, dressing, making and finishing this one article of bread.'[17] The account continues for seven pages, and each detail is new or at least unfamiliar, and reminds us of the vast ignorance that separated production and consumption in the London of Defoe's day, an ignorance that has inevitably increased since then, and that surely explains much of the fascination we find in reading the detailed descriptions of Crusoe's island labours.

Rousseau was very much aware of these factors. In his political and economic writings the development of the arts and sciences past the stage of patriarchal simplicity, and the consequent growth of the division of labour, urbanization, and the political state, are the villains.[18] One deplorable result is to separate manual from mental labour. For Rousseau's purposes, therefore, *Robinson Crusoe* was a valuable corrective to the unnatural intellectualism which society inflicts upon the middle class.

Progressive education and the arts and crafts movement owe a good deal to Rousseau's pages on *Robinson Crusoe* in *Émile*. Educationalists try to rectify many of the results of the division of labour and of urbanization, by including in the curriculum many of the practical and manual activities which Crusoe pursued on the island, and which Rousseau recommended for his pupil. In the adult sphere, many reformers have attempted to bridge the gap between the allegedly inventive, satisfying and humanizing processes of primitive methods of production, and the dehumanizing effects of most economic activities under capitalism. The Arts and Crafts movement, for example, and the cult of the rough edge, are two of the most obvious attempts to remedy the social and esthetic effects of the division of labour in industrial capitalism with an artificial primitivism in technique and way of life. The same attempted diagnosis and remedy—in which one can often detect a residue of moral and religious overtones—can be traced in many of the modern forms of leisure activity. It seems typical of our civilization to try to palliate the distortions of specialization by re-introducing the basic economic processes in the guise of recreations. In school, and in later life, it is

17. *Life*, p. 130.
18. See Arthur Lovejoy, 'The Supposed Primitivism of Rousseau's *Discourse on Inequality*', *Essays in the History of Ideas* (Baltimore, 1948).

suggested, by such pursuits as gardening, home-weaving, woodwork, the keeping of pets, we can all partake of Crusoe's character-forming satisfactions.

There are other aspects of the glorification of labour which are relevant to the function of *Robinson Crusoe* as a myth. Many political reformers since Rousseau have been occupied with the idea of rectifying the effects of the division of labour in the whole of the economic and political system. Both on the right and the left they have tried to realize in practice, by new social arrangements, the ideal of the dignity of labour.

For Marx, man and man's universe are the products of work, and his political system was designed with the idea that human labour under changed conditions could undo the contemporary estrangement of most men from their labour, and recreate a society where all economic activities would increase each individual's moral stature. William Morris and the Guild Socialists in advocating a return to a simpler communal economy suggested a different road: but they were trying to achieve the same moral end, and accepted, in the main, Marx's analysis of the real conditions of human labour in the society of their day. And on the right, Samuel Smiles, for example, was also trying to persuade us that hard work even in the present state of society is the key to all: that 'labor omnia vincit.'[19] Much of Carlyle's political theory and moral teaching derives from his idea that the great lesson is 'Know what thou canst work at.' All these and many others—educationalists, moralists, social and political reformers, publicists, economic theorists—seem to base themselves upon a dogma which finds its supreme narrative realization on Crusoe's island.

The reader's ignorance of the basic processes of production is not the only source of the appeal of Crusoe's island labours. He is also affected by the obscure ethical and religious overtones which pervade Defoe's intense concentration upon each stage of Crusoe's exertions. Eventually, they fasten upon our imaginative life a picture of the human lot as

---

19. Smiles gives this epigraph to his delightfully entitled *Life and Labour or Characteristics of Men of Industry, Culture and Genius,* attributing it to Virgil. Virgil actually wrote, of the coming of the Age of Iron:

> labor omnia vicit
> improbus et duris urgens in rebus egestas. *(Georgics,* I, 145-6)

The time-hallowed misquotation is an interesting example of the forces which have made *Robinson Crusoe* into a myth. That labour does and always will conquer all is a modern view which cannot be derived from Virgil. There seems no reason to consider *vicit* as a gnomic perfect: Conington remarks that 'the poet is narrating, not uttering a sentiment' although he approves of the general characterization of the *Georgics* as a 'glorification of labor.' (*P. Vergili Maronis Opera* . . . (London, 1881), I, 151-5). F. Plessis and P. Lejay comment acidly: 'Le poëte n'éxalte pas le travail pour lui-même, ce qui est une affectation toute moderne, une idée d'Encyclopédiste, mais pour ses résultats.' (*Œuvres* (Paris, 1945), p. 29). L. P. Wilkinson, in a recent article, writes, 'The text of Virgil's Gospel of Work was not *laborare et orare,* as some have suggested, but *laborare et vivere.*' ('The Intention of Virgil's *Georgics,*' Greece and Rome, XVIII (1950), 24.) Virgil's interpretation of the end of the Golden Age, bears obvious resemblances to the Christian, and especially Protestant, welcome to the loss of Eden; as Adam says in *Paradise Lost,* 'Idleness had been worse.' See also A. Lovejoy and G. Boas, *Primitivism and Related Ideas in Antiquity* (Baltimore, 1935), p. 370.

heroic only when productive, and of man as capable of redemption only through untiring labour. As we read we share in an inspiring and yet wholly credible demonstration of the vitality and interest of all the basic economic pursuits. If we draw a moral, it can only be that for all the ailments of man and his society, Defoe confidently prescribes the therapy of work.

The extent both of Defoe's concern with labour, and that of the whole ideology of our culture, is certainly unprecedented. Older cultural traditions would probably have seen *Robinson Crusoe* as a glorification of the purely contingent (if not wholly deplorable) aspects of human experience. Certainly most of their myths, the Golden Fleece, Midas, and the Rheingold are concerned, not with the process by which people ordinarily manage to subsist, but with the sudden magical seizure of wealth: they are inspired by the prospect of never having to work again.

Defoe's interest in labour is part of the ideology of a new and vast historical process. The dignity of labour is ultimately the creed of the religion of capitalism. In this religion Marx figures as the arch-schismatic who—like all heretics—became so by taking one part of the creed too seriously and trying to apply it universally and inconveniently.

It is impossible to deal summarily with this creed. But some attention to that part of it which is directly related to the creation of *Robinson Crusoe* seems necessary.

It is no accident that the idea of the dignity of labour sounds typical of the Victorian Age, for it was then that the new ideology was most publicly and variously established. But actually, of course, the Gospel of Work was by no means new even in 1719. In Greece, Cynics and Stoics had opposed the denigration of manual labour which is a necessary part of a slave-owning society's scale of values. In the Christian tradition labour had never been a dishonourable estate. In the sixteenth century, Protestantism, in harmony with the obscure needs of social and economic change, revived and expanded an old belief until it loomed much larger in the total picture of the human lot. The Biblical view that labour was a curse for Adam's disobedience was displaced by the idea that hard work—untiring stewardship of the gifts of God—was a paramount ethical obligation.

The extent of this shift of values can be measured by comparing Defoe's attitude to work with that of Sir Thomas More. In More's *Utopia* hours of work are limited to six, and all surpluses of production are redistributed in the form of extra holidays.[20] Defoe, in *The Complete Tradesman,* proposes very long hours, and insists that leisure activities, even an inordinate craving for sermons, must be kept in check.[21] The same tendency can be observed in the practice of Robinson Crusoe, to whom More's ideal would have seemed moral laxness. For Crusoe hard work seems to be a condition of life itself, and we notice that the arrival of Friday is a signal, not for increased leisure, but for expanded production.

20. *Ideal Commonwealths*, ed. H. Morley (London, 1899), pp. 97, 101.
21. *The Complete English Tradesman* (Oxford, 1841), I, 32-4. See also, A. E. Levett, 'Daniel Defoe,' *Social and Political Ideas of Some English Thinkers of the Augustan Age*, ed. F. J. C. Hearnshaw (London, 1928), p. 180.

One of the reasons for the canonization of *Robinson Crusoe* is certainly its consonance with the modern view that labour is both the most valuable form of human activity in itself, and at the same time the only reliable way of developing one's spiritual biceps. Defoe's version of this attitude is at times overtly religious in tone. Crusoe's successful improvisations, his perfectly controlled economy, foreshadow his ultimate standing in the divine design. Defoe has taken the idea from his own dissenting milieu, and from its conduct books, whose message has been made familiar to us today in the writings of Weber, Troeltsch and Tawney, and given it a fascinating narrative form.

The combination of this aspect of the ideology of Ascetic Protestantism, or Puritanism, with a kind of return to nature, is particularly happy. Defoe thereby embodies in the same story two historically associated aspirations of the bourgeois class with whom he and his hero have been long and justly identified. In his epic of individual enterprise he bequeathed them both a programme of further economic action, and a figure on whom to project a quasi-religious mystique which retained from the ebbing fervours of Calvinism its essential social and economic teaching. The programme of action is Empire: and it includes, as we have seen, temporary submission to primitivism, or at least to the lure of the wide open places. The mystique is one which distracts attention from the enormous and rapidly growing differences between the kinds of work and their economic rewards, by lumping them together under the one word 'labour,' and erecting a creed which bestows the same high 'dignity' on *all* forms of activity which are subsumed under that one word.

That the mystique of the Dignity of Labour helped to ensure the later success of *Robinson Crusoe* as a myth seems certain. It needed a gospel. But much of what Defoe actually wrote had to be overlooked. This may seem surprising, since Defoe, the complacent apologist of nascent industrial capitalism, certainly approved of the new ideology. But as a writer his eye was so keenly on the object, and second thoughts so rarely checked the flow of his pen, that he reported, not his wishes, but the plausible image of the moment, what he knew people would actually do. So it is that he tells us much which, if analysed, questions not only the simple message of the myth, but even some of his own cherished beliefs. And as these details do not protrude, we must consider them a little more closely.

On the desert island Robinson Crusoe turns his forsaken estate into a triumph. This is a flagrant unreality. Other castaways in the past, including Defoe's main model, Alexander Selkirk, were reduced to an extremely primitive condition, and in the space of a few years.[22] Harassed by fear, dogged by ecological degradation, they sank more and more to the level of animals: in some authentic cases they forgot the use of speech, went mad or died of inanition. One book which Defoe had almost certainly read, *The Voyages and Travels of J. Albert de Mandelso,* tells of two such cases: of a Frenchman who, after two years of solitude

22. A. W. Secord, *Studies in the Narrative Method of Defoe* (Illinois, 1924), p. 26.

on Mauritius, tore his clothing to pieces in a fit of madness brought on by a diet of raw tortoise;[23] and of a Dutch seaman on St. Helena who disinterred the body of a buried comrade and set out to sea in the coffin.[24]

Defoe's readers, perhaps, from their own ordinary experiences of solitude, may suspect as much, even if in a less dramatic form. But as they read *Robinson Crusoe* they forget that isolation can be painful or boring, that it tends in their own lives towards apathetic animality and mental derangement. Instead, they rejoice to find that isolation can be the beginning of a new realization of the potentialities of the individual. Their inertias are cheered by a vicarious participation in Crusoe's twenty-three years of lonely and triumphant struggle. They imagine themselves to be sharing each representative step in his conquest of the environment, and perform with him a heartening recapitulation of humanity's success story.

To all who feel isolated or who get tired of their job—and who at times does not?—the story has a deep appeal and sends our critical faculties asleep. Inspired by the theme, and blinded, perhaps, by our wishes and dreams, we forget the subtle ways by which a consolatory unreality has been made to appear real.

The psychological unreality has its complement in the material one. The normal economic picture—that known to most of Defoe's readers—has been tampered with, unobtrusively but decisively. Defoe's hero—unlike most of us—has been endowed with the basic necessities for the successful exercise of free enterprise. He is not actually a primitive or a proletarian or even a professional man, but a capitalist. He owns, freehold, an estate which is rich, though unimproved. It is not a desert island in the geographical sense; it is merely barren of owners or competitors, and, above all, the very event which brings him there, the shipwreck, which is supposed to be a retributive disaster, is in fact a miraculous present of the means of production, a present rendered particularly felicitous by the death of all the other passengers. Crusoe complains that he is 'reduced to a state of nature'; in fact he secures from the wreck 'the biggest magazine of all kinds . . . that ever was laid out . . . for one man.'[25]

The possession of this original stock, which Defoe's imitators usually retain, usually on a more lavish and less utilitarian scale, is the major practical unreality overlooked by many of his admirers of the classic idyll of individual enterprise. Yet it alone is enough to controvert the myth's wishful affirmation of a flagrant economic naivety—the idea that anyone has ever attained comfort and security entirely by his own efforts.

The myth demanded that the storm be presented as a tragic peripety, although it is really the *deus ex machina* which makes its message plausible. Some such legerdemain was necessary before solitary labour could even appear to be not an alternative to a death sentence, but a solution to the perplexities of economic and social reality.

23. Ibid., p. 28.
24. Ibid.
25. *Life*, p. 60.

The dignity of labour is salvaged, then, under the most apparently adverse conditions, mainly because Crusoe has been lucky with capital stock. One wonders whether his 'instinct of workmanship' would have been of any avail if he had really begun from scratch. Certainly Johann Heinrich Campe, the head master of the *Philanthropium* at Dessau, felt that there was a logical objection here which should be countered. He acted on Rousseau's suggestion that only the island episode was improving, and produced a *Nouveau Robinson* for the young which superseded Defoe's original version both in France and Germany. In it, the stock of tools was omitted.[26]

This version imposes a severe strain on the credulity of its readers; at least on that of anyone who does not live in a *Philanthropium*. But even if we grant the possibility of an isolated man reaching a high technological level unaided, there remain other more drastic difficulties in interpreting *Robinson Crusoe* as a myth of autarkic individual enterprise—difficulties based on the fact that the island is, after all, an island, and that whatever happens there is exceptional and does not seem to happen anywhere else.

On the island there is—with one exception to which we shall return —only real wealth. The perplexities of money and the price mechanism do not exist. There is there, as perhaps nowhere else, a direct relation between production and consumption. That is one obvious reason why we should not argue from it to our society; another follows from the fact that Crusoe did not want to go to the island, and once there, doesn't want to stay. The fact that he is forced to be a model of industry does not mean that he likes work. Actually, in the total setting of the trilogy, it becomes quite clear that Crusoe regards his little profits on the island only as a consolation prize. What he wanted (and later obtained) were unearned increments from the labour of others. In Brazil, he had soon tired even of the tasks of a sugar plantation owner, and it was his quest of the more spectacular rewards of the slave trade which took him to the island.[27] To use Max Weber's distinction, he preferred the speculative rewards of 'adventurer's capitalism' to the uneventful, though regular, increments which are typical of the modern economic order.[28] And after Crusoe leaves the island, he again succumbs to the lure of foreign trade, which at that time gave the highest and quickest returns on capital.[29] It is only on his island that Crusoe shows the regulated diligence combined with accurate planning and stocktaking which is so important in modern economic organization. Defoe knew this theoretically; he dealt with such matters in his economic manuals. But he

26. See Mann, *Robinson Crusoë en France*, pp. 85-101. It was this version which H. H. Gossen used in deriving economic laws from *Crusoe* (W. Stark, *The Ideal Foundations of Economic Thought* (London, 1948), p. 159): and was probably that of Frédéric Bastiat, *Harmonies Économiques* (Bruxelles, 1850), pp. 99f, 214f.

27. *Life*, pp. 40-2. See also, *Farther Adventures*, p. 66, where Defoe shows his awareness of the dangers of this type of enterprise by attributing it to idle ne'er-do-wells.

28. Weber, *The Protestant Ethic and the Spirit of Capitalism*, trans. T. Parsons (London, 1930), pp. 21, 74-8 and *The Theory of Economic and Social Organization*, trans. T. Parsons and A. M. Henderson (New York, 1947), pp. 50-2, 279ff.

29. A. L. Merson, 'The Revolution and the British Empire,' *The Modern Quarterly*, IV (1949), 152.

himself had not been able to carry out his economic ideals into prac-tice. They were to be realized only on Crusoe's 'island of despair' which is actually a utopia, though of a new and peculiar kind.

Most utopias have been based upon the ideal of a more harmonious relationship among men. Those of Plato and More are wholly social in inspiration. They, and many later utopias, are also characterized by a certain static quality, and by the fact that people seem to do much less work and get much more for it than in the real world. But this new utopia is the answer, not to the easy and expansive yearnings of the heart for individual happiness and social harmony, nor even to Crusoe's acquisitive instincts; it is the answer only to a very rigorous conception of what kind of life Defoe feels is good for other people.

Crusoe, in fact, has been stranded in the utopia of the Protestant Ethic. There temptation, whether economic or moral, is wholly absent. Crusoe's energies cannot be deflected, either by the picnic promises of pastoral utopias, or by the relaxing and uneconomic piety of the hermits and mystics who are the heroes of an earlier form of Christianity, heroes whose faith is measured by their certainty that 'God will provide.' On Crusoe's island, unremitting toil is obligatory; there, and only there, it is instinct both with moral value and calculable personal reward.

If we look further afield for economic motivation in Defoe, if we leave the island, we find a very different picture. The other adventures of Robinson Crusoe, and the lives of Defoe's other heroes and heroines do not point in the direction of the dignity of labour. Defoe knew very well that the normal social conditions of his time caused very different adjustments to the environment. Moll Flanders, Roxana, and Colonel Jacque satisfy their needs in ways which no one would propose for imi-tation. Indeed their exploits demonstrate quite another type of political economy, and point the moral that—to those outside Crusoe's island, and without his heaven-bestowed capital—'La propriéte, c'est le vol.'[30]

Defoe, then, is a realist about the individual and his economic environ-ment. He has no illusions about the dignity of the labours of most people in the England of his day. He expressed their lot in a moving passage which William Morris used as epigraph to his lecture on 'The Art of the People'; 'And the men of labour spend their strength in daily struggling for bread to maintain the vital strength they labour with: so living in a daily circulation of sorrow, living but to work, and work-ing but to live, as if daily bread were the only end of a wearisome life, and a wearisome life the only occasion of daily bread.'

If we wish to trace in Defoe any universal and overriding idea it is certainly not that of the dignity of labour as a social fact or even as a moral dogma. The key to the basic motivation of his characters and the hypothesis that best explains their history both apply to Crusoe. For he is only a special case of economic man. Just as the doctrine of the dignity of labour can be understood as the optimistic and deluding myth which hides the realities involved in the division of labour, so the fortitude of Defoe's isolated man withdraws from general attention the

30. J. Sutherland points out that on the island, although stealing is impossible the satisfactory emotions of successful theft are suggested by the looting of the wreck. *Defoe* (London, 1937), p. 232.

true lineaments of that lonely and unlovely archetype of our civilization, *homo economicus,* who is also mirrored in Robinson Crusoe.

Homo economicus is, of course, a fiction. There has long been a conflict about the utility of the abstraction. Briefly, the classical political economists found in the idea of Robinson Crusoe, the solitary individual on a desert island, a splendid example for their system-building. On the other hand, their critics who, like Marx, were concerned to prove that economics can be a guide to reality only when it is a historical and a social science, have denied the relevance of Robinson Crusoe to any realistic economic thinking.

Marx began his polemic against classical political economy by insisting on the social nature of production. He, therefore, attacked the starting points of Adam Smith and Ricardo—the isolated hunters and fishers, who were, he said, 'Robinsonades,' and belonged to 'the insipid illusions of the Eighteenth Century.'[31] Later, in *Capital,* he appropriated Crusoe to support his own theory of value. For Crusoe, 'in spite of the variety of his work . . . knows that his labour whatever its form, is but the activity of one and the same Robinson, and consequently, that it consists of nothing but different modes of human labour . . . All the relations between Robinson and the objects that form this wealth of his own creation, are here so simple and clear as to be intelligible without exertion.'[32] But it is only on the island that the value of any object is directly proportional to the quantity of labour expended upon it. In Western capitalism the rewards of labour and the price of commodities are subject to market considerations which are capricious and unjust, especially to labour.[33] The use of Crusoe as an example therefore distracts attention from the dark realities of the economic system as it is.

Marx does not make the useful polemic point which Crusoe's fortunate acquisition of capital might have afforded him. Nor does he mention the extent to which his personality embodies the moral evils which he ascribed to capitalism. This is no doubt because he is using Crusoe only as an example of one particular theme, and not for any general purpose. For actually Crusoe exemplifies another aspect of Marx's thought; the process of alienation by which capitalism tends to convert man's relationships with his fellows, and even to his own personality, into commodities to be manipulated.

This view of economic man is not, of course, limited to Marx. Max Weber's idea that the Protestant Ethic involves a thorough systematization of behavior according to rational norms of personal profit is very similar,[34] and so is Tawney's picture of the acquisitive society composed

---

31. *A Contribution to the Critique of Political Economy* (1st ed., 1859: New York, 1904), pp. 265-6.

32. Chap. I, section iv.

33. Defoe had experienced this for himself. His bookseller, Taylor, owned the whole share of all three parts of *Robinson Crusoe* and is said to have made his fortune by it. (Hutchins, *Robinson Crusoe and Its Printing,* p. 185.) Defoe worked indefatigably for most of his seventy years of life, and though he was at times rich, he died alone, hiding from a creditor. (Sutherland, *Defoe,* pp. 269-74.)

34. Weber, *Theory of Economic and Social Organization,* pp. 191-249 *et passim.*

of individuals pursuing their individual interests without any recognition of social or moral solidarity.[35] But these theoretical formulations had long before been anticipated by literary realization. For, as an ironic commentary upon the myth, the book of *Robinson Crusoe* depicts in its casual reports of the hero's behavior and of his occasional parenthetic reflections, the shameless and pervasive impact of the cash nexus upon the character and personal relationships of the archetypal economic man. Defoe has supplied the antidote to the myth of his unwitting creation—not only in the incidental unrealities of the plot mentioned above, but also in the sombre touches which are an overt part of his picture of the personality of the protagonist.

Crusoe treats his personal relationships in terms of their commodity value. The Moorish boy, Xury, for example, helps him to escape from slavery, and on another occasion offers to prove his devotion by sacrificing his own life. Crusoe very properly resolves 'to love him ever after,'[36] and promises 'to make him a great man.' But when chance leads them to the Portuguese trader, and its Captain offers Crusoe sixty pieces of eight—twice Judas's figure—he cannot resist the bargain and sells Xury into slavery. He has momentary scruples at the betrayal, it is true, but they are soon economically satisfied by securing from the Captain a promise 'to set him free in ten years if he turn Christian.'[37] Remorse later supervenes, but only when the tasks of his island existence renew his need for a slave.[38]

Slaves, of course, were his original objective in the voyage which brought him to the island. And eventually Providence and his own exertions provide him with Man Friday, who answers his prayers by 'swearing to be my slave for ever.'[39] The unsolicited promise is prophetic, and the development of the relationship is instructive. Crusoe does not ask Friday his name, he gives him one; and there is throughout a remarkable lack of interest in Friday as a person, as someone worth trying to understand or converse with. Even in language—the medium whereby human beings may achieve something more than animal relationships with each other—Crusoe is a strict utilitarian. 'I likewise taught him to say yes and no,'[40] he tells us, though as Defoe's contemporary critic Gildon not unjustly remarked,[41] Friday still speaks pidgin English at the end of their long association.

Yet Crusoe regards the relationship as ideal. In the period alone with Friday he was 'perfectly and completely happy, if any such thing as complete happiness can be found in a sublunary state.'[42] A functional silence, apparently, adds to the charms of the idyll, broken only by an occasional 'No, Friday' or an abject 'Yes, Master.' Man's social nature

35. R. H. Tawney, *The Acquisitive Society* (London, 1921), p. 32.
36. *Life*, p. 27.
37. Ibid., p. 36.
38. Ibid., p. 164.
39. Ibid., p. 226.
40. Ibid., p. 229.
41. *Robinson Crusoe Examin'd and Criticis'd;* . . . ed. P. Dottin (London and Paris, 1923) pp. 70, 78, 118.
42. *Life*, pp. 245-6.

is wholly satisfied by the righteous bestowal, or grateful receipt, of benevolent but not undemanding patronage.[43]

Only one doubt ruffles Crusoe's proprietary equanimity. He becomes obsessed with the fear that Friday may be harbouring an ungrateful wish to return to his father and his tribe. But the fear proves groundless and they leave the island together. Crusoe later avoids any possible qualms about keeping Friday in servitude by the deferred altruism of a resolution 'to do something considerable for him, if he outlived me.'[44] Fortunately, no such sacrifice is called for, as Friday dies at sea, faithful to the end, and rewarded only by a brief word of obituary compassion.

Crusoe's attitude to women is also marked by an extreme inhibition of what we now consider to be normal human feelings. There are, of course, none on the island, and their absence is not deplored. When Crusoe does notice the lack of 'society,' he prays for company, but it is for that of a male slave. With Friday, he is fully satisfied by an idyll without benefit of woman. It is an interesting break from the traditional expectations aroused by desert islands, from the *Odyssey* to the *New Yorker*.

Defoe's view of the individual was too completely dominated by the rational pursuit of material self-interest to allow any scope either for natural instinct or for higher emotional needs. Even when Crusoe returns to civilization, sex is strictly subordinated to business. Only after his financial position has been fully secured by a further voyage does he marry, 'and that not either to my disadvantage or dissatisfaction.'[45]

Some of Crusoe's colonists have the same attitude. He tells how they draw lots for five women, and strongly approves of the outcome: 'He that drew to choose first . . . took her that was reckoned the homeliest and eldest of the five, which made mirth enough among the rest . . . but the fellow considered better than any of them, that it was application and business that they were to expect assistance in as much as anything else; and she proved the best wife of all the parcel.'[46]

The conflict is put very much in Weber's terms.[47] Sex is seen as a dangerously irrational factor in life which interferes with the pursuit of rational self-interest: and economic and moral worth in the male does not guarantee him a profitable matrimonial investment. On his colony 'as it often happens in the world (what the wise ends of God's Providence are in such a disposition of things I cannot say), the two honest fellows had the two worst wives; and the three reprobates, that were scarce worth hanging, . . . had three clever, diligent, careful and ingenious wives.'[48] It is therefore no accident that love plays a very minor part in Crusoe's own life, and is eliminated from the scene of his greatest triumphs.

43. The Crusoe-Friday relationship is representative in many other ways. Not least in showing how the quest for the white man's burden tends to end in the discovery of the perfect porter and personal servant.
44. *Farther Adventures*, p. 133.
45. *Life*, p. 341.
46. *Farther Adventures*, p. 77.
47. Max Weber, *Essays in Sociology*, trans. H. H. Gerth and C. Wright Mills (New York, 1946), p. 350.
48. *Farther Adventures*, p. 78.

One could illustrate the ideology of *homo economicus* at much greater length from *Robinson Crusoe*. Everything is measured from the rational, a-social, and anti-traditional standards of individual self-interest, and some of the results are not pleasant. But these results are surely lamentable, but necessary, corollaries of the social process which the story reflects; and the common tendency to overlook them in the hero must be attributed to the obscure forces that guard the idols of our society and shape its myths.

Malinowski has said that 'myth is . . . an indispensable ingredient of all culture.'[49] It would indeed appear to be so, but I have no wish to be numbered among those who would prove our common humanity by putting us back on a level with the Trobriand islanders. The aim of this essay is rather to do something they don't do; that is, scrutinize one small item of our cultural repertoire in the hope of clarifying its role in the past and present of our society.

Much has had to be omitted. The appeal of the adventure in itself, for example, and the theological aspect of the story, which modifies the picture considerably. Some of the social and economic matters have been treated somewhat cavalierly. The case of Robinson Crusoe as *homo economicus* has been somewhat oversimplified. For Defoe does suggest on at least one occasion (the famous episode when Crusoe comes across a hoard of gold on the island and, after declaiming on its uselessness, 'upon second thoughts' takes it away)[50] the irrationality of the goals which shape the character of economic man and which affect his actions more powerfully than his own understanding of his real needs. And, of course, in a wintry sort of way, Crusoe has his pleasures. He does not, as Selkirk had done, dance with the goats, but he does at least occasionally supplement occupational by recreational therapy. Still, it seems true to say that the reality of Defoe's masterpiece, its ultimate referent, is economic man. So that if we seek a general meaning for his solitude it must be the social atomization which *homo economicus* brings in his train. That, surely, is the main historical basis of this metaphor of human solitude which has haunted the western consciousness. And the need to obscure the regrettable social and psychological corollaries of the rise of economic individualism must explain much of the very general disinclination to see the darker side of Defoe's hero.

It is certainly curious to observe how all but universal has been the reluctance to challenge Crusoe as a model for imitation and inspiration. In some cases there may be other explanations for this. The myth of national character, for example. Some foreign commentators have had ulterior motives in presenting Robinson Crusoe as the typical Englishman. Marx calls him a 'true-born Briton';[51] and Dibelius echoes the impeachment of a nation of shopkeepers with more obvious venom.[52] For France, de Vogüé, in his study of what he calls 'Le livre anglais,'

49. *Myth in Primitive Psychology*, p. 125.
50. *Life*, p. 62.
51. *Capital*, chap. I, section vi.
52. *Englische Romankunst* (Berlin, 1910), I, 36.

though more polite, is equally disparaging by implication.[53] What is curious is to find that most English writers, too, have tended to accept Crusoe as the typical Englishman, apparently undeterred by any of his anti-social idiosyncrasies.

There have been occasional dissentients. Dickens, for example, was revolted by Crusoe's attitude to the death of Friday, and to women generally; and he wrote in a letter that Defoe must have been a 'precious dry and disagreeable article himself.'[54] Ruskin—another critic of the mentality of industrial capitalism—uses the phrase 'a very small, perky, contented, conceited, Cock-Robinson-Crusoe, sort of life.'[55] Yet on the whole, Crusoe has been accepted as the typical Englishman by his fellow-countrymen, although, as it happens, Defoe made his father 'a foreigner of Bremen.'

In some ways, of course, the character of Robinson Crusoe is a national one. Courage, practical intelligence, not making a fuss, these are not the least of the virtues, and their combination in Crusoe does seem to be according to an English pattern. But these virtues cannot be regarded as exemplary and sufficient. Dickens wrote of *Robinson Crusoe* that it is 'the only instance of a universally popular book that could make no one laugh and no one cry.'[56] This suggests the major flaw. Defoe's epic of the stiff upper lip does not propose a wholly satisfactory ideal. For Crusoe's merits are combined with a stolid and inhibited self-sufficiency which is disastrous both for the individual and for society. That is Crusoe's *hubris*—a defect not unlike Rousseau's 'hypertrophie du moi.'

There is, even on Crusoe's own showing, very little content or peace in this way of life. Pascal said that the misery of man can be traced from a single fact, his inability to stay still in his own room. Crusoe can never stay still. His brisk and businesslike exterior cannot wholly conceal the deadening compulsion of an alienation which is assuaged only by ceaseless economic activity. He is modern economic man putting a poker face on the fate that Pascal found intolerable, 'Nothing else offering, and finding that really stirring about and trading, the profit being so great, and, as I may say, certain, had more pleasure in it, and more satisfaction to the mind, than sitting still, which, to me especially, was the unhappiest part of life. . . .'[57] So, in the *Farther Adventures*, he sets out on yet another lucrative Odyssey.

His author, deeply implicated in the character that Walter de la Mare has called Defoe's 'Elective Affinity,'[58] appears to approve. But he certainly does not see his work in an optimistic vein: 'Nothing else offering . . .' suggests why. Defoe wrestles with the meanings of his creation in the essay 'On Solitude' which begins the *Serious Reflections*. The essay is inconclusive, and there are several different strands of thought in it. But the bitterness of isolation as the primordial fact repeatedly moves Defoe to a great fervour of communication. One of the passages seems a partic-

53. *Revue des Deux Mondes*, October 1st, 1895. As is Jean Giraudoux in *Suzanne et le Pacifique* (Paris, 1921), pp. 228-33.
54. John Forster, *Life of Charles Dickens*, rev. J. W. T. Ley (London, 1928), p. 611.
55. Peter Quennell, *John Ruskin* (London, 1949), p. 15.
56. Loc. cit.
57. p. 214.
58. *Desert Islands and Robinson Crusoe* (London, 1930), p. 7.

ularly moving commentary on the isolation which the pursuit of individual self-interest creates in the human spirit.

> What are the sorrows of other men to us, and what their joys? Sometimes we may be touched indeed by the power of sympathy, and a secret turn of the affections; but all the solid reflection is directed to ourselves. Our meditations are all solitude in perfection; our passions are all exercised in retirement; we love, we hate, we covet, we enjoy, all in privacy and solitude. All that we communicate of those things to any other is but for their assistance in the pursuit of our desires; the end is at home; the enjoyment, the contemplation, is all solitude and retirement; it is for ourselves we enjoy, and for ourselves we suffer.[59]

The loneliness of economic man was a tragic fact. Many Stoic or Christian thinkers might have said 'We love, we hate . . . all in privacy and solitude.' But 'we covet, we enjoy' is characteristic of a later ideology. To the solitude of the soul which so many have expressed, Defoe adds 'all we communicate of those things to any other is but for their assistance in the pursuit of our desires.' A rationally-conceived self-interest makes a mockery of speech, and suggests silence.

So, although *Robinson Crusoe* is a mutation of a very ancient theme, its specific cause and nature are wholly modern. And now that it is possible to see fairly clearly the realities of which Crusoe is the menacing symbol, we must surely question his desirability as an ideal prototype. What has happened in the last 200 years has shown that where Defoe's new culture-hero is admitted into the pantheon of myth, he soon crowds out or subjugates the other figures, whether comic or tragic, round whom have gathered those more generous aspirations that occasionally mitigate the bitterness of history.

59. *Serious Reflections of Robinson Crusoe,* ed. G. A. Aitken (London, 1902), pp. 2-3.

Lee T. Lemon

BILLY BUDD: *THE PLOT AGAINST THE STORY*

Billy Budd rubs against the grain, and it rubs intensely and persistently enough to be irritating. Our sympathies are all with the innocent Billy, and we are accustomed to having authors exploit our sympathies directly. Most typically, a pattern of meaning emerges from a narrative because our responses to the pattern of values embodied in the hero and his story are reinforced by the thematic implications of the setting, characterization, tone, symbolism, authorial intrusions, and so on. If there is an ironic discrepancy between hero and theme, we expect an author to let us know what it is.

In a relatively simple novel like *For Whom the Bell Tolls*, Robert Jordan seems to embody Hemingway's ethic, and Jordan's world is conveniently built to make that ethic appear acceptable. If I may simplify somewhat, we know that Jordan is good because he is for Good Things and against Bad Things; and where the morality of the things is doubtful, we judge it by Jordan's response. Generally, we sympathize with Jordan because he is on the side of humanity; and because we sympathize, we judge the world as he judges it. This, at least, is the way Hemingway's novel seems designed to work. Similarly, when we have a rogue hero, as in Fielding's *Jonathan Wild*, we know which way our sympathies are supposed to run because the hero's actions and fate are in accord with the context the author has created.

Even in much more complicated works like *Light in August* or *Crime and Punishment*, the context in which the hero acts out his drama still generally supports the value system implicit in that drama. Our responses to Raskolnikov may be more complex than our responses to Robert Jordan, but the patterns of value Dostoevsky provides for him and his world in the novel are compatible. If a generous spirituality is good in Sonia, it is also good in Raskolnikov; if progressivism is evil for Lebeziatnikov, it is equally evil for Raskolnikov.

From *Studies in Short Fiction* (June 1964).

The Russian Formalist critic Victor Shklovskij[1] originated a distinction that may help explain my meaning. The distinction is between *story*
and *plot:* the story is the sequence of events in their causal-temporal relationship; whatever falls outside that relationship or distorts it belongs to
the plot. All literary narratives have both, and they can be roughly separated by reducing the narrative to its essential story pattern—that "A
happened, which caused B, which in turn caused C . . ." and so on. A
novel may have two or more related stories, as in *Light in August* or
Vanity Fair. Thus if one were telling Becky Sharp's "story," much of the
detail about Amelia would be totally irrelevant in tracing Becky's fate.
Likewise, much of the description of clothes, social customs, Thackeray's
intrusions, and the like, would be irrelevant. All such irrelevancies
would, however, be part of the plot.

My point is that in most narratives story and plot involve the same,
or at least compatible, patterns of sympathy and revulsion. In *Vanity
Fair* it seems clear that Thackeray wants us to be repelled by Becky's
grasping ambition. The plot—including the material centering around
Amelia—directly reinforces this theme. We know how bad Becky is partly
by her effect on Amelia, partly by the contrast between the two women,
partly by the dictums of Thackeray's that "All is vanity," and partly by
the emptiness of her temporary success. Quite simply, the plot reinforces
the thematic implications of the story.

I shall argue that in *Billy Budd* the thematic implications of the plot
and those of the story are often in direct opposition and that this causes
much of the confusion about the book. But I want to argue further that
the opposition is itself functional and leads to a more subtle and more
mature theme than could either aspect alone.

Put in its most general terms, *Billy Budd* is the familiar story of a
young man forced into strange circumstances who, having unintention-
ally incurred the enmity of a person more powerful than himself, is hounded
until he strikes out in self-defense and is murdered by society. From the
outline of the story, nothing could be clearer than that our sympathies
are to be with Billy and against society. When society kills innocence,
right thinking men bristle naturally, and authors make such natural
responses the basis of their themes. Moreover, Melville goes to great
lengths to impress his readers with Budd's innocence and society's guilt;
parts of the plot, in other words, work conventionally to reinforce the
sympathies and revulsions aroused by the story. Others work ambiguously,
and still others work unconventionally—that is, against the story. I shall
begin with what seem the most conventionally used elements of the plot
and work through to the more unconventional.

For a number of reasons, Melville develops Claggart, the antagonist,
least ambiguously. In the story he is unalloyed evil. He hates Billy for
no reason, plots against him, and tries to destroy him; nothing in the
cause and effect sequence of the story alleviates Claggart's evil—he even

---

1. *Razvertyvanie sjuzheta* and Tristram Shandy *Stern'a i teorija i romana* (*Plot Develop-
ment* and *Sterne's* Tristram Shandy *and the Theory of the Novel*), published separately in
Petrograd, 1921. These and other Russian Formalist essays have been translated into
English by L. T. Lemon and M. J. Reis; their first printing in English will be by the
University of Nebraska Press in 1965.

lacks all normal human motivation. In the plot, Melville goes out of his way to inform the reader that Claggart is born with "a depravity according to nature"; he is one of those "madmen, . . . of the most dangerous sort"[2] whose very rationality is a threat. On the level of plot he assumes a specific symbolic identity that comes as much from what we do not know about him as from what we do know. He appears to be a man "who for reasons of his own was keeping incog" (p. 64). None of the crew's speculations on Claggart's origins reflects credit on him. He is possibly a swindler and certainly not a native Englishman; the only hint as to his nationality is the word *chevalier,* which suggests that he is French and therefore, in the context of *Billy Budd,* an enemy of the established social order. We know as little of Claggart's background "as an astronomer knows about a comet's travels prior to its first observable appearance in the sky." (p. 67)

I am belaboring what we do not know about Claggart, because we lack the same information about Billy. Like Claggart, he has no antecedents, although he appears to be unalloyed English, with "a mother eminently favored by Love and the Graces" and a noble father. But a curious exchange occurs when Billy is questioned about his parents:

> ". . . . Who was your father?"
> "God knows, Sir." (p. 51)

On the strength of this I shall not attempt to make Billy into a Christ figure; at this point I merely want to emphasize that Melville is at great pains to hint that neither he nor Claggart is of this world, as if Melville were preparing us for a confrontation of a good and an evil whose purity is unalloyed by anything earthly.[3]

The purity of Claggart's evil is so beyond the range of human experience that Melville cannot trust himself to present it dramatically; instead, he stops the story at Chapter 11 to speculate on natural depravity and to suggest a radical discontinuity between the moral and the social worlds. To understand Claggart, "to pass from a normal nature to him one must cross 'the deadly space between'" (p. 74). Possibly "to know the world and to know human nature [are] . . . two distinct branches of knowledge," so that one may know either and yet know "little or nothing of the other" (p. 75). In fact, natural depravity or complete moral evil has so little to do with the everyday business of the world that society fosters the former and condemns the latter.

Symbolically (hence still on the level of plot) Claggart is linked with the serpent of the Garden of Eden. Claggart's henchman gains the attention of pre-lapsarian Billy by saying "Hist," and again, "Hist, hist!" (p. 82)—the sound of a serpent. When Claggart himself confronts Billy, "the first mesmeristic glance was one of serpent fascination" (p. 98); when the sailors carry away the dead Claggart, "it was like handling

---

2. Herman Melville, *Billy Budd: Sailor (An Inside Narrative),* Harrison Hayford and Merton M. Sealts, Jr., eds. (Chicago, 1962). All references are to this text, the first definitive edition of *Billy Budd.*

3. Captain Vere, on the other hand, is earthly. As the novel's representative of social order it is appropriate that Melville tells us much about his background.

a dead snake" (p. 99). Both the narrative thread of the story and the supplementary details of the plot combine to condemn Claggart, as in any conventional narrative. The plot serves merely to specify symbolically the nature of Claggart's evil.

The same conventional plot-story relationship holds true for Billy, but only in part. The story requires that we sympathize with this example of hounded innocence, and the plot defines that sympathy by defining its object. I have already pointed out that Billy, like Claggart, is not of this world. "God knows" who his father is, and he is constantly referred to as a kind of noble savage. The "natural regality" (p. 43) of his type specifically contrasts with Claggart's "natural depravity." His virtues are strength and beauty rather than the more civilized understanding and cunning. It should not be necessary to press the point that whenever Billy is compared to something, it is always something either before or beyond civilization. Claggart, who the narrator tells us is "intellectually capable of adequately appreciating the moral phenomenon presented in Billy Budd" understands that Billy is "nothing more than innocent" (p. 78). If we try to make a Christ or an Adam of Billy, we are attributing both too much and too little to him; symbols, even literary and mythic symbols, are seldom mutually convertible. At most we can say that Billy is Christ-like and Adam-like in his innocence and Christ-like in his role as victim.

Melville further specifies the innocence as both moral and social. His moral innocence makes the conflict with Claggart inevitable; his social innocence dooms him. He is, no matter how regrettably, "Baby Budd" in a social world that requires manhood. It is fitting that the world in which Baby Budd is most at home is the world of the *Rights-of-Man* which, Melville tells us, is named after Paine's book; the world of the rights of man is a "natural" world just as Budd is a "natural" man. On board the *Rights-of-Man*, discipline, which would seem to be social if anything is, is clearly and certainly presented as natural. It is not enforced by authority (the honest but rather ineffectual Captain Graveling) but rather by Billy: " 'Not that he preached to them or said or did anything in particular; but a virtue went out of him, sugaring the sour ones' " (p. 47). Even when Billy quiets the last trouble maker, Red Whiskers, he does it naturally by instinctively striking out, not by civilized or social means. The natural world—or, if the oxymoron is permissible, natural society—is better for Billy's presence. Yet Billy himself leaves that world with no regrets, as if Melville were telling us that Billy himself knows that he is twenty-one and must become a man. Thus he has no complaints when he is separated from his rights and impressed on board the *Bellipotent*, a warship in hostile waters and so a fitting symbol for society at its most organized and most authoritarian. As he changes ships, he shouts, " 'And good-bye to you too, old *Rights-of-Man*' " (p. 49). He is, in fact, leaving the world of natural rights. The lieutenant, the representative of authority at this point, "roars," " 'Down, Sir!' "

All of this plot material functions quite conventionally, enlisting our sympathies with the hero and defining them. But a question about Billy should be taking form: can the natural man assume the responsibilities of the social man? The plot tells us that he cannot. Perhaps the most telling incident is his response to the temptation by Claggart's hench-man.[4] Billy is utterly confused, for this is "the first time in his life that he had ever been personally approached in underhand intriguing fashion" (p. 83). More important than his confusion, however, is his refusal to report the incident; because of his "novice magnanimity" he feels that informing "would savour overmuch of the dirty work of a telltale" (p. 85). His attitude here is essentially adolescent; he neither understands the importance of the event nor conceives of a duty higher than that to his private moral code. Equally important, he lies to Red Pepper, telling him that the tempter was only an afterguardsman on the prowl, and lies again at the court-martial. Both times, and this is significant, Billy lies deliberately, so deliberately that he even overcomes his speech impediment. On the second occasion,

> The reply lingered . . . the question immediately recalling to Billy's mind the interview with the afterguardsman in the fore-chains. But an innate repugnance to playing a part at all approaching that of an informer against one's shipmates—the same erring sense of uninstructed honor which had stood in the way of his reporting the matter at the time, though as a loyal man-of-war's man it was incumbent on him, and failure so to do, if charged against him and proven, would have subjected him to the heaviest of penalties; this, with the blind feeling now his that nothing really was being hatched, prevailed with him. When the answer came it was a negative. (pp. 106–07)

I have quoted this passage at length because in it the narrator (whom we have no reason to distrust; I find the arguments that the narrator is ironic singularly unconvincing) specifically accuses Billy of a crime punishable by death. The crime can be thought of narrowly in terms of severe military justice; but it can also be thought of broadly as Billy's failure to protect the society he has joined. Billy is not only irresponsible, he is not responsible—in the sense in which children and feeble-minded persons are not responsible.

I am being very hard on Billy because critics generally have been too easy on him. And with good reason, for as I have shown, the story and much of the plot material built around him are designed to make him appealing. To state the case somewhat more fairly, Baby Budd has morally and intellectually never left the world of the *Rights-of-Man*, although we are told that at twenty-one he bade the rights good-bye and cheerfully entered the world of social responsibility, of duties as contrasted with rights.

To put this in a way hinted at earlier, Melville is opposing two ethical systems, the natural and the social, and he makes the former as attractive as possible by his description of the relaxed informality aboard Captain Graveling's ship and by the "natural regality" of Billy, the representative of the natural. Unfortunately, Billy has outgrown the natural,

4. I would include the temptation scene as part of the plot rather than the story because it is inconsequential; Claggart does not refer to it when he accuses Billy and, on the level of the story, it results in no further action.

although in his simplicity he does not understand that he has to make a choice—or better, that by the mere fact that he is twenty-one a choice has been made and that he has been placed in a social world where responsibilities must be accepted.

It might be instructive to compare the responses of students to both *Billy Budd* and *Walden*. I have found that students usually dislike *Walden* because (once we decide that Thoreau probably did not expect all mankind to settle by a pond) their good sense tells them that a society of individualists would be intolerable; if each man marches to his own drummer, each stumbles over the other. Yet they accept *Billy Budd*, failing to see that Billy instinctively follows Thoreau's advice—he settles issues that affect others on a purely personal basis. In a sense, we may read *Billy Budd* as Melville's final answer to Thoreau, Emerson, Paine, and in general to that whole strain of ultra-individualistic feeling that pervaded nineteenth-century American thought.

At the end Billy seems finally to accept his social responsibility, not passively (as is usually argued) but actively. Actually, for all his innocence, Billy is not a passive creature. When taunted loutishly on board the *Rights*, he strikes out at his tormentor; when accused falsely by Claggart, he again strikes out. He may not be subtle enough to detect covert harassment (as the incident of the bags and the episode at the mess show), but he is certainly a man who defends himself when he is unjustly imposed upon. Yet he does not lash out when Captain Vere tells him that he must hang. On the contrary, Melville does everything within his power to show that Billy accepts Vere's judgment, even to the point of guessing at what might have happened when Vere told Billy of his sentence after the court-martial: "Not without a sort of joy, indeed, he might have appreciated the brave opinion of him implied in his captain's making such a confidant of him" (p. 115). Does Billy's joy come from his natural and personal response to the meeting of two individuals? Or does it come from his sensing that acceptance of Vere's jurisdiction has placed him within the social system? I do not know, and the sections of the text dealing with Billy help very little. Billy's final exclamation, "God bless Captain Vere" (p. 123), could support either alternative, although the fact that the crew echo it, and thereby affirm their allegiance to the Captain and through him to society, supports the second.

If I have been reading aright—in outline, if not in all details—what we have seen is a growing opposition of the values implicit in the story by those in the plot. The villain of the story is the naturally depraved Claggart, the hero the naturally good Billy; the action of the story is designed to arouse our *natural* responses towards villains and heroes. But as the plot thickens we find just enough emotional correspondence between it and the story to help the latter along and to keep the reader reminded of his natural emotional reactions; additional elements of the plot seem calculated to evoke an unnatural, a *social*, response. Nowhere is this better illustrated than in the development of Captain Vere.

The story of Billy's hanging requires that Vere have certain characteristics, for not everyone has conviction enough to demand the death of an appealing and innocent young man. The story requires that Vere have a certain hardness, a certain stubbornness, and a quickness of judgment coupled with prudence. The plot gives Vere these qualities, but qualifies them in important ways. Vere is "always . . . mindful of the welfare of his men, but never tolerating an infraction of discipline" (p. 60). His convictions are "settled," yet settled against a floodtide of opinion "which carried away as in a torrent . . . minds by nature not inferior to his own" (pp. 62-63). He is also "resolute" (p. 60) and "bluff" (p. 63). If one reads the section on Vere quickly enough and wants to make a villain of him, one can conclude that Vere is a prejudiced, cowardly, and inhuman martinet—precisely the kind of man who would kill Billy. Yet each of the unfavorable traits is qualified. His prejudice is "disinterested" (p. 63) and comes from reading writers "free from cant and convention" (p. 62); an officer who keeps discipline, yet is "mindful of the welfare of his men" is, I believe, an exceptionally fine officer; I shall say more about the cowardice later.

The implied adverse criticism of Vere is—and I believe this point is crucial—just sufficient to substantiate the value system implicit in the story. It is there simply because without it Vere would not be the man to demand Billy's death; without it, the story would be unconvincing. What is far more interesting is the material that is irrelevant to the story, the material that qualifies and perhaps even reverses our attitude towards Vere's severity. Perhaps I can summarize briefly by noting that the story requires a *Captain* Vere and all the military sternness of that rank; the story does not require a *Starry* Vere and all the intellectuality, dreaminess, and idealism suggested by *Starry*.

Actually, Melville works the plot very hard to make Starry Vere appealing; he must, because in terms of the story he is a villain. Since there is a great deal of controversy about the goodness or evil of Vere, I shall present the strongest evidence of Vere's essential goodness before taking up the more dubious. Most obvious is Vere's conversation with Billy after the court-martial—the scene that Melville, in a sense, did not write. The usual argument at this point, that Billy is Christ and Vere Pilate, fails because Vere's decision to confront the condemned is most un-Pilate like and because the specific biblical allusion is to Isaac and Abraham, the sacrificial son and the father mournfully going about what he believes is God's will. The Pilate analogy probably carries over from the trial scene, in which Vere convinces the jury that Billy must hang by appealing to expediency, much as Pilate acted expediently when he turned Jesus over to the mob. Yet here the analogy breaks down quickly. Vere does not refuse to judge; he insists upon judging, and even forces a judgment against the will of the court. And furthermore, Melville explicitly shows that Vere's own decision is not based on expediency. Vere ignores naval custom, Melville tells us, by appointing an officer of the Marines to the court because he thinks the officer "a judicious person, thoughtful, and not altogether incapable of grappling with a difficult case unprecedented in his prior experience," although Vere does have misgivings (pp. 104-105). Vere does understand that the case is beyond the experience of the usual officer, tries to choose the best court he can, but must settle for what he can get. When he argues his case, he is forced to present two distinct arguments. At first he tries to argue the moral issue, which, bluntly, is the difference between natural justice and social justice and the necessity of accepting the latter within the framework of society. Vere argues from expediency only after noticing that "the three men moved in their seats, less convinced than agitated. . . . Perceiving which, the speaker paused for a moment; then abruptly changing his tone, went on" (p. 111). Vere clearly argues from expediency only as a last resort, only because his listeners understand no other argument. If the officers could have understood Vere's moral argument, Billy's hanging would have been unnecessary—the moral universe would be the social universe.

A number of other elements, major and minor, seem clearly designed to make Vere appealing. He quickly recognizes Claggart's evil and is as repelled by it as the reader is; he is equally quick in recognizing Billy's moral innocence. Generally, he is described as exceptional, as superior in all ways to his fellow officers.

With one exception, and with that exception we turn to the less obviously pro-Vere elements. The exception is the passage on Nelson, and the issue is whether Vere is compared or contrasted with the great admiral. The problem is an important one, because the whole section on Nelson is totally irrelevant to the story except, if the purpose is to contrast, to prepare for Vere as villain by showing that he is not the man Nelson was. The telling passage is this: "it was thought that an officer like Nelson was the one, not indeed to terrorize the crew into base subjection, but to win them, by force of his mere presence and heroic personality, back to an allegiance if not as enthusiastic as his own yet as true" (p. 59). It would seem, on the surface, that Vere does "terrorize the crew into base subjection," unless it be remembered that, with Billy in their hearts, they bless Vere after the hanging.[5] Furthermore, the quality that Melville seems to admire most in Nelson is his lack of "personal prudence" (p. 58), which Nelson proves by being shot down on the deck of his ship, just as Vere is. The obvious point, I believe, is that Vere compares favorably with "the greatest sailor since our world began." (p. 58)

At first sight, the fears of the surgeon concerning Vere's sanity would seem at least as damaging as the comparison with Nelson, but again the difficulties not only vanish when placed in their proper light, but the incident puts Vere in even a better position. The surgeon, who we are told is "as yet unappraised of the antecedents," was profoundly discomposed and wondered if Vere were "unhinged" (pp. 101-102). This seems damning, especially since a surgeon would be the most likely person to assess Vere's sanity; but Melville is at great pains to inform us that the surgeon is incapable of understanding. He, not Vere, is like Pilate, for despite his conviction of Vere's guilt he does not act. Immediately thereafter we learn that few dare to pronounce on a man's sanity except professional experts "for a fee" (p. 102). The surgeon, clearly, is not a man to be trusted. Later the surgeon and the purser discuss Billy's stillness at the moment of the hanging; the surgeon doubts anything that is not scientific, which is another way of saying that he has no moral understanding, which is another way of saying that he is the person least qualified to express judgment on any moral issue. Actually, the whole tone of the conversation between the surgeon and the purser shows the latter's com-

---

5. The difficulty here might result from the unfinished state of the manuscript of *Billy Budd*.

plete obtuseness and perhaps thereby insists on Vere's sanity, especially since Melville has told us that Vere and Billy share "in the rarer qualities of our nature—so rare indeed as to be all but incredible to average minds however much cultivated." (pp. 114-15)

Even though the bulk of the plot material relating to Vere either clearly or indirectly presents him as an ideal, the final meaning of *Billy Budd* is not the simple acceptance of Vere and the social morality he represents. To show the complexity both of Melville's acceptance and of his technique, I shall retell the *story* once more, and then repeat it, the second time emphasizing the elements of the plot. The story is that a young sailor, impressed aboard a British man-o'-war, incurs the unmotivated enmity of one of the crew, is falsely accused by him, kills him in a flash of instinctive anger, and is tried and hanged. The story, along with those elements of the plot which support it, especially the many allusions to Billy's natural innocence and Claggart's natural depravity, recognizes that evil exists in the world and that it is powerful enough to destroy the good; the story is bleakly pessimistic.

The plot, though, is a different matter. Baby Budd, who has just reached the age of manhood, is forced to go from the *Rights-of-Man* to His Majesty's Ship the *Bellipotent,* commanded by Edward (guardian of the realm) Fairfax (fair facts) Vere (truth, manliness). Baby Budd is tempted by the serpent; although he does not yield to the temptation, he does yield to his naive (primitive, natural) nature by refusing to act responsibly. He is accused of a crime of which he is not guilty (a formal, "social" mutiny; he is guilty of a private mutiny), and kills the accuser-tempter-serpent. The Captain forces a court-martial and accuses Baby Budd of the right crime—failure to accept his social responsibility—but is forced to punish him for the technical crime because of the limited understanding of his officers. Billy is eventually executed, and Vere is mortally wounded in a successful engagement with the *Athée* (the *Atheist*). Is it too much to suggest that the battle with the *Athée* is an externalization of Vere's personal engagement with Billy? Billy, after all, is a creature of the *Rights-of-Man*, a ship named after a book written in defense of the French Revolution. If so, then Billy, like the French Revolution, is an instance of the impossibility of translating an ideal morality into a less than ideal social world.

The opposition between the story and the major elements of the plot, then, embodies the conflict in Melville's own mind between the claims of natural moral law and social law; and further, the growing attention he gave to Vere as the manuscript grew and the sheer bulk and importance of those plot elements that run counter to the thematic implications of the story show that Melville was forced—reluctantly, regretfully, and even painfully—to the realization that man, because he must live in the social world, must abide by its laws.

Arthur Mizener

CHARACTER AND ACTION IN THE CASE OF CRISEYDE

A good deal of attention has been devoted to the question of Chaucer's intention when he created the character of Criseyde. Almost all answers have as their starting point a common assumption: that Chaucer was doing his best to create a unified character in the modern sense of the phrase. They start, that is, from the assumption that Chaucer meant Criseyde's character and actions to appear all of a piece and from the fact that he made her false to Troilus in the end. Only two conclusions are possible on the basis of these premises: either Chaucer intended Criseyde's character to appear compatible with her betrayal of Troilus from the first, or he intended it to appear to change during the course of the narrative in response to the events. The first of these conclusions, with its assumption as to Chaucer's conception of things, is the one most frequently encountered.

Professor Root, for example, concludes that Criseyde was intended to appear calculating, emotionally shallow, and a drifter from the first. Concrete evidence for hypotheses of this general type can be provided only by making very subtle psychological analyses of carefully selected details of the poem, on the tacit assumptions that Chaucer (1) thought of Criseyde as living a very complex inner life and (2) deliberately chose to reveal the nature of that inner life clearly only by the most indirect hints. Professor Root speaks of the line 'Tendre herted, slydynge of corage'[1]— which Chaucer took over from Benoit—as if this were the key to Criseyde's character.[2] It is difficult enough to believe that Chaucer would put the whole burden of clarifying Criseyde's motive for betraying Troilus on a half line near the end of the poem, and even more difficult to believe that he could have meant it to outweigh the import of the preceding five and one half lines, even if it be assumed that this passage is intended as an

From *PMLA*, LIV (March 1939) 65-81. Reprinted by permission of the Modern Language Association.

1. v, 825.—All references are to *Chaucer's Troilus and Criseyde*, ed. R. K. Root (Princeton, 1926).

2. *The Poetry of Chaucer* (Boston, 1922), p. 114. 'Slydynge of corage' is interpreted as meaning emotionally shallow and inclined to be fickle (see Professor Root's note to this line in his edition of the poem).

explanation of Criseyde's motives rather than a simple listing of the general qualities of her character.

But the main difficulty with this type of explanation is not the doubtfulness of these interpretations of details. It must be shown either (1) that Chaucer meant them as the essence of his intention, the rest of the poem to the contrary notwithstanding, or (2) that the hypothesis which is in accord with these interpretations fits the implications of the rest of the poem. The first of these alternatives is manifestly impossible. And it is impossible, too, to show in detail that the calm, essentially innocent but prudent, and finally deeply moved woman of the early part of the poem was intended to appear so morally instable that her betrayal of Troilus is a natural consequence of her character.

Professor Kittredge's more convincing explanation also suffers from the fact that he tries to find in Criseyde's character the cause of her unfaithfulness: 'As Cressida is at the beginning, such is she to the end; amorous, gentle, affectionate, and charming altogether, but fatally impressionable and yielding.'[3] Is it possible to believe that Chaucer intended to convey such an impression when he lengthened Boccaccio's period of wooing, when he was so careful to point out that Criseyde did not fall in love suddenly and to describe her admirable conduct in her difficult situation in Troy? Are not all these changes made so that Criseyde shall not appear 'impressionable and yielding' at the beginning? Yet only by believing that she is meant to appear some such thing as this can we explain her unfaithfulness on the assumption Professors Root and Kittredge make.[4]

It may appear gratuitous to say that Criseyde is unfaithful because the story makes her so, but it is just the insufficient attention given to this possibility which has made it seem necessary to prove that there was from the start some tragic flaw in her character which motivated her betrayal of Troilus.[5] The purpose of this essay is to suggest a different hypothesis of Chaucer's conception of character and its relation to events from the one which previous critics have used, and to test that hypothesis by analyzing Criseyde. This hypothesis is that for Chaucer a character consisted in a group of unchanging fundamental qualities, and that the relation between such a character and the events of the narrative was one of congruence rather than of cause and effect. This hypothesis is the outgrowth of a conviction that Chaucer's chief interest

3. *Chaucer and his Poetry* (Cambridge, 1915), p. 135. 'Baffling alike to us and to herself' (*ibid.*, p. 126), he adds elsewhere, as if Chaucer intended us not to be able to understand her.

4. Mr. C. S. Lewis's more recent analysis of the meaning of Criseyde (*The Allegory of Love*, pp. 179-190) is of this general type. According to Mr. Lewis we are meant to see Criseyde as from beginning to end governed by an almost pathological fear ('a dash of what is now called mazochism'); this theory leads him to argue that Chaucer meant the reader to see Criseyde's remarks at the last meeting of the lovers as 'desperate speeches in which Creseide, with pitiful ignorance of her self, attempts to assume the role of comforter . . .' and that he meant her resolutions to return to Troy after she had reached the Greek camp to be seen by the reader as 'desperate efforts to rise above herself.'

5. 'Emphasis cannot be too strong when placed upon the fact that in *Troilus and Criseyde* an absolutely inescapable necessity governs the progress of the story.' W. C. Curry, 'Destiny in Chaucer's *Troilus*,' *PMLA*, XLV (1930), 152.

was in the action rather than in the characters.[6] If this conviction be valid, the arrangement of his narrative was determined primarily by a desire to develop fully the dramatic possibilities of the action, not by a desire to reveal the characters of the personages in the narrative by making motivation the significant aspect of it. The subtlety and richness of such a narrative, in so far as it is a matter of character alone, will be, not in the reader's sense that each episode is a further revelation of profoundly analyzed motives, but in his sense of how perfectly Chaucer has visualized a character of unchanging fundamental qualities in a series of situations which are there because they are necessary to the action. Certainly everyone will agree that Chaucer knew, and knew how to show the reader, precisely how a character of a certain kind would respond in a given situation. The point in question, therefore, is not the subtlety of Chaucer's observation of humanity but only whether he intended us to take each observation as a hint toward the efficient causes of the successive situations of the narrative or as part of the adequate realization of the character in a situation the efficient cause of which lay elsewhere. It is a question of whether Chaucer does not, for the sake of the action, sometimes omit what is necessary for a complete explanation of events in terms of characters, sometimes distort what needs to be clear for that purpose, and even put into the mouths of various characters remarks which are appropriate to them on no theory of character.

Chaucer's method of characterization is, in this view, essentially static: a character is presented, that is, shown as made up of certain characteristics such as pity or generosity; and then, by the events of the story, it is placed in various circumstances in which it always acts in accord with these characteristics. Chaucer's characters do not change or develop under the impact of experience; they display various aspects of an established set of characteristics as the progress of the narrative places them in varying circumstances. Conversely, the events of the narrative are not determined by the particular moral qualities ascribed to the characters. It would not occur to a mind which conceived of the relationship of character and event in this fashion to ask how a person

6. The allied problem of the connection between Chaucer's conception of character on the one hand and of Fortune and Destiny on the other is far too complex to be taken up here. But see W. C. Curry, 'Destiny in Chaucer's *Troilus,' PMLA,* xlv (1930), 129-168; H. R. Patch, 'Troilus on Determinism,' *Speculum,* vi (1931), 225-243; and William Farnham, *The Medieval Heritage of Elizabethan Tragedy* (Berkeley, 1936), especially pp. 155-157. Professor Patch, if I understand him correctly, argues that any narrative in which there is not 'the interplay of free motivation' is 'the spectacle of the action of irresponsible puppets.' If this line of reasoning be valid, then it must follow from the argument of this essay that Chaucer was a complete determinist, a conclusion which is certainly open to question. But Professor Patch's line of reasoning seems to me not only to involve a confusion of literal and metaphorical statements (it is only by metaphor that one can speak meaningfully of any characters as 'irresponsible puppets' since literally speaking all characters are just that) but also to over-simplify the problem by assuming that there must be a direct connection between an author's narrative method and his philosophic opinions. Some kind of connection no doubt always exists, but surely it is not such that one can conclude that all narratives except those which provide a tight cause-and-effect relationship between the characters and the events are evidence of their author's disbelief in the freedom of the human will and the responsibility of human beings for their own acts.

who exhibited a certain character in one set of circumstances could possibly have acted so as to get himself into certain other circumstances; because in this conception the personages of the narrative do not get themselves into circumstances; the circumstances are primarily determined by the necessities of the action.

Whatever the advantages of the modern method, devised for a narrative in which the primary interest is the revealing of character, there can be no question that it involves the sacrifice of many of the dramatic effects which were possible with Chaucer's method. One such effect of major importance is the tragic emphasis Chaucer is able to manage in the Fifth Book; but on a smaller scale such effects are to be found everywhere in the poem.

Our conviction that in real life or in a psychological novel the Criseyde of the Fifth Book must have been different from the Criseyde of the early books to act as she did is no doubt true. And that Chaucer should have intended to imply no causal interaction between what Criseyde does and what she is therefore runs counter to all our habits of thought on this subject. Yet Chaucer's poem, looked at without prejudice, offers, I believe, no evidence that he intended Criseyde's unfaithfulness to appear either the cause of a change, or the consequence of an established vice, in the character he presents to us. In fact, there are grounds for an initial presumption to the contrary, for it is only if there is a contrast between what she is and what she does that Criseyde's fate is tragic. A Criseyde whose fall is the product either of an inherent vice or of a change for the worse in her character is at best an object of pathos. The argument here is, then, that from the beginning to the end of the poem Criseyde, whenever described or shown in action,

> sobre was, ek symple, and wys withal,
> The best ynorisshed ek that myghte be,
> And goodly of hire speche in general,
> Charitable, estatlich, lusty, and fre;
> Ne nevere mo ne lakkede hire pite;
> Tendre herted, slydynge of corage; . . .

Criseyde's first prolonged appearance in the narrative is the interview with Pandar in the Second Book. Before that her beauty is described and a brief account is given of her conduct at the time Calchas left Troy. Chaucer departs radically from Boccaccio in this scene when he introduces the long preliminary skirmish between Pandar and Criseyde. This addition permits him, among other things, to present at leisure Criseyde's character: her charm, intelligence, feminine simplicity, and sensitiveness. Having established the character, Chaucer then returns to Boccaccio for the main outline of the action.

In the matter of character, as in so many other matters,[7] an adequate explanation of Boccaccio's poem is not necessarily an adequate explanation of Chaucer's. By this time Chaucer has created a fixed character and, even when he translates directly, the effect against such a back-

7. See Karl Young, 'Chaucer's "Troilus and Criseyde" as Romance,' *PMLA*, LIII (1938), p. 39.

ground is very different from that in Boccaccio, for what Chaucer borrows operates in a different context. This different effect is no accident, but the deliberately planned consequence of Chaucer's art. In the scene where Pandar reveals Troilus's love, for example, Chaucer's Criseyde senses that Pandar is about to say something important and lowers her eyes just before he tells of Troilus's love; in Boccaccio the revelation is made before Criseyde exhibits any signs of embarrassment.[8] By this slight change Chaucer makes his heroine appear, unlike Boccaccio's, both modest and sensitive to the implications of a social situation. In Chaucer's account, too, Criseyde's subsequent question as to how Pandar discovered Troilus's love impresses the reader as a typical example of the innocent curiosity which is generally believed to be characteristic of women under these circumstances. But in Boccaccio Criseyde, having just subscribed heartily to Pandar's 'gather ye rosebuds' speech, then adds:

> But let us now stop thinking of this, and tell me whether I may still have solace and joy [giuoco] of love, and in what way thou didst first take note of Troilus.

Boccaccio's Criseyde is a practical young lady arranging an affair. Chaucer, using much the same material, so arranges it as to convey a very different impression of his heroine. The delicacy and complexity of this scene can hardly be exaggerated, and it is difficult to see how anyone can find evidence in the character presented for Criseyde's later action. Only the supposed necessity for finding weaknesses in her can have led people to read them into this fine rendering of an admirable woman.

The implications of the next scene are not so obvious and will probably be determined ultimately on the basis of the reader's conception of Chaucer's main intentions. A great deal has been made of it as evidence for Criseyde's cold-blooded, calculating nature. But to call Criseyde's consideration of all the factors involved in her acceptance or refusal of Troilus calculating seems to me possible only if one fails to recognize the difficulty and complexity of her situation. She would not appear either sober or prudent if she were to rush into the affair without considering that in her precarious situation in Troy, Troilus might easily have her 'in despit,' or without thinking over carefully the disadvantages of the change.

A more significant point about this scene, however, is the fact that Chaucer does not motivate Criseyde's falling in love. In Boccaccio Troilus does not go by her house until after her meditation and only then Criseyde 'praised to herself his manner, his pleasing actions, and his courtesy, and so suddenly was she captivated that she desired him above every other good.' This apparently struck Chaucer as producing an undesirable effect, for he shifted this scene so that it comes before Criseyde's meditation. It was not that Chaucer saw any psychological inadequacy in love-at-first-sight, for he used it without hesitation in the

8. II, 38. The references to Boccaccio are to *The Filostrato of Giovanni Boccaccio*, trans. N. E. Griffin and A. B. Myrick (Philadelphia, 1929).

case of Troilus. Nor does he, in Criseyde's case any more than in Troilus's, describe a gradual change in her psychological attitude leading eventually to her being in love. He simply states, quite flatly, that the process was gradual. This change was not made, then, so that Chaucer might describe Criseyde's development from one state of mind to another.

Chaucer is anxious, however, that Criseyde's attitude in this scene should appear congruous with her established character, and that is the positive consequence of his shifting the location of Troilus's ride past Criseyde's house in the sequence of the narrative. In Boccaccio Criseyde's meditation follows immediately upon Pandar's revelation that some one, not known to her personally, is in love with her. She thus appears to be weighing the joys of love (of a sort) against its risks, and the reader gains the impression that she is a shrewd and sensual young lady for whom the sight of Troilus's elegant person in the end turns the scales. In Chaucer's poem, on the other hand, despite his protest that Criseyde's glimpse of Troilus was only the beginning of love, we come to her soliloquy with a vivid memory of Criseyde gazing out the window at Troilus and wondering 'who yaf me drynke?' This soliloquy, as a result of Chaucer's change in the narrative sequence, is bound to be read as the thoughts of a person already in love with Troilus. If Chaucer's purpose was to reveal the development of Criseyde's character, then he has either deliberately and unaccountably tried to confuse the reader at this point or he has without deliberation blundered into doing so. For he has created an impression of Criseyde's feelings the existence of which he himself denies. If on the other hand his purpose was to make us read Criseyde's soliloquy, not as 'cool calculation' but as the meditation of a prudent but tender-hearted woman in love, and at the same time to make us remember her as having fallen in love slowly, then this shift in the sequence of the narrative is masterly.

The first exchange of letters between Troilus and Criseyde also raises the question of how Chaucer intended the reader to interpret Criseyde's attitude. Critics have believed that this scene was intended by Chaucer to illustrate Criseyde's tendency to drift into things. There is no drifting earlier in the poem, for no one with a knowledge of courtly love can doubt Criseyde's sincere belief in Pandar's threat that unless she yields a little both he and Troilus will die. Criseyde yields there quite deliberately to what appears to her serious necessity; she does not drift. And in this scene she conducts herself as any intelligent but modest lady would. When she accepts Troilus's letter she consciously takes the first step on the long road to the goal of courtly love; the way in which she at first refuses this letter shows she is perfectly aware of what it means to accept it. And when she writes Troilus she takes quite consciously again (as Chaucer himself tells us) another.

In both Chaucer and Boccaccio Troilus's letter is given, and then Criseyde laughs; in Boccaccio she laughs at this speech of Pandar's:

A strange thing is this to consider that at what is most desired by her sex each lady should, in the presence of others, show herself annoyed and vexed. I have spoken to thee so much of this matter that thenceforth thou shouldst not play the prude with me.

No such speech is the cause of Criseyde's laughter in Chaucer, given her established and now familiar character in this situation it is very evident that she is incapable of the light-hearted cynicism of Boccaccio's heroine. At the same time she must act deliberately. Chaucer's task is to make her appear definite but neither cynical nor immodest. The definiteness is there, for not only the embarrassment at the moment when Pandar gives her the letter, but the tacit assumption on his part after dinner that she has read it are evidence that they both clearly understood the implications of Criseyde's taking the letter. Yet even in Chaucer's times those implications had their embarrassing side for such a genteel if unhypocritical lady as Criseyde. She therefore attempts to prevent their appearing as it were naked between Pandar and herself by smiling and remarking

> em, I preye,
> Swich answere as yow list youre self purveye;
> For, trewely, I nyl no lettre write.

And Pandar, realizing that this is not really a refusal at all but an exhibition of tact, accepts the turn Criseyde is trying to give the conversation and replies in kind with an equally tactful little joke. 'Therwith she lough, and seyde: "go we dyne."' The subtlety with which Chaucer visualizes and communicates the attitude of his character in this situation can probably not be exaggerated. But there is nothing in that attitude which suggests a character capable of the ultimate betrayal of Troilus, and nothing in Chaucer's narrative which justifies the assumption that he intended it to suggest such a character.

The decorous slowness with which Criseyde falls in love is further emphasized by Chaucer's introducing a second scene in which Troilus passes by her house and by his carefully pointing out that it is far too soon for Criseyde to consider yielding to Troilus, a thing she does not do for a considerable time. Criseyde, when she sees Troilus pass by for the second time, definitely becomes very much in love, and from this point on Chaucer assumes that we understand that fact.

When Criseyde encounters Troilus at Deiphebus's house she acts exactly as we should expect, calmly and with a complete understanding of the situation and the meaning of all that is said. She loves Troilus and she is perfectly clear as to what that involves. It is difficult to imagine how Chaucer, short of showing her making the advances, could have done more to prevent her appearing to 'drift genially with circumstance,' for the progress in the relations of the two lovers made at Deiphebus's house is almost entirely due to her. Her acceptance of Troilus is characteristically deliberate and unambiguous, for all its delicacy. Certainly there was no question in the minds of Pandar and Troilus of Criseyde's meaning or of the magnitude of her decision.

As a question of character there is no necessity for Pandar's elaborate scheme for bringing Troilus and Criseyde together. But by inventing this scene Chaucer adds a tensely dramatic situation to the action. The introduction of this material is justified on these grounds; it cannot be justified on the grounds that the development of the character demanded it. For if Chaucer had been interested in the changes in Criseyde's mind which led up to her attitude at the moment Pandar came in with his cock and bull story about Orestes, he would have centered his attention in that. But he does not, and the result for the reader who does is unhappy. Chaucer, so the explanation runs, makes it clear that Criseyde sees through Pandar when, while inviting her to his house for supper, he implies that Troilus is out of town. But if Criseyde's action through the events of the night at Pandar's house must be explained in terms of a Criseyde who knew all along that Pandar was manoeuvering her into Troilus's arms, then her attitude, when Pandar comes in with his tale of Troilus's jealousy, must be put down as pure hypocrisy. Can any one read this last passage and believe that Chaucer meant Criseyde to appear hypocritical in her protestations?

If, however, we assume that this scene was introduced primarily because it is necessary to the complete development of the action, and not because it plots a point on the curve of Criseyde's gradual demoralization, and look at Chaucer's portrayal of Criseyde in this scene, not as his attempt to reveal what characteristic in her caused the scene to occur, but as his attempt to visualize how a woman of the type he has shown Criseyde to be all along would act if placed in this situation, then, it seems to me, the full subtlety of Chaucer's portrayal becomes clear. Every single word and gesture fits Chaucer's fixed character perfectly, reasserts with apparently inexhaustible variety of detail one or another of the qualities which he has already ascribed to her. She is seriously concerned at Troilus's jealousy and eager to explain to him. For, believing Pandar's tale, she assumes that an explanation is what is required. It is her affection for Troilus which finally makes her do what Pandar says will satisfy Troilus, however foolish it may seem to her. Her eagerness to help Troilus when he faints is again not the acting of hypocrisy but the result of sincere and affectionate anxiety. And at last there is her famous flash of humor when Troilus takes her in his arms.

Every word of Criseyde's in the scene is just what would be expected from the woman Chaucer has described, were she placed in the situation of the story. In that sense, psychology of the subtlest kind abounds, but in the sense that what she says is an explanation of her past or future behavior it does not. If an attempt, for example, is made to consider Criseyde's statement that she would not be there had she not yielded long before as an explanation of her state of mind during what has preceded, rather than as a reassertion of her sense of humor, there is again the necessity of explaining her attitude when Pandar tells of Troilus's jealousy. Once again only the assumption that she was playing the hypocrite will serve, and Chaucer has given us every reason to suppose Criseyde is quite sincere when she offers to see Troilus the next day and explain everything. There is not an ounce of hypocrisy in Criseyde up to this point; what reason could there be for Chaucer's making her suddenly acquire it? And yet there is no escaping a belief in her hypocrisy unless it is accepted that Chaucer had no intention of revealing

Criseyde's motives here, but only of keeping her attitude consonant with her established character.

Somewhat similar motives have been read into the scene the next morning when Pandar comes to Criseyde's room and asks with assumed anxiety if the rain has disturbed her sleep. This beautiful presentation of two witty but tactful people has been considered as evidence that Criseyde was not much in love with Troilus,[9] since she can joke about it. But to this Professor Kittredge's answer is sufficiently devastating: 'It is ridiculous to accuse her of insincerity in her love for Troilus. To be sincere, it is not necessary to be either solemn or stupid.'[10]

The ending of the poem, especially the Fifth Book, shows most clearly Chaucer's method and its purpose. It is Criseyde who, true to her character, offers most of the practical suggestions when it comes to making plans for her return, it is she who brings hope and wisdom and a plan to the final meeting of the lovers; while Troilus, true to his character also, does little except tell of his love and sorrow. That Criseyde is to be thought of not as a deliberate hypocrite or facile optimist, but as perfectly sincere and determined to return soon cannot be questioned, for Chaucer is careful to tell us these things in his own words. That is, the woman in this scene is exactly the same as she is in every other place in the poem, just as the man is. Yet in the face of Chaucer's word that Criseyde means all she says, she says a great many things which, while they are exactly what we expect from the character, cannot be brought into accord with her later conduct. They are true to her character in the circumstances in which they are spoken, and they both heighten the tragic effect of the parting and emphasize by their very sincerity the tragic irony of the scene.

But if Criseyde's words here are not meant as hypocrisy or the self-deception of a weak and shallow nature, perhaps the discrepancy between her professions and subsequent actions may be reconciled (and the tragic irony removed) by arguing that she encountered overwhelming obstacles to her plans when she got to the Greek camp and that it was impossible for her to return to Troy:

> . . . she soon discovers that she has matched her woman's wit, not against her dotard father merely, but against the doom of Troy. No pretexts avail, not because Calchas suspects her plot, but because he knows that the city is destined to destruction.[11]

This line of reasoning, unfortunately, ignores Chaucer's poem. For it is after Criseyde has realized the hopelessness of persuading her father that she finally determines to return to Troy in spite of all the difficulties she has been running over in her mind.

Mr. Graydon has worked out with great ingenuity the most probable chronology of the Fifth Book; Chaucer (for good reasons) deliberately obscures the evidence for it and once even professes ignorance of it.

9. Joseph M. Beatty, Jr., 'Mr. Graydon's "Defense of Criseyde," ' *SP*, XXVI (1929), 472.
10. G. L. Kittredge, *op. cit.*, p. 133.
11. G. L. Kittredge, *op. cit.*, p. 120.

But if Chaucer had any chronology in mind at all, it must have been some such one as Mr. Graydon suggests. As nearly as can be determined Criseyde's second letter, which practically states she will not return, is written more than two months after her departure, and her yielding to Diomede comes about two years after her departure.

But all through the Fifth Book Chaucer avoids this chronological sequence. His purpose is to describe the sorrow of Troilus, and to heighten the tragic appearance of that sorrow, and the arrangement of the narrative for that purpose inevitably involves what seems to the reader who is looking for an orderly development and explanation of character, an unaccountable confusion of the chronology of events. The whole story of Criseyde is presented at the beginning of the Fifth Book down to the time she gives herself to Diomede, a period of about two years. Chaucer then goes back to the ninth day after her departure from Troy and takes up his description of Troilus's sorrow. By concealing such chronological references as he gives and by telling of Criseyde's fall in comparatively few words, Chaucer gives the impression that that fall is very rapid. With this defection and its apparent undignified haste fresh in the reader's mind, he describes Troilus on the Trojan walls sighing his soul towards the Grecian tents, pathetically confident that each approaching figure is Criseyde. Chaucer has arranged the sequence of the events in the narrative in the order which will give the maximum effectiveness to the tragic scene. This arrangement hopelessly muddles in the reader's mind any possible chronology, so necessary if we are to follow the development of Criseyde's character. Yet Troilus's sorrow would be infinitely less pathetic if Chaucer were to say: 'And as a matter of fact, just about this time Criseyde was courageously determining to return to Troy.' If Chaucer had centered his purpose in the development of the characters, something like that would have been necessary, but since his purpose was to create a tragic action, it was not only unnecessary but highly undesirable.

All through these final scenes this purpose is apparent. Criseyde, rather surprisingly, has by far the larger number of protestations of love and loyalty. They were not meant to prove her either a hypocrite or a moral weakling. Each of them is true to Chaucer's static characterization of her, and each of them, against the background of the reader's knowledge of the future, has an ironic effect in terms of the action. Troilus accuses Criseyde of disloyalty long before she has actually contemplated any such thing. This accusation was certainly not intended by Chaucer to prove Troilus's unreasoning jealousy, as Mr. Graydon argues, but merely to give the impression that the fatal conclusion of the action was rapidly and irresistibly approaching. As soon as Criseyde is out of Troy, Pandar suddenly becomes certain she will never return. No reason for this opinion is given, and it utterly contradicts his previous serious and considered praise of Criseyde's integrity. This change of front is unmotivated. It serves the purpose of heightening by contrast the tragic irony of Troilus's confidence that Criseyde will return; it is not a hint of Criseyde's motive for not returning.

There is, finally, the crux of the poem so far as this question of Criseyde's character is concerned, that is, her unfaithfulness. Her soliloquy on the ninth night in the Greek camp is so similar to her earlier meditation on whether she ought to yield to Troilus or not that it is difficult to avoid comparing them. In each she considers carefully all the facts involved and in each reaches a definite decision; in the latter soliloquy her decision is that she will go to Troy in spite of all the difficulties. It is not easy to see how the woman presented in this soliloquy differs in any fundamental respect from the woman of the earlier parts of the poem. And the difficulty of believing Chaucer meant this speech to be taken as an indication that Criseyde was 'calculating' is as great as the difficulty of believing that that was his intention in writing her soliloquy on love in Book Two. Furthermore, instead of describing a change in her attitude subsequent to this soliloquy which we are to take as the cause of her staying with the Greeks, Chaucer merely states in five brief lines that she did stay, that two months later she was still in the Greek camp. Criseyde's failure to return to Troy is one of the necessary events in the story Chaucer is telling. The whole structure of the poem at this point shows that he did not think of it as determined by Criseyde's character.

Nor does Chaucer, in any serious psychological sense, motivate Criseyde's physical betrayal of Troilus. She betrays Troilus because the action requires it, because she had to if the tragic possibilities of the main action, 'the double sorwe of Troilus,' were to be worked out completely, and not because of anything in her character which made that betrayal inevitable. Chaucer says she is guilty, but he never shows us a woman whose state of mind is such as to make the reader believe her capable of betraying Troilus. In fact, Chaucer carefully avoids showing the reader Criseyde at all from the time when she makes her last statement of loyalty to Troilus to the time when she expresses her grief at her betrayal of him. He even refuses to say that 'she yaf hym [i.e., Diomede] hire herte,' and there is what appears to be a conscious effort on Chaucer's part to blur Criseyde's inconstancy in the reader's mind as much as he can without destroying belief in it altogether. The nearest Chaucer comes to offering on his own account (as apart from dramatically presenting) a reason for Criseyde's betrayal of Troilus is to hint at one in the stanza in which he explains why she did not return to Troy. But this reason is not psychologically reconcilable with the character displayed by Criseyde. No conceivable character capable of acting as Criseyde did for this reason can be brought into accord with the woman presented in the first four and one half books of the poem or with the woman who was grief-stricken 'whan that she falsed Troilus.'

The Criseyde we are shown, both before and after the event of her yielding to Diomede, displays exactly the same characteristics we have associated with Criseyde since the beginning of the narrative. It is difficult to believe that Chaucer was not conscious of the consequences of this arrangement of the narrative. It leaves us knowing that Criseyde has betrayed Troilus and yet visualizing her, as we have from the start, as gentle, tender-hearted, loving and honorable. In other words, Chaucer's arrangement is calculated to leave our sense of Criseyde's character as little affected as possible by our knowledge of her act, it does the best it can to prevent our substituting for the Criseyde we have known all along the character we must invent if we are successfully to imagine Criseyde's yielding to Diomede.

The hypothesis that Chaucer meant to ascribe to Criseyde a character calculated to explain her betrayal of Troilus seems to me to break down most completely at this most crucial point. For one thing, it is so incompatible with Chaucer's treatment of this part of the narrative that in order to set it up in the first place the critic must rewrite the poem in his imagination, at least to the extent of adding a new scene. For another, it requires proof that Chaucer has shown Criseyde as consistently 'impressionable and yielding' or psychopathically terrified from the first, and it seems to me impossible to present this proof without distorting the implications of the first four books of the poem. Finally, such an explanation prevents the reader from seeing Criseyde as a tragic figure. If Criseyde's character is such as to be a complete explanation of her betrayal of Troilus then she is at best merely pathetic; it is only if there is a contrast between what she seems to the reader to be and what he knows her to have done that she becomes tragic. It may be argued, of course, that Chaucer invented her only as an instrument for producing the tragedy of Troilus, but if he intended Criseyde, in addition, to be tragic in her own right, then he must have aimed at this contrast between what she is and what she does, a contrast which we destroy if we insist on seeing her as no better than she should be.

In real life as we believe it to be or in a psychological novel that contrast would be impossible. For in these worlds deeds are the outward manifestations of a process of which the inward manifestations are congruous thoughts and feelings. In them, therefore, people cannot approach and look back upon an act of inconstancy rebelling against it with their whole natures, any more than they can take this attitude while committing murder. But Chaucer's Criseyde, not living in such a world, can and does rebel against her own act, Chaucer shows her as horrified at her disloyalty, regretful of the loss of her good name and greatly admiring Troilus. Is not this precisely the attitude to be expected from the woman portrayed in the first four books of the poem had she to face the situation in which Criseyde finds herself? Chaucer could scarcely have portrayed her in this fashion had he meant us to think of her character as now degenerated to the point where her betrayal of Troilus is the perfect manifestation of it, and he certainly would not have so portrayed her, here or elsewhere, had he meant us to think of her as capable of that betrayal from the start.

From this point forward Chaucer's arrangement of the narrative is governed by his wish to emphasize the sorrow of Troilus. Criseyde's suffering and her hope that she may yet return to Troy, even though she has overstayed her ten days, are presented just before Chaucer describes her thoughts as she decides—Troilus and Troy being forgotten—to remain in the Greek camp. This sequence is incongruous, so far as any explanation of her character goes, but it strengthens the pathos of her peroration on Troilus which follows and so heightens the tragedy.

When Criseyde's first letter from the Greek camp is summarized, Chaucer very definitely gives the impression that the letter is not quite honest, and advises Troilus to give up any hope of Criseyde. This impression is contrary to what we can, if we wish, prove to be the 'facts,' for Chaucer tells us elsewhere that the letter was written about two months after Criseyde's departure, and on Chaucer's own say-so she was at that period not at all entangled with Diomede and probably had not yet ceased to hope she might return to Troy. But these 'facts' must not be allowed to obtrude here, for they would interrupt the steady and fatal progression of Troilus's tragedy. The 'false' impression that Chaucer gives furthers that tragedy; it makes us sympathize with Troilus's growing belief that Criseyde has been unfaithful to him, and that is Chaucer's purpose.

The same method is followed with Criseyde's second letter. There is no way of knowing exactly when it was written or whether Criseyde is lying. Chaucer does not even bother to provide this information so vital to a complete understanding of Criseyde's character. The letter is part of Troilus's fate; it completes his tragedy.

So, it seems to me, Criseyde is meant to be taken. Her character is a combination of subtly observed characteristics, and the illusion of reality that character leaves on a reader's mind is the result, not of Chaucer's painstaking motivation of every event from within the character, but rather of the variety and concreteness with which he puts these characteristics on display in any scene in which the character is presented. The character of Criseyde is primarily an instrument for, and a unit in, a tragic action; it is therefore statically conceived and is related to the action by congruence rather than by cause and effect. For both Troilus and Criseyde are the victims of an act determined, not by Criseyde's character, but by the dramatic necessities of the action.

Outlook

J. Hillis Miller

THE CREATION OF THE SELF
IN GERARD MANLEY HOPKINS

Seen from one point of view Hopkins' work is some dozen nearly perfect lyrics. Seen from another perspective it is a heterogeneous collection of documents: poems, fragments of poems, letters, notebooks, undergraduate papers, lecture notes, incomplete commentaries, sermons, and so on. But within this seemingly chaotic mass we can detect a certain persistent structure. It is not a structure of abstract thought, nor is it a pattern of concrete images. To create this structure the world of sense perception has been transformed, through its verbalization, into the very substance of thought, and, one may say, into the very substance of Hopkins himself. This paper has as its limited objective the attempt to reveal this pervasive imaginative structure. One of its chief limitations is the necessity of describing discursively and seriatim what is really the nontemporal interior world of Hopkins, the total context in which any single poem exists and has its real meaning.

I

I find myself both as man and as myself something most determined and distinctive, at pitch, more distinctive and higher pitched than anything else I see.[1]

It would seem that the problem of individuation is solved for Hopkins with his first awareness of himself. No one has had a more intense apprehension of the uniqueness and substantiality of his own identity. Hopkins' version of the Descartean *Cogito* is: "I taste myself, therefore I exist." "My selfbeing," says Hopkins, "my consciousness and feeling of myself, that taste of myself, of *I* and *me* above and in all things . . . is more distinctive than the taste of ale or alum, more distinctive than the smell of walnutleaf or camphor, and is incommunicable by any means to another man (as when I was a child I used to ask myself: What must it be to be someone else?)."[2]

From *Journal of English Literary History* (December 1955), 293–319. Reprinted by permission of The Johns Hopkins Press.

1. Humphrey House, ed., *The Notebooks and Papers of Gerard Manley Hopkins* (London, 1937), p. 309.
   2. *Id.*

The self for Hopkins, in the very first moment in which it recognizes itself, recognizes itself not as a lack, an appeal, but as a plenitude. It does not need to seek something outside of itself as a source of its life, because that life has already been given. One finds oneself, from the beginning, a "throng and stack of being, so rich, so distinctive."[3] No one could be less like Mallarmé, for whom the moment of selfconsciousness was the moment of a paralyzing sense of emptiness. Nor does self-awareness for Hopkins depend, as it does in the long tradition coming down from Locke, on sense perception of the external world. Much less does it depend on a *relation* to that world. No, Hopkins' *Cogito* is neither a purely intellectual self-consciousness arrived at by putting in doubt and separating from oneself everything which seems to come from the outside, nor is it the Lockean self-awareness which springs out of psychological nothingness in the moment of sensation. It is, like the first, entirely independent of the exterior world, since, for Hopkins, "when I compare myself, my being myself, with anything else whatever, all things alike, all in the same degree, rebuff me with blank unlikeness; so that my knowledge of it, which is so intense, is from itself alone."[4]

The first moment of self-awareness is, then, not a thought, but a deeply organic sense experience which permeates the whole being, as in the famous formula of Condillac: "I am odor of rose." But it is a "taste of *oneself,*" not of anything whatsoever which comes from the outside: "The development, refinement, condensation of nothing shows any sign of being able to match this to me or give me another taste of it, a taste even resembling it."[5] The self is already fully existent as soon as one is aware of oneself at all, and seems to form an eternally subsisting tasting of oneself which prolongs itself from moment to moment as long as one endures. Since it remains exactly the same through time, it is apparently indestructible. If it extends beyond disembodied consciousness, it is only to include a minimal sense of one's incarnation, minimal because it is a sense of incarnation in a simple, spaceless body which is wholly undifferentiated, wholly made up of a single taste.

The Hopkinsian self is, then, positive and definite, and it is vividly *sensed,* in the same way that objects in the exterior world are sensed. Intrinsic identity is a primary datum for man. He does not need to *do* anything at all to come into existence or to guarantee himself continued existence. And this intense possession of the sensation of self is the occasion of an elated joy at one's interior richness and at one's independence. If Hopkins' "taste of myself" reminds one of Sartre's "nausea," it is more because of the striking difference than because of the similarity. Sartre's nausea is digust at the deeply organic sense of one's contingency, of the fact that one is not a free spirit, but is trapped in the flesh and enmeshed in a world of meaningless things. What is in Sartre a sickening sense of one's imprisonment in one's own unjustifiable material form is in Hopkins cause for rejoicing. For Hopkins the fact that "human nature" is "more highly pitched, selved, and distinctive than anything in the world" is proof that man is "life's pride

---

3. *Id.*
4. *Id.,* p. 310.
5. *Id.*

and cared-for crown."[6] Man is, it seems, sufficient unto himself, like God.

But beneath the rejoicing in Hopkins at the uniqueness and self-subsistence of each human individual there is another current of thought, a current wonder at this uniqueness, a wonder which shades off into a question, one of the fundamental metaphysical questions, a question which reinstates all the problems. If nothing "explains" or "resembles" this "unspeakable stress of pitch," if I "taste self but at one tankard, that of my own being," "from what then do I with all my being and above all that taste of self, that selfbeing, come?"[7]

II

The proof of the existence of God for Hopkins is neither from the evidence of the external world, nor from direct intuition. It is a logical deduction from the fact of one's own uniqueness:

> Nothing finite then can either begin to exist or eternally have existed of itself, because nothing can in the order of time or even of nature act before it exists or exercise function and determination before it has a nature to "function" and determine, to selve and instress, with.[8]

And if this is true for all created things, how much more true for human beings is it that they cannot be selfcreated and self-existent. In a radical about-face Hopkins sees that his apparently so independent self must, on the evidence of its very nature, depend on something outside of itself, must draw its existence from "one of finer or higher pitch and determination than itself."[9] So here, almost in the moment of rejoicing over the distinctiveness of the "taste of oneself," strikes the "terror" of God.[10] For if the Creator could do so much, so can he undo, or do with his creatures as he wishes. For Hopkins, "a self is an absolute which stands to the absolute of God as the infinitesimal to the infinite."[11] The question becomes, then, "What relation do I or should I have to this Being who is so infinitely my superior and so 'dangerous'[12] to me?"

The answer is simple and total: "Man was created. Like the rest then to praise, reverence, and serve God; to give him glory."[13] But how do God's creatures "give him glory"? Merely by being themselves, by *doing* themselves. Selfhood is not a static possession, but an activity:

> Each mortal thing does one thing and the same:
> Deals out that being indoors each one dwells;

6. W. H. Gardner, ed., *Poems of Gerard Manley Hopkins,* Third Edition (New York, 1948), p. 73.

7. *Notebooks,* p. 310.

8. *Id.,* p. 312.

9. *Id.,* p. 309.

10. *Poems,* p. 56.

11. *Notebooks,* p. 331.

12. *Poems,* p. 73.

13. *Notebooks,* p. 303.

Selves—goes itself; myself it speaks and spells;
Crying *What I do is me: for that I came.*[14]

But it is just here that a radical division among God's creatures appears. Each non-human creature exists in the absolute security of being unable to do other than what it came for. It cannot choose *not* "to fling out broad its name,"[15] and, in doing so, "make [God] known," "tell of him," "give him glory."[16] "What they can *they always do.*"[17] But if man can *mean* to give God glory, he can, necessarily, mean *not* to give him glory. His complete fulfillment of his nature, the selving for which he came, is radically contingent. If the full accomplishment of his being puts him "beyond all visible creatures,"[18] so also he can, because of his free will and its accompanying self-consciousness utterly fail to be, in a way no other of God's creatures can. So then, within the very development of Hopkins' apprehension of the nature of his self-being an amazing transformation takes place. What had seemed so solid and definite turns out to be merely a "positive infinitesimal,"[19] something that both exists and does not exist, like a point on a line. It is the mere potentiality of being, a self "intrinsically different from every other self," but a self to which a "nature" must be added.[20] What had seemed so self-subsistent is really very much like the Mallarméan "néant"; it is "nothing, a zero, in the score or account of existence":[21] "For the self before nature is no thing as yet but only possible; with the accession of a nature it becomes properly a self, for instance a person."[22]

Now we can see how the fearful experience recorded in the "terrible sonnets," utter paralysis of the will, and the accompanying spiritual vertigo, is possible, perhaps even necessary, given the premises of Hopkins' universe. Only the self-conscious mind of man can utterly fail to be and plunge downward into the abyss of complete nothingness, and only the mind of man can experience the terror of that plunge:

O the mind, mind has mountains; cliffs of fall
Frightful, sheer, no-man-fathomed. Hold them cheap
May who ne'er hung there. Nor does long our small
Durance deal with that steep or deep.[23]

And if it is only man who can taste himself, can be aware of his own being, it is also only man for whom that self-taste can be a terrifying experience of his isolation from God and from all things, an experience of complete enclosure within the prison of his own self-tormenting self:

14. *Poems*, p. 95.
15. *Id.*
16. *Notebooks*, p. 303.
17. *Id.*
18. *Id.*, p. 303.
19. *Id.*, p. 322.
20. *Id.*
21. *Id.*
22. *Id.*, p. 325.
23. *Poems*, p. 107.

> I am gall, I am heartburn. God's most deep decree
> Bitter would have me taste: my taste was me[24]

The self which had seemed so solid, so enduring and self-subsistent discovers not only that it is created, but that it absolutely requires help from outside itself in order to be, since to be necessarily means being able to selve, to *do* one's proper being. Without some relation to something outside oneself, man may remain paralyzed, a mere "positive infinitesimal," unable to transform possibility into actuality. Exiled within itself, caged in itself, the self discovers that far from sufficing to itself, it is, in its isolation, entirely impotent, as impotent as a eunuch. It is "time's eunuch,"[25] that is, it is wholly unable to project into the future an action and then carry that action out. Instead of a growth, change, accomplishment matching the passage of time and filling it, such as we find in non-human creatures, man in his desolation finds that he is plunged into a subterranean darkness where time has lengthened out into an endless succession of empty moments, each one of which, because of its emptiness, seems itself to be lifelong:

> What hours, O what black hoùrs we have spent
> This night! what sights you, heart, saw; ways you went!
> And more must, in yet longer light's delay.
>   With witness I speak this. But where I say
> Hours I mean years, mean life.[26]

In this extremity, any possibility of help will be grasped. Perhaps that non-human world of creatures who "always do what they can," even though it rebuffs man with "blank unlikeness," may serve in some way to rescue man from his dizzy plunge into the abyss, from the utter cessation of the forward movement of his life. What is the relation of man to nature in Hopkins?

III

There is evident in Hopkins, from the earliest fragmentary notebooks onward, an interest in the exact nature of things in the external world which is extraordinary even in a century to which nature meant so much.

Hopkins' primary relation to nature was what perhaps remains man's most profound reaction to the external world: it was simply the astonished recognition that each perceived object is *there*, exists as a stubborn, irreducible fact. "But indeed," says Hopkins, "I have often felt . . . that nothing is so pregnant and straightforward to the truth as simple *yes* and *is.*"[27] No one has felt more deeply and consciously this wonder at the mere existence of things, and no one has tried more earnestly to cherish that wonder and make it persist throughout as the basic ingredient of his relation to the world.

24. *Id.*, p. 110.
25. *Id.*, p. 113.
26. *Id.*, p. 109.
27. *Notebooks*, p. 98.

This attitude toward nature reminds one, of course, of the fidelity to the minute particulars of nature in Hopkins' contemporaries, the Pre-Raphaelites. Hopkins' own beautiful landscape drawings are very Pre-Raphaelite in their ornate realism. Often a sketch will accompany a detailed verbal description in the *Journal*. And the *Journal* itself is largely made up of the impersonal recording of observed phenomena:

> Clouds however solid they may look far off are I think wholly made of film in the sheet or in the tuft. The bright woolpacks that pelt before a gale in a clear sky are in the tuft and you can see the wind unravelling and rending them finer than any sponge till within one easy reach overhead they are morselled to nothing and consumed—it depends of course on their size.[28]

There is in this a naturalism, an empiricism, even a nominalism, which seems to exclude any theory that objects in nature are parts of a coherent whole. What is, is what it is, and there seems to be nothing more to say about it. In any individual act of perception the whole world is reduced to the self and the observed scene, and one can only assert truthfully what one has oneself experienced. There is an implicit rejection of authority, of *a priori* ideas, the same rejection that was behind the growth of modern science, the same rejection that is one of the central motivations of romanticism. The Hopkins who wrote such passages in his journal might have said, with Keats, "O for a Life of Sensations rather than of Thoughts," and "I can never feel certain of any truth but from a clear perception of its Beauty." In order to reach truth one must begin all over again each time, reject all received opinions and make oneself energetically passive.

But what does Hopkins find outside of himself through this process of long and hard *looking?* He discovers that each thing is uniquely itself, that each thing has its own distinct nature, a nature which is never repeated. This individuality is manifested in things by the freshness and sharpness of their outline or pattern. Hopkins' nature is a nature with clearly defined edges. It is a nature without blurring or smudging, a nature in which each thing stands out vividly as though it were surrounded by perfectly translucent air. And air can reach all the surfaces of even the smallest and most intricate object, so abrupt is the frontier between the object and its surroundings:

> Wild air, world-mothering air,
> Nestling me everywhere,
> That each eyelid or hair
> Girdles; goes home betwixt
> The fleeciest, frailest-flixed
> Snowflake[29]

Hopkins' word for the design or pattern which is the perceptible sign of the unique individuality of a thing is "inscape." I give only one

28. *Id.*, p. 140.
29. *Poems*, p. 99.

example among a great many: "Below at a little timber bridge I looked at some delicate fly shafted ashes—there was one especially of single sonnet-like inscape."[30] But an "inscape" need not be a single object. It can be a *group* of objects which together form a pattern. Nevertheless, this form of inscape, too, is not a mere extrinsic organization of disparate parts, but is the manifestation of an inner, organic unity. Nor is inscape only discovered through the sense of sight (although that sense certainly predominates in Hopkins). The use of synesthesia in Hopkins' poetry is matched by an explicit analysis in the *Journal* of the way the unitary inscape of a single object may be perceived by all the senses. The passage begins: "The bluebells in your hand baffle you with their inscape, made to every sense."[31] "Inscape," then, is always used in contexts wherein the oneness, the organic unity, of a single object or group of *composed* objects is seen. And it is always associated with distinctness of outline, with words like "sharp," "wiry" and "crisp." Each object in Hopkins' world is distinctly itself, separated starkly from every other object in the universe. And it is not, like the nature of Tennyson and Rilke, seen as suspended statically and mutely in an eternal and fateful present which seems to be in the very act of fading suddenly away into non-existence. Nature in Hopkins is neither static nor does it hauntingly slip beyond the observer's immediate grasp. It is seen as present to the observer and as acting directly upon him without any intervening distance or vacancy. It does not somehow escape the spectator by withdrawing in upon itself. And even a natural scene which might seem to ask to be treated as static and inanimate is perceived by Hopkins as the center of a vital activity, even of a *personal* activity: "The mountain ranges, as any series or body of inanimate like things not often seen, have the air of persons and of interrupted activity."[32]

Natural objects, then, are not dead, but are sustained from within by a vital pressure. They are not static but ceaselessly active, even when they are apparently motionless. It is this inner pressure, permeating all nature, which is the true source of inscape and what is actually manifested by it. The word is *in*-scape, the outer manifestation or "scape" of an inner principle or activity—not the mere external pattern which things make and which is pleasing to the eye as design: "*All the world is full of inscape* and chance left free to act falls into an order as well as purpose: looking out of my window I caught it in the random clods and broken heaps of snow made by the cast of a broom."[33] "There lives the dearest freshness deep down things."[34] "Fineness, proportion of feature, comes from a moulding force which succeeds in asserting itself over the resistance of cumbersome or restraining matter."[35] Some of Hopkins' drawings are startlingly like Chinese paintings: their swirling whirlpool patterns seem to manifest an ubiquitous spiritual force rolling

30. *Notebooks*, p. 211.
31. *Id.*, p. 145.
32. W. H. Gardner, ed., *Poems and Prose of Gerard Manley Hopkins* (London, 1953), p. 115.
33. *Notebooks*, pp. 173, 174.
34. *Poems*, p. 70.
35. C. C. Abbott, ed., *Further Letters of Gerard Manley Hopkins* (London, 1938), p. 159.

through all nature. Hopkins' nature, as much as Coleridge's or White-head's, is the locus of a vital process, the explosive meeting-point of a spiritual elan and the stubborn resistance of matter. It is a nature which is in ceaseless activity and which manifests an extreme tension between the inner energy and the restraining outward form. The inscape is the meeting place of these two.

But for the inner energy itself Hopkins uses another word, a word which suggests not the outer design or pattern of a thing, but that very energy which upholds it from within: "all things are upheld by instress and are meaningless without it," wrote Hopkins in an undergraduate essay on Parmenides.[36] Just as the apparently unique and solid "taste of self" which was discovered in the first moment of awareness turned out to be a mere "positive infinitesimal," so nature, apparently so full of sharply defined distinctive objects, turns out to be upheld by a single permeating spirit. This spirit is God himself: "As we drove home the stars came out thick: I leant back to look at them and my heart opening more than usual praised our Lord to and in whom all that beauty comes home."[37] Even more striking is a passage from Hopkins' unpublished retreat notes of 1882. In this passage all the solid world is dissolved into expression of God. It is a passage which seems at the furthest pos-sible remove from the naturalism, the humble scientific observation of nature with which Hopkins began: "God's utterance of Himself in Him-self is God the Word, outside Himself in this world. The world then is word, expression, news of God. Therefore its end, its purpose, its pur-port, its meaning and its life and work is to name and praise him."[38] Nature, then, for Hopkins as for the Middle Ages, is the "book of na-ture" in which we may read "news of God." But there is one crucial difference: the medieval doctrine of analogy has almost disappeared from Hopkins. For the Christian of the Middle Ages each object in the natural world repeated some particular aspect of the supernatural world. It was thus a means of knowing that supernatural world in detail. For Hopkins all the world is "charged with the grandeur of God," and we know through the things of this world simply the power and presence of God, not details of the supernatural world.

It is easy to see now why Hopkins was so elated when in 1872 he discovered Duns Scotus' *Commentaries on the Sentences of Peter Lombard*, and why in that year he could write: "just then when I took in any in-scape of the sky or sea I thought of Scotus."[39] Hopkins found in Scotus confirmation of the theory of nature and of the human self which he al-ready held. Hopkins had always felt that the unique individuality of a thing or person was really a part of it, part of its form and not merely a result of the matter in which the form was actualised as Aristotle and St. Thomas maintained. He had always felt that one knows in the act of perception not, by means of the Aristotlean or Thomistic *"Species intel-ligibilis,"* the mere *"quidditas"* or *"whatness"* of a thing, but its distinc-tive individuality, its "thisness." In the Scotian doctrine of the *haecceitas*

36. *Notebooks*, p. 98.
37. *Id.*, p. 205.
38. Quoted in W. A. M. Peters, S.J., *Gerard Manley Hopkins* (London, 1948), p. 175.
39. *Notebooks*, p. 161.

or individualizing form, which makes an object not simply a member of a species, a pine tree, for example, but this particular unrepeatable pine tree, Hopkins found his own deepest apprehension of the world systematized. And perhaps even more importantly Hopkins felt that through the immediate sense perception of things in the world he could know God directly as the "instress" that upheld each thing. He did not want a world of abstract "ideas" or "forms" ("pinetreeness," "bluebellness" and so on) to intervene between himself and God. Paradoxically, the Scotian metaphysic, which, from one perspective at least, seems perilously close to nominalism,[40] was actually a much better basis for Hopkins' view of the universe as "news of God" than would have been the Aristotelian theory of forms. Only a world in which God himself is directly present without intermediary in each one of his creatures can be "expression, news of God" in the way Hopkins deeply felt it to be: "All things," he wrote, "therefore are charged with love, are charged with God and if we know how to touch them give off sparks and take fire, yield drops and flow, ring and tell of him."[41]

IV

"*If* we know how to touch them." The perception of the instress in natural objects, then, is contingent on something in the observer. The true theme of Hopkins' *Journal* and of his nature poems is not nature alone but the man-nature relationship. Hopkins has a striking phrase for the "bridge," the dynamic interaction, he felt to exist between subject and object: he called it the "stem of stress between us and things."[42] This tension, as between two magnets, is absolutely necessary to "bear us out and carry the mind over."[43] Subject and object share one thing at least in common: their possession of the inward energy of instress. This intrinsic spiritual force flashes out from objects; it rays forth from them. Each object is not merely the tense withholding of a spiritual charge. This charge leaps out at the slightest provocation, and all objects are thereby potentially in touch with one another. The world in Hopkins is a vast network of electrical discharges given and received by objects which are an inexhaustible source of the divine energy:

> The world is charged with the grandeur of God.
> It will flame out, like shining from shook foil.[44]

But human beings too are charged with energy: "Honour is flashed off exploit," says Hopkins,[45] and "self flashes off frame and face."[46] Perception, as in Whitehead, is only a special case of the dynamic interaction between all objects. In the moment of perception a "stem of stress" is created between subject and object to which the subject

40. See Bernard Landry, *La Philosophie de Duns Scot* (Paris, 1922), *passim.*
41. *Notebooks,* p. 342.
42. *Id.,* p. 98.
43. *Id.*
44. *Poems,* p. 70.
45. *Id.,* p. 112.
46. *Id.,* p. 104.

contributes as much as does the object: "What you look hard at seems to look hard at you."[47] Hopkins' epistemology, like that of the Pre-Socratics (whom he had read), is based ultimately on the "theory of sensation by like and like."[48] Only if the beholder is able to return stress for stress will the moment of knowledge, the moment of the coalescence of subject and object, take place.

Hopkins almost always mentions both the subject and object in his descriptions of nature. He not only describes the bluebells, he says: "I caught as well as I could while my companions talked the Greek rightness of their beauty."[49] "I caught." It is an active berb, suggesting the energetic grasp of the mind on things. The phrase echoes through the *Journal* and the poetry; it is Hopkins' special term for the strenuous activity of perception: "I caught this morning morning's minion, kingdom of daylight's dauphin, dapple-dawn-drawn Falcon."[50]

Just as Hopkins' self-awareness is an organic taste of himself, not a dry lucidity, so his grasp of the external world in the dynamic moment of instress is as much emotional as intellectual. It is a total possession of the object by the thinking, feeling, sensing subject. The object is internalized by the subject. Hence Hopkins speaks repeatedly of instress as something deeply *felt*, not merely intellectually realized: "But such a lovely damasking in the sky as today I never felt before."[51] "Looking all round but most in looking far up the valley I felt an instress and charm of Wales."[52] One gathers from the constant use of this word and of the word "caught" a strong sense of the precariousness of these experiences. They are reported with a tone of elation, as though they were rare occurrences of success among many failures.

And sometimes indeed the instress does fail to come. It depends on just the proper conditions in the perceiver and in what is perceived: in the perceiver a certain freshness of vision and a singleness of concentration on the object perceived: "Unless you refresh the mind from time to time you cannot always remember or believe how deep the inscape in things is."[53] For the instress to come it must be as if there were nothing else in the world but the present moment of ecstatic communication with what is directly present to the senses. Hopkins differs from the romantic poets generally in that there is in his writings almost no interest in affective memory, in the linkage to a moment in the past by means of intense perception in the present. Each moment recorded in the *Journal* and in the poems is sufficient unto itself. There is a kind of radical discontinuity in Hopkins' temporal existence. It proceeds by a series of vivid perceptions. Each is distinct from all the others and each fades away almost immediately to be replaced by another or sometimes by mere vacancy and lassitude. If a relation between past and present *via* memory appears in Hopkins at all it is almost always in

47. *Notebooks*, p. 140.
48. *Id.*, p. 102.
49. *Id.*, p. 174.
50. *Poems*, p. 73.
51. *Notebooks*, p. 143.
52. *Id.*, p. 210.
53. *Id.*, p. 140.

the form of a lament for the irretrievable fading away of the ecstacy of instress when it is past: "Saw a lad burning big bundles of dry honey-suckle: the flame (though it is no longer freshly in my mind) was brown and gold."[54] The *Journal* entries were often written down long after the event recorded from notes made at the time. In the few cases where the notes themselves exist we can sense a frantic attempt to capture some portion at least of what is known to be fleeting and fragile. And are not the *Journal* and the poems themselves ultimately to be defined as the attempt to give through words some form of permanence to what were actually unique, instantaneous and unrepeatable experiences? There is implicit in the very form of the *Journal* and of the poems a deep anguish at the inevitable passing away of these moments. The loss of these experiences is painful because it is the loss of what the person himself is at that moment. We can detect in the *Journal* both the anxious attempt to give these fleeting moments some permanence in words *and* the obsessive urge to have more and more and more of them. Hopkins can think of no more painful form of self-mortification and penance than to deprive himself of the repetition of one of these experiences.[55]

But sometimes even if the precious activity of instressing is permitted and desired it will not come. Not only must one banish the past and future and live wholly in the moment, one must also banish the awareness that any other person exists: "Even with one companion ecstacy is almost banished: you want to be alone and to feel that, and leisure— all pressure taken off."[56] One can see clearly and explicitly here what is sometimes obscured in other projects of founding one's self-identity on a direct relationship to nature: such a project is, strictly speaking, amoral. It does not exist in what Kierkegaard called the "ethical" realm. For Hopkins, as for Keats and Wordsworth, the self is formed not through inter-personal relations but through experiences of non-human nature, experiences which simply ignore the existence of other human beings. Hopkins' *Journal* and his greatest poems are the record of experiences of absolute isolation from other people.

But even to be alone, in the moment, isolated from past and future and from all other human beings is not always enough. There may be simply a failure of the sensibility, a failure which in some people is total and permanent: "I thought how sadly beauty of inscape was unknown and buried away from simple people and yet how near at hand it was if they had eyes to see it and it could be called out everywhere again."[57]

And sometimes it is the *object* which for one reason or another fails to offer itself to perception, fails to flash itself outwards in the stress that can be counterstressed by the poet. This fact is perceived when a change in a natural object makes it possible to detect an inscape that has been present all the time, but hidden: "This is the time to study inscape in the spraying of trees, for the swelling buds carry them to a

54. *Id.,* p. 159.
55. See *Id.,* p. 199.
56. *Id.,* p. 111.
57. *Id.,* p. 161.

pitch which the eye could not else gather."[58] "I caught as well as I could [in the bluebells] . . . a notable glare the eye may abstract and sever from the blue color of light beating up from so many glassy heads, which like water is good to float their deeper instress in upon the mind."[59] "Float their deeper instress in upon the mind"! How different this is from the perception, at a *distance*, that each individual thing is its distinct self and has an inscape. Now Hopkins wants to possess that external perception, to internalize it, to "float it in upon the mind" across the stem of stress between subject and object.

When the communication is total perceiver and perceived come into intimate contact, interpenetrate and coalesce. This experience is the true theme of the early nature poems, of "Spring," "The Starlit Night," "The Sea and the Skylark," and "Hurrahing in Harvest." The effect of this experience on the self is, in the etymological sense of the word, "ecstacy": the self leaps outside of itself and creates a new self by means of a substantial identification with all of perceived nature:

> These things, these things were here and but the beholder
>   Wanting; which two when they once meet,
> The heart rears wings bold and bolder
>   And hurls for him, O half hurls earth for him off under his
>   feet.[60]

> v
> Another night from the gallery window I saw a brindled heaven, the moon just marked—I *read* a broad careless inscape flowing throughout.[61]
> The [elms'] tops are touched and *worded* with leaf.[62]

On the one hand, natural objects are intelligible; they can be read by man as though they were not simply objects, but *signs*. On the other hand, they are *mute* signs. They only speak when there is a human being present to read them. Man gives natural objects a voice and a language. In "reading" them, and in bodying forth that meaning in words man gives nature something it does not possess, selfconsciousness and a tongue to speak that awareness:

> And what is Earth's eye, tongue, or heart else, where
> Else, but in dear and dogged man?[63]

The true "stem of stress" between man and nature is the word itself. At the point of fusion, where subject meets object and coalesces with it, is born the word. Words have for Hopkins a magic quality of attaining the object, wresting from it its meaning and making that meaning a permanent possession for man. "To every word meaning a thing

---

58. *Id.*, p. 141.
59. *Id.*, p. 174.
60. *Poems*, p. 75.
61. *Notebooks*, p. 158, my italics.
62. *Id.*, p. 190, my italics.
63. *Poems*, p. 96.

and not a relation," wrote Hopkins in a brief paper on words dated 1868, "belongs a passion or prepossession or enthusiasm which it has the power of suggesting or producing, but not always or in everyone."[64] In one sense, all Hopkins' efforts in his poetry were towards the creation of a continuum of words which would, like a proper name, convey the "prepossession," to use his word, of a unique individual experience. All Hopkins' poetry is based on the fundamental discovery that words can imitate things, re-present them in a different form, rescue them from the ceaselessly moving realm of nature and translate them into the permanent realm of words. Words can, Hopkins discovered, "catch" things, "stall" them, as he said,[65] and transform them into spiritual stuff. Metaphors were not, for him, "poetic lies," nor were words arbitrary signs. Hopkins discovered what certain contemporary poets, philosophers and anthropologists are making their central theme: in the word subject and object merge and we touch the object in a way we never can without naming it. The word is not an arbitrary label; it carries the object alive into the heart. Each different word for the "same thing" transmits to the mind a slightly (or radically) different aspect of reality. Each new word is a window through which a new portion of reality is revealed. To name a thing is to perceive it. This thing is not subjective, not "imposed" by the mind "outwards."[66] It is "really there," but is only perceived when it is so named. We only truly *see* the world when we have represented it in words. Metaphor, onomatopoeia, compound words, inversion, functional shift, and all the other special techniques of verbal representation are only modes of the universal operation of verbal *mimesis*. All the seemingly idiosyncratic methods of Hopkins' poetry are, in one way, directed towards the perfect imitation in words of the object perceived in all its concreteness and in all its energetic activity.

But if words for Hopkins face outwards towards the object, they also face inwards towards the mind. Even in the earliest of Hopkins' writings we can see another fundamental obsession: a fascination for words in themselves, for their etymology, for their multiplicity of meanings, for their abstract "prepossession" without any reference to particular experiences. Hopkins was very sensitive to the inscape of words in themselves, taken in isolation from their meaning. He was fascinated by the fact that the same word can in different contexts carry the "prepossession" of entirely different realities: "Sky peak'd with tiny flames. . . . Altogether peak is a good word. For sunlight through shutter, locks of hair, rays in brass knobs etc. Meadows peaked with flowers."[67] If Hopkins was the most nature-intoxicated poet of the Victorian period, he was also the poet most fascinated by words in themselves, by words not as the signs of an external reality but as the signs of certain definite spiritual states.

Accordingly, alongside the theory and practice of poetry as *mimesis*

64. *Notebooks,* p. 95.
65. For a use of this word, see *Notebooks,* p. 127: "these images . . . once lodged there are stalled by the mind like other images."
66. *Id.,* p. 154.
67. *Id.,* p. 32.

we can observe a very different notion, a notion of poetry as a thing to be contemplated for its own sake and without any reference to the external world: "But as air, melody, is what strikes me most of all in music and design in painting, so design, pattern or what I am in the habit of calling 'inscape' is what I above all aim at in poetry."[68] Inscape, said Hopkins, is "the very soul of art."[69] It is what makes a work of art "beautiful to individuation," that is, it gives a poem or a painting the kind of distinctness, uniqueness, *haecceitas,* possessed by a natural object. "Inscape," then, has two very different meanings. It can refer to the willed design of a human artifact as well as to the pattern into which natural objects fall without any human intervention.

Hopkins sought to achieve in his poetry an organic unity in which each part would be interrelated to all the other parts, and thus transcend its isolation as the name of an external object: "Repetition, *oftening, over-and-overing, aftering* of the inscape must take place in order to detach it to the mind and in this light poetry is speech which alters and oftens its inscape, speech couched in a repeated figure and verse as spoken sound having a repeated figure."[70] "Tout le mystère est la," said Mallarmé, in terms that Hopkins himself might have used, "établir les identités secrètes par un deux à deux qui ronge et use les objêts, au nom d'une centrale pureté."[71] For Hopkins, as for Mallarmé, the repetition or parallelism which establishes "secret identities" between one part of a poem and another was for the sake of a "central purity," a central purity which Hopkins called the total inscape of the poem. Here we have moved very far indeed from the notion of poetry as the *mimesis* of the external world, as the violent point of contact between subject and object. All the density of texture in Hopkins' verse is as much for the sake of creating its own self-sufficient durée or "sliding inscape," as it is to express the packed energy and radiance which some event in nature contains. If the extreme use of various forms of "over-and-overing" in Hopkins, assonance, alliteration, internal rhyme, Welsh *cynghanedd* and so on, is in one sense all for the purpose of representing nature, it is in another sense wholly indifferent to external nature and all calculated to "detach the mind" and "carry" the "inscape of speech for the inscape's sake."

Inscape in poetry is "the essential and only lasting thing";[72] it is "species or individually distinctive beauty of style."[73] But it is only attained *via* the individuality of the poet himself: "Every poet," says Hopkins, "must be original and originality a condition of poetic genius; so that each poet is like a species in nature (*not* an *individuum genericum* or *specificum*) and can never recur."[74] Each poet, then, is very like each

68. C. C. Abbott, ed., *Letters of Gerard Manley Hopkins to Robert Bridges* (London, 1935), p. 60.

69. C. C. Abbott, ed., *Correspondence of Gerard Manley Hopkins and Richard Watson Dixon* (London, 1935), p. 135.

70. *Notebooks,* p. 249.

71. Letter to Vielé Griffin, August 8, 1891, quoted in G. Poulet, *La Distance Intérieure* (Paris, 1952), p. 343.

72. *Further Letters,* p. 225.

73. *Id.*

74. *Id.,* p. 222.

inanimate object in that he is a *species,* not a *genus,* a *haecceitas,* not a *quidditas.* "No doubt my poetry errs on the side of oddness," wrote Hopkins, ". . . Now it is the virtue of design, pattern, or inscape to be distinctive and it is the vice of distinctiveness to become queer. This vice I cannot have escaped."[75] We can see now that when Hopkins said that he aimed above all at "inscape" in poetry he meant not simply that he aimed at pattern, design, organic unity, but that he aimed at these because only through them could poetry be the affirmation and actualization of his own identity. So in the headnote of the sonnet to Henry Purcell, Purcell is praised for having "uttered in notes the very make and species of man as created in him and in all men generally."[76] But in the poem itself the bow to St. Thomas is forgotten and Purcell's music is praised not as manifesting "man generally," but as the expression of an absolutely unique self, Purcell's own "archespecial . . . spirit":

> It is the forgèd feature finds me; it is the rehearsal
> Of own, of abrúpt sélf there so thrusts on, so throngs the ear.[77]

But at the center of the project of individuation by means of "poeting" there lies a double flaw, a flaw which leads to the faltering and ultimate total collapse of the project. In this collapse, Hopkins is left bare again, "no one, nowhere," enclosed within the unpierced walls of his own impotent taste of self.

VI

This collapse can be seen from two perspectives. The poet, it is true, however much he may be apparently imitating the external world in his poetry, is actually speaking himself, *doing* himself. The poet poets. But this "poeting" is accomplished after all through words that have meanings, that remain signs even when they are used for the sake of their own inscapes. A poem is not an act of absolute self-creation. Without the external world it could not exist; however independent it may be it must remain, to be successful, a faithful representation of the external world. The success of this reliance on the external world will depend on the stability and solidity of that world itself.

Hopkins' nature, so densely packed with distinctly singular objects, each sustained by the instress of an inexhaustible energy would seem perfectly suited to such a dependence on it. Nevertheless, we can see a disastrous transition in Hopkins' apprehension of nature. At first it seems full of solid, static, enduring objects, objects which cannot help but be themselves and which cannot cease to be themselves. But it becomes apparent that these things are in continual movement. Nature is not only full of kinetic energy, it is also a nature in process which is the dynamic expending of that energy. One remembers the clouds in "Hurrahing in Harvest" which are continually made and unmade, "moulded ever and melted across skies."[78] It is only in some kind of

75. *Letters to Bridges,* p. 60.
76. *Poems,* p. 84.
77. *Id.,* p. 85.
78. *Poems,* p. 74.

movement that things can radiate their inexhaustible energy outwards. But there seems nothing ominous about the discovery that things are not fixed eternally in a single inscape.

Yet in two magnificent poems of Hopkins' maturity, "Spelt from Sibyl's Leaves" and "That Nature is a Heraclitean Fire and of the Comfort of the Resurrection," there is a complete reversal of the earlier feeling of the permanent distinctiveness of things. What had begun as the simple perception that the inscapes of things are in a continual process of change becomes an anguished recognition that the "forgéd features" of things are ultimately utterly destroyed. Never has the perception of nature as a shifting flux of birth and death been expressed with more intensity. As in Parmenides, "unmeaning (ἀδαῆ) night, thick and wedgèd body"[79] which inevitably follows day and hides the perceptible forms of things is taken as the symbol of that absolute non-being which will inevitably overtake all created things, all *mortal* beauty:

> Earnest, earthless, equal, attuneable, ' vaulty, voluminous, . . . stupendous
> Evening strains to be tíme's vást, ' womb-of-all, home-of-all, hearse-of-all night.
>
> . . . For earth ' her being has unbound, her dapple is at an end, as—
> tray or aswarm, all throughther, in throngs; ' self ín self steepèd and páshed—qúite
> Disremembering, dísmémbering ' áll now.[80]

Only if we know how much Hopkins cherished the "original definiteness and piquant beauty of things"[81] can we understand fully what violence of regret, what "pity and indignation,"[82] there is in the image of "self ín self steepèd and páshed." It is a dynamically *experienced* image of the return of all individuated forms to the "thick and wedgèd body" of primordial chaos. In that chaos every self will be blurred, smeared, inextricably mixed in the other selves. Nature will be, in Hopkins' striking coinage, "all throughther." The suggestion that a complete phrase such as "each interpenetrated through and through with the others" has been collapsed into "throughther" makes it a perfect *mimesis* of the event described. One feels the forms of the collapsed words straining to differentiate themselves, just as the identities being crushed into chaos resist desperately the unbinding of their being.

In the poem called "That Nature is a Heraclitean Fire" another of the Pre-Socratic symbols is used, fire, the symbol of the energy of being, "ethery flame of fire" as Hopkins calls it in his essay on Parmenides.[83] In this poem all the thousand forms in which this energy manifests itself are seen to be impermanent as clouds or as straws in a bonfire,

79. *Notebooks,* p. 102.
80. *Poems,* p. 104.
81. *Further Letters,* p. 72.
82. *Poems,* p. 112.
83. *Notebooks,* p. 102.

and are continually being destroyed and replaced by other forms. "God gave things," wrote Hopkins, "a forward and perpetual motion."[84] If "Spelt from Sibyl's Leaves" is the frightening vision of night as dismembering, the later poem is a hymn to day as destructive fire, a fire in which "million-fuèled, nature's bonfire burns on."[85] The very energy of Being, its fire, what seemed to inhere within things and to sustain them in selfhood turns out to be itself the source of their undoing. For that energy drives things on to an activity of selving that eventually consumes them, unselves them, transforms them out of all resemblance to their former selves. Only the "ethery flame of fire" remains constant, that and the activity of change itself, the ceaseless metamorphosis of one form into another.

How, then, can an identification of oneself with external nature be used to establish a permanent identity if nature is as unstable as the day which moves every moment closer towards the tomb of night, as quick to change and as destructive as fire, and if it is to this universal flux that we must testify in our poems?

VII

The evidence from the other side is equally fatal. If nature fails man, man fails nature and fails himself even more totally. His relation to nature can be far different from the reverent and concentrated attention which "floats its instress in upon the mind." If natural objects lack stability and permanence, so even more completely does man. In non-human nature the law is transformation, flux, but the law for man is absolute destruction, since his identity, though incarnated, is too subtle, too spiritual, to retain its distinctness through even so many changes as a tree or flower will endure. The final lesson man learns from nature is that he, too, is part of nature and that this means but one thing for him: death. If all objects are burned in nature's bonfire, man is simply annihilated in that same fire:

> But quench her bonniest, dearest ' to her, her clearest-selvèd spark
> Man, how fast his firedint, ' his mark on mind, is gone!
> Both are in an unfathomable, all is in an enormous dark
> Drowned.[86]

Even if a man could achieve through the poetizing of his perception of nature an unwavering and permanent identity, it would be all dismembered and unbound in a moment at his death.

But even within the limits of earthly life the project is bound to fail. As we have seen, the ability to "instress" nature is intermittent and can be replaced in a moment by the most agonizing spiritual impotence. If the self is unable to selve, as it often is, it will be cut off entirely from the world which can give it such delight. In times of spiritual dry-

84. *Id.,* p. 347.
85. *Poems,* p. 112.
86. *Id.*

ness, of spiritual paralysis, the self is locked entirely within its self-torment and cut off entirely from the outside world:

> I cast for comfort I can no more get
> By groping round my comfortless, than blind
> Eyes in their dark can day or thirst can find
> Thirst's all-in-all in a world of wet.[87]

The proper image of spiritual aridity is not of a thirsty man in a desert but of a thirsty man in the midst of water he cannot drink; it is not the image of a man straining to see in the darkness but of a blind man in the midst of light which he cannot see.

There was something ominous in the double orientation of words, and in the split in Hopkins between poetry as *mimesis* and poetry as "the inscape of speech for the inscape's sake." Words can become not the point of fusion of subject and object, but the locus of their most absolute and permanent division. Words, instead of reaching out to things, touching them, and *giving* them over to man, can become merely the opaque walls of his interior prison:

> . . . Only what word
> Wisest my heart breeds dark heaven's baffling ban
> Bars or hell's spell thwarts. This to hoard unheard
> Heard unheeded, leaves me a lonely began.[88]

Cast outwards by the mind to capture the object, words may fall endlessly through a shadowy void and never touch anything at all, neither things nor the God within things:

> . . . my lament
> Is cries countless, cries like dead letters sent
> To dearest him that lives alas! away.[89]

The end point of Hopkins' long dialogue with nature is a complete reversal of the ecstatic mood of "Hurrahing in Harvest." He is cut off entirely from nature and lives in the utter isolation of his spiritual inertia, "this tormented mind / With this tormented mind tormenting yet."[90] His state is very like that of the damned who are also imprisoned in the corrosive contemplation of their own limits. "Against these acts of its own," wrote Hopkins, "the lost spirit dashes itself like a caged beast and is in prison, violently instresses them and burns, stares into them and is the deepest darkened."[91]

VIII

If all the positive ways of self-affirmation fail, perhaps there is one final way, a way through the center of the deepest despair and spiritual

87. *Id.*, p. 111.
88. *Id.*, p. 109.
89. *Id.*
90. *Id.*, p. 110.
91. Peters, *op. cit.*, p. 177.

abnegation: the creation of one's true self by self-sacrifice. The cruci-fixion, central moment of history, was the act whereby Christ "annihi-lated himself."[92] Christ was most Christ, the Mediator and Saviour of mankind, when he thus sacrificed himself, just as the windhover is most windhover when it renounces its sovereignty of the air and dives earth-ward.

Hopkins in his later years planned a treatise on sacrifice. It was never published, but it is clear from texts scattered throughout his work what he would have said. Non-human things can praise God simply by being themselves, by "dealing out that being indoors each one dwells." Only man in order to praise God and win salvation must cease to be himself. Only through such a total change of his essential being can man escape the damnation of being "no one, nowhere, / In wide the world's weal," exiled within himself, separated from all, dwell-ing in "the barren wilderness outside of God,"[93] condemned to taste his own self eternally. Only by ceasing to be oneself and becoming Christ can a man avoid an existence which is a continual dizzy falling away in time:

> I am soft sift
> In an hourglass—at the wall
> Fast, but mined with a motion, a drift,
> And it crowds and it combs to the fall.[94]

In the subtle and elaborate investigation of free will and grace in the "Commentary on the Spiritual Exercises of St. Ignatius Loyola" Hopkins devises a brilliant metaphor to define this transformation. The actual pitch of self existing at any moment in each person is only one self out of an infinity of possible selves. It is like one cross-section out of all the possible ones of a three-dimensional solid. It is one "cleave of being" out of the total "burl of being." This "burl of being" is as much really part of a person, though only potential, as his actual self. The transformation of the self when it becomes Christ is the abandon-ment of one cleave of being and the actualizing of another potential one. For every man, and even Satan himself, has at least one potential cross-section which coincides with Christ.

But how can this transformation be brought about? For man of his own power can do absolutely nothing to move himself from one "cleave of being" to another. There is only one answer: by God's grace, "which lifts the receiver from one cleave of being to another and to a vital act in Christ."[95] Hopkins' concept of grace seems to relate him rather to Post-Reformation theologies than to Thomistic Catholicism. For a Thomist, the initial act of creation gives a man's soul an indestructible permanence. He cannot cease to be himself, even if he veers to one of the extremes of mortal sin or sainthood. Grace, in the Thomistic view, does not exert its power on the permanent identity of a man's being,

---

92. *Letters to Bridges*, p. 175.
93. *Notebooks*, p. 344.
94. *Poems*, p. 56.
95. *Notebooks*, p. 337.

but only upon the variations of his temporal existence. But grace for Hopkins is precisely a *transubstantiation* of the person's innermost being. It is "an exchange of one whole for another whole, as they say in the mystery of Transubstantiation, a conversion of the whole substance into another substance, but here it is not a question of substance; it is a lifting him from one self to another self, which is a most marvellous display of divine power."[96] "It is not a question of substance," says Hopkins, but it is difficult to say what else it is, this total transformation from one self to another self, "through the gulf and void between pitch and pitch of being."[97]

Where then is free will? It would seem that there is nothing left for God's creature to do but to pray for grace. But in what Hopkins calls the "least sigh of desire," the "aspiration,"[98] of man towards God a tiny corner is left for man's free will. "Correspondence" is the key word in Hopkins' theory of grace. Just as man's salvation is won by achieving a correspondence to Christ, so the only action on man's part that makes this occur is the minute movement of volition whereby he wills to correspond with God's grace: "and by this infinitesimal act the creature does what in it lies to bridge the gulf fixed between its present actual and worser pitch of will and its future better one."[99] This "correspondence with grace and seconding of God's designs"[100] is man's tiny bit contributed towards the creation of his own best self.

But even when transubstantiated into Christ a man still remains himself, since it is that mere positive infinitesimal which the man is aware of in his first self-consciousness which is so filled with Christ. The proper figure for the achieved transformation is of a hollow shell or vessel which is everywhere inhabited by Christ and brought into positive being by Christ: "This too," writes Hopkins, "but brings out the nature of the man himself, as the lettering on a sail, or the device upon a flag are best seen when it fills."[101]

However, this metamorphosis of man into Christ remains until his death contingent, in jeopardy. It depends on God's continual gift of fresh grace and on man's continual "saying Yes"[102] to God.[103] Only at the Resurrection will man be securely and permanently transformed, soul and body, into Christ: whence the "comfort of the Resurrection," the only real comfort for man:

> . . . Flesh fade, and mortal trash
> Fall to the residuary worm; ˈworld's wildfire, leave but ash:
> In a flash, at a trumpet crash,
> I am all at once what Christ is, ˈsince he was what I am, and

96. *Id.*, p. 329.
97. *Id.*, pp. 334, 335.
98. *Id.*, p. 333.
99. *Id.*, p. 333.
100. *Id.*, p. 344.
101. *Id.*, p. 343.
102. *Id.*, p. 333.
103. See Hopkins' beautiful image for God's continual *sustaining* of man in stanza four of "The Wreck of the Deutschland" (*Poems*, p. 56).

> This Jack, joke, poor potsherd, ' patch, matchwood, immortal
> diamond,
>   Is immortal diamond.[104]

We must leave Hopkins here, at the extreme point of his despair and hope, turned far from nature and from poetry, standing aghast at the sight of a world that is visibly disintegrating and being consumed, as at the last trump. We leave him with nothing but the "comfort of the Resurrection," the hope of that miracle of transubstantiation which will change man from the mere impure carbon of matchwood to immortal diamond, change him, that is, from one allotropic form of himself to another so different that if there is any secret continuity between the two it is only in that the same null potentiality of being, is, in each case, actualized by God, actualized by God in ways that are as far apart as the whole distance from hell to heaven.

104. *Poems,* p. 112.

Samuel Holt Monk

THE PRIDE OF LEMUEL GULLIVER[1]

Gulliver's Travels is a complex book. It is, of course, a satire on four aspects of man: the physical, the political, the intellectual, and the moral. The last three are inseparable, and when Swift writes of one he always has in view the others. It is also a brilliant parody of travel literature; and it is at once science fiction and a witty parody of science fiction. It expresses savage indignation at the follies, vices, and stupidities of men, and everywhere implicit in the book as a whole is an awareness of man's tragic insufficiency. But at the same time it is a great comic masterpiece, a fact that solemn and too-sensitive readers often miss.

A friend once wrote me of having shocked an associate by remarking that he had laughed often on rereading *Gulliver's Travels.* 'What should I have done?' he asked me. 'Blown out my brains?' I am sure that Swift would have approved my friend's laughter. To conclude that *Gulliver's Travels* expresses despair or that its import is nihilistic is radically to misread the book. All of Swift's satire was written in anger, contempt, or disgust, but it was written to promote self-knowledge in the faith that self-knowledge will lead to right action. Nothing would have bewildered him more than to learn that he had led a reader to the desperate remedy of blowing out his brains. But the book is so often called morbid, so frequently have readers concluded that it is the work of an incipient madman, that I think it worth while to emphasize the gayety and comedy of the voyages as an indication of their author's essential intellectual and spiritual health. True, seventeen years after finishing *Gulliver's Travels,* Swift was officially declared *non compos mentis.* But his masterpiece was written at the height of his powers, and the comic animation of the book as a whole rules out the suspicion of morbidity and mental illness.

From *The Sewanee Review,* LXIII (1955), 48-71. Copyright 1955 by the University of the South. Reprinted by permission of Samuel Holt Monk.

1. Students of Swift will recognize my very great indebtedness to the work of other critcs and scholars. It would be pedantic to acknowledge borrowings so numerous and so self-evident. I hope that it is sufficient here to acknowledge this general indebtedness and to express my gratitude to those who, over a period of twenty-five years, have helped me to better understand Jonathan Swift.

We laugh and were meant to laugh at the toy kingdom of the Lilliputians; at the acrobatic skills of the politicians and courtiers; at the absurd jealousy of the diminutive minister who suspects an adulterous relationship between his wife and the giant Gulliver. We laugh at the plight of Gulliver in Brobdingnag: one of the lords of creation, frightened by a puppy, rendered ludicrous by the tricks of a mischievous monkey, in awe of a dwarf; embarrassed by the lascivious antics of the maids of honor; and at last content to be tended like a baby by his girl-nurse. We laugh at the abstractness of the philosophers of Laputa, at the mad experimenters of Balnibarbi. And I am sure that we are right in at least smiling at the preposterous horses, the Houyhnhnms, so limited and so positive in their knowledge and opinions, so skilled in such improbable tasks as threading needles or carrying trays, so complacent in their assurance that they are 'the Perfection of Nature.' Much of the delight that we take in *Gulliver's Travels* is due to this gay, comic, fanciful inventiveness. Swift might well say in the words of Hamlet: 'Lay not that flattering unction to your soul/That not your trespass but my madness speaks.' Swift did not wish us to blow out our brains; he did wish us to laugh. But beyond the mirth and liveliness are gravity, anger, anxiety, frustration—and he meant us to experience them fully.

For there is an abyss below this fantastic world—the dizzying abyss of corrupt human nature. Swift is the great master of shock. With perfect control of tone and pace, with perfect timing, he startles us into an awareness of this abyss and its implications. We are forced to gaze into the stupid, evil, brutal heart of humanity, and when we do, the laughter that Swift has evoked is abruptly silenced. The surface of the book is comic, but at its center is tragedy, transformed through style and tone into icy irony. Soft minds have found Swift's irony unnerving and depressing and, in self-protection, have dismissed him as a repellent misanthrope. Stronger minds that prefer unpalatable truths to euphoric illusions have found this irony bracing and healthful.

Before I discuss the book itself it is necessary to speak of certain ideas and tendencies that were current in Swift's world. *Gulliver's Travels* was written at the height of that phase of European civilization which we know as the Enlightenment, and the Enlightenment was the first clearly defined manifestation of modernity—the modernity of which our age may be the catastrophic conclusion. Swift wrote always in opposition to the Enlightenment and as an enemy of 'modernism.' He detected with uncanny prescience the implications of such characteristic ideas as the following: (1) Rationalism, especially Cartesianism, with its radical tendency to abstract truth into purely intellectual concepts, and its bold rejection of the experience and wisdom of the past. Swift doubted the capacity of human reason to attain metaphysical and theological truth. A safer guide in this life seemed to him to be what he called 'common forms,' the *consensus gentium,* the time-approved wisdom of the race. (2) Experimental and theoretical science, fathered by Bacon and Galileo, vindicated by Newton, and propagandized and nourished by the Royal Society. The science of Swift's day was predominantly concerned with physics and astronomy. Swift, I think, could not imaginatively relate to the moral—*i.e.*, the totally human—life of man the efforts of an astronomer to plot the trajectory of a comet or of a physicist to comprehend a universe that is 'really' no more than abstract mass, extension, and motion. Moreover science gave sanction to the idea of progress, deluding men with the promise of an ever-expanding and improving future, which to Swift seemed necessarily chimerical, man being limited as he is. And finally science unwittingly fostered the secularization of society and of human values, promising men mastery of nature and the abolition of all mysteries, and, by implication at least, of religion. Swift was a religious man. (3) The new conception of man, which was the result of both rationalism and science. It taught the essential goodness of human nature in a sentimental and optimistic tone of voice that irritated Swift and compelled him to reply with all his powers in *Gulliver's Travels*. (4) The new moneyed wealth of England, based upon trade and speculation and bolstering up the national importance of the middle class. Swift regarded this wealth and its owners as irresponsible and dangerous to the state. Divorced from land and the responsibilities implied in the ownership of land, it seemed to him abstract and at the same time frighteningly ambitious; and he had to look only to London and the Court to be assured that this new, vulgar, wealthy class was corrupting both the individual and the social and political institutions of England. (5) The increasing power of centralized government—in Swift's day a few ministers, the Crown and the court. To Swift, such power seemed necessarily evil since it was divorced from concrete human needs.

Why was Swift inimical to these tendencies—all of which are familiar aspects of our world today? Very simply, I think, because he was a Christian and a humanist. As a Christian he believed that man's fallen nature could never transcend its own limitations and so fulfil the hopes of that optimistic age; as a humanist he was concerned for the preservation of those moral and spiritual qualities which distinguish men from beasts and for the health and continuity of fruitful tradition in church, state, and the sphere of the mind. As both Christian and humanist, he knew that men must be better than they are and that, though our institutions can never be perfect, they need not be corrupt. The 'savage indignation' which motivates all of Swift's satires arises from his anger at the difference between what men are and what they might be if they only would rise to the full height of their humanity. If he indulged no Utopian hopes, he also never gave way to cheap cynicism.

Two famous letters, written in the fall of 1725, the year before *Gulliver's Travels* was published, tell us much about Swift's state of mind at this time. In the first, to Pope, he writes:

> . . . when you think of the world, give it one lash the more at my Request. I have ever hated all Nations, Professions, and Communities; and all my love is towards Individuals; for Instance, I hate the Tribe of Lawyers, Physicians . . . Soldiers, English, Scotch, French, and the rest. But principally I hate and detest that animal called Man, although I heartily love John, Peter, Thomas, and so forth. This is the system upon which I have

governed myself many Years . . . and so I shall go on until I have done with them. I have got Materials toward a Treatise, proving the falsity of that Definition, *Animal rationale* and to show that it should be only *rationis capax*. Upon this great foundation of Misanthropy (although not in Timon's Manner) the whole building of my travels is erected; and I will never have Peace of Mind until all honest Men are of my Opinion. . . .

This letter makes three important points.

(1) Swift's life and letters support his assertion that he could and did love individuals. His hatred was directed against abstract man, against men existing and acting within semi-human or dehumanized racial or professional groups. Apparently he felt that when men submerge their individual judgments and moral beings in such groups, they necessarily further corrupt their already corrupted natures. When for example an individual thinks or acts or feels not as a free moral agent responsible to God, but as a politician, a lawyer, a bishop, he abrogates to some degree his humanity. He becomes the instrument of a force that is larger than himself, but not so large as the moral law: and in so doing he becomes at least potentially evil. We hear a great deal today of group dynamics, group psychology, and mass communication. Swift would oppose these forces on the ground that they abridge the freedom which is necessary to the completely moral and responsible life.

(2) Swift dissociates his 'misanthropy' from that of Plutarch's Timon of Athens, the hero of Shakespeare's plays, who withdrew in bitter disillusionment merely to rail in solitude against mankind. Swift knew how sterile such an attitude is. His own satire is seldom merely invective. It is not paradoxical to say that it arises from philanthropy, not misanthropy, from idealism as to what man might be, not from despair at what he is.

(3) Swift rejects the definition of man as *animal rationale* in favor of the definition *animal capax rationis*. I think that he has Descartes in mind here, Descartes, who apparently had forgotten that God made man a little lower than the angels (pure intelligences) and consequently capable of only enough reason to order his world here and to find his way, with God's grace, to the next. The second letter, to Pope and Bolingbroke, amplifies this point.

> I tell you after all I do not hate Mankind, it is *vous autres* who hate them, because you would have them reasonable Animals, and are angry at being disappointed: I have always rejected that Definition, and made another of my own. I am no more angry with——than I was with the Kite that last Week flew away with one of my Chickens; and yet I was pleased when one of my servants shot him two days after.

Swift argues that the man really in danger of becoming a misanthrope is he who holds an unrealistic view of the potentialities of human nature and who expects that men can somehow transcend their limitations and become, shall we say, angels. In the phrase *vous autres*, Swift includes all the secular, scientific, deistic, optimistic—in a word, liberal—thinkers of the Enlightenment; and he turns in anger from them. The philanthropist will not be angry when he has to recognize the corruptions and limitations of human nature; he will settle for a creature who is *capable* of reason and will do the best he can with him. The word *capable* is a positive concept, not a negative one. It imposes a sort of moral imperative on man to exploit his capability to its fullest. As Swift makes plain in *Gulliver's Travels,* this task is large enough to occupy the whole attention of man. It is fallacious and stupid to attribute to our race qualities that it can never possess. To do so is pride, the besetting sin of men and angels, the sin that disrupts the natural and supernatural order of God's creation. The theme of pride looms large in all four voyages.

Seven years after the publication of *Gulliver's Travels,* Pope published his well-known comment on the tragic duality of man:

> Placed on this isthmus of a middle state,
> A being darkly wise, and rudely great:
> With too much knowledge for the Sceptic side,
> With too much weakness for the Stoic's pride,
> He hangs between; in doubt to act, or rest;
> In doubt to deem himself a God, or Beast;
> In doubt his Mind or Body to prefer;
> Born but to die, and reas'ning but to err;
> Alike in ignorance, his reason such,
> Whether he thinks too little, or too much:
> Chaos of Thought and Passion, all confused:
> Still by himself abused, or disabused;
> Created half to rise, and half to fall;
> Great lord of all things, yet a prey to all;
> Sole judge of Truth, in endless Error hurl'd:
> The glory, jest, and riddle of the world!

The idea that man occupies an anomalous, a middle, state in creation was a familiar one in Swift's day. The whole of living creation was conceived to be carefully ordered and subtly graded in one vast 'chain of being,' descending from God, through an almost infinite number of pure intelligences, to man, and thence through the lower animals to microscopic forms of life, which finally end in nothing. Man occupies the most uncomfortable position in this chain, since to a limited degree he shares the intelligence of higher creatures, and to an unlimited degree the sensuality of animals. He is the middle link because he is the transitional point between the purely intelligent and the purely sensual. With Pope, with Addison, and a number of other writers this image, for reasons which we shall not inquire into, became one of the chief supports of the optimism of the Enlightenment—optimism concerning God, nature, and man. To Pascal, in his moving 72nd *Pensée,* it had suggested tragic thoughts about the disproportion of man. Swift used it as an instrument of comedy, or irony, and of satire. In three of the four voyages, it plays an important role.

So much for background. Let us turn to the book. The first character to demand our attention is Gulliver himself. He is the narrator, the principal actor. We see through his eyes, feel his feelings, share his thoughts. We are in his company from first to last, and it is important that we come to know him as quickly as possible. What is he like and what is his role in the book? He is first of all a bit of a bore, for his mind is irritatingly circumstantial and unimaginative: observe the numerous insignificant biographical details which he gives us in the first pages of the book. Gradually, however, we come to like him and to enjoy his company. In all respects he is an average good man. He has had some university education both at Cambridge and at Leyden, where he studied medicine. He is observant (and we eventually come to be grateful for his gift of close observation and circumstantial reporting, once he has something worth observing and reporting), reasonably intelligent, thoroughly capable in an emergency, and both brave and hopeful. If he lacks imagination and inventiveness, so much the better; for we can be sure that what he tells us, no matter how strange, is true. He is simple, direct, uncomplicated. At the outset he is full of naive good will, and, though he grows less naive and more critical as a result of his voyaging among remote nations, he retains his benevolence throughout the first three voyages. It is a pity that so fine an example of the bluff, good-natured, honest Englishman should at last grow sick and morbid and should be driven mad—but that, I am afraid, is what befalls him.

All of this Gulliver is; but let us notice carefully what he is NOT. He is NOT Jonathan Swift. The meaning of the book is wholly distorted if we identify the Gulliver of the last voyage with his creator, and lay Gulliver's misanthropy at Swift's door. He is a fully rendered, objective, dramatic character, no more to be identified with Swift than Shylock is to be identified with Shakespeare. This character acts and is acted upon; he changes, he grows in the course of his adventures. Like King Lear, he begins in simplicity, grows into sophistication, and ends in madness. Unlike King Lear he is never cured.

The four voyages 'into several remote nations of the world' are so arranged as to attain a climactic intensification of tone as we travel through increasing darkness into the black heart of humanity. But the forward movement is interrupted by the third voyage, a macabre scherzo on science, politics, economics as they are practiced by madmen— Swift's term for those who misuse and abuse human reason. Observe that the tone of each voyage is established by the nature of the event that brings about the adventure: in the first voyage (the most benign and the gayest) accident, or at worst, the carelessness of the lookout, accounts for the shipwreck; in the second, much more savage in tone, Gulliver is left alone in a strange land, through the cowardice of his shipmates; in the third, he is captured and later abandoned by pirates (evil in action); in the fourth, his crew of cutthroats mutinies, seizes the ship, and leaves him to starve on a near-by island. Gulliver thus describes this crew to his Houyhnhnm master:

> I said they were Fellows of desparate Fortunes, forced to fly from the Places of their Birth, on Account of their Poverty and their Crimes. Some were undone by Lawsuits; others spent all they

had in Drinking, Whoring, and gaming; others fled for Treason; many for Murder, Theft, Poisoning, Robbery, Perjury, Forgery, Coining false Money; for committing Rapes and Sodomy; for flying from their Colours, or deserting to the Enemy; and most of them had broken Prison. . . .

The good ship *Adventure* was a little world which housed the whole of unregenerate human nature.

It is best to consider the first two voyages together and to notice how effectively Swift uses the idea of the great chain of being. Pascal, writing of man's disproportion, had asked: 'For in fact, what is man in nature? A nothing in comparison with the Infinite, an All in comparison with the Nothing, a mean between nothing and everything.' Swift transposes this theme into another key, and makes it the major instrument of his satire. In the first two voyages, Gulliver is made aware of his disproportion; placed on this isthmus of a middle state, in the voyage to Lilliput he looks down the chain of being and knows himself an awkward, if kindly, giant in that delicate kingdom; in the voyage to Brobdingnag he looks up the chain and discovers a race of 'superior beings,' among whom his pride shrivels through the humiliating knowledge of his own physical insignificance. The emphasis here is upon size, the physical; but it is none the less notable that Lilliputia calls into operation Gulliver's engaging kindliness and gentleness, and that Brobdingnag brings out his moral and physical courage. Though comically and tragically disproportioned, man has moral virtues which he can and does exercise.

But Swift's satire is a two-edged sword. What of the inhabitants of these strange lands? They too are disproportioned. From the start the Lilliputians win our interest and liking: these pigmies ingeniously capture the Hercules whom chance has cast on their shore; they humanely solve the problem of feeding him; their pretty land and their fascinating little city take our fancy. But in the end what do they prove to be? prideful, envious, rapacious, treacherous, cruel, vengeful, jealous, and hypocritical. Their primitive social and political systems have been corrupted; they are governed by an Emperor who is ambitious totally to destroy the neighboring kingdom, and by courtiers and ministers who are chosen not for their fitness for office, but for their skill in walking the tightrope, leaping over sticks or creeping under them. 'Climbing,' Swift once remarked, 'is performed in the same Posture with Creeping.' These little people, like Gulliver himself, are an instance of the disproportion of man. Their vices, their appetites, their ambitions, their passions are not commensurate with their tiny stature. They appear to Gulliver as he and his kind must appear to the higher orders of beings— as venomous and contemptibly petty.

In Brobdingnag we meet creatures ten times the size of Europeans, and we share Gulliver's anxiety lest their moral natures be as brutish as their bodies. But the reverse is true; and through a violent and effective shift of symbol, tone, and point of view, Gulliver, who seemed lovable and humane among the Lilliputians, appears an ignominious and morally insensitive being in contrast to the enlightened and benevolent

Brobdingnagians. Since Gulliver represents us, his shame, unsufficiency, and ludicrousness are ours.

When the peasants discover him, they feel both curiosity and repulsion: the farmer picks him up 'with the Caution of one who endeavors to lay hold on a small dangerous Animal in such a Manner that it shall not be able either to scratch or to bite him, . . .' Gulliver fears that his captor may dash him to the ground, 'as we usually do any little hateful Animal which we have a Mind to destroy.' The change in tone and intent is obvious.

Gulliver is submitted to one humiliation after another, but he is still capable of a fatuous blindness to the defects of European society, and when the King questions him about England he describes with uncritical enthusiasm its class system, its constitution, its laws, its military glory, and its history. In the questions which the king asks and which Gulliver meets with only an embarrassed silence, the voice of morality is heard condemning the institutions of the modern world. And the verdict of a moral being on European man is given in words as icy as controlled contempt can make them: 'But, by what I have gathered from your own Relation, and the Answers I have with much Pains wringed and extorted from you; I cannot but conclude the Bulk of your Natives to be the most pernicious Race of little odious Vermin that Nature ever suffered to crawl upon the Surface of the Earth.'

Such a conclusion is inevitable, for the King is high-minded, benevolent, and, in Swift's sense of the word, rational: i.e., he and his people think practically, not theoretically; concretely, not metaphysically; simply, not intricately. Brobdingnag is a Swiftian Utopia of common good sense and morality; and Gulliver, conditioned by the corrupt society from which he comes, appears naive, blind, and insensitive to moral values. His account of the history of England in the seventeenth century evokes the King's crushing retort:

> . . . it was only an Heap of Conspiracies, Rebellions, Murders, Massacres, Revolutions, Banishments; the very worst Effects that Avarice, Faction, Hypocrisy, Perfidiousness, Cruelty, Rage, Madness, Hatred, Envy, Lust, Malice and Ambition could produce.

Notice the carefully arranged disorder of that list, the calculated avoidance of climax. This is a favorite device of Swift: the irrational, the appetitive, the evil nature of man *is* disorder.

The King is horrified when Gulliver offers him a way to complete dominion over his subjects by teaching him to make gunpowder. And Gulliver, speaking as a European, feels contemptuous surprise. 'A strange Effect of *narrow Principles* and *short Views!*' The King is baffled by the concept of political *science*—how can the *art* of government be reduced to a science?

> He confined the knowledge of governing within very *narrow Bounds;* to common Sense and Reason, to Justice and Lenity, to the Speedy Determination of Civil and criminal Causes; with some other obvious Topicks which are not worth considering. And he gave it

for his Opinion; that whoever could make two Ears of Corn, or two Blades of Grass to grow upon a Spot of Ground where only one grew before would deserve better of Mankind, and do more essential Service to his Country, than the whole Race of Politicians put together.

The learning of the Brobdingnagians is simple and practical, 'consisting only in Morality, History, Poetry, and Mathematicks.' Observe that Swift omits metaphysics, theoretical science, and theology from the category of useful knowledge.

Swift's attack on pride in the first two voyages is made more powerful because of his brilliant use of the chain of being. In so far as we recognize ourselves in the Lilliputians or in Gulliver in Brobdingnag, we become aware of our pettiness—of the disproportion of our race and of the shocking difference between what we profess and what we are. But Swift uses the good giants to strike an unexpected blow at human vanity and to introduce a motif which he employed with deadly effect in the last voyage. That motif is disgust, of which, as T. S. Eliot has remarked, he is the great master. Philosophers of the century were never tired of admiring the beautiful perfection of the human body, its intricateness, its perfect articulation, its happy appropriateness to the particular place that men occupy in the scheme of things. But how does this glorious body appear to lesser creatures—say to an insect? Swift forces us to answer by making us share Gulliver's disgust at the cancerous breasts and lousy bodies of the beggars; at the blotched color, the huge pores, the coarse hairs, and the nauseous odors of the maids of honor. Such is the skin, presumably, that the Brobdingnagians love to touch. Our beauty is only apparent; our disproportion is real.

The third voyage has always been considered the least successful; that may well be, but it is none the less interesting. Structurally it is loosely episodic, lacking unity of action and tone. Into it Swift seems to have put all the material that he could not work into the other three voyages. It is a fantasia on two themes which Swift treats under a single metaphor: the metaphor is science, the themes are politics and the abuse of reason. In short, the voyage is a digression on madness, on the divorce of man and good sense in the modern world.

At this point, I fear, it is necessary to defend Swift, since he will seem merely stupid and prejudiced to a generation that enjoys the blessings of television, the common cold, and the hydrogen bomb. Moreover, to liberals he will appear an unenlightened political reactionary. I have said earlier that in my opinion Swift distrusted science because it seemed irrelevant to the moral life of man. Though no scientist, he was not an ignoramus. He had read contemporary science—Descartes, Newton, and the yearly *Transactions of the Royal Society*. The Flying Island is conceived on sound scientific principles; some of the mad experiments of the scientists of Balnibarbi are grotesque distortions of ideas actually advanced by members of the Royal Society. The philosophers of the Flying Island are lost in the abstractness of mathematics, music, and astronomy to the great neglect of all practical reality, including their wives. The very tailors measure Gulliver for clothes by abstruse mathematical processes and contrive a suit which fits him not at all. Swift lived before the age of applied science, but I do not think that he would be surprised to learn that modern citizens of his Flying Island contrived the most significant event of the twentieth century—Hiroshima.

It is also necessary to apologize for Swift's political views. He was a Tory, a conservative—opprobrious terms today. In economics he was an agrarian; in politics a royalist; in religion a high churchman. He disapproved the founding of the National Bank; could make no sense of a national debt, a gadget invented in his time; he distrusted the new moneyed wealth, the ancestor of modern capitalism, which increased the political power and importance of the merchant class, and he found his distrust justified in 1720 by the disastrous collapse of South Sea stocks. Innovation and experimentation in politics he detested and fought. He would have hated the improvisations of the New Deal; he would have deplored the vast powers of our Federal Government; he would have loathed the whole program of the Labor Party in Britain. And were he alive, he would fight the abstract state of this century with every weapon within reach.

Too many liberals are unaware of the fact that a man may be a non-liberal without being illiberal; that he may distrust the abstract power of government, the theoretical formulae of economists, politicians, and social scientists and the like without ceasing to be actively and effectively concerned for human welfare. Swift was a Tory who fought valiantly and at times successfully for the oppressed. Living in Ireland, contemptuous of the Irish, detesting their Catholicism, he none the less became their champion against the oppression and exploitation of his adopted country by the English Court and Parliament. He is one of the heroes of modern Ireland because he first gave effective expression to Irish nationalism. He earned the right to the last sentence of the epitaph which he composed for his own tombstone: *Abi Viator / et imitare, si poteris / Strenuum pro virili / Libertatis Vindicatorem.*

The Flying Island is not only a trope for science; it is also a mordant image of the concentration of political power in the hands of a clique remote from human needs, motivated by pure theory, and given to experiment and improvisation. Laputa (perhaps, as has been suggested, Spanish *La Púta,* 'the whore') is a symbol of such government: it is controlled by madmen who govern scientifically, not morally; it is a *flying* island, and hence out of touch with subject territories, which it exploits and tyrannizes over by means of what we call today air power; it can withhold sun and rain as a punitive device, or can harass through bombing raids, or even tyrannously crush all opposition by settling its great weight upon the land below. One contrasts this form of government with that of the wise and good King of Brobdingnag.

When Gulliver visits the subject land of Balnibarbi, which is of course England, he sees the result of statism.

> The People in the Streets walked fast, looked wild, their Eyes fixed, and were generally in Rags. We passed through one of the Town Gates, and went about three Miles into the Country,

where I saw many Labourers working with several Sorts of Tools in the Ground, but was not able to conjecture what they were about; neither did I observe any Expectation either of Corn or Grass, although the Soil appeared to be excellent.

This is what comes of experimentation in government and of financial speculation. It strongly suggests the memories that some of us have of the great depression. A modern Tory used it effectively as the basis of an attack on the post-war Labor Government.

But there are other ills consequent to the abstract state. Too great a concentration of power leads to tyranny; tyranny breeds fear; fear breeds the obnoxious race of spies and informers. The abstract state becomes the police state.

I told him that in the Kingdom of *Tribnia* [Britain], by the Natives called *Langden* [England], where I had sojourned some time in my Travels, the Bulk of the People consist in a manner wholly of Discoverers, Witnesses, Informers, Accusers, Prosecutors, Evidences, Swearers; together with their several subservient and subaltern Instruments; all under Deputies. The Plots in that Kingdom are usually the Workmanship of those Persons who desire to raise their own Character of profound Politicians; to restore new Vigour to a crazy Administration; to stifle or divert general Discontents; to fill their Pockets with Forfeitures; and raise or sink the Opinion of publick Credit, as either shall best answer their private Advantage. It is first agreed and settled among them, what suspected Persons shall be accused of a Plot: then, effectual Care is taken to secure all their Letters and Papers, and put the Criminals in Chains. These Papers are delivered to a Set of Artists, very dexterous in finding out the mysterious Meanings of Words, Syllables, and Letters. For Instance, they can decypher a Close-stool to signify a Privy-Council; a Flock of Geese, a Senate; a lame Dog, an Invader; a Codshead, a [King]; the Plague, a Standing Army; a Buzzard, a Prime Minister; the Gout, a High Priest; a Gibbet, a Secretary of State; a Chamber pot, a Committee of Grandees; a Sieve, a Court Lady; a Broom, a Revolution; a Mouse-trap, an Employment; a bottomless Pit, The Treasury; a Sink, the C[our]t; a Cap and Bells, a Favourite; a broken Reed, a Court of Justice; an empty Tun, a General; a running Sore, the Administration.

One cannot read that passage without thinking of certain testimony given of late years in Washington.

Such are the fruits of madness—of that pride which impels us to trust our reason beyond its proper scope and which suggests that we can build a heavenly city on earth on principles divorced from humanity and morality.

The climactic fourth voyage is the great section of *Gulliver's Travels*. It has provoked violent attacks on Swift and his book, entirely, I think, because it has been misunderstood. It has offended the unreflective and pious Christian, the sentimentalist, and the optimist. Thackeray, lecturing to the ladies in London in 1851, the year in which the Great Exhibition seemed to give the lie to every opinion that Swift held, may serve as an example, by no means unique, of the capacity of this voyage to shock. He advised his ladies not to read the last voyage, and to hoot the Dean. And the meaning that he found in it was 'that man is utterly wicked, desperate, and imbecile, and his passions are monstrous, and his boasted power mean, that he is and deserves to be the shame of brutes, and ignorance is better than his vaunted reason.' 'It is Yahoo language,' he continues, 'a monster gibbering shrieks and gnashing imprecations against mankind . . . filthy in word, filthy in thought, furious, raging, obscene.'

The legend of Swift as a savage, mad, embittered misanthrope largely rests upon this wrong-headed, sensational reading of the last voyage. In my opinion the work is that of a Christian-humanist and a moralist who no more blasphemes against the dignity of human nature than do St. Paul and some of the angrier prophets of the Old Testament. Swift has been misunderstood for several reasons.

1. The sheer intensity and violent rhetoric of the voyage are overwhelming and may well numb the critical sense of certain readers.

2. Gulliver in the frenzy of his mad misanthropy has been too facilely identified with Swift. Gulliver speaks for Gulliver and not for his creator in the final pages of the book, and careful reading should reveal the plain fact that he becomes the victim of Swift's irony as he grows to hate the human race. The final pages of the book are grimly comic.

3. The primary symbols of the voyage have been totally misunderstood. The Houyhnhnms have been regarded as Swift's ideal for man, and the Yahoos have been identified as his representation of what men are. Neither of these opinions, I believe, is correct.

Let us begin with the Houyhnhnms and the Yahoos. In the first two voyages Gulliver is shown uncomfortably situated on the isthmus of a middle state between the very large and the very small. In this voyage he also stands on an isthmus, but now it is between the purely rational and the purely sensual—between Houyhnhnm and Yahoo. Neither of these symbols can stand for man, since Gulliver himself is the symbol of humanity. Unfortunately for poor Gulliver, he shares somehow in the nature of both extremes. Swift simply isolates the two elements that combine in the duality of man, the middle link, in order to allow Gulliver to contemplate each in its essence.

Does Swift recommend that Gulliver should strive to become a Houyhnhnm? We discover that in every sense Houyhnhnmland is a rationalistic Utopia. The Houyhnhnms are the embodiment of pure reason. They know neither love nor grief nor lust nor ambition. They cannot lie; indeed they have no word for lying and are hard put to it to understand the meaning of *opinion*. Their society is an aristocracy, resting upon the slave labor of the Yahoos and the work of an especially-bred servant class. With icy, stoical calm they face the processes of life—marriage, childbirth, accident, death. Their society is a planned society that has achieved the mild anarchy that many Utopian dreamers have aspired to. They practice eugenics, and since they know no lust, they control the size of their population; children are educated by the state; their agrarian economy is supervised by a democratic council; government is entirely conducted by periodic assemblies. The Houyhnhnms feel natural human affection for each other, but they love every one equally. It is all very admirable, but it is remote from the possibilities of human life.

Does Swift intend us to accept this as his ideal way of life? He who loved and hated and fought and bled internally through *saeva indignatio?* I think not. The Houyhnhnms resemble Cartesians and are clearly stoics. 'Neither is *Reason* among them a Point problematical as with us,' reports Gulliver, 'where Men can argue with Plausibility on both Sides of a Question; but strikes you with immediate Conviction; . . .' This is the Houyhnhnm version of Descartes' rational intuition of clear and distinct ideas. Now Swift was anti-Cartesian from his first published satire, for the simple reason that he held that Descartes was self-deluded and that man's reason was incapable of the feats that Descartes attributed to it. The Houyhnhnms are stoics, and Swift recorded his view of stoicism in *Thoughts on Various Subjects:* "The Stoical Scheme of supplying our Wants, by lopping off our Desires, is like cutting off our Feet when we want Shoes.' It is Gulliver, not Swift, who is dazzled by the Houyhnhnms and who aspires to rise above the human condition and to become pure intelligence as these horses and the angels are.

The most powerful single symbol in all Swift is the Yahoos. They do not represent Swift's view of man, but rather of the bestial element in man—the unenlightened, unregenerate, irrational element in human nature. Hence the Houyhnhnms classify Gulliver with them; hence the female Yahoo wishes to couple with him; hence despite his instinctive recoiling from them, Gulliver has to admit with shame and horror that he is more like them than he is like the Houyhnhnms. This I think is clear. Because of his neglect or misuse of human reason, European man has sunk nearer to the Yahoo pole of his nature than he has risen toward the Houyhnhnm pole. The seeds of human society and of human depravity, as they exist in Europe, are clearly discerned in the society and conduct of the Yahoos. Gulliver looks into the obscene abyss of human nature unlighted by the frail light of reason and of morality, and the sight drives him mad.

Repelled by what he sees, he, not Swift, identifies the Yahoos with man; and he, not Swift, turns misanthrope. Since he will not be a Yahoo he seeks to become, as nearly as possible, a Houyhnhnm. But he can do so only by denying his place in and responsibility to humanity, by aspiring above the middle link, which is man, to the next higher link, that of the purely rational. The wise Houyhnhnm, to whom he gives his terrifying account of European man and society, concludes that 'the corruption of reason' is worse than brutality itself, and that man is more dangerous than the Yahoo. This is profoundly true. But its effect on Gulliver is to awaken loathing of all that is human.

Lear, gazing on the naked, shivering Edgar, disguised as a Tom o' Bedlam, cries: "Thou art the thing itself; unaccommodated man is no more but such a poor, bare, forked animal as thou art.' And in that intense moment, he goes mad. Something of the same thing befalls Gulliver. He thinks he has seen the thing itself. Though the Houyhnhnms never acknowledge that he is more than an unusually gifted Yahoo, he aspires to their rationality, stoicism, and simple wisdom; and persuaded that he has attained them, he feeds his growing misanthropy on pride, which alienates him not only from his remote kinsmen, the Yahoos, but eventually from his brothers, the human race. Looking back with nostalgia on his lost happiness in Houyhnhnmland, he recalls:

> I enjoyed perfect Health of Body, and Tranquility of Mind; I did not feel the Treachery or Inconstancy of a Friend, nor the Injuries of a secret or open Enemy. I had no Occasion of bribing, flattering, or pimping, to procure the Favour of any great Man, or of his Minion. I wanted no Fence against Fraud or Oppression: Here was neither Physician to destroy my Body, nor Lawyer to ruin my Fortune: No Informer to Watch my Words and Actions, or forge Accusations against me for Hire: Here were no Gibers, Censurers, Backbiters, Pickpockets, Highwaymen, Housebreakers, Attorneys, Bawds, Buffoons, Gamesters, Politicians, Wits, Spleneticks, tedious Talkers, Controvertists, Ravishers, Murderers, Robbers, Virtuosos; no Leaders or Followers of Party and Faction; no Encouragers to Vice, by Seducement or Examples: no Dungeon, Axes, Gibbets, Whippingposts, or Pillories; No cheating Shopkeepers or Mechanicks; No Pride, Vanity or Affection: No Fops, Bullies, Drunkards, strolling Whores, or Poxes: No ranting, lewd, expensive Wives: No stupid, proud Pedants: No importunate, over-bearing, quarrelsome, noisy, roaring, empty, conceited, swearing Companions: No Scoundrels raised from the Dust upon the Merit of their Vices; or Nobility thrown into it on account of their Virtues: No Lords, Fiddlers, Judges or Dancing-masters.

From the moment that the banished Gulliver despairingly sets sail from Houyhnhnmland, his pride, his misanthropy, his madness are apparent. Deluded by his worship of pure reason, he commits the error of the Houyhnhnms in equating human beings with the Yahoos. Captured by a Portuguese crew and forced to return from sullen solitude to humanity, he trembles between fear and hatred. The captain of the ship, Don Pedro de Mendez, like Gulliver himself, shares the nature of the Houyhnhnm and the Yahoo; and like the Gulliver of the first voyage he is tolerant, sympathetic, kindly, patient, and charitable; but Gulliver can no longer recognize these traits in a human being. With the myopic vision of the Houyhnhnms, he perceives only the Yahoo and is repelled by Don Pedro's clothes, food, and odor. Gradually, however, he is nursed back to partial health, and is forced to admit in the very accent of his admired horses, that his benefactor has a 'very good *human* Understanding.' But the Gulliver who writes this book is still under the control of his *idée fixe,* and when we last see him he prefers the smell and conversation of his two horses to the company of his wife and children. This is misanthropy in Timon's manner, not Swift's. In the brilliant and intricately ironic coda with which the book ends, Swift directs his savage, comic gaze straight at Gulliver and his insane pretensions.

> My Reconcilement to the *Yahoo*-kind in general might not be so difficult, if they would be content with those Vices and Follies only which Nature hath entitled them to. I am not in the least provoked at the Sight of a Lawyer, a Pickpocket, a Colonel, a Fool, a Lord, a Gamester, a Politician, a Whoremunger, a Physician, an Evidence, a Suborner, an Attorney, a Traytor, or the like: This is all according to the due Course of Things: But when I behold a Lump of Deformity, and Diseases both of Body and Mind, smitten with *Pride,* it immediately breaks all the Measures of my Patience; neither shall I ever be able to comprehend how such an Animal and such a Vice could tally together.

The grim joke is that Gulliver himself is the supreme instance of a creature smitten with pride. His education has somehow failed. He has voyaged into several remote nations of the world, but the journeys were not long, because of course he has never moved outside the bounds of human nature. The countries he visited, like the Kingdom of Heaven, are all within us. The ultimate danger of these travels was precisely the one that destroyed Gulliver's humanity—the danger that in his explorations he would discover something that he was not strong enough to face. This befell him, and he took refuge in a sick and morbid pride that alienated him from his species and taught him the gratitude of the Pharisee—'Lord, I thank Thee that I am not as other men.'

Swift himself, in his personal conduct, displayed an arrogant pride. But he was never guilty of the angelic, dehumanizing pride of Gulliver, who writes in a letter to his Cousin Sympson:

> I must freely confess, that since my last Return, some corruptions of my *Yahoo* Nature have revived in me by Conversing with a few of your Species, and particularly those of my own Family, by an unavoidable Necessity; else I should never have attempted so absurd a Project as that of reforming the *Yahoo* Race in this Kingdom; but, I have now done with all such visionary Schemes for ever.

Jonathan Swift was stronger and healthier than Lemuel Gulliver. He hated the stupidity and the sinfulness and the folly of mankind. He could not accept the optimistic view of human nature that the philosophers of the Enlightenment proposed. And so he could exclaim to his contemporaries: 'O wicked and perverse generation!' But, until he entered upon the darkness of his last years, he did not abandon his fellow man as hopeless or cease to announce, however indirectly, the dignity and worth of human kind.

Point of view

John M. Major

THE PERSONALITY OF CHAUCER THE PILGRIM

Much of the fascination—and complexity—of the General Prologue to the *Canterbury Tales* may be attributed to the elusiveness of Chaucer's point of view. Is the "I" of the General Prologue Chaucer the man, Chaucer the poet, or a *persona* created for the situation by the poet? In order to arrive at a satisfactory interpretation of either the Prologue or the *Tales* as a whole, we have first to decide as best we can who it is that is reporting to us the appearance, characters, actions, conversations, and stories of himself and his fellow pilgrims.

In a brilliant essay of a few years ago, E. Talbot Donaldson proposed that Chaucer the pilgrim was a fictional creation of Chaucer the poet, with a distinct personality of his own which was very unlike that of his creator. This pilgrim is an amiable, exceedingly naive bourgeois who admires success of every kind, but especially material success; who uncritically accepts the values of the upper class, as these are embodied in the Knight, the Prioress, the Monk, and the Friar; and who recognizes virtue and wickedness only when they are thoroughly obvious. It is a mistake, Professor Donaldson believes, "to see in the Prologue a reporter who is acutely aware of the significance of what he sees but who sometimes, for ironic emphasis, interprets the evidence presented by his observation in a fashion directly contrary to what we expect. The proposition ought to be expressed in reverse: the reporter is, usually, acutely unaware of the significance of what he sees, no matter how sharply he sees it." The implied contrast between this man's obtuse innocence and the sophisticated clarity of Chaucer's own outlook is what, in Professor Donaldson's opinion, chiefly makes for the poet's "wonderfully complex, ironic, comic, serious vision of a world."[1]

That so fresh and stimulating a theory should have enjoyed wide acceptance is quite understandable. And yet finally, I believe, so many

From *PMLA*, LXXV (June 1960), 160-162. Reprinted by permission of the Modern Language Association.

1. E. Talbot Donaldson, "Chaucer the Pilgrim," *PMLA*, LXIX (1954), 928-936. The same main points are repeated in the recent *Chaucer's Poetry*, ed. E. T. Donaldson (New York, 1958), pp. 877-881.

things in the Prologue do not fit within this theory that we are forced to construct a very different kind of Narrator from the one Professor Donaldson has represented.

It can hardly be denied that the Narrator of the General Prologue is a *persona* of some sort. Few would argue that the man Chaucer (or the poet Chaucer, if you will) was literally present on the famous pilgrimage to Canterbury; that would be carrying the requirements of realism to a quite unnecessary length even for modern tastes. And it goes without saying that all fiction, even that told in the first person ostensibly by the author himself, of necessity excludes the author from literal participation in the action. Narrative literature like the *Canterbury Tales* or the *Decameron* or *Gulliver's Travels* is fiction, certainly, regardless of the fact that the authors choose to enclose their stories within a realistic framework. For the reader the problem is not to discover that the author has a spokesman, but to try to catch from the spokesman's words and the tone of his voice the "real" viewpoint held by the author himself. This problem becomes especially difficult when one is dealing with an habitual ironist like Jonathan Swift or Jane Austen or Geoffrey Chaucer.

Granted that Chaucer does employ a *persona* in the *Canterbury Tales;* still, he does not employ him very consistently. Time and again in the General Prologue information about the other pilgrims that the Narrator, as a human being of limited knowledge, cannot possess is readily furnished by the author himself. The point of view shifts back and forth quite unrealistically between that of a first-person Narrator with restricted vision and that of an omniscient author.[2] This fact by itself ought to signify that Chaucer's *persona* just barely has an existence of his own—that he is, actually, little more than a shadowy extension of the poet himself, put forth and withdrawn to suit the poet's needs. If Chaucer had taken the pains to fashion a Narrator such as Professor Donaldson has invented, a fully conceived human being with a distinct personality the opposite of Chaucer's own, he would surely have allowed that Narrator to function all of the time, instead of only intermittently. Otherwise, there would seem to be little reason for his existing at all.

If, on the other hand, we think of the Narrator as a kind of *alter ego* of the poet himself, with just so many shades of difference as allow for ironic play, no difficulty is raised by the alternating points of view. This Narrator reveals himself to be, like his creator, perceptive, witty, sophisticated, playful, tolerant, detached, and, above all, ironic. Such a man is very well aware of the significance of what he observes, though he may show his awareness by subtle means.

These means would, however, have a much stronger appeal for the sophisticated readers and audience for whom Chaucer wrote the *Tales* than would the rather thin joke, the crude device, that relies for its effectiveness on an exaggerated difference between poet and *persona*.

2. See Ben Kimpel, "The Narrator of the *Canterbury Tales*," *ELH*, xx (1953), 77-86; also Edgar Hill Duncan, "Narrator's Points of View in the Portrait-sketches, Prologue to the *Canterbury Tales*," in *Essays in Honor of Walter Clyde Curry* (Nashville, 1954), pp. 77-101.

One of the strongest arguments against a credulous Narrator, it seems to me, is that he would have to be credulous to the point of stupidity and would therefore cease to be credible, let alone interesting. Surely it is incredible that a person of even a very low intelligence should fail to recognize that he was contradicting himself when he applauded both the Monk's refusal to "swynken with his handes . . . As Austyn bit" (A 186-187)[3] and the Plowman's, the "trewe swynkere's," willingness to work without pay "For Cristes sake, for every povre wight" (A 537). Or when he admired in one breath the Friar's skill in begging from the poor widow who "hadde noght a sho" (A 253) her last farthing and in the next breath the Parson's charity in giving from his own small substance "Unto his povre parisshens" (A 488). Throughout the Prologue one set of values is being opposed to another, with the most deliberate, though subtle, craft: generosity and charity are set against greed and self-indulgence; temperance and austerity against lechery, gluttony, and extravagance in dress; honesty against thievery and double-dealing; piety against corruption and worldly vanity; and so on, with many variations and interchanges. Only a complete fool could observe and report these things without realizing that they were antithetical.

That the real *persona*, who is far from being a fool, understands what he sees ought to be clear from a number of indications. Not that he is given to moralizing; Chaucer the pilgrim, like his companion the Parson, has a wide tolerance of human weakness, and he can warm up to almost all of his fellow pilgrims, especially if they are convivial. Most of what he observes, both the good and the bad, he reports with a straight face, that is, with deliberate irony. I can see no other way of interpreting those remarks of his that are delivered with such shocking suddenness and such murderous innocence—like his mock approbation of the Friar's shunning of beggars and lepers: "It is nat honest, it may nat avaunce" (A 246); or of the Monk's distaste for study and labor: "How shal the world be served?" (A 187). The same deliberate irony is powerfully at work in a whole series of passages in which lines of a quiet innocence suddenly reveal themselves, through the Narrator's sly use of juxtaposition and seeming irrelevance, to have a satirical purpose. The Prioress is "so charitable and so pitous"—that she weeps over a dead mouse (A 143-145). The Monk would make a fine abbot —because he is virile and has a stable full of splendid horses (A 167-168). The Friar is a "noble post" to his order—because he arranges marriages for the young women he has seduced (A 212-214); he is also courteous and humble—when it profits him to be so (A 249-252). The Wife has been a "worthy womman" all her life—witness her five husbands (A 459-460).

No innocent could have hit the mark so many times accidentally. Alexander Pope, one recalls, gains some of his finest satirical effects through the same devices of antithesis and anticlimax.

These passages cited and many others in the General Prologue can only have been devised in a vein of *conscious* irony, by a man who is

3. Citations from Chaucer in my text are to *The Works of Geoffrey Chaucer*, ed. F. N. Robinson, 2nd ed. (Boston, 1957).

sufficiently acute to be able to handle the mode. It is impossible otherwise to account for lines like that referring to the Friar—"Ther nas
no man nowher so vertuous" (A 251)—coming, as it does, in the
midst of other lines that so obviously and even heavily point up the
Friar's greed and hypocrisy. To argue that Chaucer the poet is the
one responsible for these satirical strokes is to beg the question. If
there is to be a Narrator who stands fully independent of the author,
who exists as an actual character in the drama, with a personality as
sharply defined as that of any of the other characters, that man has to
be permitted to do all of the narrating, and to do it in his own style,
as dictated by the kind of man he is.

It would be singularly odd if the Narrator, alone of all the pilgrims,
were blind to the faults of the Monk, the Friar, and most of the other
churchmen who are present. In one place after another in the *Tales*
the proverbial bad habits of the medieval clergy—the same bad habits
which the Narrator is supposed not to recognize in his religious companions—are mentioned freely and bluntly and without apology by
several of the pilgrims, some of whom, at least, would not be considered
particularly bright specimens of humanity. Even the ecclesiastical members of the pilgrimage seem to acknowledge and accept the unflattering
public image of themselves, for they do not object or seek to exclude
themselves from the general censure. The town parson in the *Reeve's
Tale* will provide for his illegitimate daughter a dowry out of church
funds, for, as the Reeve satirically puts it, "hooly chirches good moot
been despended / On hooly chirches blood, that is descended" (A
3983-84). (Incidentally, is not the tone of these lines precisely that of
the lines quoted earlier to illustrate the Narrator's employment of conscious irony? And yet no one would accuse the Reeve of being a sim-
pleton ignorant of the import of what he says.) Following the Shipman's
tale about a cozening and fornicating monk, the Host jocularly warns
his male companions not to let monks into their houses. Not only does
the Host show no concern lest his remarks may have offended the
churchmen who are present; he even calls upon the gentle Prioress
for the next tale. She, at least, is sensitive to the low reputation of her
calling; the abbot in her story is "an hooly man, / As monkes been—
or elles oghte be" (B 1832-33). In the Prologue to the *Monk's Tale* the
Host jokes with the Monk about the latter's lusty physique; the brawny
men are all in the church, he complains, which "maketh that oure
wyves wole assaye / Religious folk, for ye mowe bettre paye / Of
Venus paiementz than mowe we" (B 3149-51). Professor Donaldson
finds in the Narrator's comment on this raillery—"This worthy Monk
took al in pacience" (B 3155)—further evidence of the Narrator's uncritical admiration for the Monk. Is it not, rather, another instance of
the Narrator's use of conscious irony, the idea being, of course, that
the Monk had no choice but to submit patiently to jokes about his
worldliness, so plain for all to see?

Many other examples could be brought in to show that Chaucer's
pilgrims as a group regard churchmen as more often sinners than not.
The Nun's Priest is subjected by the Host to the same coarse raillery
as was the Monk, but he, too, takes it without protest. The Wife of

Bath delivers a thrust at lecherous friars; the Friar exposes the greed and dishonesty of summoners and makes passing reference to lustful priests and a venal archdeacon; the Canon's Yeoman tells about a rascally canon who defrauds a fellow churchman while pretending to teach him alchemy. All these examples and others show plainly that by general consensus Chaucer's pilgrims—and no doubt the fourteenth-century public whom they represent—looked on the average churchman as derelict in his vows and duties. Their jibes, some good-natured, some rough, must be in part meant for the ears of those churchmen who are their traveling companions, one or another of whom exhibits most of the vices that are so pointedly mentioned. If these vices are apparent to all the other pilgrims, even the duller-witted ones, why should they not be apparent to the Narrator as well? To deny him this elementary mental accomplishment would be to convict him of almost unbelievable stupidity.

By the same token, if the Narrator can neither use irony himself nor detect it in others, he misses the whole point of the tales told by such associates as the Nun's Priest, the Manciple, the Merchant, and the Clerk. A man so thick-skulled might better have stayed at home. Certainly he would be an extraordinary choice for recorder of some of the wittiest and most subtle stories ever told. One would think it would require a fairly high intelligence simply to follow these stories and record their nuances accurately.

The continuing use of deliberate irony by a *persona* whose outlook is almost indistinguishable from Chaucer's own helps to explain other problems in interpretation. It explains, for example, the Narrator's fondness for superlatives. This is not a mark of naïveté. The triple negative in his statement about the Friar, that "Ther nas no man no-wher so vertuous," is almost as neat an example of irony as the Nun's Priest's "I kan noon harm of no womman divyne" (B 4456). Further-more, of the many superlatives in the *Canterbury Tales*, a few are literal, a few are ironic, but most are simply a narrative device and are so employed by the various tellers of the tales. As Kemp Malone has remarked, the custom in story-telling has always been "to make the characters heroic, larger than life, extraordinary rather than ordinary people"; in following this custom, Professor Malone notes, Chaucer was also conforming to the practices of the fourteenth century.[4]

It is an ironic, playful Narrator who also deprecates his own intel-ligence and literary skill. This is of course one of Chaucer's standard jokes on himself, like the jokes about his corpulence; it crops up every-where—in the *House of Fame*, the *Parliament of Fowls*, *Troilus and Cris-eyde*, and the *Legend of Good Women* (Malone, pp. 153-155). The same self-styled booby recites the "drasty" tale of *Sir Thopas* and the long-winded *Melibeus*, in a spirit of pure, rollicking fun aimed at amusing the readers, burlesquing fashionable romances (and dull sermons?), pulling the legs of the other pilgrims, showing up the Host for a fraud-ulent literary critic,[5] and, finally, with superb daring, laughing at the

4. Kemp Malone, *Chapters on Chaucer* (Baltimore, 1951), pp. 166-168.
5. See R. M. Lumiansky, *Of Sondry Folk: The Dramatic Principle in the "Canterbury Tales"* (Austin, 1955), pp. 83-95.

whole pretentious scheme of his author's composition. It is all of a piece, and to see Chaucer the pilgrim as anyone other than a marvelously alert, ironic, facetious master of every situation is to misread the *Canterbury Tales*.

Allegory

Yvor Winters

HAWTHORNE AND THE PROBLEM OF ALLEGORY

> "At the moment of execution—with the halter about his neck and while Colonel Pyncheon sat on horseback, grimly gazing at the scene—Maule had addressed him from the scaffold, and uttered a prophecy, of which history as well as fireside tradition, has preserved the very words. 'God,' said the dying man, pointing his finger, with a ghastly look, at the undismayed countenance of his enemy. 'God will give him blood to drink!'"
>
> —THE HOUSE OF THE SEVEN GABLES

Of Hawthorne's three most important long works—*The Scarlet Letter, The House of the Seven Gables,* and *The Marble Faun*—the first is pure allegory, and the other two are impure novels, or novels with unassimilated allegorical elements. The first is faultless, in scheme and in detail; it is one of the chief masterpieces of English prose. The second and third are interesting, the third in particular, but both are failures, and neither would suffice to give the author a very high place in the history of prose fiction. Hawthorne's sketches and short stories, at best, are slight performances; either they lack meaning, as in the case of *Mr. Higginbotham's Catastrophe,* or they lack reality of embodiment, as in the case of *The Birthmark,* or, having a measure of both, as does *The Minister's Black Veil,* they yet seem incapable of justifying the intensity of the method, their very brevity and attendant simplification, perhaps, working against them; the best of them, probably, is *Young Goodman Brown.* In his later romances, *Septimius Felton, Dr. Grimshaw's Secret, The Ancestral Footstep,* and *The Dolliver Romance,* and in much of *The Blithedale Romance* as well, Hawthorne struggles unsuccessfully with the problem of allegory, but he is still obsessed with it.

Hawthorne is, then, essentially an allegorist; had he followed the advice of Poe and other well-wishers, contemporary with himself and posthumous, and thrown his allegorizing out the window, it is certain that nothing essential to his genius would have remained. He appears to have had none of the personal qualifications of a novelist, for one

Reprinted from *In Defense of Reason* by Yvor Winters by permission of the publishers, Alan Swallow and Routledge & Kegan Paul Ltd. Copyright 147, 1960 by Yvor Winters.

thing: the sombre youth who lived in solitude and in contemplation in Salem, for a dozen years or more, before succumbing to the charms and propinquity of Miss Sophia Peabody and making the spasmodic and only moderately successful efforts to accustom himself to daylight which were to vex the remainder of his life, was one far more likely to concern himself with the theory of mankind than with the chaos, trivial, brutal, and exhausting, of the actuality. Furthermore, as we shall see more fully, the Puritan view of life was allegorical, and the allegorical vision seems to have been strongly impressed upon the New England literary mind. It is fairly obvious in much of the poetry of Emerson, Emily Dickinson, Byrant, Holmes, and even Very—Whittier, a Quaker and a peasant alone of the more interesting poets escaping; Melville, relatively an outsider, shows the impact of New England upon his own genius as much through his use of allegory as through his use of New England character; and the only important novelist purely a New Englander, aside from Hawthorne, that is, O. W. Holmes, was primarily concerned with the Puritan tendency to allegory, as its one considerable satirist, yet was himself more or less addicted to it.

These matters are speculative. That New England predisposed Hawthorne to allegory cannot be shown; yet the disposition in both is obvious. And it can easily be shown that New England provided the perfect material for one great allegory, and that, in all likelihood, she was largely to blame for the later failures.

The Puritan theology rested primarily upon the doctrine of predestination and the inefficaciousness of good works; it separated men sharply and certainly into two groups, the saved and the damned, and, technically, at least, was not concerned with any subtler shadings. This in itself represents a long step toward the allegorization of experience, for a very broad abstraction is substituted for the patient study of the minutiae of moral behavior long encouraged by Catholic tradition. Another step was necessary, however, and this step was taken in Massachusetts almost at the beginning of the settlement, and in the expulsion of Anne Hutchinson became the basis of governmental action: whereas the wholly Calvinistic Puritan denied the value of the evidence of character and behavior as signs of salvation, and so precluded the possibility of their becoming allegorical symbols—for the orthodox Calvinist, such as Mrs. Hutchinson would appear to have been, trusted to no witness save that of the Inner Light—it became customary in Massachusetts to regard as evidence of salvation the decision of the individual to enter the Church and lead a moral life. "The Puritans," says Parkes, "were plain blunt men with little taste for mysticism and no talent for speculation. A new conception was formulated by English theologians, of whom William Ames was the most influential. The sign of election was not an inner assurance; it was a sober decision to trust in Christ and obey God's law. Those who made this sober decision might feel reasonably confident that they had received God's grace; but the surest proof of it was its fruit in conduct; complete assurance was impossible. It was assumed that all was the work of grace; it was God, without human coöperation, who caused the sober decision to be made. But in actual practice this doctrine had the effect of unduly magnifying man's ability to save himself, as much as Calvin's conception had unduly minimized it; conversion was merely a choice to obey a certain code of rules, and did not imply any emotional change, any love for God, or for holiness, or any genuine religious experience; religion in other words was reduced to mere morality."[1] Objective evidence thus took the place of inner assurance, and the behavior of the individual took on symbolic value. That is, any sin was evidence of damnation; or, in other words, any sin represented all sin. When Hester Prynne committed adultery, she committed an act as purely representative of complete corruption as the act of Faustus in signing a contract with Satan. This view of the matter is certainly not Catholic and is little short of appalling; it derives from the fact, that although, as Parkes states in the passage just quoted, there occurred an exaggeration of the will in the matter of practical existence, this same will was still denied in the matter of doctrine, for according to doctrine that which man willed had been previously willed by God.

The belief that the judgment of a man is predestined by God, and the corollary that the judgment of a good man, since all men are either good or bad, purely and simply, is the judgment of God, may lead in the natural course of events to extraordinary drama; and this the more readily if the actors in the drama are isolated from the rest of the world and believe that the drama in which they take part is of cosmic importance and central in human destiny. Andrews writes: "The belief that God had selected New England as the chosen land was profoundly held by the Puritans who went there. Winthrop himself in 1640 wrote to Lord Saye and Sele of 'this good land which God hath found and given to his people,' adding that 'God had chosen this country to plant his people in.' Cotton in his sermon, *God's Promise to His Plantation* (London, 1634), devotes much space to the same idea—'This place is appointed me of God.'"[2] And Schneider writes on the same subject: "No one can live long in a Holy Commonwealth without becoming sensitive, irritable, losing his sense of values and ultimately his balance. All acts are acts either of God or of the devil; all issues are matters of religious faith; and all conflicts are holy wars. No matter how trivial an opinion might appear from a secular point of view, it became vital when promulgated as a theological dogma; no matter how harmless a fool might be, he was intolerable if he did not fit into the Covenant of Grace; no matter how slight an offense might be, it was a sin against Almighty God and hence infinite. Differences of opinion became differences of faith. Critics became blasphemers, and innovators, heretics."[3] And again: ". . . the mind of the Puritan was singularly unified and his imagination thoroughly moralized. The clergy were, of course, the professional moral scientists, but the laymen were no less dominated by such mental habits. The comman man and illiterate shared with

---

1. *The Puritan Heresy*, by H. B. Parkes, The Hound and Horn V-2, Jan.-March 1932, pages 173-4. See also *The Pragmatic Test* by H. B. Parkes, The Colt Press, San Francisco.
2. *The Colonial Period of American History*, by Charles M. Andrews; Yale University Press, 1934, Vol. I, page 386, note 2.
3. *The Puritan Mind*, by H. W. Schneider; Henry Holt, 1930, pages 51-2.

the expert this interest in divining God's purposes in the course of events. No event was merely natural; it was an act of God and was hence charged with that 'numinous' quality which gives birth to both prophetic insight and mystic illumination."[4] And again: "Nature was instructive to them only in so far as it suggested the hidden mysterious operations of designing agents. God and devil were both active, scheming, hidden powers, each pursuing his own ends by various ministrations, and natural events were therefore to be understood only in so far as they showed evidence of some divine or diabolical plot."[5]

Now according to the doctrine of predestination, if we interpret it reasonably, Hester merely gave evidence, in committing adultery, that she had always been one of the damned. This point of view, if really understood, could never have led to the chain of events which Hawthorne described in *The Scarlet Letter;* neither could it have led to the events of the actual history of New England. It is at this point that we must consider that fluid element, history, in connection with dogma, for Hester, like the witches who so occupied the Mathers, was treated as if she had wilfully abandoned the ways of God for the ways of Satan. This final illogicality introduces the element of drama into the allegory of *The Scarlet Letter* and into the allegorical morality of the Puritans.

The English Puritans who settled Massachusetts were socially the product of centuries of the type of ethical discipline fostered by the Catholic and Anglo-Catholic Churches. They may have denied the freedom of the will and the efficaciousness of good works by lip, but by habit, and without really grasping the fact, they believed in them and acted upon them. Edwards exhorts sinners to repent while preaching the doctrine of the inability to repent; the Mathers wrestled with demons physically and in broad daylight, and quite obviously felt virtuous for having done so; in fact, to such a pass did Puritanism come, that Melville's Ahab, who wilfully embarks upon the Sea of Unpredictability in order to overtake and slay the Spirit of Evil—an effort in which he is predestined and at the end of which he is predestined to destruction—appears to us merely the heroic projection of a common Puritan type. The Puritan may be said to have conceived the Manicheistic struggle between Absolute Good and Absolute Evil, which he derived through the processes of simplification and misunderstanding which have already been enumerated, as a kind of preordained or mechanical, yet also holy combat, in which his own part was a part at once intense and holy and yet immutably regulated.

There were at least two motives in the new environment which tended to intensify the effect of habit in this connection: one was the inevitable impulse given to the will by the exaltation attendant upon a new religious movement; the other was the impulse given by the supremely difficult physical surroundings in which the new colonies found themselves. Foster writes on these points: "The first Puritans, sure in their own hearts that they were the elect of God, found the doctrine necessary to sustain them in the tremendous struggle through which they passed. . . . Hence the doctrine nerved to greater activity; and it

4. Ibid., page 48.
5. Ibid., pages 42-3.

produced a similar effect during the first period of the promulgation of Calvinism, among every nation which accepted the system."[6] The force of the will was strengthened at the beginning, then, at the same time that its existence was denied and that reliance upon its manner of functioning (that is, upon good works) was, from a doctrinal standpoint, regarded as sin. The will, highly stimulated, but no longer studied and guided by the flexible and sensitive ethical scholarship of the Roman tradition, might easily result in dangerous action.

Andrews speaks of this subject as follows: "The dynamic agency . . . the driving force which overrode all opposition, legal and otherwise, was the profound conviction of the Puritan leaders that they were doing the Lord's work. They looked upon themselves as instruments in the divine hand for the carrying out of a great religious mission, the object of which was the rebuilding of God's church in a land—the undefiled land of America—divinely set apart as the scene of a holy experiment that should renovate the church at large, everywhere corrupt and falling into ruins. This new and purified community was to be the home of a saving remnant delivered from the wrath to come and was to serve as an example to the mother church of a regenerated form of faith and worship. It was also to become a proselyting center for the conversion of the heathen and the extension of the true gospel among those who knew it not. In the fulfillment of this mission the Puritans counted obstacles, moral and physical, of no moment. Theirs was a religious duty to frustrate their enemies, to eradicate all inimical opinions, religious and political, and to extend the field of their influence as widely as possible. Once they had determined on their rules of polity and conduct, as laid down in the Bible and interpreted by the clergy, they had no doubts of the justness and rightness of their course. The means employed might savor of harshness and inequity, but at all costs and under all circumstances, error, sin, and idolatry, in whatever form appearing and as determined by themselves, must be destroyed. In the process, as events were to prove, a great many very human motives played an important part in interpreting the law of God, and personal likes and dislikes, hypocrisy, prejudice, and passion got badly mixed with the higher and more spiritual impulses that were actively at work purging the church of its errors."[7]

Over a long period, however, the doctrine of predestination would naturally lead to religious apathy, for it offered no explicit motive to action; and this is precisely that to which it led, for after the Great Awakening of the middle of the eighteenth century, itself a reaction to previous decay in the Church, the Church lost power rapidly, and by the opening of the nineteenth century was succumbing on every hand to Unitarianism, a mildly moralistic creed, in which the element of supernaturalism was minimized, and which, in turn, yielded rapidly among the relatively intellectual classes to Romantic ethical theory, especially as propounded by the Transcendentalists. "It has never been a good

6. *A Genetic History of the New England Theology,* by Frank Hugh Foster; University of Chicago Press, 1907; page 29.

7. Charles M. Andrews, op. cit., Vol I, pages 430-1.

way to induce men to repent," says Foster, "to tell them that they cannot."[8] Or at least the method has never been highly successful except when employed by a rhetorician of the power of Edwards, or by an orator of the effectiveness of Whitefield; and the effect can scarcely be expected long to outlive the immediate presence of the speaker. The Unitarians, in depriving the ethical life of the more impressive aspects of its supernatural sanction, and in offering nothing to take the place of that sanction, all but extinguished intensity of moral conviction, although their own conviction—we may see it portrayed, for example, in *The Europeans,* by Henry James, and exemplified in the lucid and classical prose of W. E. Channing—was a conviction, at least for a period, of the greatest firmness and dignity. Emerson eliminated the need of moral conviction and of moral understanding alike, by promulgating the allied doctrines of equivalence and of inevitable virtue. In an Emersonian universe there is equally no need and no possibility of judgment; it is a universe of amiable but of perfectly unconscious imbeciles; it is likewise a universe in which the art of the fictionist— or for that matter, any other art—can scarcely be expected to flourish. A fictionist who has been in any considerable measure affected by Emersonian or allied concepts, or even who is the product of the historical sequence which gave rise to Emerson, is likely to find himself gravely confused and may even find himself paralyzed; and we have only to read such a document, to cite a single example, as *The New Adam and Eve,* to realize that Hawthorne's own moral ideas, in spite of his intense but conflicting moral sentiments, and in spite of his professed dislike for Emerson's philosophy, were much closer to the ideas of Emerson than to those of Edwards.

Now in examining Hawthorne, we are concerned with two historical centers: that of the first generation of Puritans in New England, in which occurs the action of *The Scarlet Letter;* and that of the post-Unitarian and Romantic intellectuals, in which was passed the life of Hawthorne.

Hawthorne, by nature an allegorist, and a man with a strong moral instinct, regardless of the condition of his ideas, found in the early history of his own people and region the perfect material for a masterpiece. By selecting sexual sin as the type of all sin, he was true alike to the exigencies of drama and of history. In the setting which he chose, allegory was realism, the idea was life itself; and his prose, always remarkable for its polish and flexibility, and stripped, for once, of all superfluity, was reduced to the living idea, it intensified pure exposition to a quality comparable in its way to that of great poetry.

The compactness and complexity of the allegory will escape all save the most watchful readers. Let us consider the following passage as a representative example. Hester has learned that the magistrates and clergy are considering whether or not she ought to be separated from her child, and she waits upon Governor Bellingham in order to plead with him:

"On the wall hung a row of portraits, representing the forefathers

8. Frank Hugh Foster, op. cit., page 29.

of the Bellingham lineage, some with armor on their breasts, and others with stately ruffs and robes of peace. All were characterized by the sternness and severity which old portraits so invariably put on; as if they were the ghosts, rather than the pictures, of departed worthies, and were gazing with harsh and intolerant criticism at the pursuits and enjoyments of living men.

"At about the center of the oaken panels, that lined the hall, was suspended a suit of mail, not, like the pictures, an ancestral relic, but of the most modern date; for it had been manufactured by a skillful armorer in London, the same year in which Governor Bellingham came over to New England. There was a steel head-piece, a cuirass, a gorget, and greaves, with a pair of gauntlets and a sword hanging beneath; all, especially the helmet and breast-plate, so highly burnished as to glow with white radiance, and scatter an illumination everywhere about the floor. This bright panoply was not meant for mere idle show, but had been worn by the Governor on many a solemn muster and training field, and had glittered, moreover, at the head of a regiment in the Pequot war. For, though bred a lawyer, and accustomed to speak of Bacon, Coke, Noye, and Finch as his professional associates, the exigencies of this new country had transformed Governor Bellingham into a soldier as well as a statesman and ruler.

"Little Pearl—who was as greatly pleased with the gleaming armor as she had been with the glittering frontispiece of the house—spent some time looking into the polished mirror of the breast-plate.

"'Mother,' cried she, 'I see you here. Look! Look!'

"Hester looked, by way of humoring the child; and she saw that, owing to the peculiar effect of the convex mirror, the scarlet letter was represented in gigantic and exaggerated proportions, so as to be greatly the most prominent feature of her appearance. In truth, she seemed absolutely hidden behind it. Pearl pointed upward, also, at a similar picture in the head-piece; smiling at her mother with the elfish intelligence that was so familiar an expression on her small physiognomy. That look of naughty merriment was likewise reflected in the mirror, with so much breadth and intensity of effect, that it made Hester Prynne feel as if it could not be the image of her own child, but of an imp who was seeking to mold itself into Pearl's shape."

The portraits are obviously intended as an apology for the static portraits in the book, as an illustration of the principle of simplification by distance and by generalization; the new armor, on the other hand, is the new faith which brought the Puritans to New England, and which not only shone with piety—"especially the helmet and breast-plate," the covering of the head and heart—but supported them in their practical struggles with physical adversaries, and which in addition altered their view of the life about them to dogmatic essentials, so that Hester was obliterated behind the fact of her sin, and Pearl transformed in view of her origin. Governor Bellingham, in his combination of legal training with military prowess, is representative of his fellow colonists, who displayed in a remarkable degree a capacity to act with great strength and with absolutely simple directness upon principles so generalized as scarcely to be applicable to any particular moral problem, which mastered moral difficulties not by understanding them, but by crushing them out.

Historically and relatively considered, Richard Bellingham might conceivably have been spared this function in the story, for of his group he was one of the the two or three most humane and liberal; but the qualities represented were the qualities of the group of which he was a leader, and were extremely evident in most of the actions of the colony. Perhaps the best—or in another sense, the worst—embodiment of these qualities is to be found in John Endecott, of whom Andrews gives the following characterization: "Endecott had few lovable qualities. He was stern, unyielding, and on some subjects a zealot. Johnson apostrophizes him as 'strong, valiant John,' whom Christ had called to be his soldier, but the Old Planters, most if not all of whom were Anglicans and demanded service according to the Book of Common Prayer, deemed themselves slaves and took in very bad part his determination to suppress the Church of England in the colony. They preferred Roger Conant, who though a less forcible man was one much easier to get along with. Endecott's later career discloses his attitude toward those who differed with him—the heathen Indian, the Quaker, the prisoner before him for judgment, and the Brownes and other upholders of the Anglican service who were disaffected with the Puritan government. It also shows his dislike of forms and devices that offended him—the Book of Common Prayer, the cross of St. George, and the Maypole. He was hard, intolerant, and at times cruel. Even the Massachusetts government caused him 'to be sadly admonished for his offense' in mutilating the flag at Salem in 1635, charging him with 'rashness, uncharitableness, indiscretion, and exceeding the limits of his calling'; and again in the same year 'committed' him for losing his temper. Endecott once apologized to Winthrop for striking 'goodman Dexter,' acknowledging that he was rash, but saying that Dexter's conduct 'would have provoked a very patient man.' The best that can be said of him has been said by Chapple ('The Public Service of John Endecott,' Historical Collections, Essex Institute), an essay in the best Palfrey manner. It is odd that Endecott should have chosen for his seal a skull and cross-bones."[9] It is interesting to observe in such a passage, as in many others, that the Puritans cannot be discussed, nor can they discuss each other, without the language employed exceeding the limits proper to predestinarians and invoking the traditional morality of the older churches; yet the attempt to ignore this traditional morality as far as might be, and, in the matter of formal doctrine, to repudiate it, unquestionably had much to do with the formation of such characters as Professor Andrews here describes and as Hawthorne in the last passage quoted from him symbolizes. The imperceptive, unwavering brutality of many of the actions committed in the name of piety in the Massachusetts colonies more than justified the curse and prophecy uttered by Matthew Maule, that God would give these Puritans blood to drink; in the name of God, they had violently cut themselves off from human nature; in the end, that is in Hawthorne's generation and

9. Charles M. Andrews, op. cit., Vol. I, page 361, note 3.

in the generation following, more than one of them drank his own heart's blood, as Hawthorne himself must have done in his ultimate and frustrated solitude, and more than one of them shed it.

It is noteworthy that in this passage from *The Scarlet Letter* Hawthorne turns his instrument of allegory, the gift of the Puritans, against the Puritans themselves, in order to indicate the limits of their intelligence; it is noteworthy also that this act of criticism, though both clear and sound, is negative, that he nowhere except in the very general notion of regeneration through repentance establishes the nature of the intelligence which might exceed the intelligence of the Puritans, but rather hints at the ideal existence of a richer and more detailed understanding than the Puritan scheme of life is able to contain. The strength of *The Scarlet Letter* is in part safe-guarded by the refusal to explore this understanding; the man who was able in the same lifetime to write *The New Adam and Eve,* to conceive the art-colony described in *The Marble Faun,* and to be shocked at the nude statues of antiquity, was scarcely the man to cast a clear and steady light upon the finer details of the soul.

The conception of the book in general is as cleanly allegorical as is the conception of the passage quoted. Hester represents the repentant sinner, Dimmesdale the half-repentant sinner, and Chillingworth the unrepentant sinner. The fact that Chillingworth's sin is the passion for revenge is significant only to the extent that this is perhaps the one passion which most completely isolates man from normal human sympathies and which therefore is most properly used to represent an unregenerate condition.

The method of allegorization is that of the Puritans themselves; the substance of the allegory remained in a crude form a part of their practical Christianity in spite of their Calvinism, just as it remained in their non-theological linguistic forms, just as we can see it in the language of the best poems of so purely and mystically Calvinistic a writer as Jones Very, a living language related to a living experience, but overflowing the limits of Calvinistic dogma; Hawthorne's point of view was naturally more enlightened than that of the Puritans themselves, yet it was insufficiently so to enable him to recover the traditional Christian ethics except in the most general terms and by way of historical sympathy, for had a more complete recovery been possible, he would not have been so narrowly bound to the method of allegory and the frustration of the later romances would scarcely have been so complete.

Once Hawthorne had reduced the problem of sin to terms as general as these, and had brought his allegory to perfect literary form, he had, properly speaking, dealt with sin once and for all; there was nothing further to be said about it. It would not serve to write another allegory with a new set of characters and a different sin as the motive; for the particular sin is not particular in function, but is merely representative of sin in general, as the characters, whatever their names and conditions may be, are merely representative of the major stages of sin—there is no escape from the generality so long as one adheres to the method. There was nothing further, then, to be done in this direction, save the composition of a few footnotes to the subject in the form of sketches.

The only alternative remaining was to move away from the allegorical extreme of narrative toward the specific, that is, toward the art of the novelist. The attempt was made, but fell short of success. In *The House of the Seven Gables* and in *The Marble Faun* alike the moral understanding of the action—and there is a serious attempt at such understanding, at least in *The Marble Faun*—is corrupted by a provincial sentimentalism ethically far inferior to the Manicheism of the Puritans, which was plain and comprehensive, however brutal. And Hawthorne had small gift for the creation of human beings, a defect allied to his other defects and virtues: even the figures in *The Scarlet Letter* are unsatisfactory if one comes to the book expecting to find a novel, for they draw their life not from simple and familiar human characteristics, as do the figures of Henry James, but from the precision and intensity with which they render their respective ideas; the very development of the story is neither narrative nor dramatic, but expository. When, as in *The Marble Faun* or *The House of the Seven Gables,* there is no idea governing the human figure, or when the idea is an incomplete or unsatisfactory equivalent of the figure, the figure is likely to be a disappointing spectacle, for he is seldom if ever a convincing human being and is likely to verge on the ludicrous. Hawthorne had not the rich and profound awareness of immediacy which might have saved a writer such as Melville in a similar predicament.

His effort to master the novelist's procedure, however, was not sustained, for his heart was not in it. In *The Blithedale Romance,* he began as a novelist, but lost himself toward the close in an unsuccessful effort to achieve allegory; the four unfinished romances represent similar efforts throughout.

His procedure in the last works was startlingly simple; so much so, that no one whom I can recollect has run the risk of defining it.

In *The Scarlet Letter* there occurs a formula which one might name the formula of alternative possibilities. In the ninth chapter, for example, there occurs the following passage: "The people, in the case of which we speak, could justify its prejudice against Roger Chillingworth by no fact or argument worthy of serious refutation. There was an aged handicraftsman, it is true, who had been a citizen of London at the period of Sir Thomas Overbury's murder, now some thirty years agone; he testified to having seen the physician, under some other name, which the narrator of the story had now forgotten, in company with Dr. Forman, the famous old conjuror, who was implicated in the affair of Overbury. Two or three individuals hinted, that the man of skill, during his Indian captivity, had enlarged his medical attainments by joining in the incantations of the savage priests; who were universally acknowledged to be powerful enchanters, often performing seemingly miraculous cures by their skill in the black art. A large number—many of them were persons of such sober sense and practical observation that their opinions would have been valuable in other matters—affirmed that Roger Chillingworth's aspect had undergone a remarkable change while he had dwelt in the town, and especially since his abode with Dimmesdale. At first, his expression had been calm, meditative, scholar-like. Now, there was something ugly and evil in his face, which they had not previously noticed, and which grew still more obvious to sight the oftener they looked upon him. According to the vulgar idea, the fire in his laboratory had been brought from the lower regions, and was fed with infernal fuel; and so, as might be expected, his visage was getting sooty with smoke."

In such a passage as this, the idea conveyed is clear enough, but the embodiment of the idea appears far-fetched, and Hawthorne offers it whimsically and apologetically, professing to let you take it or leave it. Another example occurs in the eighteenth chapter; Dimmesdale and Hester are sitting in the forest, planning the flight which ultimately is never to take place, and Pearl, the symbolic offspring of the untamed elements of human nature, and hence akin to the forest, which, in the Puritan mind, was ruled by Satan in person, plays apart: "A fox, startled from his sleep by her light footstep on the leaves, looked inquisitively at Pearl, as doubting whether it were better to steal off or renew his nap on the same spot. A wolf, it is said—but here the tale has surely lapsed into the improbable—came up and smelt of Pearl's robe, and offered his savage head to be patted by her hand. The truth seems to be, however, that the mother-forest, and these wild things which it nourished, all recognized a kindred wildness in the human child." Similarly, in *The Marble Faun,* one never learns whether Donatello had or had not the pointed ears which serve throughout the book as the physical symbol of his moral nature; the book ends with the question being put to Kenyon, who has had opportunities to observe, and with his refusing to reply.

This device, though it becomes a minor cause of irritation through constant recurrence, is relatively harmless, and at times is even used with good effect. If we reverse the formula, however, so as to make the physical representation perfectly clear but the meaning uncertain, we have a very serious situation; and this is precisely what occurs, in some measure toward the close of *The Blithedale Romance,* and without mitigation throughout the four unfinished romances. We have in the last all of the machinery and all of the mannerisms of the allegorist, but we cannot discover the substance of his communication, nor is he himself aware of it so far as we can judge. We have the symbolic footprint, the symbolic spider, the symbolic elixirs and poisons, but we have not that of which they are symbolic; we have the hushed, the tense and confidential manner, on the part of the narrator, of one who imparts a grave secret, but the words are inaudible. Yet we have not, on the other hand, anything approaching realistic fiction, for the events are improbable or even impossible, and the characters lack all reality. The technique neither of the novelist nor of the allegorist was available to Hawthorne when he approached the conditions of his own experience: he had looked for signals in nature so long and so intently, and his ancestors before him had done so for so many generations, that, like a man hypnotized, or like a man corroded with madness, he saw them; but he no longer had any way of determining their significance, and he had small talent for rendering their physical presence with intensity.

Percy Boynton,[10] in quoting the following passages from *Septimius Felton*, refers to it as a self-portrait: "As for Septimius, let him alone a moment or two, and then they would see him, with his head bent down, brooding, brooding, his eyes fixed on some chip, some stone, some common plant, any commonest thing, as if it were the clew and index to some mystery; and when, by chance startled out of these meditations, he lifted his eyes, there would be a kind of perplexity, a dissatisfied, foiled look in them, as if of his speculations he found no end."

It is in this generation and the next that we see most clearly and bitterly the realization of Maule's prophecy. These men were cut off from their heritage, from their source of significance, and were abnormally sensitive to the influence of European Romanticism. In Emerson[11] the terms of New England mysticism and of Romantic amoralism were fused and confused so inextricably that we have not yet worked ourselves free of them. In Poe, a man born without a background, New England or any other, Romantic doctrine was introduced directly, in a form free of theological terminology, but in a form none the less which would tend in the long run to support the influence of Emerson. In Melville, the greatest man of his era and of his nation, we find a writer superior at certain points in his career—in books such as *Moby Dick* and *Benito Cereno*, for example—to the confusion and apparently understanding it; at other points—in books like *Mardi* and *Pierre*, —succumbing to the confusion; at all points in his career made to suffer for the confusion of contemporary literary taste; and at the end, settling himself in silence, a figure more difficult to face than the later Hawthorne—more difficult, because more conscious, more controlled, and more nearly indifferent.

In Henry Adams we see the curse at work most clearly: intellectual but inconsecutive, unable to justify any principle of action, yet with a character of the highest, a character which demanded not only just action but its justification, he was damned to a kind of restless torment; in which, though an historian of great learning and of high academic distinction, he transformed the Middle Ages by a process of subtle falsification, into a symbol of his own latter-day New England longing; in which, though a stylist of great power and precision, he propounded the aesthetic theory that modern art must be confused to express confusion;[12] in which, though a philosopher of a sort, he created one of the most unphilosophical theories of history imaginable, as a poetic symbol of his own despair. In the suicide of Henry Adams' wife it is conceivable that we see the logical outcome of his own dilemma, an outcome in his own case prevented by the inheritance of character, which, like the inheritance of confusion, was bequeathed him by early New England.[13]

In *The Scarlet Letter*, then, Hawthorne composed a great allegory; or,

10. *Literature and American Life*, by Percy H. Boynton; Ginn and Co., 1936; page 518.
11. This subject is fully discussed by H. B. Parkes, The Hound and Horn, V-4, July-Sept. 1932, pages 581-601, and *The Pragmatic Test*.
12. See the last three or four pages of *Mont Saint-Michel and Chartres*.
13. This idea is very ably defended by Katherine Simonds, The New England Quarterly, December, 1936.

if we look first at the allegorical view of life upon which early Puritan society was based, we might almost say that he composed a great historical novel. History, which by placing him in an anti-intellectual age had cut him off from the ideas which might have enabled him to deal with his own period, in part made up for the injustice by facilitating his entrance, for a brief time, into an age more congenial to his nature. Had he possessed the capacity for criticizing and organizing concepts as well as for dramatizing them, he might have risen superior to his disadvantages, but like many other men of major genius he lacked this capacity. In turning his back upon the excessively simplified conceptions of his Puritan ancestors, he abandoned the only orderly concepts, whatever their limitations, to which he had access, and in his last work he is restless and dissatisfied. The four last romances are unfinished, and in each successive one he sought to incorporate and perfect elements from those preceding; the last, *The Dolliver Romance,* which he had sought to make the best, had he lived, is a mere fragment, but on the face of it is the most preposterous of all. His dilemma, the choice between abstractions inadequate or irrelevant to experience on the one hand, and experience on the other as far as practicable unilluminated by understanding, is tragically characteristic of the history of this country and of its literature; only a few scattered individuals, at the cost of inordinate labor, and often impermanently, have achieved the permeation of human experience by a consistent moral understanding which results in wisdom and in great art. If art is to be measured by the greatness of the difficulties overcome—and the measure is not wholly unreasonable, for there can scarcely be virtue without a comprehension of sin, and the wider and more careful the comprehension the richer the virtue—then these few writers are very great indeed. Hawthorne, when he reversed his formula of alternative possibilities, and sought to grope his way blindly to significance, made the choice of the later Romantics; and his groping was met wherever he moved by the smooth and impassive surface of the intense inane.

Elliott B. Gose, Jr.

PURE EXERCISE OF IMAGINATION:
ARCHETYPAL SYMBOLISM IN **LORD JIM**

Although there is an obvious virtue in a plot which moves directly through time and space, the final justification of form is how well it conveys the author's theme, his vision of life. Conrad experimented with form: we must keep in mind his habitual refusal, beginning with *Lord Jim,* to follow a straight time sequence. In *Lord Jim,* Marlow the narrator is responsible for the complexity of time shifts which characterizes both the Patna and Patusan episodes. And the fact that the plot does break into two discrete actions makes the form of *Lord Jim* a special problem. Thematically, this break is compensated by a myriad of small parallelisms in action and image. While enlightening, the binding quality of such parallelisms (much noted by critics recently) goes only part way toward remedying the split. A more satisfactory approach to the problem is to assume that the two episodes represent the necessary embodiment of Conrad's conception. I would say that, in *Lord Jim,* Conrad came the closest he ever did in his attempt "to render the highest kind of justice" not only "to the visible universe" as he affirms in the Preface to *The Nigger of the "Narcissus,"* but also to the invisible universe within. In the same preface, Conrad asserts that "the artist descends within himself, and in that lonely region of stress and strife, if he be deserving and fortunate, he finds the terms of his appeal." And "his appeal is made . . . to that part of our nature which . . . is . . . kept out of sight." In *Lord Jim,* Conrad's aim and his triumph was to explore the world of the imagination more thoroughly than he had in *Heart of Darkness* or ever would again.

We can approach that attempt by contrasting the opposed conceptions of the two halves of the book. The *Patna* episode is informed by the assumption that the beliefs men share govern their fate, while the Patusan sequence is informed by the possibility that one man's imagination can determine his fate. The Western world in which the *Patna* was built is dominated by Marlow's moral principles; the Eastern world of Patusan appears to function according to Jim's application of Stein's romantic prescription. Marlow delivers his code in Chapter v, imme-

From *PMLA,* LXXIX (March 1964), 137-147. Reprinted by permission of the Modern Language Association.

diately after his introduction. Jim, he says, is "one of us," and consequently should have "that inborn ability to look temptations straight in the face—a readiness unintellectual enough, goodness knows, but without pose—a power of resistance . . . —an unthinking and blessed stiffness before the outward and inward terrors . . . backed by a . . . belief in a few simple notions."[1]

Marlow's belief is in "the craft of the sea . . . the craft whose whole secret could be expressed in one short sentence, and yet must be driven afresh every day into young heads till it becomes the component part of every waking thought—till it is present in every dream of their young sleep!" (p. 37). The implications of this statement are far reaching. A good sailor must be alert and conscious of detail. In fact he must reshape his unconscious life in the image of his consciousness of the outside. This formulation therefore stands directly opposed to Stein's basic principle that "a man that is born falls into a dream like a man who falls into the sea" (p. 184). Stein advises living from the dream, *submitting* to the destructive element. In opposition, Marlow, speaking for what we may call Western materialism, depends on the ingenuity of man to fashion ships that ride over the destructive element of the sea, depends on the alertness and cooperation of man to keep the destruction from affecting him. Of the situation that precipitated Jim's jump from the *Patna*, Marlow says, "It was all threats, all a terribly effective feint, a sham from beginning to end, planned by the tremendous disdain of the Dark Powers whose real terrors, always on the verge of triumph, are perpetually foiled by the steadfastness of men" (p. 105). Man's hope rests on the bond which Conrad celebrated in two separate paragraphs of his preface to *The Nigger:* "that feeling of unavoidable solidarity . . . which binds men to each other and all mankind to the visible world." Marlow himself uses the phrase "the solidarity of the craft" (p. 113) and judges Jim by his failure to live up to it: "The real significance of crime is in its being a breach of faith with the community of mankind, and from that point of view he was no mean traitor" (p. 135).

The value of the bond between men is easily appreciated, but for Conrad the bond with the visible universe was equally important. Simply, a sailor must be responsive to the elements and to his ship. But Jim fails even here. "He had to bear the criticism of men, the exactions of the sea, and the prosaic severity of the daily task that gives bread— but whose only reward is in the perfect love of the work. This reward eluded him" (p. 7). Instead of a concern for the demanding but necessary routine of the ship or for his duty to the passengers, Jim spends his time in daydreams of heroism. These dreams are intensified when he arrives in the East. He is lulled by "the softness of the sky, the languor of the earth, the bewitching breath of the Eastern waters. There were perfumes in it, suggestions of infinite repose, the gift of endless dreams" (p. 9).

Appropriately enough, those who live in the East have evolved a religion which includes this gift of the region. The eight hundred Moslem pilgrims stream on to the *Patna* "urged by faith and the hope of

1. P. 36 of the Rinehart edition, edited by Robert B. Heilman. Page references will hereafter be given in my text.

paradise." "At the call of an idea," they go, "the unconscious pilgrims of an exacting belief" (p. 11). The pilgrims have made the dream their reality. They are as true to it as Marlow is to the demands of his reality and are therefore as successful in achieving their goal. The opposition between Western and Eastern man can be seen initially then, as the opposition already mentioned between conscious and unconscious. In fact the pigrims' way of life embodies one version of Stein's philisophy; they have so far submitted to the unconscious as to be identified with the sea. They "spread on all sides over the deck, flowed forward and aft, overflowed down the yawning hatchways, filled the inner recesses of the ship—like water filling a cistern, like water flowing into crevices and crannies, like water rising silently even with the rim" (p. 11). Western man, on the other hand, rises above the sea, as comes out in one of several contrasts Conrad makes between the Western and Eastern ways of life. "The Arab standing up aft, recited aloud the prayer of travellers by sea. He invoked the favour of the Most High upon that journey, implored His blessing on men's toil and on the secret purposes of their hearts; the steamer pounded in the dusk the calm water of the Strait; and far astern of the pilgrim ship a screw-pile lighthouse, planted by unbelievers on a treacherous shoal, seemed to wink at her its eye of flame, as if in derision of her errand of faith" (p. 12). The lighthouse is the epitome of Western man, symbolizing as it does his attempt to penetrate the darkness, to enable himself to steer a safe course through the dangerous unknown, to safeguard the future by rearranging the materials of nature and giving them conscious shape through the light of reason and the inductive method. It winks in derision at the faith of the pilgrims because where they give themselves up to an inscrutable God (the word Islam means *submission*), Western man sets out to subdue the unknown, to impose the light of conscious reason on all dark and treacherous realms.

Probably the major image pattern of the novel is that based on the light-dark opposition. We have already seen that "the Dark Powers," in the form of a storm, set the scene for Jim's jump "into an everlastingly deep hole" (p. 96). The problem of the second half of the book might then be phrased: can Jim climb back out to the sunlight. Marlow's observations in Patusan do not bode well. Watching the moon rise, he observes, "it is to our sunshine, which—say what you like—is all we have to live by, what the echo is to the sound: misleading and confusing whether the note be mocking or sad. It robs forms of matter —which, after all, is our domain—of their substance, and gives a sinister reality to shadows alone" (p. 213). Marlow insists that Jim's reality comes from the world of sunlight, as is brought out when Marlow leaves Patusan. Jim "was white from head to foot, and remained persistently visible with the stronghold of the night at his back." Finally he was "only a speck, a tiny white speck, that seemed to catch all the light left in a darkened world" (p. 292). The connection between Jim and the sun is also observable in the first half of the book. There the sun functions not just as the source of light but as a pitiless god. "Every morning the sun . . . emerged with a silent burst of light . . . pouring the concentrated fire of his rays on the pious purposes of the men, glided past on his descent, and sank mysteriously into the sea. . . . The ship . . . held on her steadfast way black and smouldering in a luminous immensity, as if scorched by a flame flicked at her from a heaven with pity. The nights descended on her like a benediction" (pp. 12-13).

But the serenity of the night only tempts Jim to a false sense of security before unleashing its dark power. After his jump into the hole, Brierly suggests, "Let him creep twenty feet underground and stay there" (p. 57). Jim feels the same about the other members of the *Patna* crew, who can no longer face the sun. They spread the boat sail over the gunwales and then, says Jim "they crept under, out of my sight, thank God!" Only he remains and without a cap to shield him from the sun. "I couldn't see the water for the glitter of the sunshine. . . . The sun crept all the way from east to west over my bare head, but that day I could not come to any harm, I suppose. The sun could not . . . kill me . . . *That* rested with me. . . . I didn't bother myself at all about the sun over my head. I was thinking as coolly as any man that ever sat thinking in the shade" (pp. 108-109).

Jim has begun to shift his allegiance from light to dark, but by a different means from the rest of the crew, by making himself independent of the authority of the sun. The sun had been personified a few pages before. Jim makes Marlow see "the lower limb of the sun clearing the line of the horizon, the tremble of a vast ripple running over all the visible expanse of the sea, as if the waters had shuddered, giving birth to the globe of light. . . . [and] the lonely sun, regardless of the speck of life, ascending the clear curve of the heaven as if to gaze ardently from a greater height at his own splendour reflected in the still ocean" (p. 106). The symbolic importance of these actions will become evident presently. That the sun is an analogue for Jim we can assume from a similar Narcissus image which is applied implicitly to Jim in the next chapter (XI). There the young seaman is pictured by Marlow "on the brink," about to be "launched to sink or swim," but for the moment "looking with shining eyes upon that glitter of the vast surface which is only a reflection of his own glances full of fire" (p. 111). Marlow goes on to speak of the loss of this illusion and its replacement by "the fellowship of the craft," the code which Jim never accepts. Marlow can accept the propriety of the sun gazing at its reflection: as the creator of life, the sun has the God-like right of viewing Himself in His creation. But for a man so to indulge himself is to invite the fate of Narcissus, a falling into the water which Marlow believes will cause death. Marlow condemns Jim most for exactly the flaw of self-centeredness.

Whatever the consequences, Jim has faced the sun and declared himself independent of it. In doing so he switched his allegiance from the temporal world of day alternating with night to a timeless world which Conrad characterizes both as deathly and as eternal. The bright stars in the black night serve as an appropriate image. Marlow begins the next chapter (XI), "He heard me out with his head on one side, and I had another glimpse through a rent in the mist in which he moved and had his being. . . . At his back was the dark night with the clear stars, whose distant glitter disposed in retreating planes lured the eye into the depths of greater darkness; and yet a mysterious light seemed to show me his boyish head, as if in that moment the youth within him had, for a moment, gleamed and expired" (p. 110).

For a more positive version of the image, we may turn to Conrad's characterization of nature as it appeared to him on his own first sea voyages: "In my early days, starting out on a voyage was like being launched into Eternity. . . . An enormous silence, in which there was nothing to connect one with the Universe but the incessant wheeling about of the sun and other celestial bodies, the alternation of light and shadow, eternally chasing each other over the sky. The time of the earth, though most carefully recorded by the half-hourly bells, did not count in reality."[2]

Rather than the ship's bell, we remember Brierly's gold chronometer, left behind when he jumped, and Jim's dropping the clock before making his successful jump in Patusan. Both men were aware of the significance of time for Western man—an objective standard, a measure of duty, and a means of continuity by which Brierly tries to affirm his fidelity even in his desertion. And in Jim's case we note an unwillingness to be tied to time, his need to jump off the mundane world on which he can never escape his guilt. Thus we have Marlow referring to Patusan as a "distant heavenly body." "Had Stein arranged to send him into a star of the fifth magnitude the change could not have been greater. He left his earthly failings behind him and that sort of reputation he had, and there was a totally new set of conditions for his imaginative faculty to work upon" (pp. 188-189). We even have the moment when he actually takes leave of earth, rendered in his jump across the stream. "The earth seemed fairly to fly backwards under his feet" (p. 219). But the process is not so simply finished; he lands in the mud and has to struggle. Then "he longed—so he said—to be back . . . mending the clock. Mending the clock—that was the idea. He made efforts, tremendous sobbing, gasping efforts, efforts that seemed to burst his eyeballs in their sockets and make him blind, and culminating into one mighty supreme effort in the darkness to crack the earth asunder, to throw it off his limbs" (p. 220).[3]

Jim's successful effort to get free of the world he cannot accept is followed by an odd incident. "He lay full length on the firm ground and saw the light, the sky. Then . . . he slept—perhaps for a minute, perhaps for twenty seconds, or only for one second, but he recollects distinctly the violent convulsive start of awakening" (p. 220). He is reborn, and in that rebirth is "alone of his kind . . . like a hunted animal . . . beplastered with filth out of all semblance to a human being." But when he gets to Doramin's settlement, he produces the ring that

2. P. 182, "Well Done," in *Notes on Life and Letters*, Medallion Edition of Conrad's works (same pagination as the Dent Uniform Edition).

3. The extent to which Conrad wished the telling of the story to form a psychic parallel to the action is indicated in one of the breaks in Marlow's narrative (at the beginning of Ch. xxxiv): "Marlow swung his legs out, got up quickly, and staggered a little, as though he had been set down after a rush through space. . . . Marlow looked at them all with the eyes of a man returning from the excessive remoteness of a dream" (p. 277).

will create a bond with Doramin and is accepted as human. "He was safe. Doramin's people were barricading the gate and pouring water down his throat; Doramin's old wife . . . 'made a to-do over me as if I had been her own son'" (p. 221).

The pattern of action is, or should be, a familiar one. In the title given by Otto Rank, it is "The Myth of the Birth of the Hero." As analyzed by Carl Jung, it throws considerable light on what Conrad was allowing Jim to strive for. Jung follows Frobenius in noting that the mythic pattern is based on the rising, setting, and reappearance of the sun. And he takes it as an attempt to describe psychic phenomena. The sun is an image of man, born at morning, strong at noon, declining to death at evening. (See Conrad's parallel image, supra.) But if man refuses to accept physical death, he can plunge into the darkness within and be reborn as the hero, providing he can meet the test posed by re-immersion in his own unconscious. As Frobenius points out, the circular direction is important: East to West for the initial movement overhead, followed by West to East, beneath the surface. Jung develops the importance of water, the substance in which the sun is plunged. "The maternal significance of water is one of the clearest interpretations of symbols in the whole field of mythology, so that even the ancient Greeks could say that 'the sea is the symbol of generation.' From water comes life. . . . [In addition] in dreams and fantasies the sea or a large expanse of water signifies the unconscious. The maternal aspect of water coincides with the nature of the unconscious, because the latter (particularly in men) can be regarded as the mother."[4]

If we think of Jim's experience on the *Patna*, we see how well Jung's version of the myth fits. Water is treated philosophically by Stein as the dream, the unconscious. On the passage westward toward Mecca, the strength of the sun is emphasized. Then after plunging into darkness, Jim moves always to the east, as Conrad stresses. In going to Patusan, he plunges even further into Stein's "destructive element." Dialectically this is natural since he is following Stein's advice and footsteps. Conrad also makes it clear in the imagery, twice in Chapter XXVI comparing the forest to a sea. But it is "a dark sleeping sea" (p. 225), which "devoured the sunshine" (p. 229), instead of reflecting it as did the ocean. The question then becomes whether Patusan is a proper place to be reborn. Marlow clearly looks on Jim's going there as a further retreat, a kind of regression. Yet regress is exactly what the hero has to do to succeed. For symbolically his withdrawal is necessary when he reaches the point where he cannot cope with the outside

4. Pp. 218-219, *Symbols of Transformation*, Harper Torchbooks. This two volume edition was printed from the same plates as the one-volume Bollingen edition. It is a revision Jung made in 1952 of the book he had originally written in 1912.

As indicated in n. 3, Marlow's sympathy with Jim often causes him to react as we imagine Jim has. In any case, one of his exchanges with Jewel presents a parallel with Jung's connection of mother, water, and emotions: "'My mother had wept bitterly before she died,' she explained. An inconceivable calmness seemed to have risen from the ground around us, imperceptibly, like the still rise of a flood in the night, obliterating the familiar landmarks of emotions. There came upon me, as though I had felt myself losing my footing in the midst of waters, a sudden dread, the dread of the unknown depths" (p. 271).

world. Marlow seems to assume the common-sense view that the value of such regression lies in the strength it will give him when he turns his attention again to the "real" world. But Conrad, who is just as much committed to humanity as is Marlow, forces his narrator to ask the ultimate romantic question: "Of all mankind Jim had no dealings but with himself, and the question is whether at the last he had not confessed to a faith mightier than the laws of order and progress" (p. 294). In other words, where does reality lie: in the objective actual or in the mind; in conscious orientation to sense data or in the unconscious forms of the creative imagination?

In *Lord Jim,* Conrad gave all the sympathy he could to the claims of the transcendent self, the romantic ego-ideal. That he was able to go as far as he did strikes me as a triumph of the imagination. For when we look at the pattern of Conrad's own life, we realize why he withheld sympathy from his first two serious attempts to portray egocentric man, James Wait, the nigger of the *Narcissus,* and Mr. Kurtz, who dwelt in the heart of darkness. Conrad's well-known statement that "the romantic feeling of reality was . . . an inborn faculty" in him is, of course, substantiated by his youthful adventures. But the collapse of his fortunes in Marseilles helps to explain his change to hardworking seaman and the checks he later put on the romantic sensibility. It must, he felt, be "disciplined by a sense of solidarity and a recognition of the hard facts of existence shared with the rest of mankind" (author's Note to *Within the Tides).* These are precisely the qualities which Marlow tells us Jim lacks. The hard facts defeat him, and the lack of a sense of responsibility to people allows him at the end to desert those who believe in him still.

Writing to Edward Garnett of his aim in *Lord Jim,* Conrad said, "I wanted to obtain a sort of lurid light out of the very events" (*Life and Letters,* I, 299). Although he tried to insist that he had not succeeded, I feel that "lurid" is quite an appropriate word to describe the second half of the book. The Patusan section is purposefully romantic, highlighted, archetypal, and is successful on that level. Taken as realistic rendering, of course, it is not successful, as the first section is for all its covert symbolism. Conrad continued to Garnett, "I've been satanically ambitious, but there's nothing of a devil in me, worse luck." We are never bound to take Conrad the letter writer at face value, and I think there is a lot of evidence that Conrad knew himself better than this. In an earlier letter to Cunninghame Grahame, speaking of the burden of consciousness, Conrad wrote, "We can't return to nature, since we can't change our place in it. Our refuge is in stupidity, in drunkenness of all kinds, in lies, in beliefs, in murder, thieving, reforming, in negation, in contempt,—each man according to the promptings of his particular devil."[5]

As an ex-Catholic, Conrad had, like Jim, rejected the idea of a God who was his author, but more important, like Marlow he had gained stability by transferring his allegiance to humanity and his sense of

5. P. 226, *Joseph Conrad: Life and Letters,* Vol. I, ed. G. Jean-Aubry (New York, 1927).

duty to his profession. Unlike the merchant marine, however, writing required that he be satanic: no one, Conrad contended, can condemn an artist for pursuing a creative aim. "In that interior world where his thought and his emotions go seeking for the experience of imagined adventures, there are no policemen, no law, no pressure of circumstance or dread of opinion to keep him within bounds" (Preface to *A Personal Record*). Or, as Marlow says of Patusan, "do you notice how, three hundred miles beyond the end of telegraph cable and mail-boat lines, the haggard utilitarian lies of our civilisation wither and die, to be replaced by pure exercises of imagination, that have the futility, often the charm, and sometimes the deep hidden truthfulness, of works of art?" (p. 244). As I see Conrad's "satanic ambition," it was to present a picture of the land of the imagination, to give a true rendering of the large and autonomous forces that reign there.

In other words, I believe Conrad constructed Patusan on principles strikingly similar to those later used by Jung to analyze the structure of what he called the collective unconscious. Briefly, Jung believed that psychic energy "that will not flow into life at the right time regresses to the mythical world of the archetypes, where it activates images which, since the remotest times, have expressed the non-human life of the gods, whether of the upper world or the lower" (*Transformation*, p. 308). Jung saw these actions as resulting from unconscious personas, "certain types which deserve the name of dominants. These are archetypes like the anima, animus, wise old man, witch, shadow, earth-mother, . . . and the organizing dominants, the self, the circle, and the quaternity, i.e., the four functions or aspects of the self or of consciousness" (*Transformation*, p. 391).

Although Jung emphasized that he postulated these dominants only after empirical observations of psychosis, dream, and fantasy, he also warned that the names he has given them, while traditional, are "as if" forms, since unconscious content cannot be directly apprehended by the conscious mind. In any case, once we are aware of these traditional personified forms, we can see them playing a part in a pattern which throws considerable light on Jim's experience in Patusan.

One of Jung's basic assertions is that, for a man, male consciousness is balanced by female unconsciousness—the anima, as Jung calls it—an autonomous archetype whose contents or effects will filter through to the conscious mind so long as it is more or less in harmony with the unconscious. Once they diverge, the unconscious faculties have to distinguish themselves, and "the figure of the (wise) old man becomes detached from the anima and appears as an archetype of the 'spirit.' He stands to her in the relationship of a 'spiritual' father, like Wotan to Brunhilde" (*Transformation*, p. 437). This guide sets the hero on the path to adventure, the chance to win through to psychic wholeness. Using the Hiawatha myth as an example, Jung outlines the subsequent heroic pattern: "This great deed of Hiawatha's, when he conquers . . . the death-bringing daemon in the guise of the negative father, is followed by his marriage with Minnehaha. He can only turn to his human side after he has fulfilled his historic destiny: firstly the transformation of the daemon from an uncontrolled force of nature into a power that is his to command; secondly the final deliverance of ego-consciousness from the deadly threat of the unconscious in the form of the negative parents" (*Transformation,* p. 353). Once successful in these tests, the hero will have the freedom to arrange some sort of psychic harmony. According to Jung, this harmony will consist of a quaternity which might be expressed as mother-father, self-wife figures. In the case of Jim, we can see Jewel as the mate, one-fourth of the quaternity Jim needs to regain psychic wholeness. The obvious father-mother figures are Doramin and his wife, who oversaw Jim's rebirth. With the support of these three, Jim goes ahead to his place as hero, Tuan Jim, the white god upon whom depends the stability and order of the chaotic land he has invaded. With Jewel's help he faces the four murderers sent by the Rajah (with Cornelius' cooperation). He kills one, his first destructive act, and goes on to organize the completely successful raid on Sherif Ali. After that triumph he refuses to kill any more and lives like an immortal in the presence of his tolerated enemies, Cornelius and the subdued Rajah.

But even after he has conquered the hostile Archetypes, the hero has to face an equal if more subtle danger—that he "will grow fast to the rocks, like Theseus and Peirithous, who wanted to abduct the goddess of the underworld. It happens all too easily that there is no returning from the realm of the Mothers" (*Transformation,* p. 310). Thus we may see Jim as simply caught. Marlow mentions this possibility as a fact several times:

"All his conquests, the trust, the fame, the friendships, the love—all these things that made him master had made him a captive, too. . . . The life of old mankind, . . . the secrets of the land, . . . the pride of his own heart . . . possessed him and made him their own to the innermost thought, to the slightest stir of blood, to his last breath" (p. 215). We can almost say that such a person has to become a victim.

And one way of becoming a victim is to submit entirely, to accept the role of saviour. Jung uses Baldur in Norse mythology as an example of this divine son who must die.

> But why should the mistletoe kill Baldur, since it is, in a sense, his sister or brother? . . . In reality he is a parasite on the mother, a creature of her imagination, who only lives when rooted in the maternal body. In actual psychic experience the mother corresponds to the collective unconscious, and the son to consciousness, which fancies itself free but must ever again succumb to the power of sleep and deadening unconsciousness. The mistletoe, however, corresponds to the shadow brother. . . . The shadow becomes fatal when there is too little vitality or too little consciousness in the hero for him to complete his heroic task.[6] (*Transformation,* p. 259)

6. "He is, as it were, only a dream of the mother, an ideal which she soon takes back into herself, as we can see from the Near Eastern 'son-gods' like Tammuz, Attis, Adonis, and Christ" (*Transformation,* p. 258).

The shadow can be encountered in what Jung calls the personal unconscious. It is dark, indicating in the individual "a certain degree of inferiority and the existence of a lower level of personality. On this lower level with its uncontrolled or scarcely controlled emotions one behaves more or less like a primitive, who is . . . singularly incapable of moral judgment."[7]

The normal sequence of self-confrontation is sketched by Jung as follows: "The shadow, although by definition a negative figure . . . [seems to be] hiding meaningful contents under an unprepossessing exterior. . . . The things that are hidden usually consist of increasingly numinous figures. The one standing closest behind the shadow is the anima, who is endowed with considerable powers of fascination and possession. She often appears in rather too youthful form, and hides in her turn the powerful archetype of the wise old man (sage, magician, king, etc.)."[8] Actually, as in Jung's own earlier example of Brunhilde and Wotan as anima and wise old man, in the experience of the hero, the sage-magician often points the way to the anima. We could say that the actual sequence is not so important as the fact that the hero cannot succeed unless he comes to terms with both his shadow (representing repressions in the personal unconscious) and his anima (representing the life force in his collective unconscious).

I contend that Jim gets to the realm of archetypes without ever coming to terms with his shadow. His jumping from the *Patna* under the surface is, of course, a conventional first step. And certainly he is faced by shadow figures frequently in his flight across the Indian Ocean. But he cannot accept the shadow of his own deed; he must always escape it. Marlow has tried without success to force Jim to acknowledge this "certain degree of inferiority," but he has to be content with giving Jim merely "the means to carry on decently the serious business of life, to get food, drink, and shelter of the customary kind while his wounded spirit, like a bird with a broken wing, might hop and flutter into some hole to die quietly of inanition there" (p. 159). Such practical help is not enough, as Marlow is finally forced to admit. "I had given him many opportunities, but they had been merely opportunities to earn his bread" (p. 173). So he passes Jim on to Stein, who is Conrad's most potent version of the archetypal wise old man:

> Often the old man in fairy tales asks questions like who? why? whence? and whither? for the purpose of inducing self-reflection and mobilizing the moral forces, and more often still he gives the necessary magical talisman, the unexpected and improbable power to succeed, which is one of the peculiarities of the unified personality in good or bad alike. But the intervention of the old man—the spontaneous objectivation of the archetype— would seem to be equally indispensable, since the conscious will

7. P. 7, "Aion," in *Psyche and Symbol*, a selection from the writing of Jung made by Violet S. de Laszlo for Anchor Books.

8. P. 270, "On the Psychology of the Trickster-Figure," Vol. IX, Part I. of the Collected Works (London, 1959).

by itself is hardly ever capable of uniting the personality to the point where it acquires this extraordinary power to succeed. ("The Phenomenology of the Spirit in Fairy Tales," *Psyche and Symbol*, pp. 75-76)

With the ring given him by Stein, Jim finally achieves a safe lodging in the world of archetypes. But as we have seen, he has to face entrapment in another hole before arriving there. He gets out of the Rajah's stockade by flying, going over the palisade "like a bird" (p. 219). In other words, his spirit insists on flying to the world of the eternal, the stars, rather than getting there by grappling with his terrestial faults. Instead of going underneath on the return journey from west to east, Jim flies back *over*, following the route of the sun, but reversing its course.

In Patusan Jim is able to do the great deeds of Hiawatha, but he is also doomed to suffer the fate of Baldur. Because no matter what route he chooses, he can gain psychic unity only by making a complete circle. In reversing his course at the farthest point west, he has simply put off until the end of the cycle the necessary confronting of the shadow, the dark representative of the mundane world. Shortly before Gentleman Brown appears, Jim tells Marlow, "I am satisfied . . . nearly. I've got to look only at the face of the first man that comes along to regain my confidence" (p. 265, ellipsis Conrad's). Although Jim faces Brown physically across the stream, he does not face squarely the moral implications of Brown. This is why Marlow can say later of Brown's gratuitous slaying of Dain Waris, "It was not a vulgar and treacherous massacre; it was a lesson, a retribution—a demonstration of some obscure and awful attribute of our nature which, I am afraid, is not so very far under the surface as we like to think" (p. 352). Marlow also comments, Jim "was overwhelmed by his own personality—the gift of that destiny which he had done his best to master" (p. 296).

Brown corresponds exactly to Jung's description of the shadow, that "lower level" of personality "with its uncontrolled . . . emotions." Before seeing Jim, he imagines that "they would work like brothers" (p. 321). And when he confronts Jim, there is "subtle reference to their common blood, and assumption of common experience; a sickening suggestion of common guilt, of secret knowledge that was like a bond of their minds and of their hearts" (p. 337). Like Jim's central attribute, Brown's evil is "derived from intense egoism" (p. 298). In describing his talk with Brown, Marlow even uses an image of rebirth: "The corpse of his mad self-love uprose from rags and destitution as from the dark horrors of a tomb" (p. 334). He is the negative brother ("brown" in spirit) and his murder of Dain Waris, the positive brother ("white" in spirit, see p. 227) leaves Patusan without its natural heir to the throne, making it impossible for Jim to leave.

But this sketching in of the archetypal characters does not really tell us why Jim fails. A fuller approach, still within the Jungian framework, lies through the light-dark images we began to investigate earlier. In the sun myth rebirth is achieved by a journey in darkness. One such journey was Jonah's in the whale, a favorite with Conrad. And in the New Testament we have the resurrection of Lazarus and Christ. That Jim follows a similar pattern is evident even in the first half of the novel. Of his leap from the *Patna,* Marlow says, "He had indeed jumped into an everlasting deep hole. He had tumbled from a height he could never scale again. By that time the boat had gone driving forward past the bows. It was too dark just then for them to see each other, and, moreover, they were blinded and half drowned with rain. He told me it was like being swept by a flood through a cavern" (p. 97). Figuratively, Jim does not emerge from that cave (or grave, see p. 104) during the rest of his life. After he returned for the trial, for instance, Marlow says, "He had passed these days on the verandah, buried in a long chair, and coming out of his place of sepulture only at meal-times or late at night, when he wandered on the quays all by himself, detached from his surroundings, irresolute and silent, like a ghost without a home to haunt" (p. 70). The parallel between Jim's situation and that of Christ in the tomb is picked up later when Jim gets to Patusan. "This is where I was prisoner for three days," he says of the Rajah's stockade. In one sense then we must see Jim as re-emerging into life in the rebirth scene already analyzed. But in another sense he never does, as other images connected with Patusan itself indicate.

As we might expect, Marlow's philosophy of life influences not only his final judgment but his very descriptions of Patusan. He is able to react favorably to some of its qualities because they show a form of solidarity, but we will find in his characterization of much of the land and of its "authors," Jim and Stein, an hostility apparent in the images connected with them. For instance, when we accompany Marlow to Stein's house for the first time, we note that only one corner of the study "was strongly lighted by a shaded reading-lamp, and the rest of the spacious apartment melted into shapeless gloom like a cavern" (p. 175). When Stein leaves that light, "his tall form, as though robbed of its substance, hovered noiselessly over invisible things with stooping and indefinite movements; his voice, heard in that remoteness where he could be glimpsed mysteriously busy with immaterial cares, was no longer incisive, seemed to roll voluminous and grave" (p. 184). It is under such ambiguous circumstances that Stein gives his famous prescription for romantic action. And when he then returns "the light had destroyed the assurance which had inspired him in the distant shadows. . . . The whisper of his conviction seemed to open before me a vast and un-certain expanse, as of a crepuscular horizon on a plain at dawn—or was it, perchance, at the coming of the night? One had not the courage to decide; but it was a charming and deceptive light, throwing the impalpa-ble poesy of its dimness over pitfalls—over graves" (p. 185). Although Stein's connection with darkness is not unexpected in view of the light-reality, dark-dream opposition we investigated earlier, its connection with a cave and the grave is somewhat ominous.

And when we move to Patusan itself, the connection between moon-light and the grave increases. Even before he goes there, Marlow real-izes that it has "been used as a grave for some sin" once before (p. 189).

And when he actually arrives in Patusan, he watches "the moon float away above the chasm between the hills like an ascending spirit out of a grave; its sheen descended, cold and pale, like the ghost of dead sunlight. There is something haunting in the light of the moon; it has all the dispassionateness of a disembodied soul, and something of its inconceivable mystery" (p. 213). It is at this point that Marlow invokes the sunlight as "all we have to live by." Still later the moon is connected with the specific grave of the past sin earlier speculated on, the grave of Jewel's mother.[9]

> I saw part of the moon glittering through the bushes at the bottom of the chasm. For a moment it looked as though the smooth disc, falling from its place in the sky upon the earth, had rolled to the bottom of that precipice: its ascending movement was like a leisurely rebound; it disengaged itself from the tangle of twigs; the bare contorted limb of some tree, growing on the slope, made a black crack right across its face. It threw its level rays afar as if from a cavern, and in this mournful eclipse-like light the stumps of felled trees uprose very dark, the heavy shadows fell at my feet on all sides, my own moving shadow, and across my path the shadow of the solitary grave perpetually garlanded with flowers.
> (p. 279)

Like Jim, the moon is described as a "disembodied soul" trying to escape from an abyss into which it has fallen.[10] The image is appropriate, for like Jim the moon tries to take the place of the sun, in a dark world of shadows. That it is possible to live in the cave while ostensibly in reality is clear from the last cave image, of Stein's rooms again, after Jewel emerges from her native land.

> They are cool on the hottest days, and you enter them as you would a scrubbed cave underground. I passed through one, and in the other I saw the girl sitting at the end of a big mahogany table, on which she rested her head, the face hidden in her arms. The waxed floor reflected her dimly as though it had been a sheet of frozen water. . . . Her white figure seemed shaped in snow; the pendent crystals of a great chandelier clicked above her head like glittering icicles. She looked up and watched my approach. I was chilled as if these vast apartments had been the cold abode of despair. (pp. 301–02)

The waters of life have frozen.

These images emphasize that in addition to choosing between light and dark, Jim is also choosing between heat and cold. The sun is both

9. For an analysis of the sinister imagery frequently associated with Conrad's women, see Part II of Thomas Moser's *Joseph Conrad, Achievement and Decline* (Cambridge, Mass., 1957), especially pp. 83-86. My own case will be that although Jewel's relation to her mother figures negatively, her relation to Jim is as positive as he will let it be.

10. Cf. Dorothy Van Ghent's treatment of this description, pp. 235-237. *The English Novel, Form and Function* (New York, 1953).

light and hot; the moon, though it lights the darkness, is cold. Marlow's strongest charge against Jim is that he could have lived in Patusan and still chosen heat. Even the jungle strives for it: "the immovable forests rooted deep in the soil, soaring towards the sunshine, everlasting in the shadowy might of their tradition, like life itself" (p. 211). But even at night there is hope and solace for man in the forest of Patusan. If the dark houses of the natives are like "a spectral herd of shapeless creatures pressing forward to drink in a spectral and lifeless stream," yet "here and there a red gleam twinkled within the bamboo walls, warm, like a living spark, significant of human affections, of shelter, of repose" (pp. 213–214). Patusan stands for the primitive beginnings of consciousness and civilization, as Marlow tries to inform the reader. He sees Jim dominating "the forest, the secular gloom, the old mankind. He was like a figure set up on a pedestal, to represent in his persistent youth the power, and perhaps the virtues, of races that never grow old, that have emerged from the gloom. I don't know why he should always have appeared to me symbolic" (p. 229). Jim has immersed himself in this old life, been reborn from its dark mud, and found a light to guide him upward to godhead.

In truth he has found two lights. The first is the cold light of eternity under which he conceived his strategy: "A star suddenly twinkled through a hole in the roof. His brain was in a whirl; but, nevertheless, it was on that very night that he matured his plan for overcoming Sherif Ali" (p. 252). The second light is the warm fire of humanity by which he actually passes his first test. "Jim's slumbers were disturbed by a dream of heavens like brass resounding with a great voice, which called upon him to Awake! Awake! so loud that, notwithstanding his desperate determination to sleep on, he did wake up in reality. The glare of a red spluttering conflagration going on in mid-air fell on his eyes" (p. 256). It is Jewel, who leads him with her torch to the storehouse where his would-be assassins are hiding. She thrusts her arm through a window to light the inside for him. "The door swung with a creak and a clatter, disclosing to his intense astonishment the low dungeon-like interior illuminated by a lurid, wavering glare. . . . 'Fire! Defend yourself,' the girl outside cried in an agonising voice. She being in the dark and with her arm thrust in to the shoulder through the small hole, couldn't see what was going on, and she dared not withdraw the torch to run round" (p. 260).

By her light Jim is in a few minutes able to kill his first man. "He found himself calm, appeased, without rancour, without uneasiness, as if the death of that man had atoned for everything. The place was getting very full of sooty smoke from the torch, in which the unswaying flame burned blood-red without a flicker" (p. 261). The other three men he forces to jump into the river. Then "Jim turned to the girl, who had been a silent and attentive observer. His heart seemed suddenly to grow too big for his breast and choke him in the hollow of his throat. This probably made him speechless for so long, and after returning his gaze she flung the burning torch with a wide sweep of the arm into the river. The ruddy fiery glare, taking a long flight through the night, sank with a vicious hiss, and the calm soft starlight descended upon them, unchecked" (p. 263). Later she tells Marlow that "she had flung the torch in the water because he was looking at her so. There was too much light, and the danger was over then—for a little time" (p. 268). Jewel realizes instinctively that Jim's love for her is not flesh and blood. Marlow sees this too. "There was nothing lighthearted in their romance: they came together under the shadow of a life's disaster, like night and maiden meeting to exchange vows amongst haunted ruins. The starlight was good enough for that story, a light so faint and remote that it cannot resolve shadows into shapes, and show the other shore of a stream. I did look upon the stream that night and from the very place; it rolled silent and as black as Styx" (p. 270). Like Jim's own personality, their love is both heroic and child-like.[11]

> "Hallo, girl!" he cried, cheerily, "Hallo, boy!" she answered at once with amazing pluck.
> This was their usual greeting to each other, and the bit of swagger she would put into her rather high but sweet voice was very droll, pretty, and childlike. (p. 278)

Another indication of the non-sexual nature of their love is the fact that they have no child, unlike Tamb Itam who married after meeting Jim, and even unlike Stein.

But whereas Stein is able to return to civilization unencumbered when his wife and daughter die, Jim will have to take Jewel, his butterfly, with him. Showing the butterfly to Marlow, Stein says, "So halt' ich's endlich denn in meinen Händen, / Und nenn' es in gewissem Sinne mein" (p. 181). And as Jim is about to go to be shot by Doramin, Jewel cries, "Ah! but I shall hold thee thus, . . . Thou art mine!" (p. 359). But he is not. We implied earlier that Jim rescued Jewel from Cornelius, but it was actually she who watched over him for a succession of nights and finally summoned him to his triumph. Similarly she tries at the end to claim him for the warmth of life, even if it means fighting for it. But Jim is too rarified. He has already made up his mind to offer himself as a sacrifice.

As Jung says, "Only out of disaster can the longing for the saviour arise—in other words, the recognition and unavoidable integration of the shadow create such a harrowing situation that nobody but a saviour can undo the tangled web of fate. In the case of the individual, the problem constellated by the shadow is answered on the plane of the anima, that is, through relatedness" ("The Trickster-Figure," p. 271). How is it that Jim has not learned from his anima, Jewel, how to "relate," to respond to others? It is certainly what she has tried to teach him, whether in leading him to the assassins, urging him to kill Brown, or demanding his impure help rather than his final pure sacrifice. But the problem is not so simple. According to Jung, for a man "the anima is and remains the representative of that part of the unconscious which

---

11. Ch. xxxiv ends with Cornelius' oft expressed, "No more than a little child." Ch. xxxv ends with Marlow's being rowed out until Jim is "no bigger than a child." Because of Jim's regression and rebirth, we have the paradox of the childish hero. Like Baldur he may be reluctant to leave his mother and grow to maturity.

can never be assimilated into a humanly attainable whole" ("The Spirit in Fairy Tales," p. 99). If Jim leaves Patusan, he will not be able to take Jewel, a half-caste, back to civilization as his wife. Yet he can accept the imperfect solution of leaving her behind no more than he can the thought of staying in a disorganized Patusan which would be a constant reminder of the harmony he almost succeeded in making permanent. He consequently takes another route, to a third universe with another anima figure, as Marlow ironically admits in his final summation: "It may very well be that in the short moment of his last proud and un-flinching glance, he had beheld the face of that opportunity which, like an Eastern bride, had come veiled to his side" (p. 362). In any case, Marlow tells us that Jim had determined "the dark powers should not rob him twice of his peace" (p. 356). Marlow had earlier criticized Jim for desiring such peace on the sinking *Patna*, although he understood its appeal: "Which of us here has not observed this, or maybe experi-enced something of that feeling in his own person—this extreme weari-ness of emotions, the vanity of effort, the yearning for rest?" (p. 76). Conrad certainly had; as he expressed it lightly in the "Author's Note" to *The Mirror of the Sea*, "I have been all my life averse from exertion." But the theme of the burden of life we can see weighing down his letters to Garnett and Cunninghame Grahame, and we can imagine it winning a temporary victory in his youthful suicide attempt. Despite, therefore, the affirmed and reaffirmed solidarity about which Conrad so frequently wrote in his non-fiction, most of his novels record its struggle with that longing which Jung seemed to have understood too. Man

> imagines his worst enemy in front of him, yet he carries the enemy within himself—a deadly longing for the abyss, a longing to drown in his own source, to be sucked down to the realm of the Mothers. His life is a constant struggle against extinction, a violent yet fleeting deliverance from ever-lurking night. This death is no external enemy, it is his own inner longing for the stillness and profound peace of all-knowing non-existence, for all-seeing sleep in the ocean of coming-to-be and passing away. Even in his highest strivings for harmony and balance, for the profundities of philosophy and the raptures of the artist, he seeks death, immobility, satiety, rest. (*Transformation*, p. 356)

So perhaps we should see Jim's self-sacrifice as a tribute to the young Conrad and to what his attempt at suicide made possible—or necessary —the later Conrad who valued so highly responsibility and human love. The conflict between these two sides of man's nature is clearly present in the possibilities open to Jim in Patusan. Even at the end he could still admit his responsibility by affirming his love for Jewel as a human being. Earlier he could have asserted it by taking action in the case of Brown (the solution advocated by Jewel and Dain Waris is clearly the correct one).

Such acceptance of responsibility would inevitably mean taking over authority from Doramin, but this has already happened in actuality. After Jim's defeat of Sherif Ali, Doramin symbolically retires "with great dignity into a bit of shade where he laid himself down to sleep covered entirely with a piece of white sheeting" (p. 235). This action does not mean that Doramin has given up his authority entirely, however. He still has the imposing flintlock pistols, which Marlow says were "a present from Stein . . . in exchange for that ring . . . Used to belong to good old M'Neil. God only knows how *he* came by them" (p. 229). They are clearly the symbol of power and authority. Who has them controls man's temporal fate; who has the ring may triumph spiritually, asserting eternal values. But Jim, though he uses a pistol to kill one assassin and the cannon to smash Sherif Ali, will not kill if he can help it. In fact, he has been consistently reluctant to use the power to destroy which must go with temporal authority. This reluctance is evident before he ever reaches Patusan in his taking a pistol but leaving the shells for it behind.

The three routes that Jim may take to solve his problem all finally focus on the same image, blood-red fire. Issuing from a gun, it is destructive and associated with the exercise of temporal authority. As the household fire or Jewel's torch, it stands for the bond of human love and is associated with the continuity of generation. As the blood of the sacrificial victim, it offers a short cut to eternity, and is associated with an unworldly spiritual purity. This central image is derived from the setting sun which warns that death is a certainty on earth. Thus before Jim's death, we are told, "the sky over Patusan was blood-red, immense, streaming like an open vein" (p. 360).

The man who chooses the hearth fire hopes to win immortality through his offspring. The man who puts his faith in a pistol acknowledges and uses destruction. But the man who chooses to become a victim disdains destructiveness and cannot accept vicarious immortality. Rather than becoming the authoritative father or responsible husband, he takes on the role of the unworthy son who redeems himself by early sacrifice and return to the mother, undifferentiated nature. During his final parting from Jim, Marlow noted how "under the low sun, glowing, darkened and crimson, like an ember snatched from the fire, the sea lay outspread, offering all its immense stillness to the approach of the fiery orb. . . . The half-submerged sun faced him; I could see its red gleam in his eyes that looked dumbly at me" (pp. 290–291). With the death of Dain Waris Jim's need to choose becomes a matter of life and death. He can admit weakness and go on living, or he can do what he does, "prove his power in another way and conquer the fatal destiny itself" (p. 357). By sacrificing his physical body to his concept of himself, Jim has finally freed himself for good from the mud and filth of the temporal world. From another point of view, he has recaptured the height of the mast of the training ship from which he once "looked down with the contempt of a man destined to shine in the midst of dangers" (p. 3). More permanently than when he captured Sherif Ali's hill, Jim has mounted, flown to the height of the stars, become the high light he longed to be. If that light has no heat, it is at least eternal, an archetype worthy of this slightly inhuman son of nature.

Imagery

Wolfgang Clemen

KING LEAR

An attempt to interpret a Shakespearian play solely on the basis of its imagery—a risky undertaking—would have the greatest chance of success if *King Lear* were the play in question. The imagery here seems to be more fully integrated into the structure of the drama and for that reason to play a more meaningful rôle than in other plays. Not only do the various sequences of imagery offer important clues to what Shakespeare sought to represent in *King Lear,* but the distribution of the images among the characters, their interrelation and their significance for the illumination of certain themes and trends of the action also help us to a better insight into the meaning of the drama. In *King Lear,* action and imagery appear to be particularly closely dependent upon each other and are reciprocally illuminating; the imagery, in fact, seems to have taken over some functions which so far—in Shakespeare's earlier plays—belonged to other mediums of dramatic expression. In the development of Shakespeare's imagery, *King Lear* therefore represents an important new stage. The present chapter tries to investigate only some of these new aspects. To explore it fully would demand a study of greater length than the scope of the present book allows.[1]

At the very first glance we perceive that the form of most of the

Reprinted by permission of the publishers from Wolfgang Clemen, *The Development of Shakespeare's Imagery.* Cambridge, Mass.: Harvard University Press, 1951 and Methuen & Co. Ltd.

1. After completing this chapter the present writer became acquainted with the book by R. B. Heilman, *This Great Stage, Image and Structure in King Lear,* Louisiana State University Press, 1948. This book, so far the most outstanding full-length study of the imagery in a single Shakespearian play, is of great importance and interest for our own investigation. Heilman's book can throw light on several points made in this chapter, in that it develops and examines more comprehensively some of the ideas upon which we here have merely touched. On the other hand, the present writer's view and approach differ in several important respects from that put forward by R. B. Heilman, so that it was not thought necessary to cancel or rewrite this chapter in spite of certain similarities the two studies may offer. Whereas Heilman's chief concern is with "patterns" or "areas" of meaning created by recurrent and interrelated imagery, which, in his view, embody "a good deal of what the drama has to say", the present writer's aim has been to examine the different functions, the distribution and the form of imagery as well as its cooperation with the other elements of dramatic art.

images and their connection with the context differ from those in the earlier plays. Formerly, the images were used as illustrations, or the metaphorical element was fused with the train of thought as a means of enhancement or elucidation. In *King Lear* we can seldom speak of such an illustrative function. The image is presented as if it existed for its own sake; it serves no other aim but to speak for itself alone. Let us look at Lear's speeches in III. ii. or in IV. vi. from this point of view: he sets image after image as independent, direct visions. The same thing holds true of the Fool. Up to now, we have found characters speaking exclusively in imagery only in moments of the greatest excitement. In *King Lear,* however, this is the case throughout many scenes; imagery is for Lear his most characteristic form of utterance.

The reason for this becomes clear if we trace Lear's development during the early scenes. The first shows us Lear still in possession of his power; he is still a member of society. He makes decisions, gives orders and makes plans, addresses the other characters of this scene, his daughters, Kent, France, etc. But the very first scene gives us a hint of how Lear is going to lose contact with this natural relation to his environment. The dialogue which he carries on with his daughters is at bottom no true dialogue, that is, a dialogue based on a mutual will to mutual understanding. Lear determines in advance the answers he will receive; he fails to adapt himself to the person with whom he is speaking. Hence his complete and almost incomprehensible misunderstanding of Cordelia. Lear takes no pains to understand what Cordelia is really trying to say; he does not consider whether her words could not have quite another meaning. He catches up only their superficial form and, because he had expected another answer, different from this, he repels the one person who in reality is nearest and dearest to him. More and more Lear loses contact with the outside world; words become for him less a means of communication with others than a means of expressing what goes on within himself. His utterances, even when addressed to other persons, take on, increasingly, the character of a monologue and become less and less part of the dramatic dialogue, although Lear (which is typical) never speaks an actual monologue himself.

The wealth of images in his speech results from this process and gives it expression; we have seen that in Shakespeare, the monologue is always the form of utterance richest in imagery. Lear gazes within himself; he no longer sees people nor what goes on about him. In madness a man is alone with himself; he speaks more to his own person than to others; where he does not speak to himself, he creates for himself a new and imaginary partner. Lear speaks to people not present, he speaks to the elements, to nature, to the heavens. Men have forsaken him; so he turns to the non-human, superhuman powers. It is one of the functions of the imagery in *King Lear* to awaken these elemental forces and to open to them the way into the play.

The characters around Lear, too, the Fool, Edgar and Kent, speak a language rich in imagery. We shall discuss later the significance of the image in their utterances. If we glance, however, at the other group of characters, Edmund, Goneril, Regan, Cornwall, we note how seldom they employ images, how different is their whole language. In contrast to Lear and his followers, we never find that peculiar form of "mono-logic dialogue" between them. They speak rationally; they address their words to their partner, and converse in a deliberate and conscious manner. They have a goal which they seek to attain and everything they have to say is bent upon this. Their language does not betray to us what is taking place within them—in the form of "imaginative vis-ions"; it reveals to us solely their aims and attitudes, and how they intend to put these into practice. Thus their language scarcely changes throughout the course of the play, whereas Lear's, Edgar's and Kent's way of speaking is constantly varied. Goneril, Regan and Edmund are the calculating,[2] cool and unimaginative people who are incapable of "creative" imagery. They have no relationship to nature, to the ele-mental powers. Their world is the world of reason; they live and speak within the narrow limits of their plans, within the limits drawn by the plot and the given moment of the action. Lear's language continually points beyond these limits. Thus the distribution of the images among the characters also gives us a hint as to their position within the play.

The middle acts of the tragedy, Acts II.-IV., are the richest in imagery. The outer action is less important here and is relegated to the back-ground. The main emphasis does not fall upon the outer course of events, upon what Regan or Goneril are planning, or what Edmund is about, but rather upon what is passing in Lear himself.[3] The outer drama has become an inner drama. Beneath the surface of the plot lies the deeper level of inner experience which gradually frees itself more and more from the sparse events of the action. The latter becomes a frame and an occasion in order that the former may take on living reality. In truth, Shakespeare has not treated this outer action with the same thoroughness and care as he usually employed in the construction of the plot. As Bradley has already pointed out,[4] the plot displays a number of inconsistencies and is not carried out clearly. Goethe found the action of *Lear* full of improbabilities and "absurd". But Shakespeare was concerned not with the "outer", but with the "inner" drama. The important thing is not what Lear does, but what he suffers, feels, and envisions with his inner eye. One of the greatest and deepest truths of this play is that we must first go through suffering before we can recognize our real selves and the truth. "I stumbled when I saw", Gloucester cries out (IV. i.); he first learned to see, when he was blind. Thus Lear, too, sees through the world of appearances not with his physical eyes; it is rather with his inner eye—in madness—that he pene-

2. Gundolf notes that Goneril, while expressing her feelings towards her father, uses the terminology of "possession and calculation." She asserts her love in terms of "nega-tive measurements" (I. i. 61) (Fr. Gundolf, *Shakespeare, Sein, Wesen und Werk*, Berlin, 1928, vol. II, p. 235). Dr. Schmetz (*op. cit.*) notes the frequent occurrence of quantitative and mercantile terms as well as the use of calculating comparatives in the language of the two sisters (cf. "disquantity," "remainder," "want," "need," "scanted," "prize," "use," "business," "safe and politic," "expense and waste of his revenues" (I. i. 72, 281–282; I. iv. 272–273, 348, 353; II. i. 102; II. ii. 121–130; II. iv. 241, 264, 266)).

3. Granville-Barker says about some of these scenes: "They pass beyond the needs of the plot, they belong to a larger synthesis" (H. Granville-Barker, *Prefaces to Shake-speare, First Series*, London, 1927).

4. Bradley, *Shakespearean Tragedy*, p. 256.

trates to the very bottom of things and recognizes their true nature, whereas he formerly let himself be blinded by their outward appearance. It is obvious that imagery is the only adequate form of expression for such an inner process.

But the term "inner drama" is not sufficient to describe accurately the peculiar shifting of emphasis—from the level of human action to another level. Much of what Lear utters in the central scenes points beyond the limits of his personal fate. Indeed, Lear's suffering and experience, although represented to us as an individual case, is meant to signify much more than something merely personal; it is meant to be an archetype of the universal. More than in any other play, the human events in *King Lear* are related to the happenings of the whole world. Bradley speaks of the "feeling which haunts us in *King Lear*, as though we were witnessing something universal—a conflict not so much of particular persons as of the powers of good and evil in the world."[5] Behind Lear's personal suffering stands the suffering of the whole world; behind the severing of the bond between Lear and his daughters stands the breakdown of all the hard-and-fast limits of the universe. This inclusive action is made clear to us by means of the imagery. The imagery gives the horizon of the individual occurrence a comprehensive perspective; it transforms human matters into mighty universal events. The elemental forces and the things of nature, as they appear so profusely in the language of Lear and his followers from the second act on, often seem to grow beyond the speakers. They assume, as it were, an individual existence, they become almost independent of the speakers. The imagery becomes the means by which these forces of nature enter into the play and take part therein as active agents. These sequences of imagery, such as are to be found, for example, in Edgar's long list of animals and plants, are not to be interpreted as the "expression" of individual inner experiences, but rather as the appearance of independent forces which belong to the play just as much as to the people. The words "atmosphere", "background", no longer suffice to designate what of nature, landscape and animal world is evoked by the imagery. This "atmosphere" here becomes a world in itself; we almost forget that it is only through the words of certain characters that life is given to this world of nature.

The non-human nature-world enters into the play in the same measure as the human world breaks down and falls to pieces. This occurs when the father is expelled by his daughters, when the son is persecuted by the father and madness dissolves human order; the firm bonds and laws of human society are destroyed; so now non-human powers, heavenly forces, lightning, thunder, rain and wind, animals and plants, enter in rich variety. This interrelationship is to be seen clearly in the structure of the play; the first act contains relatively little nature-imagery; in the second act it begins to grow, and it attains to its height in the third and fourth acts, which show us the forsaken Lear in his madness.

In the first scene of the play we may study the peculiar nature of

5. *Shakespearean Tragedy*, p. 262.

"dramatic imagery," consisting in preparing for later issues and giving hints of the further development of the action. For the reasons explained above, the first scene is relatively poor in images; but where they do occur, their appearance is significant.

When Lear appears for the first time upon the stage and communicates to the assembled court and to his daughters his intention to divide the kingdom, he says:

> and 'tis our fast intent
> To shake all cares and business from our age;
> Conferring them on younger strengths, while we
> Unburthen'd *crawl* toward death.
> (I. i. 39)

crawl awakens a definite notion. Taken from the realm of animal life, crawling suggests a wounded, tired, perhaps hunted animal dragging itself nearer to death. Lear, at this point still in full possession of his royal authority, employs the metaphor ironically; he has as yet no knowledge of the fate which will actually cast him out and bring him down to the level of the animals.

We find the next metaphorical passage of this scene when Lear irrevocably disinherits Cordelia:

> Let it be so; thy truth, then, be thy dower:
> For, by the sacred radiance of the sun,
> The mysteries of Hecate, and the night;
> By all the operation of the orbs
> From whom we do exist, and cease to be;
> Here I disclaim all my paternal care,
> (I. i. 110)

Lear's security is shaken for the first time by Cordelia's misunderstood renouncement. It is no mere chance that Lear at just this moment should turn to the non-human powers, call upon them and repudiate his fathership in their name. This reveals his relationship to the elemental powers: it is awakened when his relationship to the human world is shaken, and it is intensified, as if by a law of nature, by every further wound and repulse he receives from this quarter. On this first occasion we have not yet the form of the direct apostrophe, but the formula of the oath. When Goneril—some scenes later—expels him, Lear again turns to those powers of the underworld. We have a preparatory abrupt flash in "Darkness and devils! Saddle my horses;" (I. iv. 274), and a few lines later, the first great explosion of this feeling in the apostrophe to nature (I. iv. 297). When Goneril reappears, we hear: "Blast and fogs upon thee," and when finally his other daughter also rejects him, the elemental forces are called upon once again:

> You nimble lightnings, dart your blinding flames
> Into her scornful eyes! Infect her beauty,
> You fen-suck'd fogs, drawn by the powerful sun,
> To fall and blast her pride!
> (II. iv. 167)

The great apostrophes to the elements in the heath scene are the culmination of this sequence; we shall discuss them later. Thus light is thrown from these later passages upon the passage in the first scene.

When Kent in the first scene repeatedly takes the part of the unjustly treated Cordelia, Lear answers impatiently:

> The bow is bent and drawn, make from the shaft.
> KENT. Let it fall rather, though the fork invade
> The region of my heart:
> (I. i. 145)

This is the first independent image of the scene; the more excited Lear becomes, the more often do images appear in his language. The form of the comparison, such as we still have in the simile of the barbarous Scythian (I. i. 118), is soon replaced by more direct and forceful metaphorical language in "Come not between the dragon and his wrath" (I. i. 123). By the well-known image of the bent bow Lear seeks to warn Kent of continuing in his contradiction; twenty lines later he seizes the sword. But beyond the significance of the moment, this image simultaneously contains dramatic irony: with the transfer of the crown to his daughters Lear has surrendered his own position and power; at this moment, without being aware of it, he has delivered himself up to his coming fate. Nothing can now recall the arrow.

When Lear threatens Kent with the sword, Kent replies:

> Kill thy physician, and the fee bestow
> Upon thy foul disease.
> (I. i. 166)

This designation as physician is also premonitory, for the title comes to full realization only in Kent's rôle in the last acts. "The foul disease," too, is forewarning; it points to the ungrateful daughters and to what they are later to signify for Lear's own feelings. Here, in this first scene, Kent is the only one who has a presentiment of this; but soon, in the second act, Lear himself will say to Goneril:

> But yet thou art my flesh, my blood, my daughter;
> Or rather a *disease* that's in my flesh,
> Which I must needs call mine: thou art a boil,
> A plague-sore, an embossed carbuncle,
> In my corrupted blood.
> (II. iv. 223)

A final example may serve to show how here, at the beginning of the play, short metaphors and hints suggest what is more fully unfolded by the imagery of the later scenes. France, the future husband of Cordelia, uses the following words in speaking to Lear of Cordelia:

> Sure, her offence
> Must be of such unnatural degree,

That monsters it, or your fore-vouch'd affection
Fall'n into taint:
(I. i. 221)

France employs the metaphor "monsters" in regard to Cordelia's al-
leged attitude, wherein lies a reproach against Lear, but at the same
time dramatic irony as well. For in the course of the play the word
"monster" will have its specific application to the ingratitude and the
inhuman behavior of the two other daughters.[6]

Thus many images in this first scene are prophetic. What Herder,
speaking more generally, said of the first scene also applies to the
imagery: "Lear . . . in the very first scene of his appearance on the
stage already bears within himself all the seeds of his destinies for the
harvest of the darkest future".[7]

The figure in the play for whom the image is an even more characteristic form of expression than for Lear, is that of the Fool. The Fool
never speaks in blank verse, indeed he never comes near the more conventional, measured and dignified manner of speech such as we find,
for example, in the first part of the first scene. From the very beginning
he has his own peculiar way of expressing himself, a manner which
marks him as an outsider. In the speech of the Fool, Shakespeare has
given the images wholly new functions. But what is the significance of
the image in his case?

We have already stated that in the very first scene Lear loses the
capacity for really understanding others in conversation; he cannot
carry on a real dialogue. The words of the others no longer reach him
or, if they do, in an ill-conveyed meaning. Lear shuts himself off; he
becomes isolated in his speech, which from now on, even in the dialogue, bears the stamp of a monologue.[8] The usual manner of speech
can therefore no longer move him; such words can neither help nor
heal Lear who, in his madness, needs help more and more. The Fool
knows this from the very beginning, and he speaks to the King in
simile, proverb and image and in rhymed adages and sayings which
have the same purpose as his images. Much of what the Fool says
Lear neither hears nor grasps, for much is indeed spoken more to the
audience than to the King. But part comes home to him and this he
does comprehend. Even if Lear replies to only a few of the Fool's utter-

---

6. To take a few examples from this image-group which was first noticed by Miss
Spurgeon (*Shakespeare's Imagery*, p. 341): to the King "ingratitude" appears as "monster"
(I. iv. 281; I. v. 41); Albany says of Goneril that she "be-monsters" her countenance,
and Albany says of all humanity:

> Humanity must perforce prey on itself,
> Like monsters of the deep.   (IV. ii. 48)

"Women will all turn monsters" cries Cornwall's angry servant after Gloucester's blinding (III. vii. 102). The symbolic meanings and ramifications of this "pattern of imagery"
have been further explored and interpreted by R. B. Heilman *op. cit.*, pp. 93-98 *et
passim*.

7. "Shakespeare" (Section 5) in *Von Deutscher Art und Kunst, Einige fliegende Blätter*,
Hamburg, 1773. Reprinted in all complete editions of Herder's works.

8. Cf. J. Gurland, *Das Gestaltungsgesetz von Shakespeares König Lear*, Würzburg, 1938.

ances, that is still no proof of what Lear may really have heard and understood. For much of the Fool's talk expects no answer. He inserts his sayings and comparisons between the speeches of the others, and he sings his little songs as an outsider, as it were—in this respect his position[9] is often similar to the chorus of the classical tragedy—and formulates most of what he says not as if it were coined to fit a particular case, or were directed at a particular person. "He that hath ears to hear let him hear!" It is the image which makes this unobtrusive parenthetical way of speaking possible. The image clothes the individual and particular case in a more general form; it may take away the sting. Between Lear and the Fool a new form of the dialogue develops which is no longer based upon rational communication, upon the simple play of question and answer, but which is a finer and more subtle interplay of shifting meanings and hints.

The more Lear becomes a victim of self-delusion and madness, the more it becomes the task of the Fool to express in epigrammatic images the unreality of Lear's behaviour, his self-deception and his error. The images of the Fool are the dry and almost trivial language of reality which is continually contrasted with Lear's separation from the outside world. In the great scenes on the heath Lear reaches heights of fantasy and emotion which far transcend human proportions; he becomes a gigantic superhuman figure whose huge dimensions threaten to overstep the limits of what may be represented upon the stage and within the scope of a drama. Here the Fool has the continual function "to keep the scene in touch with reality" (Granville-Barker).[10] For no matter how tremendously the horizon spread out before us in these scenes may widen, the presentation of the play never loses itself in a sphere of the fantastically unreal. Lear himself, as Granville-Barker has shown, returns again and again to intimate, earthly things, he again and again resorts to simplicity and actuality.[11] But it is especially the little sayings and similes of the Fool pertaining to the triviality of every day which counterbalance the gigantic dimensions of Lear's feelings and ideas. The Fool understands how to reduce Lear's behaviour to the simplest, most uncomplicated images of actuality, so that the state of affairs becomes perfectly obvious. Thus, for example, by means of the trivial simile of the egg which Lear has divided to give away both halves (the two crowns) he shows how simple is the division of the kingdom and the relinquishment of the royal power (I. iv. 173). In spite of this simplicity, the Fool's images may have a complex meaning and may give us hints of things still hidden.[12] This passage, thirty lines later, harks back to the image just mentioned: "thou hast pared

9. In almost every Shakespearian tragedy there is the figure of the objective observer who interprets the action from a standpoint outside the dramatic action. In *King Lear* there is, in addition to the Fool, Kent, who serves as an objective observer, as does also in a certain manner Edgar.

10. "King Lear" (H. Granville-Barker, *Prefaces to Shakespeare, First Series,* London, 1927).

11. "Shakespeare has, besides, to carry us into strange regions of thought and passion, so he must, at the same time, hold us by familiar things," *op. cit.,* p. 158.

12. How many hidden meanings are suggested by the utterances of the Fool is shown by Edmund Blunden in his essay, "Shakespeare's Significances," in A. Bradby, *Shakespeare Criticism,* 1919–1935, London, 1937.

thy wit o' both sides and left nothing i' the middle. Here comes one o' the parings" (I. iv. 206). The voluntary dispossession of property is seen as a relinquishing of reason. The ceding of both halves of the land without leaving anything for himself was like the paring of reason on both sides without leaving anything in the middle—so blind and foolish. Thus the rapid transition to "paring" becomes comprehensible; Goneril represents the half of the kingdom given away and at the same time, through her, Lear will go mad. Thus many of the Fool's other images serve to light up the situation with a single flash and, furthermore, to draw the obvious conclusions and to clothe in the universally intelligible language of the proverb what the language of the action is unable to epitomize so convincingly (cf. I. iv. 124; I. v. 8; I. v. 30; II. iv. 7; II. iv. 68; III. vi. 13).

At first glance, the images of the Fool, gathered as they are from the unexciting sphere of everyday common sense and often expressing trivial commonplaces, seem to stand in contrast to the great issues of the Lear drama. Fateful predestinations, even aberrations of such tragic weight and such great pathos—thus we could argue—may not be viewed from a merely utilitarian or common-sense standpoint. But it is precisely these simple, uncomplicated conclusions which form the path by which Lear and we, the audience, are led to a deeper and more moving recognition of the ultimate truth.

The effect of image, rhymed proverb and maxim is different from the effect of the direct admonition. Images as well as proverbs can convey a meaning in a manner more impersonal and universally valid. Images, as they are employed by the Fool, free the action from the narrow restrictions of the moment—they assist in producing a detached attitude of mind. The little songs which the Fool sings, further enhance this quieting effect which liberates us and creates this detachment; "the greater the force of the truth, the lighter, the calmer and the more detached appears the form".[13] The songs of the Fool as well as his images indicate a relaxation and a diminution of the suspense in the structure of the scenes—this being, indeed, to a large degree the function of the Fool. If we recall to mind the early Elizabethan tragedies, the *Spanish Tragedy* or *Titus Andronicus,* we see that such relaxation and counterbalancing are there entirely wanting: everything moves in extremes, every gesture, every word, every action is aimed at achieving the highest possible degree of glaring and bloody effect. In the later Elizabethan drama the Fool with his songs belongs, of course, to the conventions. But nowhere else are he and his forms of utterance employed in so profound a manner, at one and the same time creating detachment and pointing beyond the immediate issue, as here in *King Lear.*

The dramatic quality of the imagery also becomes apparent in the way the dynamic presence of nature in the heath scenes is prepared for very early through allusions and hints; on the other hand, the raging storm continues to sound in the words of the characters long afterwards in later scenes. As early as Edgar's monologue in II. iii. we have

13. Gurland, *Das Gestaltungsgesetz von Shakespeares König Lear,* Würzburg, 1938, p. 60.

an introduction to the great heath scene. Edgar's language—from the moment he begins to play the madman—is full of references to the world of nature, and in this respect differs greatly from the unimaginative utterances characteristic of Edmund. His monologue displays many a little touch which summons to the mind the picture of the heath-landscape: happy hollow of a tree; pins, wooden pricks, nails, sprigs of rosemary; poor pelting villages, sheep-cotes and mills—to select just a few lines out of the scene. In the following act also his deliberately confused talk greatly assists the creation of a powerful nature-atmosphere. To quote two examples:

> through ford and whirlipool, o'er bog and quagmire
> (III. iv. 53)

or:

> who drinks the green mantle of the standing pool

When he says that he is ready "to outface / The winds and persecutions of the sky" (I. iii. 14), his words are parallel to, and anticipate Lear's assertion in the next scene:

> No, rather I abjure all roofs, and choose
> To wage against the enmity o' the air;
> To be a comrade with the wolf and owl,
> (II. iv. 211)

In Lear's language, too, the forces of nature make their appearance before they become grim reality in the third act: "You nimble lightnings" (II. iv. 167). Especially the following line is already suggestive of the atmosphere of the heath:

> You fen-suck'd fogs, drawn by the powerful sun.

The Fool sings:

> That sir which serves and seeks for gain,
>   And follows but for form,
> Will pack when it begins to rain,
>   And leave thee in the storm.
>   (II. iv. 79)

At the end of the scene the coming of the storm is announced more definitely: "'twill be a storm" (II. iv. 290); "the night comes on, and the black winds do sorely ruffle:" (II. iv. 304). In the next scene Lear is not yet shown us in person, but we are first apprised by the Gentleman of how the King fares:

> KENT. Where's the king?
> GENTLEMAN. Contending with the fretful element;
>   Bids the wind blow the earth into the sea,

Or swell the curled waters 'bove the main,
That things might change or cease;

               tears his white hair,
Which the impetuous blasts, with eyeless rage,
Catch in their fury, and make nothing of;
Strives in his little world of man to out-scorn
The to-and-fro conflicting wind and rain.
              (III. i. 3)

The dramatic value of this brief description is apparent. Lear's appearance in the following scene is so overwhelming, and so far surpasses, in every respect, what we are accustomed to seeing and hearing upon the stage, that we must be prepared for this moment. The great heath-scene (III. ii.) demands the utmost of our own creative powers of imagination; unprepared, we would be unable to comprehend it. Lear's apostrophes to the elements transform the detached description of the Gentleman into living dramatic dialogue:

Blow, winds, and crack your cheeks! rage! blow!
You cataracts and hurricanoes, spout
Till you have drench'd our steeples, drown'd the cocks!
You sulphurous and thought-executing fires,
Vaunt-couriers to oak-cleaving thunderbolts,
Singe my white head! And thou, all-shaking thunder,
Smite flat the thick rotundity o' the world!
Crack nature's moulds, all germens spill at once,
That make ingrateful man!
              (III. ii. 1)

In this series of images, Lear's relation to the elements finds its most direct expression. Lear can scarcely be said to be still speaking to the Fool or to Kent; his real partners in converse are the forces of nature. In this act, through Lear's words, they become acting characters. It is interesting to note that single motifs of this apostrophe to the elements appeared previously, but that they now achieve a more universal significance; in the first act Lear had asked nature[14] to make Goneril forever barren. Now all mankind shall become unfruitful, everything shall be destroyed. To Lear's prophetic fantasy, the breaking of the natural bond between himself and his daughters, appears as a rent running through the whole of the universe.[15] Just as human nature overstepped its limits, so do the elements now transcend their boundaries—this is a fundamental idea, which appears in the imagery again

14. For the different meanings of "nature" in *King Lear* and in sixteenth-century literature see John F. Danby, *Shakespeare's Doctrine of Nature, A Study of King Lear*, London, 1949. For further comment on the significance of "nature" in *King Lear* cf. Heilman *op. cit.*, p. 115, and George Gordon, *Shakespearean Comedy and other Studies*, London, 1944, p. 124.
15. The symbolic implications of the imagery relating to this theme have been explored by R. B. Heilman in his chapter on "The Breach of Nature," *op. cit.*, p. 89.

and again. Thus the Gentleman had already said: at Lear's command, the waters should overflow the earth and the earth should sweep into the sea. At the end of the act we again find an image of this kind, this time used by Gloucester:

> The sea, with such a storm as his bare head
> In hell-black night endured, would have buoy'd up,
> And quench'd the stelled fires.
> (III. vii. 59)

The storm is reflected by the individual characters of this scene in various ways. For Lear it has the greatest symbolical significance and reality; hence he speaks of "the tempest in my mind." What passes outside, goes on within himself. Kent stands aside, he is the observer, who, with experience and quiet contemplation, takes note of all that occurs:

> Since I was man,
> Such sheets of fire, such bursts of horrid thunder,
> Such groans of roaring wind and rain, I never
> Remember to have heard:
> (III. ii. 46)

> The tyranny of the open night's too rough
> For nature to endure.
> (III. iv. 2)

The Fool strikes the note of the storm in his little song:

> With hey, ho, the wind and the rain,
> (III. ii. 75)

and, finally, Edgar mirrors the weather in the twice repeated "Through the sharp hawthorn blows the cold wind" (III. iv. 47). And even after this tempest scene is long past, it still lives on in the memory. Thus Lear's recollection: "When the rain came to wet me once, and the wind to make me chatter; when the thunder would not peace at my bidding"; (IV. vi. 102), or Cordelia's words in the next scene:

> Was this a face
> To be opposed against the warring winds?
> To stand against the deep dread-bolted thunder?
> In the most terrible and nimble stroke
> Of quick, cross lightning?
> (IV. vii. 32)

The elements of nature not only help to create the atmosphere, but they also have symbolical significance and a definite "function." This also holds true of the animal-imagery. The wealth of animal-images in

King Lear has often been emphasized.[16] Thus Bradley sums up the effect of these animal-images: "As we read, the souls of all the beasts in turn seem to have entered the bodies of these mortals; horrible in their venom, savagery, lust, deceitfulness, sloth, cruelty, filthiness; miserable in their feebleness, nakedness, defencelessness, blindness; and man, 'consider him well,' is even what they are". Miss Spurgeon, in her subtle analysis of the "dominating image" in *King Lear*,[17] shows how these animal-images, too, "because portrayed chiefly in angry or anguished action, very distinctly augment the sensation of horror and bodily pain". G. Wilson Knight, in his chapter on "The Lear Universe",[18] explains at length how the animal-imagery helps to illustrate the "revulsion from humanity" and other basic themes of the tragedy. It is interesting to note how these animal-images make their appearance in considerable number from a definite moment in the play on. That is in the heath-scenes of the third act. Nature, the landscape, the world of animals come to life after the world of man has failed; since his fellow-men have cast him out, the aged king turns to nature. But this involves an increasing influence of the low and animal element in contrast to the dimming of the human mind and consciousness, as we are to see it represented to us in Lear's insanity and Edgar's madness. We must discriminate, however, between the low and repulsive animal-images, such as are uttered by Edgar and the Fool, and the higher animals, which populate the forest. Lear's prophecy, "to be a comrade with the wolf and the owl" (II. iv. 213) is the cue for their coming to life.

The beasts of prey, to which the thankless daughters are frequently compared,[19] often appear without any definite reference to characters of the play, but nevertheless have the significance outlined above. Edgar's seemingly irrelevant list has surely this meaning: "hog in sloth, fox in stealth, wolf in greediness, dog in madness, lion in prey" (III. iv. 96). Likewise this statement of the Fool: "He's mad that trusts in the tameness of a wolf" (III. vi. 20). Another thought which is expressed by the animal-imagery, is: in such fearful weather even the animals of the forest would fare better than Lear (III. i. 12), some shelter would have been offered even to the howling wolves or the enemy's dog (III. vii. 63; IV. vii. 36). It is significant that Lear, too, when he seeks a comparison with his own state, draws upon animal-imagery:

> Thou'ldst shun a bear;
> But if thy flight lay toward the raging sea,
> Thou'ldst meet the bear i' the mouth.
>   (III. iv. 9)

One act later Lear is called:

16. First by J. Kirkman in *New Shakespeare Society Transactions*, 1877; Bradley, *Shakespearean Tragedy*, p. 266 sqq.; Spurgeon, *Shakespeare's Imagery*, p. 342; G. Wilson Knight, *The Wheel of Fire*, p. 194 sqq. For further comment on the animal-imagery in *King Lear* see Heilman, *op. cit.*, p. 93 ("The Animal in Man"). Audrey Yoder's book, *Animal Analogy in Shakespeare's Character Portrayal* (New York, 1947), became accessible to the author only after completion of this book.
17. *Shakespeare's Imagery*, p. 342.
18. *The Wheel of Fire*, p. 194ff.
19. Cf. Bradley, *op. cit.*, p. 207.

>   a gracious aged man,
> Whose reverence the head-lugg'd bear would lick,
>   (IV. ii. 41)

Edgar's language fairly teems with repulsive, low animals: "Poor Tom, that eats the swimming frog, the toad, the tadpole, the wall-newt and the water; . . . swallows the old rat and the ditch-dog" (III. iv. 137). Mice, rats, salamander and mongrel (III. vi. 71) complete the list. Not only in his outward appearance but also in his language Edgar is meant to impress us as an image of bestiality. The fact that Lear meets with him on the heath has symbolical meaning. Himself cast out and left defenceless to the untrammelled winds, he meets in Edgar the worst extremity of the outcast. His own condition, and above and beyond that, the insignificance of man in general, his similarity to the animal, become apparent to Lear:[20] "unaccommodated man is no more but such a poor, bare, forked animal as thou art" (III. iv. 111).

This comparison of man with the lowly animal finds its most significant expression in Gloucester's words, culminating in the well-known comparison:

> I' the last night's storm I such a fellow saw;
> Which made me think a man a worm: . . .
>
> .   .   .   .
>
> As flies to wanton boys, are we to the gods,
> They kill us for their sport.
>   (IV. i. 36)

Many animal-comparisons of the Fool, too, are meant to stress the fact that men may fare no better than the animals; when he sees Kent in the stocks, he remarks: "Horses are tied by the heads, dogs and bears by the neck, monkeys by the loins, and men by the legs" (II. iv. 7). Otherwise, however, most of the animal comparisons employed by the Fool are aimed to show how dumb animals, in spite of their want of reason, still fare better and act more sensibly than unintelligent human beings. Even animals would not be so foolish and devoid of instinct as Lear, when he gave his kingdom away (cf. I. iv. 124, 177, 235, 244; I. v. 26).

Lear's inner development is portrayed in images more than that of any other character in Shakespeare.[21] The great apostrophes to the

---

20. This recurrent theme in the imagery has been further traced and interpreted by R. B. Heilman, *op. cit.*, p. 67 sqq.

21. We must distinguish here between the rôle of the imagery to denote certain characteristic traits in a person and its function to give expression to a change in his mind. Whereas the latter function, as shown above, is very marked and noteworthy, the former, i.e. the characterization of a person through consistent features of the imagery, is less important in *King Lear*, than, for instance, in *Othello* or *Hamlet*. As was shown in the last passage, certain fundamental themes of the play are taken up in the imagery of several characters who all in turn contribute to the progressive disclosure of the play's meaning through imagery and action.

For certain features in Lear's personality (his manifold interests, his classical education, his love of English scenes, and his knowledge of hunting, tournament and warfare) as revealed through his imagery see Edmund Blunden, "Shakespeare's Significances" in *Shakespeare Criticism*, 1919–1935, ed. A. Bradby, London, 1937.

elemental forces of nature in the scenes on the heath have already revealed a significant change in Lear. The images of the next scenes, in which the King goes mad, are again illuminating for Lear's state of mind. The swiftly passing images, logically unconnected with each other, which we hear Lear utter, correspond to the abnormal mental state of the King; they are the adequate form of perception and expression of a lunatic. "It is his mind which is laid bare," Charles Lamb said as an interpretation of these strange speeches—especially in the fourth act. Lear's insanity should not be dismissed as simple craziness. It is rather another manner of perception, by means of which, however, Lear now sees and recognizes what formerly remained concealed to him, as long as he was sane. These images are the fragments of his inner visions, which have not yet attained to the form of thoughts; they have not yet been transformed, ordered and connected in logical sequence and in the service of clear statement.[22] Many images in the fourth act become more comprehensible if light is thrown upon them from previous passages. In the great scene on the heath we hear Lear cry out:

> Let the great gods,
> That keep this dreadful pother o'er our heads,
> Find out their enemies now. Tremble, thou wretch,
> That hast within thee undivulged crimes,
> Unwhipp'd of justice: hide thee, thou bloody hand;
> Thou perjured, and thou simular man of virtue
> That art incestuous:
>   (III. ii. 50)

The sins of earth pass before Lear's inner eye as visionary images— the thanklessness of his daughters brings him to the thanklessness and unrighteousness of the whole world. At first judge of his daughters (cf. the judgement scene played in madness with the Fool and Kent, III. vi.), Lear becomes in the fourth act the judge of all creatures. From the passage quoted above there runs a connecting link to IV. vi. 165:

> Thou rascal beadle, hold thy bloody hand!
> Why dost thou lash that whore? Strip thine own back;

Lear, having experienced in his personal world the destruction of human right and order, thus gains insight into the common injustice and frailty of all mankind. His fancy now sees examples of this everywhere in the world. License appears to him in the form of animal-images (IV. vi. 114) and in the vision of the "simpering dame" (IV. vi. 120); injustice and mendacity in the image of the railing judge (IV. vi. 154), of

22. Regarding these passages A. Somerville says in his book *Madness in Shakespearean Tragedy*, London, 1929: "What really happens, however, is that the thoughts from his subconscious mind run too rapidly for expression in words, and sentences that should appear as associating links necessary to make the whole speech coherent, are left out." In general, however, it is a rather dubious procedure to seek to judge Shakespeare's characters from the point of view of modern psychology.

the beggar running from the farmer's dog (IV. vi. 158), of the hypo-critical beadle, and of the magnificent robes which cover vice (IV. vi. 168). In madness Lear has won eyes for reality. His inner eye pierces the outer appearance and penetrates to the true nature of things.

Lear's recovery in the fifth act, too, is clearly reflected in the imagery. Peaceful and delicate things have taken the place of the unclean and repulsive images, and his language is connected, musical and gentle:

> We two alone will sing like birds i' the cage:
> When thou dost ask me blessing, I'll kneel down,
> And ask of thee forgiveness: so we'll live,
> And pray, and sing, and tell old tales, and laugh
> At gilded butterflies,
> (v. iii. 9)

This mood, however, is again interrupted by the terrible and painful experience of Cordelia's death. The fourfold "Howl" when Lear "re-enters with Cordelia dead in his arms" recalls the animal-imagery, and in the next lines spoken by Lear the gigantic and powerful nature of Lear is once again given expression through imagery:

> Had I your tongue and eyes, I'ld use them so
> That heaven's vault should crack.
> (v. iii. 258)

Lear translates all feelings into bodily terms. His imagery thus conveys to us the impression of immense physical force[23] or, if mental suffering is to be expressed, of immense physical pain. The imagery thus helps to intensify and sharpen the poignancy of the spiritual experience through which Lear has to pass.[24] The above image is the last link in a chain which runs through the whole drama.[25]

23. After having been told that Regan and her husband refuse to appear, Lear threatens:

> bid them come forth and hear me,
> Or at their chamber-door I'll beat the drum
> Till it cry sleep to death. (II. iv. 118)

24. This also applies to the perhaps most famous image used by Lear:

> . . . but I am bound
> Upon a wheel of fire, that mine own tears
> Do scald like molten lead. (IV. vii. 46)

25. The frequency of metaphors and images expressing bodily pain and tension was first noted by Miss Spurgeon (*op. cit.*, p. 338). She goes so far as to consider these images of "bodily and generally anguished motion" as the "one overpowering and dom-inating continuous image" in *King Lear*.

Diction

I. A. Richards

THE INTERACTIONS OF WORDS

There should be an ancient saying, "If you talk too much about words, your tongue will become a stone." More than once in this lecture you will see why. I have been minded again and again to change my title or dodge the topic. "Whereof we cannot speak, thereof we must be silent," remarked Ludwig Wittgenstein some twenty years ago, but men have gone on investigating languages in which to talk about that silence.

What are these words we talk with and talk so much about? Taking poetry to be an affair of the interactions of words, how far will we get in a discussion of poetry if we are in real doubt about what words are and do?

This essay threatens thus to become an attempt to define "a word." I am extremely loath to inflict that upon you. The definition of "a word" has been a task from which the best authorities have rightly shrunk, an obligation which has made even psychologists into mystics and left the adepts in linguistics at a loss. But when the subject has been tactlessly raised, how are we to avoid it? How are we to conceive the interactions of words without forming as clear a conception as we can of the words themselves?

"As clear a conception as we can!" But what are these *conceptions* and how can they be *clear?* The implications of this word "conception," if we take it literally and thereby awaken it to full metaphoric liveliness, are a philosophy of poetic language—as Plato pointed out, in the *Phaedrus* (277). It is true he calls them "scientific words" there, but he was concerned with "the dialectic art" which I arbitrarily take here to have been the practice of a supreme sort of poetry—the sort which was to replace the poetry he banished from the Republic. Here is the passage. "Noble it may be to tell stories about justice and virtue; but far nobler is a man's work, when finding a congenial soul he avails himself of the dialectic art to sow and plant therein scientific words, which

Reprinted from *The Language of Poetry* by Allen Tate, ed., by permission of Princeton University Press. Copyright, 1942, by Princeton University Press. Printed in the United States of America by Princeton University Press, at Princeton, New Jersey.

are competent to defend themselves, and him who planted them, and are not unfruitful, but bear seed in their turn, from which other words springing up in other minds are capable of preserving this precious seed ever undecaying, and making their possessor ever happy, so far as happiness is possible to man." Plato is fond of this sort of language. If you look for it you will find it everywhere in the *Republic,* used with a frankness which embarrassed his Victorian translators.

What are these conceptions through which words, by uniting, bring new beings into the world, or new worlds into being? A truly philosophic definition of "a word" would be, I suppose, an all-purpose definition. I am hoping for no such thing—only for a definition useful for our purpose: the study of the language of poetry. But limits to that are not easily set. However, I can escape some of the most dreadful parts of the undertaking by assuming frankly that our purposes are not those of psychology or of linguistics. Their troubles come in part from the uses for which they require their definitions of "a word." Poetics has a different set of purposes and needs a different sort of definition. If so, I can work at it without the tedious attempt to relate it to the other definitions that other studies need. Philosophically speaking, this leaves Poetics "up in the air"; but that is perhaps where, in the present state of philosophy, it will be safest.

But very likely someone will already be saying, "Wait a moment. Are these troubles real or only philosophic? Do we really need any definition poetic or otherwise? Are not most of us in fact clear enough about what poetry and words in general are and do? This marvelous, this miraculous thing we call our language works somehow for us and within us; the better, it may well be, for our not knowing too much about it. Our digestions, to take a humble parallel, do not depend, fortunately, on our knowledge of physiology. Don't our poetic difficulties also arise with particular instances only? Isn't this pretense that we never understand what we are saying or how we say it rather like witchcraft—an epidemic invented to give employment to specialists in its treatment?"

"I would meet you upon this honestly." Such questionings can be barren. To ask "What is a word and how does it work?" may do us no good. On the other hand, there is a sense in which this question is the very foundation, the source, the origin, the ἀϱχή (to use Plato's word), the starting point and final cause of the intellectual life. But I do not know how, in *words,* to distinguish the idle from the vital question here.

In the philosophy of poetry this vital question is not a question of fact but one of choice or decision. In that, it is like the fundamental definitions of mathematics. Facts, by themselves, do not, in any simple direct way, settle what we should define "a word" to be. Facts, which we are aware of and can compare only through words, come later. None the less our definition must let the facts be facts. We do well to be humble here; this "What is a word?" is one of the founding questions—along with "What am I?" "What is a fact?" and "What is God?"—on which all other questions balance and turn. The art of entertaining such questions, and of distinguishing them from other questions which we might ask with the same sounds, is the dialectic study of poetry. And the founding questions—those that establish and maintain our state as men—are themselves poetic. But that might mean so many false things that I tremble as I say it.

Still, the other ways of saying it, and ways of guarding it, suffer equal danger. If I add, for example, that this poetic basis of ours is no matter of *mere make-believe,* well, we have the varying possible ways of understanding that richly mysterious phrase, "make-believe," before us. "Mere make-believe." Here is a notable example of the interaction of words. Just where do its disparaging or mocking implications come from? Are beliefs *not* to be made (i.e., forced)? Is *that* the point? Or is it the poor quality of the belief so made? Are beliefs which *we* make not genuine? Must the world, something not ourselves, make them for us? And if so, *which* world will we trust to do that? The world of tradition, of theology, or current public opinion, of science, or one of the worlds of poetry? Which will give us the beliefs we need? Is that the question, or is it the inferior quality of such beliefs which is being mocked, the immature craftsmanship, the inexperience which knows too little about either the materials or the purpose of the belief?

All this and more is to be considered in asking seriously if the poetic basis of our world is make-believe. This phrase, *make-believe,* like a good watch dog, warns us off sternly—if we have no proper business with these premises. But if we were their master, it would be silent. There is another possibility of course. In the Chinese story the stone-deaf visitor remarked, "Why do you keep your dog up so late? He did nothing but yawn at me as I came through the gate."

However, if we know what we are doing, and what the phrase "make-believe" is doing—and it has several senses which should alarm us for one which is safe because true—we may say that our world rests on make-belief or—to use a more venerable word—on faith. But it is *our* world, mind you, which so rests, our world in which we live as men, so different from the bullet's world, in which *it* travels. And yet our world includes the bullet.

I have been trying with all this to revive for you the sense of the word "maker," in which a poet may be seriously said to be a maker. This is the sense in which poetry matters because it is creative—not the sense in which we say it is "creative" because we feel it matters. The poet is a maker of beliefs—but do not give here to "belief" the first meaning that comes to mind, for it is as true that for other senses of "belief" poetry has nothing to do with them. What does the poet *make* and what does his work *create?* Himself and his world first, and thereby other worlds and other men. He makes through shaping and molding, through giving form. But if we ask what he shapes or molds or gives form to, we must answer with Aristotle that we can say nothing about that which has no form. There are always prior forms upon which the poet works, and how he takes these forms is part of his making. He apprehends them by taking them into forms of more comprehensive order. To the poet as poet, his world is the world, and the world is his world. But the poet is not always poet. All but the greatest poets in the most favorable societies seem to have to pay for being poets. Of recent poets, Yeats has put this best:

The intellect of man is forced to choose
Perfection of the life or of the work,
And if it take the second must refuse
A heavenly mansion, raging in the dark.
When all that story's finished, what's the news?
In luck or out, the toil has left its mark:
That old perplexity, an empty purse
Or the day's vanity, the night's remorse.

The work of the poet is the maintenance and enlargement of the human spirit through remaking it under changing circumstances; through molding and remolding the ever-varying flux. The molds are sets of words, interacting in manifold ways within a language. At first sight this old Platonic image of the mold looks crude. What could be less like a mold than a word—which endlessly changes its work with its company as we all may note if we care to look? But the mold metaphor —the dominant metaphor of the Greek invention of education—is there to shock us into thought. The poetic problem is precisely the maintenance of stability *within* minds and correspondence *between* them. It is *not* how to get the flux into molds supposed somehow to be fixed already; but how to recreate perpetually those constancies (as of sets of molds) upon which depend any order, any growth, any development— any changes, in fact, other than the chance-ridden changes of chaos.

It is through the interactions of words within a language that a poet works. In a sense all literary men are inquiring concretely into the detail of this in all their work, but let us try to take a more general and comprehensive view before going on to contrast two types of verbal interactions. If I can show you how I conceive words, the rest will be easier. First I spoke of the *question*, "What is a word?", not of any answer to it, as one of the founding forces, and as thereby poetic. Answers to it of many sorts can be contrived and offered. Linguistics and psychology in their different divisions have many very different answers and the debate between them, as studies aspiring to become sciences (in various senses of "science"), must be a long one. But these answers would answer different questions from my poetic "What is a word?" That question is nourished by awareness of them, but it is not reducible to them. It is not answered by an exhaustive dictionary or encyclopedia article on the word *Word*. That would answer only the set of historical, factual, linguistic, psychological, religious, metaphysical and other questions which I am trying—by these very odd means—to distinguish from the poetic question. With any of these questions, it would be shocking —would it not?—to suggest that its answer is one and the same with itself. But the poetic question has to be its own master—as virtue is its own reward, to cite the wider rule of which this is an example. As an answer it is aware that it is a bundle of possibilities dependent on other possibilities which in turn it in part determines; as a question it is attempting through its influence on them to become more completely itself. It is growing as a cell grows with other cells. It is a conception. It is being "divided at the joints" and recombined. "Attempting" and "growing" are not metaphors here. A word, a question or its answer, does all that we do, since we do all that in the word. Words are alive as our other acts are alive—though apart from the minds which use them they are nothing but agitations of the air or stains on paper.

A word then by this sort of definition is a permanent set of possibilities of understanding, much as John Stuart Mill's table was a permanent possibility of sensation. And as the sensations the table yields depend on the angle you look from, the other things you see it with, the air, your glasses, your eyes and the light . . . so how a word is understood depends on the other words you hear it with, and the other frames you have heard it in, on the whole setting present and past in which it has developed as a part of your mind. But the interactions of words with one another and with other things are far more complex than can be paralleled from the case of the table—complex enough as those are. Indeed they are not paralleled anywhere except by such things as pictures, music or the expressions of faces which are other modes of language. Language, as understood, is the mind itself at work and these interactions of words are interdependencies of our own being.

I conceive then a word, as poetry is concerned with it, and as separated from the mere physical or sensory occasion, to be a component of an act of the mind so subtly dependent on the other components of this act and of other acts that it can be distinguished from these interactions only as a convenience of discourse. It sounds nonsense to say that a word is its interactions with other words; but that is a short way of saying the thing which Poetics is in most danger always of overlooking. Words only work together. We understand no word except in and through its interactions with other words.

Let me now come down to detail. I invite you to compare two very different types of the interactions of words in poetry: I will read the first twelve lines of Donne's *First Anniversary*.

An Anatomy of the World
The First Anniversary

Wherein
By occasion of the untimely death of Mistress
Elizabeth Drury, the frailty and the decay of this whole world
is represented.

When that rich Soule which to her heaven is gone,
Whom all do celebrate, who know they have one,
(For who is sure he hath a Soule, unlesse
It see, and judge, and follow worthinesse,
And by Deedes praise it? hee who doth not this,
May lodge an In-mate soule, but 'tis not his.)
When that Queene ended her progresse time,
And, as t'her standing house to heaven did climbe,
Where loath to make the Saints attend her long,
She's now a part both of the Quire, and Song,
This world, in that great earthquake languished;
For in a common bath of teares it bled.

Let us compare with that the first stanza of Dryden's

ODE: *To the Pious Memory of the accomplished young lady, Mrs. Anne Killigrew, excellent in the two sister arts of Poesy and Painting*

Thou youngest virgin-daughter of the skies,
Made in the last promotion of the blest;
Whose palms, new pluck'd from Paradise,
In spreading branches more sublimely rise,
Rich with immortal green above the rest:
Whether, adopted to some neighboring star,
Thou roll'st above us, in thy wandering race,
Or, in procession fixt and regular,
Mov'd with the heaven's majestic pace;
Or, call'd to more superior bliss,
Thou tread'st with seraphims the vast abyss:
Whatever happy region is thy place,
Cease thy celestial song a little space;
Thou wilt have time enough for hymns divine,
Since Heaven's eternal year is thine.
Hear, then, a mortal Muse thy praise rehearse,
      In no ignoble verse;
But such as thy own voice did practice here,
When thy first-fruits of Poesy were given,
To make thyself a welcome inmate there;
While yet a young probationer,
      And candidate of Heaven.

In the Donne, I suggest, there is a prodigious activity between the words as we read them. Following, exploring, realizing, *becoming* that activity is, I suggest, the essential thing in reading the poem. Understanding it is not a preparation for reading the poem. It is itself the poem. And it is a constructive, hazardous, free creative process, a process of conception through which a new being is growing in the mind. The Dryden, I suggest, is quite otherwise. No doubt there are interactions between the words but they are on a different level. The words are in routine conventional relations like peaceful diplomatic communications between nations. They do not induce revolutions in one another and are not thereby attempting to form a new order. Any mutual adjustments they have to make are preparatory, and they are no important part of the poetic activity. In brief Dryden's poem comes before our minds as a mature creation. But we seem to create Donne's poem.

Donne's poem is called *The First Anniversary* because he wrote it a year after the death of Elizabeth Drury. He was going to write a similar poem every year but only wrote one other. His latest editor, Mr. John Hayward (in the Nonesuch Edition) says this "concluded the series of preposterous eulogies." Whether Mr. Hayward thinks them preposterous, whether they are eulogies, and whether, if we took them as such, they would be preposterous—are questions I leave till later.

Opinion about them has always been mixed. Ben Jonson is reported to have said that "they were prophane and full of blasphemies; that he told Mr. Donne if it had been written of the Virgin Marie it had been something; to which he answered that he described the Idea of a Woman, and not as she was." That is a helpful hint. It points to the Platonism in the poem. But Mr. Hayward comments: "However this may be, the subject of the two poems was a real woman, a child rather, who died in 1610 at the age of fifteen." Two things are worth a word here. Doubtless, in one sense, Elizabeth Drury is the subject; but in a more important sense, the subject of the poem, what it is about, is something which only a good reading will discover. That discovery here is the poetic process. Secondly, when Mr. Hayward says "a child rather," he is being twentieth century, not seventeenth century. A fifteen year old girl was a woman for the seventeenth century. In Donne's poem *Upon the Annunciation and the Passion* he writes of the Virgin Mary:

> Sad and rejoyc'd shee's seen at once, and seen
> At almost fiftie and at scarce fifteene.

For Donne the Annunciation came to Mary when she was "scarce fifteene." Elizabeth's youth is of course no bar—rather the reverse—to Donne's taking her very seriously as a symbol.

Dryden's *Ode* has long been an anthology piece. Dr. Johnson called it "the noblest Ode that our Language produced" and "the richest complex of sounds in our language." A modern critic has called this "a judgment then bold but now scarcely intelligible." There are seventy-five years between the poems.

Now let us consider the lines in detail and especially this question, "How closely should we be examining them in our reading?" I will take Dryden first. You may guess perhaps that even in taking him first here I am expressing a judgment between them.

How near should we come to the *Ode?* The only way to find out is by experimenting. Public declamation—the style of reading which the *Ode* suggests as right—does not invite close attention to the meaning. The façade of a public building is not to be studied with a handglass. Gulliver, you remember, thought nothing of the complexions of the Brobdingnagian ladies. Let us try looking a little closer.

> *Thou youngest virgin-daughter of the skies*

Why "youngest virgin-daughter"? "Youngest" may here mean "new-born"; but then, why *virgin?* New-borns are necessarily virgins. And why, then, "daughter of the skies"? Do we need especially to be reminded that daughters of the skies—in Christian mythology—as denizens of Paradise, are virgins? On earth she was a virgin, it is true. In Heaven, there is neither marriage nor giving in marriage. And there is no special relation to the Virgin. We gain nothing by such ponderings here. Again:

> *Whose palms, new pluck'd from Paradise,*
> *In spreading branches more sublimely rise,*
> *Rich with immortal green above the rest:*

Why *from* Paradise? Has she left it? Why not *in* Paradise? The answer might be in terms of resonance of the line.

But why should these palms of hers *more sublimely* rise? or be "rich with immortal green *above the rest*"? Do Paradisaic palms wilt and fade like florist's goods here on earth? Or does the row of palms get greener and greener, richer and richer, loftier and loftier, as we get further along the line from the first saints?

Clearly these questions and all others of the sort are quite irrelevant and out of place. We are looking too close, looking for a kind of poetic structure, an interaction of the words which is not there and is not needed for the proper purpose of the poem.

The same thing would appear if we questioned similarly Dryden's suggestions about what she is doing and where she is: on a planet, "in thy wandering race" or on a fixed star "in procession fixt and regular." Or if we wondered whether "the vast abyss" so described seems a *happy* region. Or again if we ask whether she need really stop singing to listen to Dryden. Or again whether Dryden really, for a moment, considers her earthly verses to have been such as his own voice is practicing here? Of course, he doesn't. Or again, if we ask whether her *verses* could possibly make her welcome *in Paradise?* Or if they would advance her as a "candidate for heaven"? Or lastly if we asked why she is called an "inmate"? We shall see later that the same word in the Donne is packed with implications.

The outcome of all such close questioning is the same. Dryden's words have no such implications and we shall be misreading him if we hunt for them. In brief, this is not a poetry of Wit—in the technical sense of the word in which Donne's verses are, as Coleridge called them,

Wit's fire and fireblast, meaning's press and screw.

On this question of wit, let us listen to Dr. Johnson a moment. He is talking about conversation and has been comparing styles of conversation with beverages. He says,

"Spirit alone is too powerful to use. It will produce madness rather than merriment; and instead of quenching thirst, will inflame the blood. Thus wit, too copiously poured out, agitates the hearer with emotions rather violent than pleasing; everyone shrinks from the force of its oppression, the company sits entranced and overpowered; all are astonished, but nobody is pleased." One might retort, "Please, why should we please?" Or, when he says, "It will produce madness rather than merriment," we might recall the link between poetry and madness that has been noted from Plato's time to Shakespeare's. Dr. Johnson had deep personal reasons for distrusting this connection. He would have replied that he was talking about conversation, social intercourse. "Instead of quenching thirst," he says, "wit will inflame the blood." Quenching thirst? "Do you converse, Sir, in order to have had enough of it?" But Dr. Johnson's prose here no more requires us to pursue such implications and interactions than Dryden's verses.

Turn now to the Donne. Let us see what minute reading brings out of that.

> *When that rich Soule which to her heaven is gone,*

rich: in two senses—possessing much (a rich man); giving much (a rich mine). Compare Coleridge:

> Oh lady, we receive but what we give
> And in our life alone does Nature live.

or Croce: "Intuition is Expression": we *have* only that which we can give out.
her heaven: again the double force; she possesses it and it possesses her, as with "her country," or "her place."

> *Whom all do celebrate, who know they have one;*

celebrate: a new word then in the sense of "praise, extol, or publish the fame of." This would be its first occurrence in that sense. Prior to 1611 it means "commemorate or perform publicly and in due form (with a ritual—as in a celebration of the Eucharist) or solemnize." There is a very serious suggestion of participation or partaking or ritual imitation. Thus, all who know they have a soul partake of that rich Soule, in knowing that (i.e., in having a soul). Then follows Donne's gloss:

> *For who is sure he hath a Soule, unlesse*
> *It see, and judge, and follow worthiness;*

sure is more than "confident, without doubts about it"; it means "safe, firm, immovable," because seeing, judging and following worthiness are themselves the very possession of a soul, not merely signs of having one. To see and judge and follow worthiness is to have a soul.
worthiness: excellence in the highest of all senses. That use was going out in Donne's time (1617).

> *And by Deedes praise it*

No verbal praise, but imitation of or participation in actual works;

> *hee who doth not this,*
> *May lodge an In-mate soule, but 'tis not his.*

in-mate: a word of very ill suggestions. We keep some of them in "an inmate of a penitentiary or an asylum." For Donne it suggests a lodger or a foreigner. Compare Milton:

> So spake the Enemie of Mankind, enclos'd
> In Serpent, Inmate bad, [*P.L.* ix, 495]

Who does not see and follow worthiness hasn't a soul but is possessed by something not truly him.
   And so often with Donne, what seems a most farfetched conceit is

no more than the result of taking a commonplace of language seriously. We say daily that a man is "not himself" or "beside himself" or "not his true self," and we do the same thing when we say he is "alienated" or call a psychopathologist an "alienist." Donne is just expanding such expressions, making their implications explicit, increasing their interaction, as heat increases chemical interaction. That is the technique of most "metaphysical poetry."

> *When that Queene ended here her progresse time,*
> *And, as t'her standing house to heaven did climbe,*

Here Donne's metaphor takes seriously the doctrine of the Divinity of Kings. The Ruler is to the body politic as the soul is to the body. Sickness or departure of the Ruler is sickness or death to the state. In fact he is just reversing the metaphor which created the doctrine of Divine Right. He adds a pun. A Queen made royal progresses through her dominions so that her subjects might come together and realize themselves as a State in her. But the soul, as in Bunyan, also makes a pilgrim's progress. Her "standing house" is where she *rests* at the end of her progress. Compare Augustine: "Thou has made us for Thyself and our souls are restless until they find their rest in Thee."

> *Where loath to make the Saints attend her long,*
> *She's now a part both of the Quire, and Song,*

A soul so conceived need not delay in joining the company of the Saints. *Quire:* How deep we could take this word you can see from Ruskin's note in *Munera Pulveris.* But the main point of the line is that the Soul becomes both a singer and the song. That goes to the heart of Aristotelianism—where the Divine thinking is one with the object of its thought. (*Metaphysics* 1075 a). It is itself that thought (or intellect) thinks, on account of its participation in the object of thought: for it becomes its own object in the act of apprehending it: so that thought (intellect) and what is thought of are one and the same. We come back here to our founding questions where the distinction between matter and activity vanishes—as it does for the modern physicist when his ultimate particles become merely what they do.

But to elucidate Donne's line it is better perhaps just to quote another poet: from the last verse of W. B. Yeats's "Among School Children" in *The Tower.*

> O Chestnut tree, great rooted blossomer
> Are you the leaf, the blossom or the bole?
> O body swayed to music, O brightening glance,
> How can we know the dancer from the dance?

or this from T. S. Eliot's *Burnt Norton:*

> At the still point of the turning world . . . at the still point,
> there the dance is,

> But neither arrest nor movement. And do not call it fixity . . .
>   Except for the point, the still point,
> There would be no dance, and there is only the dance.

Donne's next line contains the word upon which, with the word *Soule* —as on two poles—the entire interpretation of this poem turns, as for that matter all philosophy must, the word *world*.

> *This world, in that great earthquake languished;*

world: not of course this planet, the earth, but this present life as opposed to the other, the realm of departed spirits. Or more narrowly "the pursuits and interests of the earthly life," as the *Oxford Dictionary* puts it, with the note, "especially in religious use, the least worthy of these." Donne was extremely fond of playing with the word "world." It is one of the chief of his wonder workers. Compare *A Valediction of Weeping:*

> On a round ball
> A workman that hath copies by, can lay
> An Europe, Afrique, and an Asia,
> And quickly make that which was nothing, All,
>   So doth each teare,
>   Which thee doth weare,
> A globe, yea world by that impression grow,
> Till thy tears mixt with mine doe overflow
> This world, by waters sent from thee, my heaven dissolved so.

That is metaphysical metaphor at its height. Philosophically it is the age-old recognition that, as Blake put it, "The eye altering, alters all." Donne, of course, plays throughout his poem on shifts between the private solipsistic world and the general public world of mundane interests. It is his general theme that both these worlds die, corrupt and disintegrate in the absence of the Soule—as defined in the parenthesis of lines 3 to 6.

Is this extravagance? Is the poem a "preposterous eulogy"? Is it not rather that Donne is saying something which if said in our everyday style would seem so commonplace that we would not notice what we were saying? If so, what was he saying? To put it with our usual crude and unilluminating briefness, he was saying that Elizabeth Drury was an example, an inspiration, and would have been to all who knew her. That looks little enough to say, *if so said.* It took a Donne to expand the implications of those two words "example" and "inspiration" into the poem. But the more we look into the poem, the more we will discover that the understanding of those two words is an understanding of the whole Platonic Aristotelian account of the fabric of things. These words take their meaning, by participation, directly from the founding questions. The best witness will be the closing lines of *The Second Anniversary:*

>   nor would'st thou be content,
> To take this, for my second yeares true Rent,

Did this Coine beare any other stampe, than his,
That gave thee power to doe, me, to say this.
Since his will is, that to posteritie,
Thou should'st for life, and death, a patterne bee,
And that the world should notice have of this:
The purpose, and th'authoritie is his;
Thou art the Proclamation; and I am
The Trumpet, at whose voyce the people came.

To read the poem rightly would be to hear and come.

Comparison

Sigurd Burckhardt

POETRY, LANGUAGE,
AND THE CONDITION OF MODERN MAN

I

One could write the history of poetry and science in two ways; like
the history of the Roman Empire, it may be told either as a series of
conquests or as a series of defenses. The Romans avoided the word "conquest"; they preferred "pacification." They found that their boundaries, wherever they were, had a way of disintegrating; the only remedy
was to pacify the area outside the boundaries. In this way Rome expanded in sheer self-defense. It is similar with science and literature;
and if the Romans' plea of self-defense strikes us as a little disingenuous,
scientists and poets, considering the meagre awards that await them,
could enter it with a good deal of justice, though in fact, since their
consciences are clean, they rather think of their expansion as conquests. Scientists—and, I believe, poets too—are engaged in a continuous effort to restore unity and cohesion to a universe—whether of
matter or of discourse—which is always threatened with disintegration.
The great scientific theories are constructs designed to reestablish universal harmony by the conquest and incorporation of troublesome new
data which the existing order had ignored and which are threatening
to throw the whole proud structure into confusion. And it is not surprising that a cosmos which has progressed from the primordial egg
through Ptolemaic spheres to an expanding universe demands constructs
of a more and more abstract and remote order, if it is to stay (concep-
tually, at any rate) in one piece. It is equally evident that a human
community which has progressed from our paradisal parents through
the Polis and Urbs to the Lonely Crowd should require, as at least one
of its ties, a language increasingly remote from the careless and carefree
certainties of every-day discourse. Just as the scientist, charged with
keeping the material universe intelligible, is, from a common-sense
point of view, absurdly sensitive to minute data which call the grand
existing order into question, so the poet is inordinately aware of any
evidence that human communion—through language—is perhaps only
an illusion; that language itself, once it is deprived of its external

From *Centennial Review* (Winter 1960), 1-15. This article appeared in two parts, the
second written by Roy Harvey Pearce.

props, may be merely a vast game of question-begging, in which we presuppose the community which we pretend to establish by speaking. Sterne's *Tristram Shandy* remains the classic document, as disquieting as it is delightful, of the ludicrous arbitrariness and solitariness of our separate minds, and of the inadequacy of ordinary language to bridge the chasm between them.

Language—which for most of us is a convenience—is the poet's be-all and end-all; that is why he cannot rest satisfied with weeping or laughing over our trust in it. Improbably he must try to get the better of it, to provide the constructs which, however indirectly and abstractly, show that language *can* be unequivocal. And while he sorrows, rejoices, prophesies, or celebrates love and beauty in full creative freedom, to this one task he is bound; whatever he is talking *about,* the very mode of his talking is a commentary on language and an attempt to overcome its paradoxes. In the end, it is for this servitude that he is rewarded and, if necessary, absolved. Time, W. H. Auden writes in his elegy on Yeats:

> Worships language and forgives
> Everyone by whom it lives;
> Pardons cowardice, conceit,
> Lays its honours at their feet.

> Time, that with this strange excuse
> Pardoned Kipling and his views,
> And will pardon Paul Claudel,
> Pardons him for writing well.

It is because poetry is, in the most radical sense, "language in action" that we cannot fully understand it except as an address, a mode of discourse, something said by someone to someone in such a way as to be unequivocal. Poetry applies the severest test to the casual assurance of its time that language is a communion; but at the same time it tries to show how language must be spoken to *be* a communion.

II

By way of showing how poets respond to the threat of disintegration, to the awareness that traditional harmonies and cohesions are no longer to be relied on, I should like to consider three poems, all on the same subject but far apart in time and in form. The first is Robert Herrick's *To Daffodils*.

> 1.   Fair Daffodils, we weep to see
>   You haste away so soon:
>   As yet the early-rising Sun
>   Has not attain'd his Noon.

Stay, stay
Until the hasting day
Has run
But to the Even-song;
And, having prayed together, we
Will go with you along.

2. We have short time to stay, as you,
We have as short a spring;
As quick a growth to meet Decay,
As you or anything.
We die,
As your hours do, and dry
Away,
Like to the Summer's rain;
Or as the pearls of Morning's dew
Ne'er to be found again.

This apostrophe to flowers is perhaps a song rather than a poem; it may be a violence to strip it of its musical envelopment. Still I think we are safe in noting two things about it as significant: that daffodils are being addressed, and that the stanzaic pattern is forbiddingly complex. The subject itself—the analogy between human and floral life—is a topos as old as the Bible; the basic rhetorical figure—the apostrophe —is equally old. But the tone is singular: a pleading, at times almost hectic, to the flowers to acknowledge the relationship which alone can make the direct address meaningful. The point in history at which an address to inanimate things ceased to be taken literally and became figurative lies in the dim past; but the point at which such an apostrophe is felt to be a positive incongruity, an artifice no longer reconcilable with the speaker's sense of reality, is very much more recent and varies from person to person, perhaps from mood to mood. Herrick, I think, reaches that point in this poem. To trace out rhyme schemes is no longer fashionable critical practice, but here we need one, because the poem is a rhymer's tour de force; it stretches almost to the breaking point our capacity for hearing the tonal correspondencies. As the speaker has difficulty in believing that human and inanimate nature are still sufficiently of a piece to talk to each other, so we have difficulty in hearing that the lines of the poem fully answer each other. German has an expressive term for lines which, in generally rhymed stanzas, remain without the fulfillment of an answering line; it calls them "orphans." There are two near-orphans in Herrick's stanza: the first and the ninth lines. Is it altogether an accident that it is the word "we" at the end of line 9 which stands in this position of almost complete bereavement (and pronounced syntactical isolation), harking back to an answering echo that has become almost too faint to hear? And again, is it an accident that in line 6 of the second stanza the flow of the verse, until then easy though varied, becomes disturbed and clogged through the juxtaposition of the words "your hours"? "Hours" itself is wilful; from the logic of the analogy we should expect a simple "you." But if we consider "hours" as a pun on the first-person-plural possessive, we see that the disturbance arises from the too close joining of the two pronouns—"we" and "you"—to join which would have seemed the very point of the poem.

We might say, then, that the poem is a splendid farewell to itself, or to its mode. This particular kind of grace, of madrigal lightness and intricacy, does not, I believe, recur in English poetry. The faith in the universal harmony of all creation, which ought to be the real substratum for such modes of speech, is only a charming fiction. And though there is hardly a limit to the fictions the poet may permit himself, fictions about his medium are forbidden him upon pain of poetic death. What makes this poem live—as the anthologies show it does— is not the fiction but rather the poet's awareness of it *as* a fiction. Because an apostrophe is a figure of *speech* in the most literal sense, and because the poet is the most conscious and responsible of speakers, he knows himself committed to something untenable, something beautiful but already beyond recall; the "Stay, stay" calls out not only to the daffodils in the first line, but also to those in the title—that is, to the poem as a whole.

Two and a half centuries separate Hopkins' elegy from Herrick's, and they tell.

SPRING AND FALL
To a Young Child

Márgarét, are you gríeving
Over Goldengrove unleaving?
Léaves, líke the things of man, you
With your fresh thoughts care for, can you?
Áh! ás the heart grows older
It will come to such sights colder
By and by, nor spare a sigh
Though worlds of wanwood leafmeal lie;
And yet you wíll weep and know why.
Now no matter, child, the name:
Sórrow's spríngs áre the same.
Nor mouth had, no nor mind, expressed
What heart heard of, ghost guessed:
It ís the blight man was born for,
It is Margaret you mourn for.

Now it is not the "we" of common humanity that speaks to flowers, but the poet who speaks to a child. The child responds to the falling of leaves somewhat as Herrick, speaking for all of us, does to the withering of the daffodils; but the poet initiates her into the harsher verities of human life and growth. He does not call Margaret's grief pointless, on the contrary: he says that she is, by intuitive wisdom, grieving over the ineluctable future time when she will no longer grieve. Thus the poem translates into an adult sensibility the kind of correspondence which formed the already precarious base of Herrick's poem. To put it somewhat baroquely, Hopkins goes about his work with a compassionate severity, destroying the fairy-tale Goldengrove in which the child still finds the objective correlative of her sorrow, and leaving in its place worlds of wanwood, but on the other hand giving that sorrow a new dignity by showing it its true object: man's—Margaret's—self.

In this separation, words and images assume a particularity which they do not have in the earlier poem. Perhaps my interpretation of Herrick's "your hours" seemed a little strained; but if it occurred in this poem, my calling attention to it would, I daresay, seem quite natural, because it would be entirely of a piece with "heart heard, ghost guessed," with wanwood and leafmeal, etc. What I take to be the first sign of disintegration in Herrick has become the dominant formal feature in Hopkins; the words do not easily blend into the total utterance, but insistently call attention to themselves as entities, as particulars, which the meter, moreover, compels us to linger over and take in fully.

This means that Hopkins has drawn the linguistic consequences of his knowledge. The relative ease with which we read Herrick's poem derives from the sense of correspondence which still structures it: where Nature is in tune with man's feelings, language need not carry a very heavy burden; the greater, encompassing harmony is pre-established, as it were. Call this harmony into question, as Hopkins does, and the burden on language immediately becomes greater. It has to exert itself to hold things together; we can see the alliterative tendons straining.

But something has been gained by the loss; as man has been turned in upon himself, so has language. In being forced to structure itself more rigorously from within, it has gained a new resilience. I will risk the assertion that the rhyme of the final couplet would have been impossible before Hopkins, except where the intention was comic; it has so work-a-day a cadence that it seems, or did seem, unavailable to serious lyric poetry. Here however, it does its work with dignity and even poignancy. Why? Mostly, I think, because the poem as a whole has prepared us to accept words as particulars, with an inherent worth. Perhaps it is a blight which has turned Goldengrove into wanwood and splendid phrases like "pearls of morning's dew" into "It is Margaret you mourn for." (Margaret, by the way, is Greek for "pearl.") But it is the human lot and the human phrase, as moving in their way as any beautiful but false compare.

That this conquest of a new linguistic province for poetry has not been a matter of course, we see from the strange second couplet. Why this painfully contorted sentence, which seems to yield nothing but a strained and inharmonious rhyme? My guess is that the principle of contortion is not a "poetic" one, in the common acceptance of that much abused term, but a purely linguistic—and thus a *truly* poetic—one. The sentence creates no effect that would speak immediately to our feelings (unless we have learned to *feel* language, as the poet does); what it does is to crowd together, at the beginning, all its nominal elements and to relegate the verbal elements to the end. Is not the point of this to show the linguistic impossibility of that pristine innocence and sense of harmony in which all things stand side by side, inviolate, substantial and yet intimately related?—a harmony so unbroken that there is no subject lording it over an object and no verb to intervene between the two, relating only what itself has separated? In a sense, the child's inarticulate, ineffable intuition of coherence is true; but the poet knows, more keenly than anyone else, that what cannot be said cannot, humanly speaking, be true. And yet it seems that what *can* be said must be false. It is at this point that the final and "vulgar" phrasing comes to the poet's rescue. In "the blight man was born for" and "Margaret you mourn for"—already anticipated in the "care for" of line 4—the form of statement which before was all but unintelligible becomes available; in a curious way subject and object have become one, and no verb separates the substantives. There has been a price to pay: the truth of language is man's truth; its limitations are man's blight; the pathetic fallacy is, humanly speaking, just that—a fallacy. But at least the truth of man's fellowship and common fate can be wrested from language, and that, as the poem proves, is no mean triumph.

THE COURSE OF A PARTICULAR

Wallace Stevens

Today the leaves cry, hanging on branches swept by wind,
Yet the nothingness of winter becomes a little less.
It is still full of icy shades and shapen snow.

The leaves cry . . . One holds off and merely hears the cry.
It is a busy cry, concerning someone else.
And though one says that one is part of everything,

There is a conflict, there is a resistance involved;
And being part is an exertion that declines:
One feels the life of that which gives life as it is.

The leaves cry. It is not a cry of divine attention,
Nor the smoke-drift of puffed-out heroes, nor human cry.
It is the cry of leaves that do not transcend themselves,

In the absence of fantasia, without meaning more
Than they are in the final finding of the ear, in the thing
Itself, until, at last, the cry concerns no one at all.

If we were asked to supply a title for Stevens' poem, it is a safe guess that we would not hit on the one chosen by the poet. Herrick's title adds nothing to our understanding which we would not know after reading the first two words of the poem; Hopkins' we might guess and do at least not puzzle over. But I doubt that we could read Stevens' poem correctly without the pointer supplied in the title; even with it it is difficult enough. This means, surely, that a confidence has become still more shaky: the confidence, let us say, of the apostrophe, of the direct address; the trust that the poet will be understood, because his voice is the common voice of man. Where Herrick says "we" and speaks to Nature and where Hopkins says "you" and speaks to a child, Stevens says not even "I" but "one"; and if he speaks to anyone, it is with a mediacy and from an isolation so great that he is bound to be diffident about being understood at all. Hence the starkly abstract title, a warning that what follows will speak for itself with an uncompromising absoluteness.

The "particular" that runs its course through the poem is the cry of the leaves—or perhaps, more cautiously, "the leaves cry." The course itself is a merciless stripping, a structured and mounting negation, until we have the thing "itself," untranscending, uncommunicative, cut off from all connection with gods, heroes, man, and even, so it seems, with that impersonal "one," who has no attributes left except the rapidly failing ability to hear and the ebbing will to be part. At first the leaves cry in a setting, temporal and spatial; but, bleak as the setting is, it is too much, is got rid of. The phrase itself must speak, or rather cry . . . what, or to whom? The "one" hearer lacks the energy and resists the temptation to hear more than is said—and nothing *is* said. The meaning of the cry would have to be contributed by the "one" and to do so would not only be an exertion, but a violation of the truth of the thing, the cry, itself. And so, finally, the particular stands naked, separate, intransitive, closed off by a full stop. It has become absolutely itself.

In this minimal integrity, the particular has to counterbalance a heavy bulk of statement—statement which, except in the first stanza, is weighed down with bureaucratic jargon. Compared with "concerning someone else," "there is a resistance involved," or "in the absence of," Hopkins' "It is Margaret you mourn for" seems the essence of purity. And so does the particular—"the leaves cry"—itself. We get the feeling that to say more than this barest of sentences is already too much, too risky, involving us, on the one hand, in fantasias of togetherness and on the other in a mode of speech so drained of all concreteness and felt reality that it seems to issue from a Hartford, Conn., office building. Anything that might smack of artifice, of vividness, is stringently avoided; even images are too much, it seems, because the human mind is so constituted that it takes images as metaphors and finds a specious consolation in the sense that things have, after all, a meaning, are related, cohere. It is this consolation Stevens deprives us of; he will not supply us with any props for our illusions. This is the language you speak, he seems to say, and consequently this is the way you are; it would be a lie to pretend that things are meaningful.

I do not, for my part, feel that the particular suffices to counterbalance the mass of negation, though I think that Stevens intends that it should. But in any case, what we have here is a poem of radical doubt and analysis, in which the poet tries to get to the minimal, the quantum of meaningful language, out of which to rebuild the universe of discourse. I do not believe that the final statement—"the cry concerns no one at all"—can be taken at face value, for in that case the poem, the act of speech which lastly it remains and through which it remains tied to the community of men, would be absurd. The only fully autonomous poetry is nonsense poetry. But perhaps the poet means to offer us a way out of this dilemma; we are to read "no one" not as "none," but as the negation of the "one" in stanzas 2 and 3, the "one" who holds off and resists being part. The stress, in other words, should be on the "one," so that the cry, not concerning one, concerns all. This would imply that the ultimate negation is the ultimate affirmation, a somewhat uneasy conclusion since it is so blatantly paradoxical. Still I suggest it as the only one which does not reduce the poet's whole enterprise to nonsense.

I distrust the practice of assigning philosophical labels to poetry, but Stevens' stripping of language to the bare bones of statement is too obviously analogous, to the existentialist's stripping man of all his attributes to be ignored. "The leaves cry" is the linguistic counterpart to the existentialist "I am"; we have here the same desperate search for the irreducible, the same will to take nothing for granted. We have observed the interiorisation of "form" from Herrick to Hopkins; with Stevens it has become pure structure. Rhyme, meter, richness of image and sound—all the devices which, being external and immediately perceptible emblems of order and splendor (however fleeting), affirm an ordered and in some sense splendid world outside of the poet's created act, a world within which he can act because he shares it with his audience—all these are no longer available. Traditionally, poetry has been in some way celebratory; however precarious the poet felt the possibility of communion to be, he celebrated the sense that it was still and once more possible. With Stevens—and much modern poetry —all the energy seems to be spent on the mere assertion that communion must be *made* possible. The act of creation has become absolute—and for this reason stark. By a curious but necessary paradox, the unlimited freedom of the absolute creator turns into the grimmest kind of necessity; it is this paradox which Stevens' particular, in the counterplay of form and content, embodies. "The leaves cry" is, as an assertion, creatively sovereign; real leaves do not *cry*. But as a *form* of statement it is terrifyingly compelled; if less were said, it would no longer be a statement at all.

The point and poignancy, then, of Stevens' poem is that it accepts, as ultimately binding, the obligation of human discourse, of statement. Elsewhere Stevens calls the poem "the cry of its occasion"; but this cry is not allowed to deteriorate into a "Howl" of despair or protest against the world. Meaninglessness—and howls, however charged with emotion, are in the strict sense meaningless—is the limit of speech, which the poet, at whatever cost of beauty or intensity, must stop short of. "Said words of the world are the life of the world"; the emphasis is on the "said," the human act which invests words with lifegiving meaning. What has thus been conquered is no more and no less than the threat of meaninglessness, which is far more formidable than the threat of falsification. Falsification Herrick could still afford to glance at, while Hopkins had to confront it fully. Of Stevens more is demanded. As Job would have found it consoling to believe that he had done something to deserve his misfortunes, because it is better to think oneself unjust than to think God capricious, so—if we can generalize from Stevens—the modern poet would find it consoling to believe that language condemned him to falsehood. For there is a way to expiate the falsehood of language—poetic form: "After great pain a formal feeling comes." But there is none I know of to conquer meaningless-ness except to dare confront it and to forge meaning from it by an act which knows itself to be both frighteningly free and fully bound by the conditions of human discourse.

III

What I have tried to show is that and how, for the poet, the con-dition of language *is* the human condition, because what we call, loosely and metaphorically, the "meaning of our lives," he tests literally against the meaning of our discourse. A theory of meaning—whether explicit or implicit—is in fact a whole philosophy, because it stipulates the all-important third party who must be the guarantor of true communion. Who or what guarantees that the meaning I attach to my words is the same as the meaning my listener derives from them? Is it a divinely pre-established harmony, a firmly and beautifully woven texture of creation, in which all creatures can have discourse with each other? Is it the more tenuous—I would say the Protestant—order, which still allows men the community of their fallen state, though the sense of *culpa* has swallowed up that of *felix?* Or is it that purely group-made, haphazardly enslaving system of mere habit, based upon a kind of probability calculus of communion, the order of jargon and slogan and conditioned response? For the poet the shift from Divine Providence to actuarial tables is a linguistic one.

In "Carrion Comfort," Hopkins cries: "Not, I'll not, carrion com-fort, Despair, not feast on thee; / Not untwist—slack they may be— these last strands of man . . ." This is anything but confident or even elegiac, but it is still grand. Though God—the sonnet ends: "I wretch lay wrestling with (my God!) my God."—has become inscrutable to the point where prayer and blasphemy are almost one; He is still there. To Stevens, I think, "these last strands of man" would be those which tie subject and verb into utterance. Metaphysical despair is no longer a possible stance; our language forbids. What should God an-swer, suppose He did answer? "Concerning your message of . . . , let me assure you that I fully appreciate your concern"? Addressed as we are by Wildroot and Vitalis ads, we cannot well sustain the faith that the hairs on our heads are counted; embedded in the solicitude and bon-homie of salesmanship, we have reason to wonder whether language can ever be more than a manipulatory device. But the archaising anath-emas of Pound are little help; whipping the money changers out of the temple was meaningful as long as they still found it profitable to set up business in the *temple*. The poet's faith and resolution and act, if it is to have meaning, is bounded by the condition of language; his business is not to scourge us in the name of dead gods and heroes, but to tell us—and this can be a quietly bitter thing—what still remains to us of true speech. Once we know this, we discover that language is not mere limit, that our condition is not unchangeable, but that both of them, truly and coldly seen, have within them creative energy. Our condition, like our language, is, or can be, *act*—minimal perhaps, but forged and integral. This possibility the poet discovers for us in the universe which is peculiarly his, but also ours, so long as we have the courage not to untwist "these last strands of man": the universe of language.

Evaluation

Samuel Taylor Coleridge

THE CHARACTERISTIC DEFECTS OF
WORDSWORTH'S POETRY

I cannot here enter into a detailed examination of Mr. Wordsworth's works; but I will attempt to give the main results of my own judgement, after an acquaintance of many years, and repeated perusals. And though, to appreciate the defects of a great mind it is necessary to understand previously its characteristic excellences, yet I have already expressed myself with sufficient fulness, to preclude most of the ill effects that might arise from my pursuing a contrary arrangement. I will therefore commence with what I deem the prominent *defects* of his poems hitherto published.

The first *characteristic, though only occasional* defect, which I appear to myself to find in these poems is the INCONSTANCY of the *style*. Under this name I refer to the sudden and unprepared transitions from lines or sentences of peculiar felicity (at all events striking and original) to a style, not only unimpassioned but undistinguished. He sinks too often and too abruptly to that style, which I should place in the second division of language, dividing it into the three species; *first,* that which is peculiar to poetry; *second,* that which is only proper in prose; and *third,* the neutral or common to both. There have been works, such as Cowley's Essay on Cromwell, in which prose and verse are intermixed (not as in the Consolation of Boetius, or the Argenis of Barclay, by the insertion of poems supposed to have been spoken or composed on occasions previously related in prose, but) the poet passing from one to the other, as the nature of the thoughts or his own feelings dictated. Yet this mode of composition does not satisfy a cultivated taste. There is something unpleasant in the being thus obliged to alternate states of feeling so dissimilar, and this too in a species of writing, the pleasure from which is in part derived from the preparation and previous expectation of the reader. A portion of that awkwardness is felt which hangs upon the introduction of songs in our modern comic operas; and to prevent which the judicious Metastasio (as to whose exquisite *taste* there can be no hesitation, whatever doubts may be entertained as to his *poetic genius)* uniformly placed the ARIA at the end of the

From *Biographia Literaria*, ed. J. Shawcross (Oxford University Press, 1907), II, 97-131. Reprinted by permission of the Clarendon Press, Oxford.

scene, at the same time that he almost always raises and impassions the style of the recitative immediately preceding. Even in real life, the difference is great and evident between words used as the *arbitrary marks* of thought, our smooth market-coin of intercourse, with the image and superscription worn out by currency; and those which convey pictures either borrowed from *one* outward object to enliven and particularize some *other;* or used allegorically to body forth the inward state of the person speaking; or such as are at least the exponents of his peculiar turn and unusual extent of faculty. So much so indeed, that in the social circles of private life we often find a striking use of the latter put a stop to the general flow of conversation, and by the excitement arising from concentered attention produce a sort of damp and interruption for some minutes after. But in the perusal of works of literary *art,* we *prepare* ourselves for such language; and the business of the writer, like that of a painter whose subject requires unusual splendor and prominence, is so to raise the lower and neutral tints, that what in a different style would be the *commanding* colors, are here used as the means of that gentle *degradation* requisite in order to produce the effect of a *whole.* Where this is not achieved in a poem, the metre merely reminds the reader of his claims in order to disappoint them; and where this defect occurs frequently, his feelings are alternately startled by anticlimax and hyperclimax.

I refer the reader to the exquisite stanzas cited for another purpose from the blind Highland Boy; and then annex, as being in my opinion instances of this *disharmony* in style, the two following:

"And one, the rarest, was a shell,
Which he, poor child, had studied well:
The shell of a green turtle, thin
And hollow;—you might sit therein,
    It was so wide, and deep."

"Our Highland Boy oft visited
The house which held this prize; and, led
By choice or chance, did thither come
One day, when no one was at home,
    And found the door unbarred."

Or page 172, vol. I.

"'Tis gone—forgotten—*let me do
My best.* There was a smile or two—
I can remember them, I see
The smiles worth all the world to me.
Dear Baby, I must lay thee down:
Thou troublest me with strange alarms;
Smiles hast thou, sweet ones of thine own;
I cannot keep thee in my arms;
For they confound me: *as it is,*
I have forgot those smiles of his!"

Or page 269, vol. I.

> "Thou hast a nest, for thy love and thy rest,
> And though little troubled with sloth
> Drunken lark! thou would'st be loth
> To be such a traveller as I.
>   Happy, happy liver!
> *With a soul as strong as a mountain river*
> *Pouring out praise to th'Almighty giver!*
> Joy and jollity be with us both!
> Hearing thee or else some other,
>   As merry a brother
> I on the earth will go plodding on
> By myself chearfully till the day is done."

The incongruity, which I appear to find in this passage, is that of the two noble lines in italics with the preceding and following. So vol II. page 30.

> "Close by a pond, upon the further side,
> He stood alone; a minute's space, I guess,
> I watch'd him, he continuing motionless:
> To the pool's further margin then I drew,
> He being all the while before me full in view."

Compare this with the repetition of the same image, in the next stanza but two.

> "And, still, as I drew near with gentle pace,
> Beside the little pond or moorish flood
> Motionless as a cloud the old man stood,
> That heareth not the loud winds as they call,
> And moveth altogether, if it move at all."

Or lastly, the second of the three following stanzas, compared both with the first and the third.

> "My former thoughts returned; the fear that kills;
> And hope that is unwilling to be fed;
> Cold, pain, and labour, and all fleshly ills;
> And mighty poets in their misery dead.
> But now, perplex'd by what the old man had said,
> My question eagerly did I renew,
> 'How is it that you live, and what is it you do?'
>
> He with a smile did then his words repeat;
> And said, that gathering leeches far and wide
> He travell'd; stirring thus about his feet
> The waters of the ponds where they abide.
> 'Once I could meet with them on every side,

'But they have dwindled long by slow decay;
'Yet still I persevere, and find them where I may.'

While he was talking thus, the lonely place,
The old man's shape, and speech, all troubled me:
In my mind's eye I seemed to see him pace
About the weary moors continually,
Wandering about alone and silently."

Indeed this fine poem is *especially* characteristic of the author. There is scarce a defect or excellence in his writings of which it would not present a specimen. But it would be unjust not to repeat that this defect is only occasional. From a careful reperusal of the two volumes of poems, I doubt whether the objectionable passages would amount in the whole to one hundred lines; not the eighth part of the number of pages. In the "EXCURSION" the feeling of incongruity is seldom excited by the diction of any passage considered in itself, but by the sudden superiority of some other passage forming the context.

The second defect I can generalize with tolerable accuracy, if the reader will pardon an uncouth and new-coined word. There is, I should say, not seldom a *matter-of-factness* in certain poems. This may be divided into, *first,* a laborious minuteness and fidelity in the representation of objects, and their positions, as they appeared to the poet himself; *secondly,* the insertion of accidental circumstances, in order to the full explanation of his living characters, their dispositions and actions; which circumstances might be necessary to establish the probability of a statement in real life, where nothing is taken for granted by the hearer; but appear superfluous in poetry, where the reader is willing to believe for his own sake. To this *accidentality* I object, as contravening the essence of poetry, which Aristotle pronounces to be σπουδαιότατον καὶ φιλοσοφώτατον γένος, the most intense, weighty and philosophical product of human art; adding, as the *reason,* that it is the most catholic and abstract. The following passage from Davenant's prefatory letter to Hobbs well expresses this truth. "When I considered the actions which I meant to describe, (those inferring the persons), I was again persuaded rather to choose those of a former age, than the present; and in a century so far removed, as might preserve me from their improper examinations, who know not the requisites of a poem, nor how much pleasure they lose, (and even the pleasures of heroic poesy are not unprofitable), who take away the liberty of a poet, and fetter his feet in the shackles of an historian. For why should a poet doubt in story to mend the intrigues of fortune by more delightful conveyances of probable fictions, because austere historians have entered into bond to truth? An obligation, which were in poets as foolish and unnecessary, as in the bondage of false martyrs, who lie in chains for a mistaken opinion. *But by this I would imply, that truth narrative and past is the idol of historians, (who worship a dead thing), and truth operative, and by effects continually alive, is the mistress of poets, who hath not her existence in matter, but in reason.*"

For this minute accuracy in the painting of local imagery, the lines in the EXCURSION, pp. 96, 97, and 98, may be taken, if not as a striking instance, yet as an illustration of my meaning. It must be some strong motive (as, for instance, that the description was necessary to the intelligibility of the tale) which could induce me to describe in a number of verses what a draughtsman could present to the eye with incomparably greater satisfaction by half a dozen strokes of his pencil, or the painter with as many touches of his brush. Such descriptions too often occasion in the mind of a reader, who is determined to understand his author, a feeling of labor, not very dissimilar to that, with which he would construct a diagram, line by line, for a long geometrical proposition. It seems to be like taking the pieces of a dissected map out of its box. We first look at one part, and then at another, then join and dove-tail them; and when the successive acts of attention have been completed, there is a retrogressive effort of mind to behold it as a whole. The poet should paint to the imagination, not to the fancy; and I know no happier case to exemplify the distinction between these two faculties. Master-pieces of the former mode of poetic painting abound in the writings of Milton, ex. gr.

> "The fig-tree; not that kind for fruit renown'd,
> But such as at this day, to Indians known,
> In Malabar or Decan spreads her arms
> Branching so broad and long, that in the ground
> The bended twigs take root, *and daughters grow*
> *About the mother tree, a pillar'd shade*
> *High over-arch'd and* ECHOING WALKS BETWEEN:
> *There oft the Indian Herdsman, shunning heat,*
> *Shelters in cool, and tends his pasturing herds*
> *At loop holes cut through thickest shade."*
> MILTON *P. L.* 9. 1100.

This is *creation* rather than *painting,* or if painting, yet such, and with such co-presence of the whole picture flash'd at once upon the eye, as the sun paints in a camera obscura. But the poet must likewise understand and command what Bacon calls the *vestigia communia* of the senses, the latency of all in each, and more especially as by a magical *penna duplex,* the excitement of vision by sound and the exponents of sound. Thus "THE ECHOING WALKS BETWEEN," may be almost said to reverse the fable in tradition of the head of Memnon, in the Egyptian statue. Such may be deservedly entitled the *creative words* in the world of imagination.

The second division respects an apparent minute adherence to *matter-of-fact* in characters and incidents; a *biographical* attention to probability, and an *anxiety* of explanation and retrospect. Under this head I shall deliver, with no feigned diffidence, the results of my best reflection on the great point of controversy between Mr. Wordsworth and his objectors; namely, on THE CHOICE OF HIS CHARACTERS. I have already declared and, I trust, justified, my utter dissent from the mode of argument which his critics have hitherto employed. To *their* question, Why did you chuse such a character, or a character from such a rank of life? the poet might in my opinion fairly retort: why with the conception of my character did you make wilful choice of mean or ludicrous associations not furnished by me, but supplied from your own sickly and fastidious feelings? How was it, indeed, probable, that such arguments could have any weight with an author, whose plan, whose guiding principle, and main object it was to attack and subdue that state of association, which leads us to place the chief value on those things in which man DIFFERS from man, and to forget or disregard the high dignities, which belong to HUMAN NATURE, the sense and the feeling, which *may* be, and *ought* to be, found in *all* ranks? The feelings with which, as Christians, we contemplate a mixed congregation rising or kneeling before their common Maker: Mr. Wordsworth would have us entertain at *all* times, as men, and as readers; and by the excitement of this lofty, yet prideless impartiality in *poetry*, he might hope to have encouraged its continuance in *real life*. The praise of good men be his! In real life, and, I trust, even in my imagination, I honor a virtuous and wise man, without reference to the presence or absence of artificial advantages. Whether in the person of an armed baron, a laurel'd bard, &c., or of an old pedlar, or still older leach-gatherer, the same qualities of head and heart must claim the same reverence. And even in poetry I am not conscious, that I have ever suffered my feelings to be disturbed or offended by any thoughts or images, which the poet himself has not presented.

But yet I object nevertheless and for the following reasons. First, because the object in view, as an *immediate* object, belongs to the moral philosopher, and would be pursued, not only more appropriately, but in my opinion with far greater probability of success, in sermons or moral essays, than in an elevated poem. It seems, indeed, to destroy the main fundamental distinction, not only between a poem and prose, but even between philosophy and works of fiction, inasmuch as it proposes *truth* for its immediate object, instead of *pleasure*. Now till the blessed time shall come, when truth itself shall be pleasure, and both shall be so united, as to be distinguishable in words only, not in feeling, it will remain the poet's office to proceed upon that state of association, which actually exists as *general;* instead of attempting first to *make* it what it ought to be, and then to let the pleasure follow. But here is unfortunately a small *Hysteron-Proteron*. For the communication of pleasure is the introductory means by which alone the poet must expect to moralize his readers. Secondly: though I were to admit, for a moment, *this* argument to be groundless: yet how is the moral effect to be produced, by merely attaching the name of some low profession to powers which are *least* likely, and to qualities which are assuredly not *more* likely, to be found in it? The poet, speaking in his own person, may at once delight and improve us by sentiments, which teach us the independence of goodness, of wisdom, and even of genius, on the favors of fortune. And having made a due reverence before the throne of Antonine, he may bow with equal awe before Epictetus among his fellow-slaves—

_____"and rejoice
In the plain presence of his dignity."

Who is not at once delighted and improved, when the POET Wordsworth himself exclaims,

> "O many are the poets that are sown
> By Nature; man endowed with highest gifts,
> The vision and the faculty divine,
> Yet wanting the accomplishment of verse,
> Nor having e'er, as life advanced, been led
> By circumstance to take unto the height
> The measure of themselves, these favor'd beings,
> All but a scatter'd few, live out their time
> Husbanding that which they possess within,
> And go to the grave unthought of. Strongest minds
> Are often those of whom the noisy world
> Hears least."
> EXCURSION, B. I.

To use a colloquial phrase, such sentiments, in such language, do one's
heart good; though I for my part, have not the fullest faith in the *truth*
of the observation. On the contrary I believe the instances to be exceedingly rare; and should feel almost as strong an objection to introduce such a character in a poetic fiction, as a pair of black swans on
a lake in a fancy-landscape. When I think how many, and how much
better books than Homer, or even Herodotus, Pindar or Eschylus,
could have read, are in the power of almost every man, in a country
where almost every man is instructed to read and write; and how restless, how difficultly hidden, the powers of genius are; and yet find
even in situations the most favorable, according to Mr. Wordsworth,
for the formation of a pure and poetic language; in situations which
ensure familiarity with the grandest objects of the imagination; but
one BURNS, among the shepherds of *Scotland,* and not a single poet of
humble life among those of *English* lakes and mountains; I conclude,
that POETIC GENIUS is not only a very delicate but a very rare plant.
But be this as it may, the feelings with which

> "I think of CHATTERTON, the marvellous boy,
> The sleepless soul, that perished in his pride;
> Of BURNS, that walk'd in glory and in joy
> Behind his plough upon the mountain-side"—

are widely different from those with which I should read a *poem,* where
the author, having occasion for the character of a poet and a philosopher
in the fable of his narration, had chosen to make him a *chimney-sweeper;*
and then, in order to remove all doubts on the subject, had *invented* an
account of his birth, parentage and education, with all the strange and
fortunate accidents which had concurred in making him at once poet,
philosopher, and sweep! Nothing but biography can justify this. If it
be admissible even in a *Novel,* it must be one in the manner of De
Foe's, that were meant to pass for histories, not in the manner of
Fielding's: in the life of Moll Flanders, or Colonel Jack, not in a Tom

Jones, or even a Joseph Andrews. Much less then can it be legitimately introduced in a *poem,* the characters of which, amid the strongest individualization, must still remain representative. The precepts of Horace, on this point, are grounded on the nature both of poetry and of the human mind. They are not more peremptory, than wise and prudent. For in the first place a deviation from them perplexes the reader's feelings, and all the circumstances, which are feigned in order to make such accidents less improbable, divide and disquiet his faith, rather than aid and support it. Spite of all attempts, the fiction *will* appear, and unfortunately not as *fictitious* but as *false.* The reader not only *knows,* that the sentiments and language are the poet's own, and his own too in his *artificial* character, *as poet;* but by the fruitless endeavours to make him think the contrary, he is not even suffered to *forget* it. The effect is similar to that produced by an epic poet, when the fable and the characters are *derived* from Scripture history, as in the *Messiah* of *Klopstock,* or in *Cumberland's Calvary;* and not merely *suggested* by it, as in the Paradise Lost of Milton. That *illusion,* contra-distinguished from *delusion,* that *negative* faith, which simply permits the images presented to work by their own force, without either denial or affirmation of their real existence by the judgement, is rendered impossible by their immediate neighbourhood to words and facts of known and absolute truth. A faith, which transcends even historic belief, must absolutely *put out* this mere poetic Analogon of faith, as the summer sun is said to extinguish our household fires, when it shines full upon them. What would otherwise have been yielded to as pleasing fiction, is repelled as revolting falsehood. The effect produced in this latter case by the solemn belief of the reader, is in a less degree brought about in the instances, to which I have been objecting, by the baffled attempts of the author to *make* him believe.

Add to all the foregoing the seeming uselessness both of the project and of the anecdotes from which it is to derive support. Is there one word, for instance, attributed to the pedlar in the "Excursion," characteristic of a *pedlar?* One sentiment, that might not more plausibly, even without the aid of any previous explanation, have proceeded from any wise and beneficent old man, of a rank or profession in which the language of learning and refinement are natural and to be expected? Need the rank have been at all particularized, where nothing follows which the knowledge of that rank is to explain or illustrate? When on the contrary this information renders the man's language, feelings, sentiments, and information a riddle, which must itself be solved by episodes of anecdote? Finally when this, and this alone, could have induced a genuine *poet* to inweave in a poem of the loftiest style, and on subjects the loftiest and of most universal interest, such minute matters of fact, (not unlike those furnished for the obituary of a magazine by the friends of some obscure *ornament of society lately deceased* in some obscure town), as

> "Among the hills of Athol he was born:
> There, on a small hereditary farm,
> An unproductive slip of rugged ground,

His Father dwelt; and died in poverty;
While he, whose lowly fortune I retrace,
The youngest of three sons, was yet a babe,
A little one—unconscious of their loss.
But, ere he had outgrown his infant days,
His widowed mother, for a second mate,
Espoused the teacher of the Village School;
Who on her offspring zealously bestowed
Needful instruction."

———————

"From his sixth year, the Boy of whom I speak,
In summer tended cattle on the hills;
But, through the inclement and the perilous days
Of long-continuing winter, he repaired
To his step-father's school,"—&c.

For all the admirable passages interposed in this narration, might,
with trifling alterations, have been far more appropriately, and with
far greater verisimilitude, told of a poet in the character of a poet;
and without incurring another defect which I shall now mention, and a
sufficient illustration of which will have been here anticipated.

Third; an undue predilection for the *dramatic* form in certain poems,
from which one or other of two evils result. Either the thoughts and
diction are different from that of the poet, and then there arises an
incongruity of style; or they are the same and indistinguishable, and
then it presents a species of ventriloquism, where two are represented
as talking, while in truth one man only speaks.

The fourth class of defects is closely connected with the former; but
yet are such as arise likewise from an intensity of feeling disproportionate to *such* knowledge and value of the objects described, as can be
fairly anticipated of men in general, even of the most cultivated classes;
and with which therefore few only, and those few particularly circum-
stanced, can be supposed to sympathize. In this class, I comprise
occasional prolixity, repetition, and an eddying, instead of progression,
of thought. As instances, see pages 27, 28, and 62 of the Poems, Vol. I.
and the first eighty lines of the Sixth Book of the Excursion.

Fifth and last; thoughts and images too great for the subject. This
is an approximation to what might be called *mental* bombast, as distinguished from verbal: for, as in the latter there is a disproportion
of the expressions to the thoughts, so in this there is a disproportion of
thought to the circumstance and occasion. This, by the bye, is a fault
of which none but a man of genius is capable. It is the awkwardness
and strength of Hercules with the distaff of Omphale.

It is a well-known fact, that bright colors in motion both make and
leave the strongest impressions on the eye. Nothing is more likely too,
than that a vivid image or visual spectrum, thus originated, may become
the link of association in recalling the feelings and images that had
accompanied the original impression. But if we describe this in such
lines, as

"They flash upon that inward eye,
Which is the bliss of solitude!"

in what words shall we describe the joy of retrospection, when the
images and virtuous actions of a whole well-spent life, pass before that
conscience which is indeed the *inward* eye: which is indeed *"the bliss
of solitude"?* Assuredly we seem to sink most abruptly, not to say bur-
lesquely, and almost as in a *medly,* from this couplet to—

"And then my heart with pleasure fills,
And dances with the *daffodils.*"
Vol. I. p. 320.

The second instance is from Vol II. page 12, where the poet, having
gone out for a day's tour of pleasure, meets early in the morning with
a knot of *gypsies,* who had pitched their blanket-tents and straw-beds,
together with their children and asses, in some field by the road-side.
At the close of the day on his return our tourist found them in the
same place. "Twelve hours," says he,

"Twelve hours, twelve bounteous hours are gone, while I
Have been a traveller under open sky,
Much witnessing of change and cheer,
Yet as I left I find them here!"

Whereat the poet, without seeming to reflect that the poor tawny
wanderers might probably have been tramping for weeks together
through road and lane, over moor and mountain, and consequently
must have been right glad to rest themselves, their children and cattle,
for one whole day; and overlooking the obvious truth, that such repose
might be quite as necessary for *them,* as a walk of the same continuance
was pleasing or healthful for the more fortunate poet; expresses his
indignation in a series of lines, the diction and imagery of which would
have been rather above, than below the mark, had they been applied
to the immense empire of China improgressive for thirty centuries:

"The weary SUN betook himself to rest:—
—Then issued VESPER from the fulgent west,
Outshining, like a visible God,
The glorious path in which he trod!
And now, ascending, after one dark hour,
And one night's diminution of her power,
Behold the mighty MOON! this way
She looks, as if at them—but they
Regard not her:—oh, better wrong and strife,
Better vain deeds or evil than such life!
The silent HEAVENS have goings on:
The STARS have tasks!—but *these* have none!"

The last instance of this defect (for I know no other than these already cited) is from the Ode, page 351, Vol. II., where, speaking of a child, "a six years' darling of a pigmy size," he thus addresses him:

"Thou best philosopher, who yet dost keep
Thy heritage! Thou eye among the blind,
That, deaf and silent, read'st the eternal deep,
Haunted for ever by the Eternal Mind,—
Mighty Prophet! Seer blest!
On whom those truths do rest,
Which we are toiling all our lives to find!
Thou, over whom thy immortality
Broods like the day, a master o'er the slave,
A presence that is not to be put by!"

Now here, not to stop at the daring spirit of metaphor which connects the epithets "deaf and silent," with the apostrophized *eye:* or (if we are to refer it to the preceding word, philosopher) the faulty and equivocal syntax of the passage; and without examining the propriety of making a "master *brood* o'er a slave," or the *day* brood *at all;* we will merely ask, what does all this mean? In what sense is a child of that age a *philosopher?* In what sense does he *read* "the eternal deep"? In what sense is he declared to be *"for ever haunted"* by the Supreme Being? or so inspired as to deserve the splendid titles of a *mighty prophet,* a *blessed seer?* By reflection? by knowledge? by conscious intuition? or by *any* form or modification of consciousness? These would be tidings indeed; but such as would presuppose an immediate revelation to the inspired communicator, and require miracles to authenticate his inspiration. Children at this age give us no such information of themselves; and at what time were we dipped in the Lethe, which has produced such utter oblivion of a state so godlike? There are many of us that still possess some rememberances, more or less distinct, respecting themselves at six years old; pity that the worthless straws only should float, while treasures, compared with which all the mines of Golconda and Mexico were but straws, should be absorbed by some unknown gulf into some unknown abyss.

But if this be too wild and exorbitant to be suspected as having been the poet's meaning; if these mysterious gifts, faculties, and operations, are *not* accompanied with consciousness; who *else* is conscious of them? or how can it be called the child, if it be no part of the child's conscious being? For aught I know, the thinking Spirit within me may be substantially one with the principle of life, and of vital operation. For aught I know, it might be employed as a secondary agent in the marvellous organization and organic movements of my body. But, surely, it would be strange language to say, that *I* construct my *heart!* or that *I* propel the finer influences through my *nerves!* or that *I* compress my brain, and draw the curtains of sleep round my own eyes! SPINOZA and BEHMEN were, on different systems, both Pantheists; and among the ancients there were philosophers, teachers of the EN KAI ΠΑΝ, who not only taught that God was All, but that this All constituted God. Yet not even these would confound the *part, as* a part, with the Whole, *as* the whole. Nay, in no system is the distinction between the individual and God, between the Modification, and the one only Substance, more sharply drawn, than in that of SPINOZA. JACOBI indeed relates of LESSING, that, after a conversation with him at the house of the poet, GLEIM (the Tyrtæus and Anacreon of the German Parnassus) in which conversation L. had avowed privately to Jacobi his reluctance to admit any *personal* existence of the Supreme Being, or the *possibility* of personality except in a finite Intellect, and while they were sitting at table, a shower of rain came on unexpectedly. Gleim expressed his regret at the circumstance, because they had meant to drink their wine in the garden: upon which Lessing in one of his half-earnest half-joking moods, nodded to Jacobi, and said, "It is *I*, perhaps, that am doing *that*," i.e. *raining!* and J. answered, "or perhaps I"; Gleim contented himself with staring at them both, without asking for any explanation.

So with regard to this passage. In what sense can the magnificent attributes, above quoted, be appropriated to a *child*, which would not make them equally suitable to a *bee*, or a *dog*, or a *field of corn:* or even to a ship, or to the wind and waves that propel it? The omnipresent Spirit works equally in them, as in the child; and the child is equally unconscious of it as they. It cannot surely be, that the four lines, immediately following, are to contain the explanation?

> "To whom the grave
> Is but a lonely bed without the sense or sight
> Of day or the warm light,
> A place of thought where we in waiting lie."

Surely, it cannot be that this wonder-rousing apostrophe is but a comment on the little poem, "We are seven?" that the whole meaning of the passage is reducible to the assertion, that a *child*, who by the bye at six years old would have been better instructed in most Christian families, has no other notion of death than that of lying in a dark, cold place? And still, I hope, not as in a *place of thought!* not the frightful notion of lying *awake* in his grave! The analogy between death and sleep is too simple, too natural, to render so horrid a belief possible for children; even had they not been in the habit, as all Christian children are, of hearing the latter term used to express the former. But if the child's belief be only, that "he is not dead, but sleepeth:" wherein does it differ from that of his father and mother, or any other adult and instructed person? To form an idea of a thing's becoming nothing; or of nothing becoming a thing; is impossible to all finite beings alike, of whatever age, and however educated or uneducated. Thus it is with splendid paradoxes in general. If the words are taken in the common sense, they convey an absurdity; and if, in contempt of dictionaries and custom, they are so interpreted as to avoid the absurdity, the meaning dwindles into some bald truism. Thus you must at once understand the words *contrary* to their common import, in order to arrive at any *sense;* and *according* to their common import, if you are to receive from them any feeling of *sublimity* or *admiration*.

Though the instances of this defect in Mr. Wordsworth's poems are so few, that for themselves it would have been scarce just to attract the reader's attention toward them; yet I have dwelt on it, and perhaps the more for this very reason. For being so very few, they cannot sensibly detract from the reputation of an author, who is even characterized by the number of profound truths in his writings, which will stand the severest analysis; and yet few as they are, they are exactly those passages which his *blind* admirers would be most likely, and best able, to imitate. But WORDSWORTH, where he is indeed Wordsworth, may be mimicked by Copyists, he may be plundered by Plagiarists; but he cannot be imitated, except by those who are not born to be imitators. For without his depth of feeling and his imaginative power his *sense* would want its vital warmth and peculiarity; and without his strong sense, his *mysticism* would become *sickly*—mere fog, and dimness!

To these defects which, as appears by the extracts, are only occasional, I may oppose, with far less fear of encountering the dissent of any candid and intelligent reader, the following (for the most part correspondent) excellences. First, an austere purity of language both grammatically and logically; in short a perfect appropriateness of the words to the meaning. Of how high value I deem this, and how particularly estimable I hold the example at the present day, has been already stated: and in part too the reasons on which I ground both the moral and intellectual importance of habituating ourselves to a strict accuracy of expression. It is noticeable, how limited an acquaintance with the masterpieces of art will suffice to form a correct and even a sensitive taste, where none but masterpieces have been seen and admired: while on the other hand, the most correct notions, and the widest acquaintance with the works of excellence of all ages and countries, will not perfectly secure us against the contagious familiarity with the far more numerous offspring of tastelessness or of a perverted taste. If this be the case, as it notoriously is, with the arts of music and painting, much more difficult will it be to avoid the infection of multiplied and daily examples in the practice of an art, which uses words, and words only, as its instruments. In poetry, in which every line, every phrase, may pass the ordeal of deliberation and deliberate choice, it is possible, and barely possible, to attain that ultimatum which I have ventured to propose as the infallible test of a blameless style; its *untranslatableness* in words of the same language without injury to the meaning. Be it observed, however, that I include in the *meaning* of a word not only its correspondent object, but likewise all the associations which it recalls. For language is framed to convey not the object alone, but likewise the character, mood and intentions of the person who is representing it. In poetry it *is* practicable to preserve the diction uncorrupted by the affectations and misappropriations, which promiscuous authorship, and reading not promiscuous only because it is disproportionally most conversant with the compositions of the day, have rendered general. Yet even to the poet, composing in his own province, it is an arduous work: and as the result and pledge of a watchful good sense, of fine and luminous distinction, and of complete self-possession, may justly claim all the honor which belongs to an attainment equally difficult and valuable, and the more valuable for being rare. It is at *all* times the proper food of the understanding; but in an age of corrupt eloquence it is both food and antidote.

In prose I doubt whether it be even possible to preserve our style wholly unalloyed by the vicious phraseology which meets us everywhere, from the sermon to the newspaper, from the harangue of the legislator to the speech from the convivial chair, announcing a *toast* or sentiment. Our chains rattle, even while we are complaining of them. The poems of Boetius rise high in our estimation when we compare them with those of his contemporaries, as Sidonius Apollinarius, &c. They might even be referred to a purer age, but that the prose, in which they are set, as jewels in a crown of lead or iron, betrays the true age of the writer. Much however may be effected by education. I believe not only from grounds of reason, but from having in great measure assured myself of the fact by actual though limited experience, that, to a youth led from his first boyhood to investigate the meaning of every word and the reason of its choice and position, Logic presents itself as an old acquaintance under new names.

On some future occasion, more especially demanding such disquisition, I shall attempt to prove the close connection between veracity and habits of mental accuracy; the beneficial after-effects of verbal precision in the preclusion of fanaticism, which masters the feelings more especially by indistinct watch-words; and to display the advantages which language alone, at least which language with incomparably greater ease and certainty than any other means, presents to the instructor of impressing modes of intellectual energy so constantly, so imperceptibly, and as it were by such elements and atoms, as to secure in due time the formation of a second nature. When we reflect, that the cultivation of the judgement is a positive command of the moral law, since the reason can give the *principle* alone, and the conscience bears witness only to the *motive*, while the application and effects must depend on the judgement: when we consider, that the greater part of our success and comfort in life depends on distinguishing the similar from the same, that which is peculiar in each thing from that which it has in common with others, so as still to select the most probable, instead of the merely possible or positively unfit, we shall learn to value earnestly and with a practical seriousness a mean, already prepared for us by nature and society, of teaching the young mind to think well and wisely by the same unremembered process and with the same never forgotten results, as those by which it is taught to speak and converse. Now how much warmer the interest is, how much more genial the feelings of reality and practicability, and thence how much stronger the impulses to imitation are, which a *contemporary* writer, and especially a contemporary *poet*, excites in youth and commencing manhood, has been treated of in the earlier pages of these sketches. I have only to add, that all the praise which is due to the exertion of such influence for a purpose so important, joined with that which must be claimed for the infrequency of the same excellence in the same perfection, belongs in full right to Mr. Wordsworth. I am far however from denying that we have poets whose *general* style possesses the same excellence, as

Mr. Moore, Lord Byron, Mr. Bowles, and, in all his later and more important works, our laurel-honoring Laureate. But there are none, in whose works I do not appear to myself to find *more* exceptions, than in those of Wordsworth. Quotations or specimens would here be wholly out of place, and must be left for the critic who doubts and would invalidate the justice of this eulogy so applied.

The second characteristic excellence of Mr. W's work is: a correspondent weight and sanity of the Thoughts and Sentiments, won—not from books, but—from the poet's own meditative observation. They are *fresh* and have the dew upon them. His muse, at least when in her strength of wing, and when she hovers aloft in her proper element,

> "Makes audible a linked lay of truth,
> Of truth profound a sweet continuous lay,
> Not learnt, but native, her own natural notes!"
>   S. T. C.

Even throughout his smaller poems there is scarcely one, which is not rendered valuable by some just and original reflection.

See page 25, vol. 2nd.: or the two following passages in one of his humblest compositions.

> "O Reader! had you in your mind
> Such stores as silent thought can bring,
> O gentle Reader! you would find
> A tale in every thing;"

and

> "I've heard of hearts unkind, kind deeds
> With coldness still returning;
> Alas! the gratitude of men
> Has oftener left me mourning"

or in a still higher strain the six beautiful quatrains, page 134.

> "Thus fares it still in our decay:
> And yet the wiser mind
> Mourns less for what age takes away
> Than what it leaves behind.
>
> The Blackbird in the summer trees,
> The Lark upon the hill,
> Let loose their carols when they please,
> Are quiet when they will.
>
> With nature never do *they* wage
> A foolish strife; they see
> A happy youth, and their old age
> Is beautiful and free!
>
> But we are pressed by heavy laws;
> And often, glad no more,
> We wear a face of joy, because
> We have been glad of yore.

If there is one, who need bemoan
His kindred laid in earth,
The household hearts that were his own,
It is the man of mirth.

My days, my Friend, are almost gone,
My life has been approved,
And many love me; but by none
Am I enough beloved."

or the sonnet on Buonaparte, page 202, vol. 2; or finally (for a volume would scarce suffice to exhaust the instances) the last stanza of the poem on the withered Celandine, vol. 2, p. 212.

"To be a prodigal's favorite—then, worse truth,
A miser's pensioner—behold our lot!
O man! that from thy fair and shining youth
Age might but take the things youth needed not."

Both in respect of this and of the former excellence, Mr. Wordsworth strikingly resembles Samuel Daniel, one of the golden writers of our golden Elizabethan age, now most causelessly neglected: Samuel Daniel, whose diction bears no mark of time, no distinction of age, which has been, and as long as our language shall last, will be so far the language of the to-day and for ever, as that it is more intelligible to us, than the transitory fashions of our own particular age. A similar praise is due to his sentiments. No frequency of perusal can deprive them of their freshness. For though they are brought into the full daylight of every reader's comprehension; yet are they drawn up from depths which few in any age are priviledged to visit, into which few in any age have courage or inclination to descend. If Mr. Wordsworth is not equally with Daniel alike intelligible to all readers of average understanding in all passages of his works, the comparative difficulty does not arise from the greater impurity of the ore, but from the nature and uses of the metal. A poem is not necessarily obscure, because it does not aim to be popular. It is enough, if a work be perspicuous to those for whom it is written, and

"Fit audience find, though few."

To the "Ode on the intimation of immortality from recollections of early childhood" the poet might have prefixed the lines which Dante addresses to one of his own Canzoni—

"Canzon, io credo, che saranno radi
  Che tua ragione intendam bene,
  Tanto lor sei faticoso ed alto."

"O lyric song, there will be few, think I,
  Who may thy import understand aright:
  Thou art for *them* so arduous and so high!"

But the ode was intended for such readers only as had been accustomed to watch the flux and reflux of their inmost nature, to venture at times into the twilight realms of consciousness, and to feel a deep interest in modes of inmost being, to which they know that the attributes of time and space are inapplicable and alien, but which yet can not be conveyed save in symbols of time and space. For such readers the sense is sufficiently plain, and they will be as little disposed to charge Mr. Wordsworth with believing the Platonic pre-existence in the ordinary interpretation of the words, as I am to believe, that Plato himself ever meant or taught it.

> Πολλά μοι ὑπ᾽ ἀγκῶ-
> νος ὠκέα βέλη
> ἔνδον ἐντὶ φαρέτρας
> φωνᾶντα συνετοῖσιν· ἐς
> δὲ τὸ πὰν ἑρμηνέων
> χατίζει. σοφὸς ὁ πολ-
> λὰ εἰδὼς φυᾷ.
> μαθόντες δέ, λάβροι
> παγγλωσσίᾳ, κόρακες ὥς,
> ἄκραντα γαρύετον
> Διὸς πρὸς ὄρνιχα θεῖον.

Third (and wherein he soars far above Daniel) the sinewy strength and originality of single lines and paragraphs: the frequent curiosa felicitas of his diction, of which I need not here give specimens, having anticipated them in a preceding page. This beauty, and as eminently characteristic of Wordsworth's poetry, his rudest assailants have felt themselves compelled to acknowledge and admire.

Fourth; the perfect truth of nature in his images and descriptions, as taken immediately from nature, and proving a long and genial intimacy with the very spirit which gives the physiognomic expression to all the works of nature. Like a green field reflected in a calm and perfectly transparent lake, the image is distinguished from the reality only by its greater softness and lustre. Like the moisture or the polish on a pebble, genius neither distorts nor false-colours its objects; but on the contrary brings out many a vein and many a tint, which escapes the eye of common observation, thus raising to the rank of gems what had been often kicked away by the hurrying foot of the traveller on the dusty high road of custom.

Let me refer to the whole description of skating, vol. I., page 42 to 47, especially to the lines

> "So through the darkness and the cold we flew,
> And not a voice was idle: with the din
> Meanwhile the precipices rang aloud;
> The leafless trees and every icy crag
> Tinkled like iron; while the distant hills
> Into the tumult sent an alien sound

Of melancholy, not unnoticed, while the stars
Eastward were sparkling clear, and in the west
The orange sky of evening died away."

Or to the poem on the green linnet, vol. I. page 244. What can be more accurate yet more lovely than the two concluding stanzas?

"Upon yon tuft of hazel trees,
That twinkle to the gusty breeze,
Behold him perched in ecstasies,
     Yet seeming still to hover;
There! where the flutter of his wings
Upon his back and body flings
Shadows and sunny glimmerings,
     That cover him all over.

While thus before my eyes he gleams,
A brother of the leaves he seems;
When in a moment forth he teems
     His little song in gushes:
As if it pleased him to disdain
And mock the form which he did feign,
While he was dancing with the train
     Of leaves among the bushes."

Or the description of the blue-cap, and of the noon-tide silence, page 284; or the poem to the cuckoo, page 299; or, lastly, though I might multiply the references to ten times the number, to the poem, so completely Wordsworth's, commencing

"Three years she grew in sun and shower," &c.

Fifth: a meditative pathos, a union of deep and subtle thought with sensibility; a sympathy with man as man; the sympathy indeed of a contemplator, rather than a fellow-sufferer or co-mate, (spectator, haud particeps) but of a contemplator, from whose view no difference of rank conceals the sameness of the nature; no injuries of wind or weather, or toil, or even of ignorance, wholly disguise the human face divine. The superscription and the image of the Creator still remain legible to *him* under the dark lines, with which guilt or calamity had cancelled or cross-barred it. Here the man and the poet lose and find themselves in each other, the one as glorified, the latter as substantiated. In this mild and philosophic pathos, Wordsworth appears to me without a compeer. Such he *is:* so he *writes.* See vol. I. page 134 to 136, or that most affecting composition, the "Affliction of Margaret —— of ——," page 165 to 168, which no mother, and, if I may judge by my own experience, no parent can read without a tear. Or turn to the genuine lyric, in the former edition, entitled "The Mad Mother," page 174 to 178, of which I cannot refrain from quoting two of the stanzas, both of them for their pathos, and the former for the fine transition in the two concluding lines of the stanza, so expressive of that deranged state, in which from the increased sensibility the sufferer's attention is abruptly drawn off by every trifle, and in the same instant plucked back again by the one despotic thought, bringing home with it, by the blending, *fusing* power of Imagination and Passion, the alien object to which it had been so abruptly diverted, no longer an alien but an ally and an inmate.

> "Suck, little babe, oh suck again!
> It cools my blood; it cools my brain:
> Thy lips, I feel them, baby! they
> Draw from my heart the pain away.
> Oh! press me with thy little hand;
> It loosens something at my chest:
> About that tight and deadly band
> I feel thy little fingers prest.
> The breeze I see is in the tree!
> It comes to cool my babe and me."

> "Thy father cares not for my breast,
> 'Tis thine, sweet baby, there to rest,
> 'Tis all thine own!—and, if its hue
> Be changed, that was so fair to view,
> 'Tis fair enough for thee, my dove!
> My beauty, little child, is flown,
> But thou wilt live with me in love;
> And what if my poor cheek be brown?
> 'Tis well for me, thou canst not see
> How pale and wan it else would be."

Last, and pre-eminently, I challenge for this poet the gift of IMAGI-NATION in the highest and strictest sense of the word. In the play of *Fancy,* Wordsworth, to my feelings, is not always graceful, and sometimes *recondite.* The *likeness* is occasionally too strange, or demands too peculiar a point of view, or is such as appears the creature of pre-determined research, rather than spontaneous presentation. Indeed his fancy seldom displays itself, as mere and unmodified fancy. But in imaginative power, he stands nearest of all modern writers to Shakespeare and Milton; and yet in a kind perfectly unborrowed and his own. To employ his own words, which are at once an instance and an illustration, he does indeed to all thoughts and to all objects

> "_____add the gleam,
> The light that never was, on sea or land,
> The consecration, and the poet's dream."

I shall select a few examples as most obviously manifesting this faculty; but if I should ever be fortunate enough to render my analysis of imagination, its origin and characters, thoroughly intelligible to the reader, he will scarcely open on a page of this poet's works without recognising, more or less, the presence and the influences of this faculty. From the poem on the Yew Trees, vol. I. page 303, 304.

> "But worthier still of note
> Are those fraternal four of Borrowdale,
> Joined in one solemn and capacious grove:
> Huge trunks!—and each particular trunk a growth
> Of intertwisted fibres serpentine
> Up-coiling, and inveterately convolved,—
> Not uninformed with phantasy, and looks
> That threaten the profane;—a pillared shade,
> Upon whose grassless floor of red-brown hue,
> By sheddings from the pinal umbrage tinged
> Perennially—beneath whose sable roof
> Of boughs, as if for festal purpose decked
> With unrejoicing berries, ghostly shapes
> May meet at noontide—FEAR and trembling HOPE,
> SILENCE and FORESIGHT—DEATH, the skeleton,
> And TIME, the shadow—there to celebrate,
> As in a natural temple scattered o'er
> With altars undisturbed of mossy stone,
> United worship; or in mute repose
> To lie, and listen to the mountain flood
> Murmuring from Glaramara's inmost caves."

The effect of the old man's figure in the poem of Resignation and Independence, vol. II. page 33.

> "While he was talking thus, the lonely place,
> The old man's shape, and speech, all troubled me:
> In my mind's eye I seemed to see him pace
> About the weary moors continually,
> Wandering about alone and silently."

Or the 8th, 9th, 19th, 26th, 31st, and 33d, in the collection of miscellaneous sonnets—the sonnet on the subjugation of Switzerland, page 210, or the last ode, from which I especially select the two following stanzas or paragraphs, page 349 to 350.

> "Our birth is but a sleep and a forgetting;
> The soul that rises with us, our life's star,
> Hath had elsewhere its setting,
>   And cometh from afar.
> Not in entire forgetfulness,
> And not in utter nakedness,
> But trailing clouds of glory do we come
> From God, who is our home:
> Heaven lies about us in our infancy!
> Shades of the prison-house begin to close
>   Upon the growing boy;

But he beholds the light, and whence it flows,
    He sees it in his joy!
The youth who daily further from the East
Must travel, still is nature's priest,
    And by the vision splendid
    Is on his way attended;
At length the man perceives it die away,
And fade into the light of common day."

And page 352 to 354 of the same ode.

"O joy that in our embers
Is something that doth live,
That nature yet remembers
What was so fugitive!
The thought of our past years in me doth breed
Perpetual benedictions: not indeed
For that which is most worthy to be blest;
Delight and liberty, the simple creed
Of childhood, whether busy or at rest,
With new-fledged hope still fluttering in his breast:—
Not for these I raise
The song of thanks and praise;
But for those obstinate questionings
Of sense and outward things,
Fallings from us, vanishings;
Blank misgivings of a creature
Moving about in worlds not realized,
High instincts, before which our mortal nature
Did tremble like a guilty thing surprised!
But for those first affections,
Those shadowy recollections,
Which, be they what they may,
Are yet the fountain light of all our day,
Are yet a master light of all our seeing;
Uphold us—cherish—and have power to make
Our noisy years seem moments in the being
Of the eternal silence; truths that wake
    To perish never:
Which neither listlessness, nor mad endeavour,
Nor man nor boy,
Nor all that is at enmity with joy,
Can utterly abolish or destroy!
Hence, in a season of calm weather,
Though inland far we be,
Our souls have sight of that immortal sea
Which brought us hither;
Can in a moment travel thither—
And see the children sport upon the shore,
And hear the mighty waters rolling evermore."

And since it would be unfair to conclude with an extract, which, though highly characteristic, must yet, from the nature of the thoughts and the subject, be interesting, or perhaps intelligible, to but a limited number of readers; I will add, from the poet's last published work, a passage equally Wordsworthian; of the beauty of which, and of the imaginative power displayed therein, there can be but one opinion, and one feeling. See "White Doe," page 5.

"Fast the church-yard fills;—anon
    Look again and they are gone;
    The cluster round the porch, and the folk
    Who sate in the shade of the prior's oak!
    And scarcely have they disappear'd,
    Ere the prelusive hymn is heard;—
    With one consent the people rejoice,
    Filling the church with a lofty voice!
    They sing a service which they feel,
    For 'tis the sun-rise of their zeal;
    And faith and hope are in their prime
    In great Eliza's golden time.

"A moment ends the fervent din,
    And all is hushed, without and within;
    For though the priest, more tranquilly,
    Recites the holy liturgy,
    The only voice which you can hear
    Is the river murmuring near.
    When soft!—the dusky trees between,
    And down the path through the open green,
    Where is no living thing to be seen;
    And through yon gateway, where is found,
    Beneath the arch with ivy bound,
    Free entrance to the church-yard ground;
    And right across the verdant sod,
    Towards the very house of God;
    Comes gliding in with lovely gleam,
    Comes gliding in serene and slow,
    Soft and silent as a dream,
    A solitary doe!
    White she is as lily of June,
    And beauteous as the silver moon
    When out of sight the clouds are driven
    And she is left alone in heaven!
    Or like a ship some gentle day
    In sunshine sailing far away—
    A glittering ship, that hath the plain
    Of ocean for her own domain.

*   *   *   *   *   *

"What harmonious pensive changes
    Wait upon her as she ranges

Round and through this pile of state
Overthrown and desolate!
Now a step or two her way
Is through space of open day,
Where the enamoured sunny light
Brightens her that was so bright;
Now doth a delicate shadow fall,
Falls upon her like a breath,
From some lofty arch or wall,
As she passes underneath."

The following analogy will, I am apprehensive, appear dim and fantastic, but in reading Bartram's Travels I could not help transcribing the following lines as a sort of allegory, or connected simile and metaphor of Wordsworth's intellect and genius.—"The soil is a deep, rich, dark mould, on a deep stratum of tenacious clay; and that on a foundation of rocks, which often break through both strata, lifting their back above the surface. The trees which chiefly grow here are the gigantic black oak; magnolia magni-floria; fraximus excelsior; platane; and a few stately tulip trees." What Mr. Wordsworth *will* produce, it is not for me to prophecy: but I could pronounce with the liveliest convictions what he is capable of producing. It is the First Genuine Philosophic Poem.

The preceding criticism will not, I am aware, avail to overcome the prejudices of those, who have made it a business to attack and ridicule Mr. Wordsworth's compositions.

Truth and prudence might be imaged as concentric circles. The poet may perhaps have passed beyond the latter, but he has confined himself far within the bounds of the former, in designating these critics, as too petulant to be passive to a genuine poet, and too feeble to grapple with him;—"men of palsied imaginations, in whose minds all healthy action is languid;—who, therefore, feed as the many direct them, or with the many are greedy after vicious provocatives."

Let not Mr. Wordsworth be charged with having expressed himself too indignantly, till the wantonness and the systematic and malignant perseverance of the aggressions have been taken into fair consideration. I myself heard the commander in chief of this unmanly warfare make a boast of his private admiration of Wordsworth's genius. I have heard him declare, that whoever came into his room would probably find the Lyrical Ballads lying open on his table, and that (speaking exclusively of those written by Mr. Wordsworth himself) he could nearly repeat the whole of them by heart. *But* a Review, in order to be a saleable article, must be *personal, sharp,* and *pointed:* and, *since then,* the poet has made himself, and with himself all who were, or were supposed to be, his friends and admirers, the object of the critic's revenge—how? by having spoken of a work so conducted in the terms which it deserved! I once heard a clergyman in boots and buckskin avow, that he would cheat his own father *in a horse.* A moral system of a similar nature seems to have been adopted by too many anonymous critics. As we used to say at school, in reviewing they *make* being rogues: and he, who complains, is to be laughed at for his ignorance of *the game.* With the pen out of their hand they are *honorable men.* They exert indeed power (which is to that of the injured party who should attempt to expose their glaring perversions and misstatements, as twenty to one) to write down, and (where the author's circumstances permit) to *impoverish* the man, whose learning and genius they themselves in private have repeatedly admitted. They knowingly strive to make it impossible for the man even to publish[1] any future work without exposing himself to all the wretchedness of debt and embarrassment. But this is all *in their vocation:* and, bating what they do in their *vocation, "who can say that black is the white of their eye?"*

So much for the detractors from Wordsworth's merits. On the other hand, much as I might wish for their fuller sympathy, I dare not flatter myself, that the freedom with which I have declared my opinions concerning both his theory and his defects, most of which are more or less connected with his theory, either as cause or effect, will be satisfactory or pleasing to *all* the poet's admirers and advocates. More indiscriminate than mine their admiration may be: deeper and more sincere it can not be. But I have advanced no opinion either for praise or censure, other than as texts introductory to the reasons which compel me to form it. Above all, I was fully convinced that such a criticism was not only wanted; but that, if executed with adequate ability, it must conduce, in no mean degree, to Mr. Wordsworth's *reputation.* His *fame* belongs to another age, and can neither be accelerated nor retarded. How small the proportion of the defects are to the beauties, I have repeatedly declared; and that no one of them originates in deficiency of poetic genius. Had they been more and greater, I should still, as a friend to his literary character in the present age, consider an analytic display of them as *pure gain;* if only it removed, as surely to all reflecting minds even the foregoing analysis must have removed, the strange mistake, so slightly grounded, yet so widely and industriously propagated, of Mr. Wordsworth's turn for SIMPLICITY! I am not half so much irritated by hearing his enemies abuse him for vulgarity of style, subject, and conception; as I am disgusted with the gilded side of the same meaning, as displayed by some affected admirers, with whom he is, forsooth, a *sweet, simple poet!* and *so* natural, that little master Charles and his younger sister are *so* charmed with them, that they play at "Goody Blake," or at "Johnny and Betty Foy!"

---

1. Not many months ago an eminent bookseller was asked what he thought of——? The answer was: "I have heard his powers very highly spoken of by some of our first-rate men; but I would not have a work of his if any one would give it me: for he is spoken but slightly of, or not at all, in the Quarterly Review: and the Edinburgh, you know, is decided to cut him up!"

Categories of criticism

M. H. Abrams

ORIENTATION OF CRITICAL THEORIES

> BOSWELL. 'Then, Sir, what is poetry?'
> JOHNSON. 'Why, Sir, it is much easier to say what it is not.
> We all *know* what light is; but it is not easy to *tell* what it is.'

> It is the mark of an educated man to look for precision in
> each class of things just so far as the nature of the subject
> admits.
>
> ARISTOTLE, *Nicomachean Ethics*

To pose and answer aesthetic questions in terms of the relation of art to the artist, rather than to external nature, or to the audience, or to the internal requirements of the work itself, was the characteristic tendency of modern criticism up to a few decades ago, and it continues to be the propensity of a great many—perhaps the majority—of critics today. This point of view is very young measured against the twenty-five-hundred-year history of the Western theory of art, for its emergence as a comprehensive approach to art, shared by a large number of critics, dates back not much more than a century and a half. The intention of this book is to chronicle the evolution and (in the early nineteenth century) the triumph, in its diverse forms, of this radical shift to the artist in the alignment of aesthetic thinking, and to describe the principal alternate theories against which this approach had to compete. In particular, I shall be concerned with the momentous consequences of these new bearings in criticism for the identification, the analysis, the evaluation, and the writing of poetry.

The field of aesthetics presents an especially difficult problem to the historian. Recent theorists of art have been quick to profess that much, if not all, that has been said by their predecessors is wavering, chaotic, phantasmal. 'What has gone by the name of the philosophy of art' seemed to Santayana 'sheer verbiage.' D. W. Prall, who himself wrote two excellent books on the subject, commented that traditional aesthetics 'is in fact only a pseudo-science or pseudo-philosophy.'

Its subject-matter is such wavering and deceptive stuff as dreams are made of; its method is neither logical nor scientific, nor quite whole-heartedly and empirically matter of fact . . . without application in practice to test it and without an orthodox terminology to make it into an honest superstition or a thoroughgoing, soul satisfying cult. It is neither useful to creative artists nor a help to amateurs in appreciation.[1]

And I. A. Richards, in his *Principles of Literary Criticism,* labeled his first chapter 'The Chaos of Critical Theories,' and justified the pejorative attribute by quoting, as 'the apices of critical theory,' more than a score of isolated and violently discrepant utterances about art, from Aristotle to the present time.[2] With the optimism of his youth, Richards himself went on to attempt a solid grounding of literary evaluation in the science of psychology.

It is true that the course of aesthetic theory displays its full measure of the rhetoric and logomachy which seem an inseparable part of man's discourse about all things that really matter. But a good deal of our impatience with the diversity and seeming chaos in philosophies of art is rooted in a demand from criticism for something it cannot do, at the cost of overlooking many of its genuine powers. We still need to face up to the full consequences of the realization that criticism is not a physical, nor even a psychological, science. By setting out from and terminating in an appeal to the facts, any good aesthetic theory is, indeed, empirical in method. Its aim, however, is not to establish correlations between facts which will enable us to predict the future by reference to the past, but to establish principles enabling us to justify, order, and clarify our interpretation and appraisal of the aesthetic facts themselves. And as we shall see, these facts turn out to have the curious and scientifically reprehensible property of being conspicuously altered by the nature of the very principles which appeal to them for their support. Because many critical statements of fact are thus partially relative to the perspective of the theory within which they occur, they are not 'true,' in the strict scientific sense that they approach the ideal of being verifiable by any intelligent human being, no matter what his point of view. Any hope, therefore, for the kind of basic agreement in criticism that we have learned to expect in the exact sciences is doomed to disappointment.

A good critical theory, nevertheless, has its own kind of validity. The criterion is not the scientific verifiability of its single propositions, but the scope, precision, and coherence of the insights that it yields into the properties of single works of art and the adequacy with which it accounts for diverse kinds of art. Such a criterion will, of course, justify not one, but a number of valid theories, all in their several ways self-consistent, applicable, and relatively adequate to the range of aesthetic

1. Foreword to *Philosophies of Beauty,* ed. E. F. Carritt (Oxford, 1931), p. ix.
2. (5th ed; London, 1934), pp. 6-7. Richards' later change of emphasis is indicated by his recent statement that ' "Semantics" which began by finding nonsense everywhere may well end up as a technique for widening understanding' (*Modern Language Notes,* LX, 1945, p. 350).

phenomena; but this diversity is not to be deplored. One lesson we gain from a survey of the history of criticism, in fact, is the great debt we owe to the variety of the criticism of the past. Contrary to Prall's pessimistic appraisal, these theories have not been futile, but as working conceptions of the matter, end, and ordonnance of art, have been greatly effective in shaping the activities of creative artists. Even an aesthetic philosophy so abstract and seemingly academic as that of Kant can be shown to have modified the work of poets. In modern times, new departures in literature almost invariably have been accompanied by novel critical pronouncements, whose very inadequacies sometimes help to form the characteristic qualities of the correlated literary achievements, so that if our critics had not disagreed so violently, our artistic inheritance would doubtless have been less rich and various. Also, the very fact that any well-grounded critical theory in some degree alters the aesthetic perceptions it purports to discover is a source of its value to the amateur of art, for it may open his senses to aspects of a work which other theories, with a different focus and different categories of discrimination, have on principle overlooked, underestimated, or obscured.

The diversity of aesthetic theories, however, makes the task of the historian a very difficult one. It is not only that answers to such questions as 'What is art?' or 'What is poetry?' disagree. The fact is that many theories of art cannot readily be compared at all, because they lack a common ground on which to meet and clash. They seem incommensurable because stated in diverse terms, or in identical terms with diverse signification, or because they are an integral part of larger systems of thought which differ in assumptions and procedure. As a result it is hard to find where they agree, where disagree, or even, what the points at issue are.

Our first need, then, is to find a frame of reference simple enough to be readily manageable, yet flexible enough so that, without undue violence to any one set of statements about art, it will translate as many sets as possible onto a single plane of discourse. Most writers bold enough to undertake the history of aesthetic theory have achieved this end by silently translating the basic terms of all theories into their own favorite philosophical vocabulary, but this procedure unduly distorts its subject matter, and merely multiplies the complications to be unraveled. The more promising method is to adopt an analytic scheme which avoids imposing its own philosophy, by utilizing those key distinctions which are already common to the largest possible number of the theories to be compared, and then to apply the scheme warily, in constant readiness to introduce such further distinctions as seem to be needed for the purpose in hand.

Some Co-ordinates of Art Criticism

Four elements in the total situation of a work of art are discriminated and made salient, by one or another synonym, in almost all theories which aim to be comprehensive. First, there is the *work,* the artistic product itself. And since this is a human product, an artifact, the second common element is the artificer, the *artist*. Third, the work is taken to have a subject which, directly or deviously, is derived from existing things—to be about, or signify, or reflect something which either is, or bears some relation to, an objective state of affairs. This third element, whether held to consist of people and actions, ideas and feelings, material things and events, or super-sensible essences, has frequently been denoted by that word-of-all-work, 'nature'; but let us use the more neutral and comprehensive term, *universe*, instead. For the final element we have the *audience:* the listeners, spectators, or readers to whom the work is addressed, or to whose attention, at any rate, it becomes available.

On this framework of artist, work, universe, and audience I wish to spread out various theories for comparison. To emphasize the artificiality of the device, and at the same time make it easier to visualize the analyses, let us arrange the four co-ordinates in a convenient pattern. A triangle will do, with the work of art, the thing to be explained, in the center.

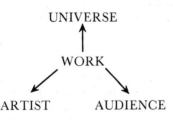

Although any reasonably adequate theory takes some account of all four elements, almost all theories, as we shall see, exhibit a discernible orientation toward one only. That is, a critic tends to derive from one of these terms his principal categories for defining, classifying, and analyzing a work of art, as well as the major criteria by which he judges its value. Application of this analytic scheme, therefore, will sort attempts to explain the nature and worth of a work of art into four broad classes. Three will explain the work of art principally by relating it to another thing: the universe, the audience, or the artist. The fourth will explain the work by considering it in isolation, as an autonomous whole, whose significance and value are determined without any reference beyond itself.

To find the major orientation of a critical theory, however, is only the beginning of an adequate analysis. For one thing, these four co-ordinates are not constants, but variables; they differ in significance according to the theory in which they occur. Take what I have called the *universe* as an example. In any one theory, the aspects of nature which an artist is said to imitate, or is exhorted to imitate, may be either particulars or types, and they may be only the beautiful or the moral aspects of the world, or else any aspect without discrimination. It may be maintained that the artist's world is that of imaginative intuition, or of common sense, or of natural science; and this world may be held to include, or not to include, gods, witches, chimeras, and Platonic Ideas. Consequently, theories which agree in assigning to the represented universe the primary control over a legitimate work of art may vary from recommending the most uncompromising realism to the most remote idealism. Each of our other terms, as we shall see, also varies, both in meaning and functioning, according to the critical theory in which it occurs, the method of reasoning which the theorist characteristically uses, and the explicit or implicit 'world-view' of which these theories are an integral part.

It would be possible, of course, to devise more complex methods of analysis which, even in a preliminary classification, would make more subtle distinctions.[3] By multiplying differentiae, however, we sharpen our capacity to discriminate at the expense both of easy manageability and the ability to make broad initial generalizations. For our historical purpose, the scheme I have proposed has this important virtue, that it will enable us to bring out the one essential attribute which most early nineteenth-century theories had in common: the persistent recourse to the poet to explain the nature and criteria of poetry. Historians have recently been instructed to speak only of 'romanticisms,' in the plural, but from our point of vantage there turns out to be one distinctively romantic criticism, although this remains a unity amid variety.

Mimetic Theories

The mimetic orientation—the explanation of art as essentially an imitation of aspects of the universe—was probably the most primitive aesthetic theory, but mimesis is no simple concept by the time it makes its first recorded appearance in the dialogues of Plato. The arts of painting, poetry, music, dancing, and sculpture, Socrates says, are all imitations.[4] 'Imitation' is a relational term, signifying two items and some correspondence between them. But although in many later mimetic theories everything is comprehended in two categories, the imitable and the imitation, the philosopher in the Platonic dialogues characteristically operates with three categories. The first category is that of the eternal and unchanging Ideas; the second, reflecting this, is the world of sense, natural or artificial; and the third category, in turn reflecting the second, comprises such things as shadows, images in water and mirrors, and the fine arts.

Around this three-stage regress—complicated still further by various supplementary distinctions, as well as by his exploitation of the polysemism of his key terms—Plato weaves his dazzling dialectic.[5] But from the shifting arguments emerges a recurrent pattern, exemplified in the famous passage in the tenth book of the *Republic*. In discussing the

3. For a subtle and elaborate analysis of diverse critical theories, see Richard McKeon, 'Philosophic Bases of Art and Criticism,' *Critics and Criticism, Ancient and Modern,* ed. R. S. Crane (The University of Chicago Press, Chicago, 1952).

4. *Republic* (trans. Jowett) x. 596-7; *Laws* ii. 667-8, vii. 814-16.

5. See Richard McKeon, 'Literary Criticism and the Concept of Imitation in Antiquity,' *Critics and Criticism,* ed. Crane, pp. 147-9. The article exhibits those multiple shifts in Plato's use of the term 'imitation' which have trapped many later commentators as successfully as they once did the rash spirits who engaged Socrates in controversy.

nature of art, Socrates makes the point that there are three beds: the Idea which 'is the essence of the bed' and is made by God, the bed made by the carpenter, and the bed found in a painting. How shall we describe the painter of this third bed?

> I think, he said, that we may fairly designate him as the imitator of that which the others make.
>
> Good, I said; then you call him who is third in the descent from nature an imitator?
>
> Certainly, he said.
>
> And the tragic poet is an imitator, and therefore, like all other imitators, he is thrice removed from the king and from the truth?
>
> That appears to be so.[6]

From the initial position that art imitates the world of appearance and not of Essence, it follows that works of art have a lowly status in the order of existing things. Furthermore, since the realm of Ideas is the ultimate locus not only of reality but of value, the determination that art is at second remove from the truth automatically establishes its equal remoteness from the beautiful and good. Despite the elaborate dialectic—or more accurately, by means of it—Plato's remains a philosophy of a single standard; for all things, including art, are ultimately judged by the one criterion of their relation to the same Ideas. On these grounds, the poet is inescapably the competitor of the artisan, the lawmaker, and the moralist; indeed, any one of these can be regarded as himself the truer poet, successfully achieving that imitation of the Ideas which the traditional poet attempts under conditions dooming him to failure. Thus the lawmaker is able to reply to the poets seeking admission to his city, 'Best of strangers—

> we also according to our ability are tragic poets, and our tragedy is the best and noblest; for our whole state is an imitation of the best and noblest life, which we affirm to be indeed the very truth of tragedy. You are poets and we are poets . . . rivals and antagonists in the noblest of dramas. . .[7]

And the poor opinion of ordinary poetry to which we are committed on the basis of its mimetic character, is merely confirmed when Plato points out that its effects on its auditors are bad because it represents appearance rather than truth, and nourishes their feelings rather than their reason; or by demonstrating that the poet in composing (as Socrates jockeys poor obtuse Ion into admitting) cannot depend on his art and knowledge, but must wait upon the divine afflatus and the loss of his right mind.[8]

The Socratic dialogues, then, contain no aesthetics proper, for neither the structure of Plato's cosmos nor the pattern of his dialectic permits

6. *Republic* x. 597.
7. *Laws* vii. 817.
8. *Republic* x. 603-5; *Ion* 535-6; cf. *Apology* 22.

us to consider poetry as poetry—as a special kind of product having its own criteria and reason for being. In the dialogues there is only one direction possible, and one issue, that is, the perfecting of the social state and the state of man; so that the question of art can never be separated from questions of truth, justice, and virtue. 'For great is the issue at stake,' Socrates says in concluding his discussion of poetry in the *Republic*, 'greater than appears, whether a man is to be good or bad.'[9]

Aristotle in the *Poetics* also defines poetry as imitation. 'Epic poetry and Tragedy, as also Comedy, Dithyrambic poetry, and most flute-playing and lyre-playing, are all, viewed as a whole, modes of imitation'; and 'the objects the imitator represents are actions. . .'[10] But the difference between the way the term 'imitation' functions in Aristotle and in Plato distinguishes radically their consideration of art. In the *Poetics*, as in the Platonic dialogues, the term implies that a work of art is constructed according to prior models in the nature of things, but since Aristotle has shorn away the other world of criterion-Ideas, there is no longer anything invidious in that fact. Imitation is also made a term specific to the arts, distinguishing these from everything else in the universe, and thereby freeing them from rivalry with other human activities. Furthermore, in his analysis of the fine arts, Aristotle at once introduces supplementary distinctions according to the objects imitated, the medium of imitation, and the manner—dramatic, narrative, or mixed, for example—in which the imitation is accomplished. By successive exploitation of these distinctions in object, means, and manner, he is able first to distinguish poetry from other kinds of art, and then to differentiate the various poetic genres, such as epic and drama, tragedy and comedy. When he focuses on the genre of tragedy, the same analytic instrument is applied to the discrimination of the parts constituting the individual whole: plot, character, thought, and so on. Aristotle's criticism, therefore, is not only criticism of art as art, independent of statesmanship, being, and morality, but also of poetry as poetry, and of each kind of poem by the criteria appropriate to its particular nature. As a result of this procedure, Aristotle bequeathed an arsenal of instruments for technical analysis of poetic forms and their elements which have proved indispensable to critics ever since, however diverse the uses to which these instruments have been put.

A salient quality of the *Poetics* is the way it considers a work of art in various of its external relations, affording each its due function as one of the 'causes' of the work. This procedure results in a scope and flexibility that makes the treatise resist a ready classification into any one kind of orientation. Tragedy cannot be fully defined, for example, nor can the total determinants of its construction be understood, without taking into account its proper effect on the audience: the achievement of the specifically 'tragic pleasure,' which is 'that of pity and fear.'[11] It is apparent, however, that the mimetic concept—the reference of a work to the subject matter which it imitates—is primary in

9. *Republic* x. 608.
10. *Poetics* (trans. Ingram Bywater) 1. 1447^a, 1448^a. On imitation in Aristotle's criticism see McKeon, 'The Concept of Imitation,' op. cit. pp. 160-68.
11. *Poetics* 6. 1449^b, 14. 1453^b.

Aristotle's critical system, even if it is *primus inter pares*. Their character as an imitation of human actions is what defines the arts in general, and the kind of action imitated serves as one important differentia of an artistic species. The historical genesis of art is traced to the natural human instinct for imitating, and to the natural tendency to find pleasure in seeing imitations. Even the unity essential to any work of art is mimetically grounded, since 'one imitation is always of one thing,' and in poetry 'the story, as an imitation of action, must represent one action, a complete whole. . .'[12] And the 'form' of a work, the presiding principle determining the choice and order and internal adjustments of all the parts, is derived from the form of the object that is imitated. It is the fable or plot 'that is the end and purpose of tragedy,' its 'life and soul, so to speak,' and this because

> tragedy is essentially an imitation not of persons but of action and life . . . We maintain that Tragedy is primarily an imitation of action, and that it is mainly for the sake of the action that it imitates the personal agents.[13]

If we refer again to our analytic diagram, one other general aspect of the *Poetics* presses on our attention, particularly when we have the distinctive orientation of romantic criticism in mind. While Aristotle makes a distribution (though an unequal one) among the objects imitated, the necessary emotional effects on an audience, and the internal demands of the product itself, as determinants of this or that aspect of a poem, he does not assign a determinative function to the poet himself. The poet is the indispensable efficient cause, the agent who, by his skill, extracts the form from natural things and imposes it upon an artificial medium; but his personal faculties, feelings, or desires are not called on to explain the subject matter or form of a poem. In the *Poetics*, the poet is invoked only to explain the historical divergence of comic from serious forms, and to be advised of certain aids toward the construction of plot and the choice of diction.[14] In Plato, the poet is considered from the point of view of politics, not art. When the poets make a personal appearance all but the major ones are dismissed, with extravagant courtesy, from the ideal Republic; upon later application, a somewhat greater number are admitted to the second-best state of the *Laws*, but with a radically diminished repertory.[15]

'Imitation' continued to be a prominent item in the critical vocabulary for a long time after Aristotle—all the way through the eighteenth century, in fact. The systematic importance given to the term differed greatly from critic to critic; those objects in the universe that art imitates, or should imitate, were variously conceived as either actual or in some sense ideal; and from the first, there was a tendency to replace Aristotle's 'action' as the principal object of imitation with such ele-

12. Ibid. 8. 1451ᵃ.
13. Ibid. 6. 1450ᵃ-1450ᵇ.
14. Ibid. 4. 1448ᵇ, 17. 1455ᵃ-1455ᵇ.
15. *Republic* iii. 398, x. 606-8; *Laws* vii. 817.

ments as human character, or thought, or even inanimate things. But particularly after the recovery of the *Poetics* and the great burst of aesthetic theory in sixteenth-century Italy, whenever a critic was moved to get down to fundamentals and frame a comprehensive definition of art, the predicate usually included the word 'imitation,' or else one of those parallel terms which, whatever differences they might imply, all faced in the same direction: 'reflection,' 'representation,' 'counterfeiting,' 'feigning,' 'copy,' or 'image.'

Through most of the eighteenth century, the tenet that art is an imitation seemed almost too obvious to need iteration or proof. As Richard Hurd said in his 'Discourse on Poetical Imitation,' published in 1751, 'All *Poetry*, to speak with Aristotle and the Greek critics (if for so plain a point authorities be thought wanting) is, properly, *imitation*. It is, indeed, the noblest and most extensive of the mimetic arts; having all creation for its object, and ranging the entire circuit of universal being.'[16] Even the reputedly radical proponents of 'original genius' in the second half of the century commonly found that a work of genius was no less an imitation for being an original. '*Imitations*,' Young wrote in his *Conjectures on Original Composition*, 'are of two kinds: one of nature, one of authors. The first we call *Originals*. . .' The original genius in fact turns out to be a kind of scientific investigator: 'The wide field of nature lies open before it, where it may range unconfined, make what discoveries it can . . . as far as visible nature extends. . .'[17] Later the Reverend J. Moir, an extremist in his demand for originality in poetry, conceived genius to lie in the ability to discover 'a thousand new variations, distinctions, and resemblances' in the 'familiar phenomena of nature,' and declared that original genius always gives 'the identical impression it receives.'[18] In this identification of the poet's task as novelty of discovery and particularity of description we have moved a long way from Aristotle's conception of mimesis, except in this respect, that criticism still looks to one or another aspect of the given world for the essential source and subject matter of poetry.

Instead of heaping up quotations, it will be better to cite a few eighteenth-century discussions of imitation that are of special interest. My first example is the French critic, Charles Batteux, whose *Les Beaux Arts réduits à un même principe* (1747) found some favor in England and had immense influence in Germany, as well as in his native country. The rules of art, Batteux thought, which are now so numerous, must surely be reducible to a single principle. 'Let us,' he cries, 'imitate the

16. *The Works of Richard Hurd* (London, 1811), II, 111-12.
17. Edward Young, *Conjectures on Original Composition*, ed. Edith Morley (Manchester, 1918), pp. 6, 18. See also William Duff, *Essay on Original Genius* (London, 1767), p. 192n. John Ogilvie reconciles creative genius and original invention with 'the great principle of *poetic imitation*' (*Philosophical and Critical Observations on the Nature, Characters, and Various Species of Composition*, London, 1774, I, 105-7). Joseph Warton, familiar proponent of a 'boundless imagination,' enthusiasm, and 'the romantic, the wonderful, and the wild,' still agrees with Richard Hurd that poetry is 'an art, whose essence is imitation,' and whose objects are 'material or animate, extraneous or internal' (*Essay on the Writings and Genius of Pope*, London, 1756, I, 89-90). Cf. Robert Wood, *Essay on the Original Genius and Writings of Homer* (1769), London, 1824, pp. 6-7, 178.
18. 'Originality,' *Gleanings* (London, 1785), I, 107, 109.

true physicists, who assemble experiments and then on these found a system which reduces them to a principle.'

That Batteux proposes for his procedure 'to begin with a clear and distinct idea'—a principle 'simple enough to be grasped instantly, and extensive enough to absorb all the little detailed rules'—is sufficient clue that he will follow in method not Newton, the physicist, but rather Euclid and Descartes. In pursuance of his clear and distinct idea, he burrowed industriously through the standard French critics until, he says ingenuously, 'it occurred to me to open Aristotle, whose *Poetics* I had heard praised.' Then came the revelation; all details fell neatly into place. The source of illumination?—none other than 'the principle of imitation which the Greek philosopher established for the fine arts.'[19] This imitation, however, is not of crude everyday reality, but of 'la belle nature'; that is, 'le vrai-semblable,' formed by assembling traits taken from individual things to compose a model possessing 'all the perfections it is able to receive.'[20] From this principle Batteux goes on, lengthily and with great show of rigor, to extract one by one the rules of taste—both the general rules for poetry and painting and the detailed rules for the special genres. For

> the majority of known rules refer back to imitation, and form a sort of chain, by which the mind seizes at the same instant consequences and principle, as a whole perfectly joined, in which all the parts are mutually sustained.[21]

Next to this classic instance of a priori and deductive aesthetics I shall set a German document, Lessing's *Laokoon*, published in 1776. Lessing undertook to undo the confusion in theory and practice between poetry and the graphic and plastic arts which, he believed, resulted from an uninquisitive acceptance of Simonides' maxim that 'painting is dumb poetry and poetry a speaking painting.' His own procedure, he promises, will be continually to test abstract theory against 'the individual instance.' Repeatedly he derides German critics for their reliance on deduction. 'We Germans have no lack of systematic books. We are the most expert of any nation in the world at deducing, from a few given verbal explanations, and in the most beautiful order, anything whatever that we wish.' 'How many things would prove incontestable in theory, had not genius succeeded in proving the contrary in fact!'[22] Lessing's intention, then, is to establish aesthetic principles by an inductive logic which is deliberately opposed to the procedure of Batteux. Nevertheless, like Batteux, Lessing concludes that poetry, no less than painting, is imitation. The diversity between these arts follows from their difference in medium, which imposes necessary differences in the objects each is competent to imitate. But

19. Charles Batteux, *Les Beaux Arts réduits à un même principe* (Paris, 1747), pp. i-viii.
20. Ibid. pp. 9–27.
21. Ibid. p. xiii. For the important place of imitation in earlier French neo-classic theories, see René Bray, *La Formation de la doctrine classique en France* (Lausanne, 1931), pp. 140ff.
22. Lessing, *Laokoon*, ed. W. G. Howard (New York, 1910), pp. 23-5, 42.

although poetry consists of a sequence of articulate sounds in time rather than of forms and colors fixed in space, and although, instead of being limited, like painting, to a static but pregnant moment, its special power is the reproduction of progressive action, Lessing reiterates for it the standard formula: 'Nachahmung' is still for the poet the attribute 'which constitutes the essence of his art.'[23]

As the century drew on, various English critics began to scrutinize the concept of imitation very closely, and they ended by finding (Aristotle to the contrary) that differences in medium between the arts were such as to disqualify all but a limited number from being classed as mimetic, in any strict sense. The trend may be indicated by a few examples. In 1744 James Harris still maintained, in 'A Discourse on Music, Painting, and Poetry,' that imitation was common to all three arts. 'They agree, by being all mimetic or imitative. They differ, as they imitate by different media. . .'[24] In 1762 Kames declared that 'of all the fine arts, painting only and sculpture are in their nature imitative'; music, like architecture, 'is productive of originals, and copies not from nature'; while language copies from nature only in those instances in which it 'is imitative of sound or motion.'[25] And by 1789, in two closely reasoned dissertations prefixed to his translation of the *Poetics*, Thomas Twining confirmed this distinction between arts whose media are 'iconic' (in the later terminology of the Chicago semiotician, Charles Morris), in that they resemble what they denote, and those which are significant only by convention. Only works in which the resemblance between copy and object is both 'immediate' and 'obvious,' Twining says, can be described as imitative in a strict sense. Dramatic poetry, therefore, in which we mimic speech by speech, is the only kind of poetry which is properly imitation; music must be struck from the list of imitative arts; and he concludes by saying that painting, sculpture, and the arts of design in general are 'the only arts that are *obviously* and *essentially* imitative.'[26]

The concept that art is imitation, then, played an important part in neo-classic aesthetics; but closer inspection shows that it did not, in most theories, play the dominant part. Art, it was commonly said, is an imitation—but an imitation which is only instrumental toward producing effects upon an audience. In fact, the near-unanimity with which post-Renaissance critics lauded and echoed Aristotle's *Poetics* is deceptive. The focus of interest had shifted, and, on our diagram, this later criticism is primarily oriented, not from work to universe, but from work to audience. The nature and consequences of this change of direction is clearly indicated by the first classic of English criticism, written sometime in the early 1580's, Sir Philip Sidney's *The Apologie for Poetry*.

23. Ibid. pp. 99-102, 64.
24. *Three Treatises*, in *The Works of James Harris* (London, 1803), i, 58. Cf. Adam Smith, 'Of the Nature of that Imitation which Takes Place in What Are Called the Imitative Arts,' *Essays Philosophical and Literary* (London, n.d.), pp. 405ff.
25. Henry Home, Lord Kames, *Elements of Criticism* (Boston, 1796), ii, i (chap. xviii).
26. Thomas Twining, ed., *Aristotle's Treatise on Poetry* (London, 1789), pp. 4, 21-2, 60-61.

> Poesy therefore [said Sidney] is an arte of imitation, for so Aristotle termeth it in the word *Mimesis*, that is to say, a representing, counterfetting, or figuring foorth—to speake metaphorically, a speaking picture: with this end, to teach and delight.[27]

In spite of the appeal to Aristotle, this is not an Aristotelian formulation. To Sidney, poetry, by definition, has a purpose—to achieve certain effects in an audience. It imitates only as a means to the proximate end of pleasing, and pleases, it turns out, only as a means to the ultimate end of teaching; for 'right poets' are those who 'imitate both to delight and teach, and delight to move men to take that goodnes in hande, which without delight they would flye as from a stranger. . .'[28] As a result, throughout this essay the needs of the audience become the fertile grounds for critical distinctions and standards. In order 'to teach and delight,' poets imitate not 'what is, hath been, or shall be,' but only 'what may be, and should be,' so that the very objects of imitation become such as to guarantee the moral purpose. The poet is distinguished from, and elevated above, the moral philosopher and the historian by his capacity to move his auditors more forcefully to virtue, since he couples 'the general notion' of the philosopher with 'the particular example' of the historian; while by disguising his doctrine in a tale, he entices even 'harde harted evill men,' unaware, into the love of goodness, 'as if they tooke a medicine of Cherries.' The genres of poetry are discussed and ranked from the point of view of the moral and social effect each is suited to achieve: the epic poem thus demonstrates itself to be the king of poetry because it 'most inflameth the mind with desire to be worthy,' and even the lowly love lyric is conceived as an instrument for persuading a mistress of the genuineness of her lover's passion.[29] A history of criticism could be written solely on the basis of successive interpretations of salient passages from Aristotle's *Poetics*. In this instance, with no sense of strain, Sidney follows his Italian guides (who in turn had read Aristotle through the spectacles of Horace, Cicero, and the Church fathers) in bending one after another of the key statements of the *Poetics* to fit his own theoretical frame.[30]

For convenience we may name criticism that, like Sidney's, is ordered toward the audience, a 'pragmatic theory,' since it looks at the work of art chiefly as a means to an end, an instrument for getting something done, and tends to judge its value according to its success in achieving that aim. There is, of course, the greatest variance in emphasis and detail, but the central tendency of the pragmatic critic

27. Sir Philip Sidney, 'An Apology for Poetry,' *Elizabethan Critical Essays*, ed. G. Gregory Smith (London, 1904), I, 158.

28. Ibid. I, 159.

29. Ibid. I, 159, 161-4, 171-80, 201.

30. See, e.g., his use of Aristotle's statement that poetry is more philosophical than history (I, 167-8), and that painful things can be made pleasant by imitations (p. 171); and his wrenching of Aristotle's central term, *praxis*—the actions which are imitated by poetry—to signify the moral action which a poem moves the spectator to practise (p. 171).

is to conceive a poem as something made in order to effect requisite responses in its readers; to consider the author from the point of view of the powers and training he must have in order to achieve this end; to ground the classification and anatomy of poems in large part on the special effects each kind and component is most competent to achieve; and to derive the norms of the poetic art and canons of critical appraisal from the needs and legitimate demands of the audience to whom the poetry is addressed.

The perspective, much of the basic vocabulary, and many of the characteristic topics of pragmatic criticism originated in the classical theory of rhetoric. For rhetoric had been universally regarded as an instrument for achieving persuasion in an audience, and most theorists agreed with Cicero that in order to persuade, the orator must conciliate, inform, and move the minds of his auditors.[31] The great classical exemplar of the application of the rhetorical point of view to poetry was, of course, the *Ars Poetica* of Horace. As Richard McKeon points out, 'Horace's criticism is directed in the main to instruct the poet how to keep his audience in their seats until the end, how to induce cheers and applause, how to please a Roman audience, and by the same token, how to please all audiences and win immortality.'[32]

In what became for later critics the focal passage of the *Ars Poetica*, Horace advised that 'the poet's aim is either to profit or to please, or to blend in one the delightful and the useful.' The context shows that Horace held pleasure to be the chief purpose of poetry, for he recommends the profitable merely as a means to give pleasure to the elders, who, in contrast to the young aristocrats, 'rail at what contains no serviceable lesson.'[33] But *prodesse* and *delectare,* to teach and to please, together with another term introduced from rhetoric, *movere,* to move, served for centuries to collect under three heads the sum of aesthetic effects on the reader. The balance between these terms altered in the course of time. To the overwhelming majority of Renaissance critics, as to Sir Philip Sidney, the moral effect was the terminal aim, to which delight and emotion were auxiliary. From the time of the critical essays of Dryden through the eighteenth century, pleasure tended to become the ultimate end, although poetry without profit was often held to be trivial, and the optimistic moralist believed with James Beattie that if poetry instructs, it only pleases the more effectually.[34]

Looking upon a poem as a 'making,' a contrivance for affecting an audience, the typical pragmatic critic is engrossed with formulating the methods—the 'skill, or Crafte of making' as Ben Jonson called it —for achieving the effects desired. These methods, traditionally comprehended under the term *poesis,* or 'art' (in phrases such as 'the art of poetry'), are formulated as precepts and rules whose warrant consists either in their being derived from the qualities of works whose success and long survival have proved their adaptation to human nature,

31. Cicero, *De oratore* ii. xxviii.
32. 'The Concept of Imitation,' op. cit. p. 173.
33. Horace, *Ars Poetica*, trans. E. H. Blakeney, in *Literary Criticism, Plato to Dryden*, ed. Allan H. Gilbert (New York, 1940), p. 139.
34. *Essays on Poetry and Music* (3d ed.; London, 1779), p. 10.

or else in their being grounded directly on the psychological laws governing the responses of men in general. The rules, therefore, are inherent in the qualities of each excellent work of art, and when excerpted and codified these rules serve equally to guide the artist in making and the critics in judging any future product. 'Dryden,' said Dr. Johnson, 'may be properly considered as the father of English criticism, as the writer who first taught us to determine upon principles the merit of composition.'[35] Dryden's method of establishing those principles was to point out that poetry, like painting, has an end, which is to please; that imitation of nature is the general means for attaining this end; and that rules serve to specify the means for accomplishing this end in detail:

> Having thus shewn that imitation pleases, and why it pleases in both these arts, it follows, that some rules of imitation are necessary to obtain the end; for without rules there can be no art, any more than there can be a house without a door to conduct you into it.[36]

Emphasis on the rules and maxims of an art is native to all criticism that grounds itself in the demands of an audience, and it survives today in the magazines and manuals devoted to teaching fledgling authors 'how to write stories that sell.' But rulebooks based on the lowest common denominator of the modern buying public are only gross caricatures of the complex and subtly rationalized neo-classic ideals of literary craftsmanship. Through the early part of the eighteenth century, the poet could rely confidently on the trained taste and expert connoisseurship of a limited circle of readers, whether these were Horace's Roman contemporaries under Emperor Augustus, or Vida's at the papal court of Leo X, or Sidney's fellow-courtiers under Elizabeth, or the London audience of Dryden and Pope; while, in theory, the voices even of the best contemporary judges were subordinated to the voice of the ages. Some neo-classic critics were also certain that the rules of art, though empirically derived, were ultimately validated by conforming to that objective structure of norms whose existence guaranteed the rational order and harmony of the universe. In a strict sense, as John Dennis made explicit what was often implied, Nature 'is nothing but that Rule and Order, and Harmony, which we find in the visible Creation'; so 'Poetry, which is an imitation of Nature,' must demonstrate the same properties. The renowned masters among the ancients wrote not

> to please a tumultuous transitory Assembly, or a Handful of Men, who were call'd their Countrymen; They wrote to their Fellow-Citizens of the Universe, to all Countries, and to all Ages. . . They were clearly convinc'd, that nothing could trans-

---

35. 'Dryden,' *Lives of the English Poets*, ed. Birkbeck Hill (Oxford, 1905), I, 410.
36. 'Parallel of Poetry and Painting' (1695), *Essays*, ed. W. P. Ker (Oxford, 1926), II, 138. See Hoyt Trowbridge, 'The Place of Rules in Dryden's Criticism,' *Modern Philology*, XLIV (1946), 84ff.

mit their Immortal Works to Posterity, but something like that harmonious Order which maintains the Universe. . .[37]

Although they disagreed concerning specific rules, and although many English critics repudiated such formal French requisites as the unity of time and place, and the purity of comedy and tragedy, all but a few eccentrics among eighteenth-century critics believed in the validity of some set of universal rules. At about mid-century, it became popular to demonstrate and expound all the major rules for poetry, or even for art in general, in a single inclusive critical system. The pattern of the pragmatic reasoning usually employed may conveniently be studied in such a compendious treatment as James Beattie's *Essay on Poetry and Music as they affect the Mind* (1762), or more succinctly still, in Richard Hurd's 'Dissertation of the Idea of Universal Poetry' (1766). Universal poetry, no matter what the genre, Hurd says, is an art whose end is the maximum possible pleasure. 'When we speak of poetry, as an *art*, we mean *such a way or method of treating a subject, as is found most pleasing and delightful to us.*' And this idea 'if kept steadily in view, will unfold to us all the mysteries of the poetic art. There needs but to evolve the philosopher's idea, and to apply it, as occasion serves.' From this major premise Hurd evolves three properties, essential to all poetry if it is to effect the greatest possible delight: figurative language, 'fiction' (that is to say, a departure from what is actual, or empirically possible), and versification. The mode and degree in which these three universal qualities are to be combined in any one species of poetry, however, will depend on its peculiar end, because each poetic kind must exploit that special pleasure which it is generically adapted to achieve. 'For the art of every *kind* of poetry is only this general art so modified as the *nature* of each, that is, its more immediate and subordinate end, may respectively require.'

> For the name of poem will belong to every composition, whose primary end is to *please,* provided it be so constructed as to afford *all* the pleasure, which its kind or *sort* will permit.[38]

On the basis of isolated passages from his *Letters on Chivalry and Romance,* Hurd is commonly treated as a 'pre-romantic' critic. But in the summation of his poetic creed in the 'Idea of Universal Poetry,' the rigidly deductive logic which Hurd employs to 'unfold' the rules of poetry from a primitive definition, permitting 'the reason of the thing' to override the evidence of the actual practice of poets, brings him as close as anyone in England to the geometric method of Charles Batteux, though without that critic's Cartesian apparatus. The difference is that Batteux evolves his rules from the definition of poetry as the

---

37. *The Advancement and Reformation of Modern Poetry* (1701), in *The Critical Works of John Dennis,* ed. E. N. Hooker (Baltimore, 1939), I, 202-3. For Dennis' derivation of specific rules from the end of art, which is 'to delight and reform the mind,' see *The Grounds of Criticism in Poetry* (1704), ibid. pp. 336ff.

38. 'Dissertation on the Idea of Universal Poetry,' *Works,* II, 3-4, 25-6, 7. For a parallel argument see Alexander Gerard, *An Essay on Taste* (London, 1759), p. 40.

imitation of *la belle nature*, and Hurd, from its definition as the art of treating a subject so as to afford the reader a maximum pleasure; and this involves his assuming that he possesses an empirical knowledge of the psychology of the reader. For if the end of poetry is to gratify the mind of the reader, Hurd says, knowledge of the laws of mind is necessary to establish its rules, which are 'but so many MEANS, which experience finds most conducive to that end.'[39] Since Batteux and Hurd, however, are both intent on rationalizing what is mainly a common body of poetic lore, it need not surprise us that, though they set out from different points of the compass, their paths often coincide.[40]

But to appreciate the power and illumination of which a refined and flexible pragmatic criticism is capable, we must turn from these abstract systematizers of current methods and maxims to such a practical critic as Samuel Johnson. Johnson's literary criticism assumes approximately the frame of critical reference I have described, but Johnson, who distrusts rigid and abstract theorizing, applies the method with a constant appeal to specific literary examples, deference to the opinions of other readers, but ultimately, reliance on his own expert responses to the text. As a result Johnson's comments on poets and poems have persistently afforded a jumping-off point for later critics whose frame of reference and particular judgments differ radically from his own. For an instance of Johnson's procedure which is especially interesting because it shows how the notion of the imitation of nature is co-ordinated with the judgment of poetry in terms of its end and effects, consider that monument of neo-classic criticism, Johnson's *Preface to Shakespeare*.

Johnson undertakes in his *Preface* to establish Shakespeare's rank among poets, and to do so, he is led to rate Shakespeare's native abilities against the general level of taste and achievement in the Elizabethan age, and to measure these abilities in turn 'by their proportion to the general and collective ability of man.'[41] Since the powers and excellence of an author, however, can only be inferred from the nature and excellence of the works he achieves, Johnson addresses himself to a general examination of Shakespeare's dramas. In this systematic appraisal of the works themselves, we find that mimesis retains for Johnson a measure of authority as criterion. Repeatedly Johnson maintains that 'this therefore is the praise of *Shakespeare*, that his drama is the mirrour of life,' and of inanimate nature as well: 'He was an exact surveyor of the inanimate world. . . *Shakespeare*, whether life or nature

39. 'Idea of Universal Poetry,' *Works*, II, 3-4. On the rationale underlying the body of Hurd's criticism, see the article by Hoyt Trowbridge, 'Bishop Hurd: A Reinterpretation,' *PMLA*, LVIII (1943), 450ff.

40. E.g., Batteux 'deduces' from the idea that poetry is the imitation, not of unadorned reality, but of *la belle nature*, that its end can only be 'to please, to move, to touch, in a word, pleasure' (*Les Beaux Arts*, pp. 81, 151). Conversely, Hurd infers from the fact that the end of poetry is pleasure that the poet's duty is 'to illustrate and adorn' reality, and to delineate it 'in the most taking forms' ('Idea of Universal Poetry,' *Works*, II, 8). For purposes of a specialized investigation into the evidences for plagiarism among poets, Hurd himself, in another essay, shifts his ground, and like Batteux, sets out from a definition of poetry as an imitation, specifically, of 'the fairest forms of things' (Discourse on Poetic Imitation,' *Works*, II, III).

41. *Johnson on Shakespeare*, ed. Walter Raleigh (Oxford, 1908), pp. 10, 30-31.

be his subject, shews plainly, that he has seen with his own eyes. . .'[42] But, Johnson also claims, 'The end of writing is to instruct; the end of poetry is to instruct by pleasing.'[43] It is to this function of poetry, and to the demonstrated effect of a poem upon its audience, that Johnson awards priority as aesthetic criterion. If a poem fails to please, whatever its character otherwise, it is, as a work of art, nothing; though Johnson insists, with a strenuous moralism that must already have seemed old-fashioned to contemporary readers, it must please without violating the standards of truth and virtue. Accordingly, Johnson discriminates those elements in Shakespeare's plays which were introduced to appeal to the local and passing tastes of the rather barbarous audience of his own time ('He knew,' said Johnson, 'how he should most please'),[44] from those elements which are proportioned to the tastes of the common readers of all time. And since in works 'appealing wholly to observation and experience, no other test can be applied than length of duration and continuance of esteem,' Shakespeare's long survival as a poet 'read without any other reason than the desire for pleasure' is the best evidence for his artistic excellence. The reason for this survival Johnson explains on the subsidiary principle that 'nothing can please many, and please long, but just representations of general nature.' Shakespeare exhibits the eternal 'species' of human character, moved by 'those general passions and principles by which all minds are agitated.'[45] Thus Shakespeare's excellence in holding up the mirror to general nature turns out, in the long run, to be justified by the superior criterion of the appeal this achievement holds for the enduring tastes of the general literary public.

A number of Johnson's individual observations and judgments exhibit a play of the argument between the two principles of the nature of the world the poet must reflect, and the nature and legitimate requirements of the poet's audience. For the most part the two principles co-operate toward a single conclusion. For example, both the empirical nature of the universe and of the universal reader demonstrate the fallacy of those who censure Shakespeare for mixing his comic and tragic scenes. Shakespeare's plays, Johnson says, exhibit 'the real state of sublunary nature, which partakes of good and evil, joy and sorrow, mingled with endless variety.' In addition, 'the mingled drama may convey all the instruction of tragedy or comedy' by approaching nearer 'to the appearance of life'; while the objection that the change of scene 'wants at last the power to move' is a specious reasoning 'received as true even by those who in daily experience feel it to be false.'[46] But when the actual state of sublunary affairs conflicts with the poet's obli-

42. Ibid. pp. 14, 39. Cf. pp. 11, 31, 33, 37, etc.
43. Ibid. p. 16.
44. Ibid. pp. 31-3, 41.
45. Ibid. pp. 9-12.
46. Ibid. pp. 15-17. See also Johnson's defense of Shakespeare for violating the decorum of character-types, by the appeal to 'nature' as against 'accident'; and for breaking the unities of time and place, by the appeal both to the actual experience of dramatic auditors, and to the principle that 'the greatest graces of a play, are to copy nature and instruct life' (ibid. pp. 14-15, 25-30). Cf. *Rambler* No. 156.

gation to his audience, the latter is the court of final appeal. It is Shakespeare's defect, says Johnson,

> that he seems to write without any moral purpose. . . . He makes no just distribution of good or evil, nor is always careful to shew in the virtuous a disapprobation of the wicked. . . It is always a writer's duty to make the world better, and justice is a virtue independant on time or place.[47]

The pragmatic orientation, ordering the aim of the artist and the character of the work to the nature, the needs, and the springs of pleasure in the audience, characterized by far the greatest part of criticism from the time of Horace through the eighteenth century. Measured either by its duration or the number of its adherents, therefore, the pragmatic view, broadly conceived, has been the principal aesthetic attitude of the Western world. But inherent in this system were the elements of its dissolution. Ancient rhetoric had bequeathed to criticism not only its stress on affecting the audience but also (since its main concern was with educating the orator) its detailed attention to the powers and activities of the speaker himself—his 'nature,' or innate powers and genius, as distinguished from his culture and art, and also the process of invention, disposition, and expression involved in his discourse.[48] In the course of time, and particularly after the psychological contributions of Hobbes and Locke in the seventeenth century, increasing attention was given to the mental constitution of the poet, the quality and degree of his 'genius,' and the play of his faculties in the act of composition. Through most of the eighteenth century, the poet's invention and imagination were made thoroughly dependent for their materials—their ideas and 'images'—on the external universe and the literary models the poet had to imitate; while the persistent stress laid on his need for judgment and art—the mental surrogates, in effect, of the requirements of a cultivated audience—held the poet strictly responsible to the audience for whose pleasure he exerted his creative ability. Gradually, however, the stress was shifted more and more to the poet's natural genius, creative imagination, and emotional spontaneity, at the expense of the opposing attributes of judgment, learning, and artful restraints. As a result the audience gradually receded into the background, giving place to the poet himself, and his own mental powers and emotional needs, as the predominant cause and even the end and test of art. By this time other developments, which we shall have occasion to talk about later, were also helping to

47. Ibid. pp. 20-21. The logic appears even more clearly in Johnson's early paper on 'works of fiction,' in *Rambler* No. 4, 1750 (*The Works of Samuel Johnson,* ed. Arthur Murphy, London, 1824, IV, 23): 'It is justly considered as the greatest excellency of art, to imitate nature; but it is necessary to distinguish those parts of nature which are most proper for imitation,' etc. For a detailed analysis of Johnson's critical methods, see W. R. Keast, 'The Theoretical Foundations of Johnson's Criticism,' *Critics and Criticism,* ed. R. S. Crane, pp. 389-407.

48. See the masterly précis of the complex movements within English neo-classic criticism by R. S. Crane, 'English Neoclassical Criticism,' *Critics and Criticism,* pp. 372-88.

shift the focus of critical interest from audience to artist and thus to introduce a new orientation into the theory of art.

Expressive Theories

'Poetry,' Wordsworth announced in his Preface to the *Lyrical Ballads* of 1800, 'is the spontaneous overflow of powerful feelings.' He thought well enough of this formulation to use it twice in the same essay, and on this, as the ground-idea, he founded his theory of the proper subjects, language, effects, and value of poetry. Almost all the major critics of the English romantic generation phrased definitions or key statements showing a parallel alignment from work to poet. Poetry is the overflow, utterance, or projection of the thought and feelings of the poet; or else (in the chief variant formulation) poetry is defined in terms of the imaginative process which modifies and synthesizes the images, thoughts, and feelings of the poet. This way of thinking, in which the artist himself becomes the major element generating both the artistic product and the criteria by which it is to be judged, I shall call the expressive theory of art.

Setting the date at which this point of view became predominant in critical theory, like marking the point at which orange becomes yellow in the color spectrum, must be a somewhat arbitrary procedure. As we shall see, an approach to the expressive orientation, though isolated in history and partial in scope, is to be found as early as Longinus' discussion of the sublime style as having its main sources in the thought and emotions of the speaker; and it recurs in a variant form in Bacon's brief analysis of poetry as pertaining to the imagination and 'accommodating the shows of things to the desires of the mind.' Even Wordsworth's theory, it will appear, is much more embedded in a traditional matrix of interests and emphases, and is, therefore, less radical than are the theories of his followers of the 1830's. The year 1800 is a good round number, however, and Wordsworth's Preface a convenient document, by which to signalize the displacement of the mimetic and pragmatic by the expressive view of art in English criticism.

In general terms, the central tendency of the expressive theory may be summarized in this way: A work of art is essentially the internal made external, resulting from a creative process operating under the impulse of feeling, and embodying the combined product of the poet's perceptions, thoughts, and feelings. The primary source and subject matter of a poem, therefore, are the attributes and actions of the poet's own mind; or if aspects of the external world, then these only as they are converted from fact to poetry by the feelings and operations of the poet's mind. ('Thus the Poetry . . .' Wordsworth wrote, 'proceeds whence it ought to do, from the soul of Man, communicating its creative energies to the images of the external world.')[49] The paramount cause of poetry is not, as in Aristotle, a formal cause, determined primarily by the human actions and qualities imitated; nor, as in neoclassic criticism, a final cause, the effect intended upon the audience;

49. *Letters of William and Dorothy Wordsworth: The Middle Years,* ed. E. de Selincourt (Oxford, 1937), II, 705; 18 Jan. 1816.

but instead an efficient cause—the impulse within the poet of feelings and desires seeking expression, or the compulsion of the 'creative' imagination which, like God the creator, has its internal source of motion. The propensity is to grade the arts by the extent to which their media are amenable to the undistorted expression of the feelings or mental powers of the artist, and to classify the species of an art, and evaluate their instances, by the qualities or states of mind of which they are a sign. Of the elements constituting a poem, the element of diction, especially figures of speech, becomes primary; and the burning question is, whether these are the natural utterance of emotion and imagination or the deliberate aping of poetic conventions. The first test any poem must pass is no longer, 'Is it true to nature?' or 'Is it appropriate to the requirements either of the best judges or the generality of mankind?' but a criterion looking in a different direction; namely, 'Is it sincere? Is it genuine? Does it match the intention, the feeling, and the actual state of mind of the poet while composing?' The work ceases then to be regarded as primarily a reflection of nature, actual or improved; the mirror held up to nature becomes transparent and yields the reader insights into the mind and heart of the poet himself. The exploitation of literature as an index to personality first manifests itself in the early nineteenth century; it is the inevitable consequence of the expressive point of view.

The sources, details, and historical results of this reorientation of criticism, in its various forms, will be a principal concern of the rest of this book. Now, while we have some of the earlier facts fresh in mind, let me indicate what happened to salient elements of traditional criticism in the essays 'What Is Poetry?' and 'The Two Kinds of Poetry,' written by John Stuart Mill in 1833. Mill relied in large part on Wordsworth's Preface to the *Lyrical Ballads,* but in the intervening thirty years the expressive theory had emerged from the network of qualifications in which Wordsworth had carefully placed it, and had worked out its own destiny unhindered. Mill's logic in answering the question, 'What Is Poetry?' is not *more geometrico,* like that of Batteux, nor stiffly formal, like Richard Hurd's; nonetheless, his theory turns out to be just as tightly dependent upon a central principle as theirs. For whatever Mill's empirical pretensions, his initial assumption about the essential nature of poetry remains continuously though silently effective in selecting, interpreting, and ordering the facts to be explained.

The primitive proposition of Mill's theory is: Poetry is 'the expression or uttering forth of feeling.'[50] Exploration of the data of aesthetics from this starting point leads, among other things, to the following drastic alterations in the great commonplaces of the critical tradition:

(1) *The poetic kinds.* Mill reinterprets and inverts the neo-classic ranking of the poetic kinds. As the purest expression of feeling, lyric poetry is 'more eminently and peculiarly poetry than any other. . .' Other forms are all alloyed by non-poetic elements, whether descriptive, didactic, or narrative, which serve merely as convenient occasions for the poetic utterances of feeling either by the poet or by one of his in-

50. *Early Essays by John Stuart Mill,* ed. J. W. M. Gibbs (London, 1897), p. 208.

vented characters. To Aristotle, tragedy had been the highest form of poetry, and the plot, representing the action being imitated, had been its 'soul'; while most neo-classic critics had agreed that, whether judged by greatness of subject matter or of effect, epic and tragedy are the king and queen of poetic forms. It serves as an index to the revolution in critical norms to notice that to Mill, plot becomes a kind of necessary evil. An epic poem 'in so far as it is epic (i.e. narrative) . . . is not poetry at all,' but only a suitable frame for the greatest diversity of genuinely poetic passages; while the interest in plot and story 'merely as a story' characterizes rude stages of society, children, and the 'shallowest and emptiest' of civilized adults.[51] Similarly with the other arts; in music, painting, sculpture, and architecture Mill distinguishes between that which is 'simple imitation or description' and that which 'expresses human feeling' and is, therefore, poetry.[52]

(2) *Spontaneity as criterion.* Mill accepts the venerable assumption that a man's emotional susceptibility is innate, but his knowledge and skill —his art—are acquired. On this basis, he distinguishes poets into two classes: poets who are born and poets who are made, or those who are poets 'by nature,' and those who are poets 'by culture.' Natural poetry is identifiable because it 'is Feeling itself, employing Thought only as the medium of its utterance'; on the other hand, the poetry of 'a cultivated but not naturally poetic mind,' is written with 'a distinct aim,' and in it the thought remains the conspicuous object, however surrounded by 'a halo of feeling.' Natural poetry, it turns out, is 'poetry in a far higher sense, than any other; since . . . that which constitutes poetry, human feeling, enters far more largely into this than into the poetry of culture.' Among the moderns, Shelley represents the poet born and Wordsworth the poet made; and with unconscious irony Mill turns Wordsworth's own criterion, 'the spontaneous overflow of feeling,' against its sponsor. Wordsworth's poetry 'has little even of the appearance of spontaneousness: the well is never so full that it overflows.'[53]

(3) *The external world.* In so far as a literary product simply imitates objects, it is not poetry at all. As a result, reference of poetry to the external universe disappears from Mill's theory, except to the extent that sensible objects may serve as a stimulus or 'occasion for the generation of poetry,' and then, 'the poetry is not in the object itself,' but 'in the state of mind' in which it is contemplated. When a poet describes a lion he 'is describing the lion professedly, but the state of excitement of the spectator really,' and the poetry must be true not to the object, but to 'the human emotion.'[54] Thus severed from the external world, the objects signified by a poem tend to be regarded as no more than a projected equivalent—an extended and articulated symbol—for the poet's inner state of mind. Poetry, said Mill, in a phrasing which anticipates T. E. Hulme and lays the theoretical groundwork for the practice of symbolists from Baudelaire through T. S. Eliot, embodies 'itself in symbols, which are the nearest possible representa-

51. Ibid. pp. 228, 205-6, 213, 203-4.
52. Ibid. pp. 211-17.
53. Ibid. pp. 222-31.
54. Ibid. pp. 206-7.

tions of the feeling in the exact shape in which it exists in the poet's mind.'[55] Tennyson, Mill wrote in a review of that poet's early poems, excels in 'scene-painting, in the higher sense of the term'; and this is

> not the mere power of producing that rather vapid species of composition usually termed descriptive poetry . . . but the power of *creating* scenery, in keeping with some state of human feeling; so fitted to it as to be the embodied symbol of it, and to summon up the state of feeling itself, with a force not to be surpassed by anything but reality.[56]

And as an indication of the degree to which the innovations of the romantics persist as the commonplaces of modern critics—even of those who purport to found their theory on anti-romantic principles—notice how striking is the parallel between the passage above and a famous comment by T. S. Eliot:

> The only way of expressing emotion in the form of art is by finding an 'objective correlative'; in other words, a set of objects, a situation, a chain of events which shall be the formula of that *particular* emotion; such that when the external facts, which must terminate in sensory experience, are given, the emotion is immediately evoked.[57]

(4) *The audience.* No less drastic is the fate of the audience. According to Mill, 'Poetry is feeling, confessing itself to itself in moments of solitude. . .' The poet's audience is reduced to a single member, consisting of the poet himself. 'All poetry,' as Mill puts it, 'is of the nature of soliloquy.' The purpose of producing effects upon other men, which for centuries had been the defining character of the art of poetry, now serves precisely the opposite function: it disqualifies a poem by proving it to be rhetoric instead. When the poet's

> act of utterance is not itself the end, but a means to an end— viz. by the feelings he himself expresses, to work upon the feelings, or upon the belief, or the will, of another—when the expression of his emotions . . . is tinged also by that purpose, by that desire of making an impression upon another mind, then it ceases to be poetry, and becomes eloquence.[58]

55. Ibid. pp. 208-9. Cf. Hulme, 'If it is sincere in the accurate sense . . . the whole of the analogy is necessary to get out the exact curve of the feeling or thing you want to express . . .' ('Romanticism and Classicism,' *Speculations*, London, 1936, p. 138).

56. Review, written in 1835, of Tennyson's *Poems Chiefly Lyrical* (1830) and *Poems* (1833), in *Early Essays*, p. 242.

57. 'Hamlet,' *Selected Essays* 1917-32 (London, 1932), p. 145.

58. *Early Essays*, pp. 208-9. Cf. John Keble, *Lectures on Poetry* (1832-41), trans. E. K. Francis (Oxford, 1912), I, 48-9: 'Cicero is always the orator' because 'he always has in mind the theatre, the benches, the audience'; whereas Plato is 'more poetical than Homer himself' because 'he writes to please himself, not to win over others.'

There is, in fact, something singularly fatal to the audience in the romantic point of view. Or, in terms of historical causes, it might be conjectured that the disappearance of a homogeneous and discriminating reading public fostered a criticism which on principle diminished the importance of the audience as a determinant of poetry and poetic value. Wordsworth still insisted that 'Poets do not write for Poets alone, but for Men,' and that each of his poems 'has a worthy purpose'; even though it turns out that the pleasure and profit of the audience is an automatic consequence of the poet's *spontaneous* overflow of feeling, provided that the appropriate associations between thoughts and feelings have been established by the poet in advance.[59] Keats, however, affirmed roundly that 'I never wrote one single line of Poetry with the least Shadow of public thought.'[60] 'A poet is a nightingale,' according to Shelley, 'who sits in darkness and sings to cheer its own solitude with sweet sounds; his auditors are as men entranced by the melody of an unseen musician. . .'[61] For Carlyle, the poet utterly replaces the audience as the generator of aesthetic norms.

> On the whole, Genius has privileges of its own; it selects an orbit for itself; and be this never so eccentric, if it is indeed a celestial orbit, we mere star-gazers must at last compose ourselves; must cease to cavil at it, and begin to observe it, and calculate its laws.[62]

The evolution is complete, from the mimetic poet, assigned the minimal role of holding a mirror up to nature, through the pragmatic poet who, whatever his natural gifts, is ultimately measured by his capacity to satisfy the public taste, to Carlyle's Poet as Hero, the chosen one who, because he is 'a Force of Nature,' writes as he must, and through the degree of homage he evokes, serves as the measure of his *reader's* piety and taste.[63]

Objective Theories

All types of theory described so far, in their practical applications, get down to dealing with the work of art itself, in its parts and their mutual relations, whether the premises on which these elements are

59. Preface to the *Lyrical Ballads*, *Wordsworth's Literary Criticism*, ed. N. C. Smith (London, 1905), pp. 30, 15-16.

60. *Letters*, ed. Maurice Buxton Forman (3d ed.; New York, 1948), p. 131 (to Reynolds, 9 Apr. 1818).

61. 'Defence of Poetry,' *Shelley's Literary and Philosophical Criticism*, ed. John Shawcross (London, 1909), p. 129.

62. 'Jean Paul Friedrich Richter' (1827), *Works*, ed. H. D. Traill (London, 1905), XXVI, 20.

63. See *Heroes, Hero-Worship, and the Heroic in History*, in *Works*, V, esp. pp. 80-85, 108-12. Cf. Jones Very's indignant denial of the inference that because the general ear takes delight in Shakespeare, 'his motive was to please. . . We degrade those whom the world has pronounced poets, when we assume any other cause of their song than the divine and original action of the soul in humble obedience to the Holy Spirit upon whom they call' ['Shakespeare' (1838), *Poems and Essays*, Boston and New York, 1886, pp. 45-6].

discriminated and evaluated relate them primarily to the spectator, the artist, or the world without. But there is also a fourth procedure, the 'objective orientation,' which on principle regards the work of art in isolation from all these external points of reference, analyzes it as a self-sufficient entity constituted by its parts in their internal relations, and sets out to judge it solely by criteria intrinsic to its own mode of being.

This point of view has been comparatively rare in literary criticism. The one early attempt at the analysis of an art form which is both objective and comprehensive occurs in the central portion of Aristotle's *Poetics*. I have chosen to discuss Aristotle's theory of art under the heading of mimetic theories, because it sets out from, and makes frequent reference back to the concept of imitation. Such is the flexibility of Aristotle's procedure, however, that after he has isolated the species 'tragedy,' and established its relation to the universe as an imitation of a certain kind of action, and to the audience through its observed effect of purging pity and fear, his method becomes centripetal, and assimilates these external elements into attributes of the work proper. In this second consideration of tragedy as an object in itself, the actions and agents that are imitated re-enter the discussion as the plot, character, and thought which, together with diction, melody, and spectacle, make up the six elements of a tragedy; and even pity and fear are reconsidered as that pleasurable quality proper to tragedy, to be distinguished from the pleasures characteristic of comedy and other forms.[64] The tragic work itself can now be analyzed formally as a self-determining whole made up of parts, all organized around the controlling part, the tragic plot—itself a unity in which the component incidents are integrated by the internal relations of 'necessity or probability.'

As an all-inclusive approach to poetry, the objective orientation was just beginning to emerge in the late eighteenth and early nineteenth century. We shall see later on that some critics were undertaking to explore the concept of the poem as a heterocosm, a world of its own, independent of the world into which we are born, whose end is not to instruct or please but simply to exist. Certain critics, particularly in Germany, were expanding upon Kant's formula that a work of art exhibits *Zweckmässigkeit ohne Zweck* (purposiveness without purpose), together with his concept that the contemplation of beauty is disinterested and without regard to utility, while neglecting Kant's characteristic reference of an aesthetic product to the mental faculties of its creator and receptor. The aim to consider a poem, as Poe expressed it, as a 'poem *per se* . . . written solely for the poem's sake,'[65] in isolation from external causes and ulterior ends, came to constitute one element of the diverse doctrines usually huddled together by historians under the heading 'Art for Art's Sake.' And with differing emphases and adequacy, and in a great variety of theoretical contexts, the objective approach to poetry has become one of the most prominent ele-

---

64. 'Not every kind of pleasure should be required of a tragedy, but only its own proper pleasure. The tragic pleasure is that of pity and fear . . .' (*Poetics* 14.1453ᵇ).

65. 'The Poetic Principle,' *Representative Selections,* ed. Margaret Alterton and Hardin Craig (New York, 1935), pp. 382-3.

ments in the innovative criticism of the last two or three decades. T. S. Eliot's dictum of 1928, that 'when we are considering poetry we must consider it primarily as poetry and not another thing' is widely approved, however far Eliot's own criticism sometimes departs from this ideal; and it is often joined with MacLeish's verse aphorism, 'A poem should not mean But be.' The subtle and incisive criticism of criticism by the Chicago Neo-Aristotelians and their advocacy of an instrument adapted to dealing with poetry as such have been largely effective toward a similar end. In his 'ontological criticism,' John Crowe Ransom has been calling for recognition of 'the autonomy of the work itself as existing for its own sake';[66] campaigns have been organized against 'the personal heresy,' 'the intentional fallacy,' and 'the affective fallacy'; the widely influential handbook, *The Theory of Literature*, written by René Wellek and Austin Warren, proposes that criticism deal with a poem *qua* poem, independently of 'extrinsic' factors; and similar views are being expressed, with increasing frequency, not only in our literary but in our scholarly journals. In America, at least, some form of the objective point of view has already gone far to displace its rivals as the reigning mode of literary criticism.

According to our scheme of analysis, then, there have been four major orientations, each one of which has seemed to various acute minds adequate for a satisfactory criticism of art in general. And by and large the historic progression, from the beginning through the early nineteenth century, has been from the mimetic theory of Plato and (in a qualified fashion) Aristotle, through the pragmatic theory, lasting from the conflation of rhetoric with poetic in the Hellenistic and Roman era almost through the eighteenth century, to the expressive theory of English (and somewhat earlier, German) romantic criticism.

Of course romantic criticism, like that of any period, was not uniform in its outlook. As late as 1831 Macaulay (whose thinking usually followed traditional patterns) still insists, as an eternal rule 'founded in reason and in the nature of things,' that 'poetry is, as was said more than two thousand years ago, imitation,' and differentiates between the arts on the basis of their diverse media and objects of imitation. Then, in an essay packed with eighteenth-century catch-lines, he ungratefully employs the mimetic principle to justify his elevation of Scott, Wordsworth, and Coleridge over the eighteenth-century poets because they imitate nature more accurately, and attacks the neo-classic rules of correctness on the ground that they 'tend to make . . . imitations less perfect than they otherwise would be. . .'[67] The mode of criticism which subjects art and the artist to the audience also continued to flourish, usually in a vulgarized form, among influential journalists such as Francis Jeffrey, who deliberately set themselves to voice the

66. See John Crowe Ransom, *The World's Body* (New York, 1938), esp. pp. 327ff., and 'Criticism as Pure Speculation,' *The Intent of the Critic*, ed. Donald Stauffer (Princeton, 1941).

67. 'Moore's *Life of Lord Byron*,' in *Critical and Historical Essays* (Everyman's Library; London, 1907), II, 622-8.

literary standards of the middle class and to preserve unsullied what Jeffrey called 'the purity of the female character.'[68]

But these are not the innovative critical writings which contributed to the predominant temper of what Shelley, in his 'Defence of Poetry,' called 'the spirit of the age'; and the radical difference between the characteristic points of view of neo-classic and romantic criticism remains unmistakable. Take such representative productions of the 1760's and '70's, as Johnson's *Preface to Shakespeare,* Kames's *Elements of Criticism,* Richard Hurd's 'On the Idea of Universal Poetry,' *The Art of Poetry on a New Plan* (of dubious authorship), Beattie's *Essays on Poetry and Music,* and the first eight *Discourses* of Sir Joshua Reynolds. Place these next to the major inquiries into poetry and art of the romantic generation: Wordsworth's Prefaces and collateral essays, Coleridge's *Biographia Literaria* and Shakespearean lectures, Hazlitt's 'On Poetry in General' and other essays, even Shelley's Platonistic 'Defence of Poetry'; then add to this group such later documents as Carlyle's 'Characteristics' and early literary reviews, J. S. Mill's two essays on poetry, John Keble's *Lectures on Poetry,* and Leigh Hunt's 'What Is Poetry?'. Whatever the continuity of certain terms and topics between individual members of the two eras, and however important the methodological and doctrinal differences which divide the members within a single group, one decisive change marks off the criticism in the Age of Wordsworth from that in the Age of Johnson. The poet has moved into the center of the critical system and taken over many of the prerogatives which had once been exercised by his readers, the nature of the world in which he found himself, and the inherited precepts and examples of his poetic art.

68. *Edinburgh Review,* VIII (1806), 459-60. On Jeffrey's use of an elaborate associationist aesthetics in order to justify the demand that an author or artist have as his aim 'to give as much [pleasure] and to as many persons as possible,' and that he 'fashion his productions according to the rules of taste which may be deduced' from an investigation of the most widespread public preferences, see his *Contributions to the Edinburgh Review* (London, 1844), I, 76-8, 128; III, 53-4. For contemporary justifications, on sociological and moral grounds, for instituting a petticoat government over the republic of letters, see, e.g., John Bowring's review of Tennyson's *Poems,* in *Westminster Review,* XIV (1831), 223; *Lockhart's Literary Criticism,* ed. M. C. Hildyard (Oxford, 1931), p. 66; Christopher North (John Wilson), *Works,* ed. Ferrier (Edinburgh and London, 1857), IX, 194-5, 228.